Oracle SOA Suite Developer's Guide

Design and build Service-Oriented Architecture
Solutions with the Oracle SOA Suite 10gR3

Matt Wright

Antony Reynolds

PUBLISHING

BIRMINGHAM - MUMBAI

Oracle SOA Suite Developer's Guide

First published: March 2009

Production Reference: 1120309

Published by Packt Publishing Ltd.
32 Lincoln Road
Olton
Birmingham, B27 6PA, UK.

ISBN 978-1-847193-55-1

www.packtpub.com

Cover Image by Vinayak Chittar (vinayak.chittar@gmail.com)

Credits

Authors

Matt Wright

Antony Reynolds

Reviewers

Jason Jones

Phil McLaughlin

Acquisition Editor

Bansari Barot

Development Editor

Swapna V. Verlekar

Technical Editor

Gagandeep Singh

Editorial Team Leader

Akshara Aware

Production Editorial Manager

Abhijeet Deobhakta

Project Team Leader

Lata Basantani

Project Coordinator

Rajashree Hamine

Indexer

Rekha Nair

Proofreader

Laura Booth

Production Coordinator

Rajni R. Thorat

Cover Work

Rajni R. Thorat

Foreword

Over the past several years, we have seen a growing momentum in the adoption of Service-Oriented Architectures, which continues to accelerate. At this point in its evolution, SOA has started to cross the chasm between the early-adopter, bleeding-edge IT architects and the mainstream IT and software development community. And what enables this progression to continue gathering steam is the sharing of knowledge, experiences, and lessons learned between the early adopters in the community and those following their footsteps. As such, I am very enthusiastic about *Oracle SOA Suite Developer Guide* because Matt Wright and Antony Reynolds are exactly the right people to share this knowledge with us.

I joined Oracle in 2004 through the acquisition of Collaxa, which is where the Oracle BPEL Process Manager came from. At Collaxa, I was responsible for all the interfaces between our SOA products and our customers and the developer community. It was very clear, shortly after the acquisition, that the Oracle field was going to be a tremendous asset to the adoption of our products, our customers' success, and to the advancement of SOA in general.

As Oracle became a leader in the SOA space over the next several years, building out a full SOA platform through continued development and further acquisitions, Antony and Matt continued to stand out as leaders among the special community of Oracle SOA field representatives. Along the way, they built a knowledge base that enabled customers to get over (and better yet, avoid...) common hurdles, and feed customer requirements back into the engineering organization. We are highly appreciative of the fact that they have undertaken the monumental task of incorporating this knowledge into a book that is built on the existing documentation, and will provide great value to experienced SOA practitioners and newbies alike.

SOA is about more than just tools, a fact that is clear even to those of us who work for software vendors. However, to be effective with any software development products, requires detailed knowledge of the products, APIs, features, and capabilities. Antony and Matt cover these basics in this book in great detail.

But even more importantly, developers need to know about edge cases, design patterns, and how these products fit into the full development life cycle. This information comes best from real-world experiences with the products, even more than from the people who build a product. It is particularly valuable that Antony and Matt focus the majority of the content in this book on deeper topics such as SOA exception handling, full life cycle support for testing, security, and migration across environments. If I had a quarter for every customer who has asked me, over the past eight years, about best practices to move their SOA composites from dev to test to production… well, let's just say you can save your quarters and read Chapter 18 instead.

Finally, even as SOA adoption matures, it is still important to understand why you are adopting SOA, what the expected benefits are, and to measure your progress toward those as objectively as possible. Today, most people state goals such as:

- Developer productivity for system-to-system integration
- Greater interoperability between systems
- Flexibility and agility that reduces the costs associated with maintenance and changing requirements
- Service re-use
- Scalability
- Enhanced business visibility and administration

I believe that this book, coming from pragmatic practitioners in the field, will specifically help developers realize these benefits from their SOA implementations by providing clear and useful information on Oracle's SOA platform.

On behalf of the Oracle SOA Engineering and Product Management team, as well as all the customers and partners who have asked for this book, we heartily thank Antony and Matt for the investment of their time and energy, and hope that this book helps you achieve your SOA goals.

David Shaffer
Vice President, Product Management
Oracle Integration
david.shaffer@oracle.com

About the authors

Matt Wright has been involved with standards-based Service-Oriented Architecture (SOA) since shortly after the initial submission of SOAP 1.1 to the W3C in 2000, and has worked with some of the early adopters of BPEL since its initial release in 2002. Since then, he has been a passionate exponent of SOA and has been engaged in some of the earliest SOA-based implementations across EMEA and APAC.

He is currently a Director of Product Management for Oracle Fusion Middleware in APAC, where he is responsible for working with organizations to educate and enable them in realizing the full business benefits of SOA in solving complex business problems. As a recognized authority on SOA, Matt is also responsible for evangelizing the Oracle SOA message and is a regular speaker and instructor at private and public events. He also enjoys writing and publishes his own blog (`http://blogs.bpel-people.com`). Matt holds a B.Sc. (Eng) in Computer Science from Imperial College, University of London.

It seems a long time ago that I first suggested to Antony that we write this book. Since that day there have been numerous twists and turns, not least the acquisition of BEA which resulted in many revisions and re-writes. Having Antony as my co-author throughout this process was invaluable; Antony's continued conviction and enthusiasm throughout was instrumental in ensuring the book finally made the light of day.

Throughout this process, everyone at Oracle has been very supportive. I would like to make a special mention to Andy Gale for guiding us in the right direction when we first suggested the idea and to John Deeb for his continual support and encouragement throughout. I would also like to express my gratitude to everyone in the SOA Development team; in particular to David Shaffer, Demed L'Her, Manoj Das, Neil Wyse, Ralf Mueller, and Mohamed Ashfar who contributed to this book in many ways.

A major part in the quality of any book is down to the reviewers, so I would like to say a big thank you to Phil McLaughlin, Jason Jones, and James Oliver for all their incredibly valuable feedback, which has made this a clearer and simpler book to read.

The staff at Packt Publishing Pvt. Ltd. helped a great deal to make this book a reality. I would like to thank Rajashree Hamine the Project Coordinator, Swapna Verlekar the Development Editor, and Gagandeep Singh the Technical Editor.

Finally, writing a book is challenging at the best of times, to do it whilst re-locating half way round the world from the UK to Australia probably isn't the best timing! So I would like to say a special thank you to my wife Natasha and my children Elliot and Kimberley for their constant support and understanding throughout this period.

Antony Reynolds has worked in the IT industry for more than 24 years, since getting a job to maintain yield calculations for a Zinc smelter while still an undergraduate. After graduating from the University of Bristol with a degree in Maths and Computer Science he worked first for a software house, IPL in Bath, England, before joining the travel reservations system Galileo as a development team lead. At Galileo he was involved in development and maintenance of workstation products before joining the architecture group. Galileo gave him the opportunity to work in Colorado and Illinois where he developed a love for the Rockies and Chicago style deep pan pizza. He joined Oracle in 1998 as a sales consultant and has worked with a number of customers in that time, including a large retail bank's Internet banking project for which he served as chief design authority and security architect.

Antony currently is lucky to work with customers on the early stages of many interesting projects, providing advice on sizing models and architecture for the SOA Suite.

Outside of work Antony is a bishop in the Church of Jesus Christ of Latter Day Saints (Mormons) and is responsible for a congregation of 350. His wife and four children make sure that he also spends time with them, playing games, watching movies, and acting as an auxiliary taxi service.

I would like to thank my wife Rowan, and my four very patient children, who have put up with their husband and father disappearing into his office in the roof far too often. Several reviewers have provided invaluable advice and assistance. Phil McLaughlin of Oracle has been a constant source of encouragement and constructive criticism as the book has homed in on its target platform. Iswarya Dhandapani of Luton Borough Council took the time to try out all my code samples and identify ones which didn't work as well as providing feedback on my chapters from the view of someone who has to use SOA Suite to provide real solutions. Oracle ACE Jason Jones came a little late to the reviewing but managed to review every chapter and made clear what worked for him and what didn't. Simone Geib of Oracle Product Management provided valuable feedback on the sections covering Oracle Service Bus. I particularly appreciated the way all the reviewers not only pointed out the problems in the book but also identified the positive parts. Edwin Khodabachian is no longer with Oracle, but his team created the BPEL Process Manager at Collaxa, which was bought by Oracle and became under Edwins guidance the foundation of the SOA Suite. Finally, I would like to express appreciation to Thomas Kurian at Oracle who had the vision of a single integrated product suite, the Oracle SOA Suite, and has always been willing to listen to provide advice and guidance to me.

About the reviewers

Jason Jones is a software architect specializing in SOA and Java technologies. Since 2003, Jason has worked for Zirous, an Oracle Certified Partner, where he currently holds the position of Senior System Architect. In 2007, Jason was named an Oracle ACE Director, a prestigious international group of Oracle experts. Jason has been accepted as a speaker at Oracle OpenWorld, IOUG COLLABORATE, ODTUG Kaleidoscope, and has a published article on OTN.

Jason's more than 8 years of experience in IT that includes SOA technologies such as BPEL, ESB, SOAP, WS-Security, XML, and Enterprise Java technologies such as Spring, Struts, JMS, JPA, Hibernate, and EJBs among many others. Jason is a Sun Certified Java Programmer (SCJP), Sun Certified Web Component Developer (SCWCD), and holds a BS in Computer Science from Iowa State University.

Jason's blog can be found at `realjavasoa.blogspot.com`.

Phil McLaughlin has 20 years of early adopter experience with the technologies associated with SOA, working with architectural models such as object orientation before they were mainstream. In the late 1980s and early 1990s this was largely with the Smalltalk programming language and associated tools but he was asked to investigate and teach Java in 1997. Since then, he has maintained his interest in the development of distributed composite applications intially with CORBA, then J2EE and more recently SOA itself.

Phil's experience of SOA spans the theoretical and practical, having been a senior lecturer in academia until 1997 specializing in object oriented software (which could reasonably be argued as providing the foundations of the SOA architectural model), and how to transfer the requisite skills to developers often struggling with new and different architectural paradigms. Since 1997, he has worked in a number of specialist consultancies covering topics such as analysis and design methods, development and implementation from the OO/SOA perspective.

Phil Joined Oracle Corporation (UK) in 2002 when Oracle acquired the TopLink persistence management framework from WebGain and since then has specialized in working with Partners/System Integrators to educate them on best practice around the use of Oracle Java technology and more recently the Oracle SOA Suite. Phil currently holds the position of Master Principal Sales Consultant in the UK SOA pre-sales team where he provides initial advice and solution mapping to customers and partners about Oracle's SOA offerings.

Phil has worked with both authors for a number of years and is very pleased that thay have decided to share their wealth of knowledge and practical experience with the wider community. For anyone working with Oracle SOA suite, this is a 'must have' book.

Table of Contents

Preface

Service-oriented architecture is not just changing how we approach application integration, but the mindset of software development as well.

Applications as we know them are becoming a thing of the past. In the future we will increasingly think of services and how those services are assembled to build complete "composite" applications that can be modified easily and quickly to adapt to a continually evolving business environment.

This is the vision of a standards-based service-oriented architecture (SOA), where the IT infrastructure is continuously adapted to keep up with the pace of business change.

Oracle is at the forefront of this vision, with the Oracle SOA Suite providing the most comprehensive, proven, and integrated tool kit for building SOA based applications.

This is no idle boast. Oracle Fusion Applications (the re-implementation of Oracle's E-Business Suite, Siebel, PeopleSoft, and JD Edwards Enterprise as a single application) is probably the largest composite application being built today and it has the Oracle SOA platform at its core.

Developers and architects using the Oracle SOA Suite, whether working on integration projects, building new bespoke applications, or specializing in large implementations of Oracle Applications will need a book that provides a hands-on guide on how best to harness and apply this technology. This book will enable them to do just that.

The initial section of the book is aimed at providing the reader with an overview of the Oracle SOA Suite and its various components, followed by a hands on introduction to each of them. This will provide the reader with a good feel for each of the components and how to use them.

Once the reader is familiar with various pieces of the SOA Suite and what they do, the next question will typically be:

What is the best way to combine/use all of these different components to implement a real world SOA solution?

Answering this question is the goal of the next section. Using a working example of an online auction site (oBay), it leads the reader through key SOA design considerations in implementing a robust solution that is designed for change. It explores topics such as:

- How to design sustainable service contracts, that is, ones that easily accommodate future change.
- How best to leverage functionality from existing systems when building business services, while still providing flexibility to plug in an alternate service provider at a later point.
- What is the right way to implement new services.
- When to use rules to implement specialized services for greater flexibility.
- The use of different interaction patterns and when to use each one.
- Strategies for data validation and error handling, whether system errors or business errors.
- Key considerations when implementing "Human Workflow".

Before an application is complete and moves from development into production, it must also meet non-functional criteria such as security, availability, and scalability requirements. The final section addresses these issues and covers considerations such as the packaging, deployment, testing, security, and administration of composite applications as well as the overall deployment of the infrastructure. Topics addressed include:

- Guidelines on packaging an application for easy deployment and movement from development to the test and production environments.
- Tips on building automated test suites that start at the component level and allow for testing of individual components and the complete assembly.
- Where are the most effective places to apply security and what options are available for securing the system.

What this book covers

The book is divided into three sections. Let us have a look at these three sections in detail.

Section 1: Getting started

This section provides an overview of the various components of the Oracle SOA Suite and gives the reader a fast-paced, hands-on introduction to each of the **key** components.

Chapter 1 gives an initial tour of the constituent parts, which make up the Oracle SOA Suite as well as detailing related elements of the Oracle Fusion Middleware stack and how they relate to the SOA Suite.

Chapter 2 provides an initial look at the Oracle BPEL Process Manager and Oracle Service Bus, by stepping us through the process of developing, deploying, and running our first service.

Chapter 3 looks at a number of key technology adapters and how we can use them to service enable existing systems.

Chapter 4 describes how we can use the Oracle Service Bus to build services that are implementation agnostic. Doing so allows us to change the service location, communication protocol, or even replace a service implementation with another, with no impact on the client.

Chapter 5 describes how we can use BPEL to assemble services to build composite services as well as how we can link together a number of services to build a long-running business process. It also introduces the concepts of synchronous and asynchronous services.

Chapter 6 looks at how human tasks can be managed through workflow activities embedded within a BPEL process.

One of the key motivations behind SOA is *Agility*, the ability of an organization to respond rapidly to changes in market conditions and hence gain a competitive advantage.

Chapter 7 introduces the concept of externalizing "decision points" in a BPEL process as business rules, allowing us to change the flow through a process without having to make any changes to the deployed process.

Chapter 8 examines how Business Activity Monitoring (BAM) can be used to give business users a real-time view into how the business process is performing.

Section 2: Putting it all together

This section uses the example of an online auction site (oBay) to illustrate how to use the various components of the SOA Suite to implement a real-world SOA based solution.

Each chapter covers a specific area that needs to be considered when developing a SOA based solution, such as the design of the service contract, validation, error handling, and message interaction patterns.

To highlight and demonstrate key design considerations, chapters use examples based on key parts of the oBay application to illustrate what's been covered, as well as providing a step-by-step guide on how to implement these techniques.

Chapter 9 introduces oBay and details the overall business requirements of the online auction site. Next, we present our outline for a typical SOA architecture, highlighting some of the key design considerations behind this. Finally, we use this to derive the overall architecture for oBay.

The first step in building a sustainable SOA based solution, that is, one that easily accommodates future change, is careful design of the service contracts. *Chapter 10* gives guidance on designing these contracts and provides strategies for managing change when it occurs.

Once we know what service we require, we need to select the appropriate way of providing it. In *Chapter 11,* we examine different approaches to this, either through service enabling an existing application, using someone else's service, or building the service from scratch.

A common question with SOA is "Where do I put my validation?" At first glance this may seem like an obvious question, but once we consider the layered approach to SOA, it soon becomes clear that there are a number of choices each with their own advantages and disadvantages. *Chapter 12* provides us with guidelines on where to put our validation and how to implement it.

Chapter 13 examines strategies for handling errors in SOA based systems. It covers system errors such as a network connection going down meaning a web service is temporarily unavailable, and business errors such as service being invoked with invalid data.

In every business process messages are exchanged between participants. So far, we have only looked at simple interactions, that is a single request followed by a reply, whether synchronous or asynchronous.

In *Chapter 14,* we look at messaging in a lot more detail. In particular, how we handle more complex interactions such as multiple requests and responses, unscheduled events, timeouts, and message correlation (both system and business).

In *Chapter 15,* we look at workflows involving complex chains of approval, including parallel approvers and the different options that are available. We also look at how we can use the Workflow Service API to integrate workflow into a user's existing user interface as an alternative to accessing it through the out of the box worklist application.

The Rules engine uses the Rete Algorithm, which was developed by researchers into Artificial Intelligence in the 1970s. In *Chapter 16,* we look at some of Rete's unique qualities, and how we can use them to implement particular categories of first class business services.

When we talk about web services, most people assume that we are going to bind (that is, connect to) the service using SOAP over HTTP. Indeed, this is often the case; however, Oracle SOA Suite supports binding to web services over multiple protocols. *Chapter 17* looks at the different bindings supported and the various advantages they have, including better support for transactions and improved performance.

Section 3: Other considerations

This final section covers other considerations such as the packaging, deployment, testing, security, and administration of composite applications as well as the overall deployment of the infrastructure.

Chapter 18 examines how to package up the various artifacts that make up a composite application in order to enable easy deployment into multiple environments such as test and production. We also look at suitable deployment topologies for the SOA Suite based on run-time requirements for high availability, disaster recovery, and scalability.

Chapter 19 looks at how to create, deploy, and run test cases that automate the testing of composite applications. Testing is dealt with at several levels: unit testing, component testing, and finally assembly testing.

Chapter 20 examines how we can centrally define policies that govern the operation of web services, such as security and access policies, auditing policies, and the management of service level agreements.

Who is this book for

The primary purpose of the book is to provide developers and technical architects with a practical guide to using and applying the Oracle SOA Suite delivering real-world SOA based applications.

It is assumed that the reader already has a basic understanding of the concepts of SOA, as well as some of the key standards in this space, including web services (SOAP, WSDL), XML Schemas, and XSLT (and XPath).

Conventions

In this book, you will find a number of styles of text that distinguish between different kinds of information. Here are some examples of these styles, and an explanation of their meaning.

Code words in text are shown as follows: "Each schema can reference definitions in other schemas by making use of the `xsd:import` directive."

A block of code will be set as follows:

```
<types>
  <schema xmlns="http://www.w3.org/2001/XMLSchema">
    <import namespace="http://xmlns.oracle.com/Echo"
            schemaLocation="Echo.xsd"/>
  </schema>
</types>
```

When we wish to draw your attention to a particular part of a code block, the relevant lines or items will be made bold:

```
<types>
  <schema xmlns="http://www.w3.org/2001/XMLSchema">
    <import namespace="http://xmlns.oracle.com/Echo"
            schemaLocation="Echo.xsd"/>
  </schema>
</types>
```

New terms and **important words** are introduced in a bold-type font. Words that you see on the screen, in menus or dialog boxes for example, appear in our text like this: "clicking the **Next** button moves you to the next screen".

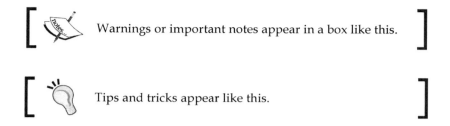

Warnings or important notes appear in a box like this.

Tips and tricks appear like this.

Reader feedback

Feedback from our readers is always welcome. Let us know what you think about this book, what you liked or may have disliked. Reader feedback is important for us to develop titles that you really get the most out of.

To send us general feedback, simply drop an email to feedback@packtpub.com, making sure to mention the book title in the subject of your message.

If there is a book that you need and would like to see us publish, please send us a note in the **SUGGEST A TITLE** form on www.packtpub.com or email suggest@packtpub.com.

If there is a topic that you have expertise in and you are interested in either writing or contributing to a book, see our author guide on www.packtpub.com/authors.

Customer support

Now that you are the proud owner of a Packt book, we have a number of things to help you to get the most from your purchase.

Downloading the example code for the book

Visit http://www.packtpub.com/files/code/3551_Code.zip to directly download the example code.

The downloadable files contain instructions on how to use them.

Errata

Although we have taken every care to ensure the accuracy of our contents, mistakes do happen. If you find a mistake in one of our books—maybe a mistake in text or code—we would be grateful if you would report this to us. By doing this you can save other readers from frustration, and help to improve subsequent versions of this book. If you find any errata, report them by visiting http://www.packtpub.com/support, selecting your book, clicking on the **let us know** link, and entering the details of your errata. Once your errata are verified, your submission will be accepted and the errata are added to the list of existing errata. The existing errata can be viewed by selecting your title from http://www.packtpub.com/support.

Piracy

Piracy of copyright material on the Internet is an ongoing problem across all media. At Packt, we take the protection of our copyright and licenses very seriously. If you come across any illegal copies of our works in any form on the Internet, please provide the location address or website name immediately so we can pursue a remedy.

Please contact us at copyright@packtpub.com with a link to the suspected pirated material.

We appreciate your help in protecting our authors, and our ability to bring you valuable content.

Questions

You can contact us at questions@packtpub.com if you are having a problem with some aspect of the book, and we will do our best to address it.

Introduction to Oracle SOA Suite

1

The Oracle SOA Suite is a large and complex piece of software. In this chapter we will provide a roadmap for your use of the SOA Suite. After a review of the basic principles of SOA we will look at how the SOA Suite provides support for those principles through its many different components. Following this journey through the components of SOA Suite, we will introduce Oracle JDeveloper as the primary development tool that is used to build applications for deployment into the SOA Suite.

Service-oriented architecture in short

Service-oriented architecture (SOA) has evolved to allow greater flexibility in adapting the IT infrastructure to satisfy the needs of business. Let's examine what SOA means by examining the components of its title.

Service

A service is a term that is understood both by the business and IT. It has some key characteristics:

- **Encapsulation**: A service creates delineation between the service provider and the service consumer. It identifies what will be provided.

- **Interface**: It is defined in terms of inputs and outputs. How the service is provided is not of concern to the consumer, only to the provider. The service is defined by its interface.

- **Contract or service level agreements**: There may be quality of service attributes associated with the service, such as performance characteristics, availability constraints, or cost.

The break-out box uses the example of a laundry service to make the characteristics of a service more concrete. Later we will map these characteristics onto specific technologies.

A clean example

Consider a laundry service. The service provider is a laundry company, and the service consumer a corporation or individual with washing to be done.

The input to the company is a basket of dirty laundry. Additional input parameters may be a request to iron the laundry as well as wash it, or to starch the collars. The output is a basket of clean washing with whatever optional additional services such as starching or ironing were specified. This defines the interface.

Quality of service may specify that the washing must be returned within 24 or 48 hours. Additional quality of service attributes may specify that the service is unavailable from 5PM Friday until 8AM Monday. These service level agreements may be characterized as policies to be applied to the service.

An important thing about services is that they can be understood by both business analysts and IT implementers. This leads to the first key benefit of service-oriented architecture.

SOA makes it possible for IT and the business to speak the same language, that of services.

Services allow us to have a common vocabulary between IT and the business.

Orientation

When we are building our systems we are looking at them from a service point of view or orientation. This implies that we are oriented or interested in the following:

- **Granularity**: The level of service interface or number of interactions required with the service, typically characterized as course grained or fine grained.
- **Collaboration**: Services may be combined together to create higher level or composite services.

- **Universality**: All components can be approached from a service perspective. For example, a business process may also be considered a service that, despite its complexity, provides inputs and outputs.

Thinking of everything as a service leads us to another key benefit of service-oriented architecture—**composability**.

 Composing new services out of existing services allows easy reasoning about the availability and performance characteristics of the composite service.

By building composite services out of existing services, we can reduce the amount of effort required to provide new functionality as well as being able to build something with prior knowledge of its availability and scalability characteristics. The latter can be derived from the availability and performance characteristics of the component services.

Architecture

Architecture implies a consistent and coherent design approach. This implies a need to understand the inter-relationships between components in the design and ensure consistency in approach. Architecture suggests that we adopt some of the following principles:

- **Consistency**: The same challenges should be addressed in a uniform way. For example, the application of security constraints needs to be enforced in the same way across the design. Patterns or proven design approaches can assist with maintaining consistency of design.

- **Reliability**: The structures created must be fit to purpose and meet the demands for which they are designed.

- **Extensibility**: A design must provide a framework that can be expanded in ways both foreseen and unforeseen. See the break out box on extensions.

Extending Antony's house

My wife and I designed our current house. We built in the ability to convert the loft into extra rooms and also allowed for a conservatory to be added. This added to the cost of the build but these were foreseen extensions. The costs of actually adding the conservatory and two extra loft rooms were low because the architecture allowed for this. In a similar way it is relatively easy to architect for foreseen extensions, such as additional related services and processes that must be supported by the business. When we wanted to add a playroom and another bathroom, this was more complex and costly as we had not allowed for it in the original architecture. Fortunately our original design was sufficiently flexible to allow for these additions but the cost was higher. In a similar way the measure of the strength of a service-oriented architecture is the way in which it copes with unforeseen demands, such as new types of business process and service that were not foreseen when the architecture was laid down. A well architected solution will be able to accommodate unexpected extensions at a manageable cost.

A consistent architecture when coupled with implementation in **SOA Standards** gives us another key benefit — **inter-operability**.

SOA allows us to build more inter-operable systems by being based on standards agreed by all the major technology vendors.

SOA is not about any specific technology. The principles of service-orientation can be applied equally well using assembler as they can in a high level language. However, as with all development it is easiest to use a model that is supported by tools and is both inter-operable and portable across vendors. SOA is widely associated with the web service or WS-* standards presided over by groups like OASIS. This use of common standards allows SOA to be inter-operable between vendor technology stacks.

Why SOA is different

A few years ago distributed object technology in the guise of CORBA and COM+ were going to provide benefits of reuse. Prior to that third and fourth generation languages such as C++ and Smalltalk based on object technology were to provide the same benefit. Even earlier the same claims were made for structured programming. So why is SOA different?

Terminology

The use of terms such as "services" and "processes" allows business and IT to talk about items in the same way, improving communication and reducing impedance mismatch between the two. The importance of this is greater than what it appears initially, because it drives IT to build and structure its systems around the business rather than vice versa.

Inter-operability

In the past there have been competing platforms for the latest software development fad. This manifested itself as CORBA and COM+, Smalltalk and C++, Pascal and C. This time around the standards are not based upon the physical implementation but upon the service interfaces and wire protocols. In addition these standards are generally text based to avoid issues around conversion between binary forms. This allows services implemented in C# under Windows to inter-operate with Java or PL/SQL services running on Oracle SOA Suite under Windows, Linux or UNIX. The major players like Oracle, Microsoft, IBM, SAP, and others are agreed on how to inter-operate together. This agreement has always been missing in the past.

WS Basic Profile

There is an old IT joke that standards are great, there are so many to choose from! Fortunately this has been recognized by the SOA vendors and they have collaborated to create a basic profile, or collection of standards, that focus on inter-operability. This is known as **WS Basic Profile** and details the key web service standards that all vendors should implement to allow for inter-operability. SOA Suite supports this basic profile as well as additional standards.

Extension and evolution

SOA recognizes that there are existing assets in the IT landscape and does not force these to be replaced, preferring instead to encapsulate and later extend these resources. SOA may be viewed as a boundary technology that reverses many of the earlier development trends. Instead of specifying how systems are built at the lowest level it focuses on how services are described and how they inter-operate in a standards-based world.

Reuse in place

A final major distinguishing feature for SOA is the concept of reuse in place. Most reuse technologies in the past have focused on reuse through libraries, at best sharing a common implementation on a single machine through the use of dynamic link libraries. SOA focuses not just on reuse of the code functionality but also upon the reuse of exiting machine resources to execute that code. When a service is reused the same physical servers with their associated memory and CPU are shared across a larger client base. This is good from the perspective of providing a consistent location to enforce code changes, security constraints, and logging policies but it does mean that performance of existing users may be impacted if care is not taken in how services are reused.

SOA Suite components

SOA Suite has a number of component parts, some of which may be licensed separately.

Services and adapters

The most basic unit of a service-oriented architecture is the service. This may be provided directly as a web service enabled piece of code or it may be exposed by encapsulating an existing resource.

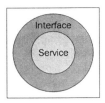

Services are defined by a specific interface, usually specified in a **Web Service Description Language (WSDL)** file. A WSDL file specifies the operations supported by the service. Each operation describes the expected format of the input message and if a message is returned it also describes the format of that message. The structure of WSDL files are described in Chapter 17.

Services are often surfaced through adapters that take an existing piece of functionality and "adapt" it to the SOA world so it can interact with other SOA Suite components. An example of an adapter is the file adapter that allows a file to be read or written to. The act of reading or writing the file is encapsulated into a service interface. This service interface can then be used to receive service requests by reading a file or to create service requests by writing a file.

Out of the box the SOA Suite includes licenses for the following adapters:

- File Adapter
- FTP Adapter
- Database Adapter
- JMS Adapter
- MQ Adapter
- AQ Adapter

The database adapter and the file adapter are explored in more detail in Chapter 3 and Chapter 11. There is also support for other non-SOAP transports and styles such as plain HTTP, REST, plain TCP/IP, and Java.

Services are the most important part of service-oriented architecture and in this book we focus on how to define their interfaces and how to best assemble services together to create composite services with a value beyond the functionality on a single atomic service.

ESB—service abstraction layer

To avoid service location dependencies it is desirable to access services through an **Enterprise Service Bus (ESB)**. This provides a layer of abstraction over the service and allows transformation of data between formats. The ESB is aware of the physical endpoint locations of services and acts to virtualize services.

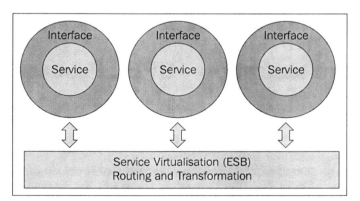

Services may be viewed as being plugged into the service bus.

An Enterprise Service Bus is responsible for routing and transforming service requests between components. By abstracting the physical location of a service an ESB allows services to be moved to different locations without impacting the clients of those services. The ability of an ESB to transform data from one format to another also allows for changes in service contracts to be accommodated without recoding client services. The service bus may also be used to validate that messages conform to interface contracts and to enrich messages by adding additional information to them as part of the message transformation process.

Oracle Service Bus and Oracle ESB

Note that the SOA Suite contains both the Oracle Service Bus (formerly AquaLogic Service Bus) and the Oracle ESB. The stated direction by Oracle is for the Oracle Service Bus to be the preferred ESB for interactions outside the SOA Suite. Interactions within the SOA Suite may sometimes be better dealt with by the Oracle ESB, which will be known as the Mediator component in the 11g release of SOA Suite, but we believe that for most cases the Oracle Service Bus will provide a better solution and so that is what we have focused on within this book. However, the current release of the Oracle Service Bus, only executes on the Oracle WebLogic platform. So when running SOA Suite on non-Oracle platforms there are two choices:

- Use only the Oracle ESB
- Run Oracle Service Bus on a separate WebLogic Server while running the rest of SOA Suite on the non-Oracle platform

We will focus on the Oracle Service Bus in this book, as that is the preferred direction for ESB functionality within the SOA Suite. Later releases of the SOA Suite will support Oracle Service Bus on non-Oracle platforms such as WebSphere.

Service orchestration—BPEL Process Manager

In order to build composite services, that is services constructed from other services, we need a layer that can orchestrate, or tie together, multiple services into a single larger service. Simple service orchestrations can be done within the Oracle Service Bus but more complex orchestrations require additional functionality. These service orchestrations may be thought of as processes, some of which are low-level processes and others are high-level business processes.

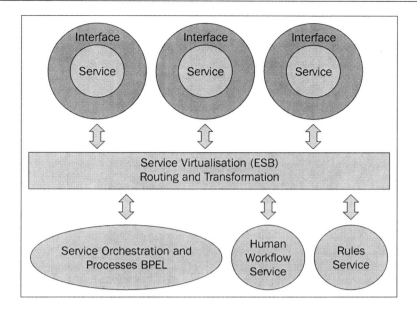

Business Process Execution Language is the standard way to describe processes in the SOA world, a task often referred to as service orchestration. The BPEL Process Manager in SOA Suite includes support for the BPEL 1.1 standard with some constructs from BPEL 2.0 also being supported. BPEL allows multiple services to be linked to each other as part of a single managed process. The processes may be short running, seconds and minutes, or long running, hours and days.

The BPEL standard says nothing about how people interact with it, but BPEL Process Manager includes a Human Workflow component that provides support for human interaction with processes.

The BPEL Process Manager may also be purchased as a standalone component, in which case it ships with the Human Workflow support and the same adapters as included in the SOA Suite.

We explore the BPEL Process Manager in more detail in Chapter 5 and Chapter 14. Human workflow is examined in Chapter 6 and Chapter 15.

Oracle also package the BPEL Process Manager with the Oracle Business Process Management (BPM) Suite. This package includes the former Aqualogic BPM product (acquired when BEA bought Fuego), now known as Oracle BPM. Oracle position BPEL as a system-centric process engine with support for human workflow while BPM is positioned as human-centric process engine with support for system interaction.

Rules

Business decision making may be viewed as a service within SOA. A rules engine is the physical implementation of this service.

SOA Suite includes a powerful rules engine that allows key business decision logic to be abstracted out of individual services and managed in a single repository. The rules engine is also included in the Oracle Application Server Enterprise Edition.

In Chapters 7 and 16 we investigate how to use the rules engine.

Security and monitoring—OWSM

One of the interesting features of SOA is the way in which aspects of a service are themselves a service. Nowhere is this better exemplified than with security. Security is a characteristic of services, yet to implement it effectively requires a centralized policy store coupled with distributed policy enforcement at the service boundaries. The central policy store can be viewed as a service that the infrastructure uses to enforce service security policy.

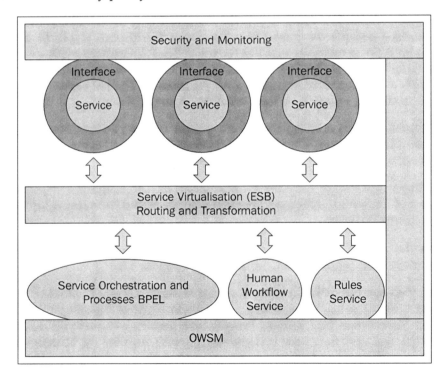

The Oracle Web Services Manager has several roles to play within an SOA. Firstly it serves as a policy enforcement point for security, ensuring that only requests that comply with policy are accepted. Secondly it provides a monitoring service to ensure that services are compliant with their service level agreements.

Security policy may also be applied through the Service Bus although policy definition is currently different between the Service Bus and OWSM the direction is for Oracle to have a common policy management in a future release.

Applying security policies is covered in Chapter 20.

Active monitoring–BAM

It is important in SOA to track what is happening in real time. Some business processes require such real-time monitoring. Users such as financial traders, risk assessors, and security services may need instant notification of business events that have occurred.

Business Activity Monitoring is part of the SOA Suite and provides a real time view of processes and services data to end users. BAM is covered in Chapter 8.

Business to business—B2B

Although we can use adapters to talk to remote systems, we often need additional features to support external services, either as clients or providers. For example, we may need to verify that there is a contract in place before accepting or sending messages to a partner. Management of agreements or contracts is a key additional piece of functionality that is provided by Oracle B2B. B2B can be thought of as a special kind of adapter that, in addition to support for B2B protocols such as EDIFACT/ANSI X12 or RosettaNet, it also supports agreement management. Agreement management allows control over the partners and interfaces used at any given point in time. We will not cover B2B in this book as the B2B space is a little at the edge of most SOA deployments.

Complex Event Processing—CEP

As our services execute we will often generate events. These events can be monitored and processed using the complex event processor. The difference between event and message processing is that messages generally require some action on their own with little or minimal additional context. Events on the other hand often require us to monitor several of them to spot and respond to trends. For example, we may treat a stock sale as a message when we need to record it and reconcile it with the accounting system. We may also want to treat the stock sale as an event, in which we wish to monitor the overall market movements in a single stock or in related stocks to decide whether we should buy or sell. The complex event processor allows us to do time based and series based analysis of data. We will not talk about CEP in this book as it is a complex part of the SOA suite that requires a complementary but different approach to the other SOA components.

SOA Suite architecture

We will now examine how Oracle SOA Suite provides the services identified above.

Top level

The SOA Suite is built on top of a Java Enterprise Edition (Java EE) infrastructure. Although SOA Suite is certified with several different Java EE servers, including IBM WebSphere, it will most commonly be used with the Oracle WebLogic Server. Currently the SOA Suite is provided with an integrated install for Oracles OC4J container but this is changing to make WebLogic the primary platform. The Oracle WebLogic Server (WLS) will probably always be the first available Java EE platform for SOA suite and is the only platform that will be provided bundled with SOA Suite to simplify installation. For the rest of this book we will assume that you are running SOA Suite on Oracle WebLogic Server. If there are any significant differences when running on non-Oracle application servers we will highlight them in the text.

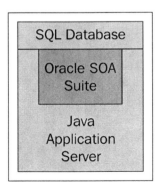

In addition to a Java EE application server the SOA Suite also requires a database. The SOA Suite is designed to run against any SQL database, but certification for non-Oracle databases has been slow in coming. The database is used to maintain configuration information and also records of runtime interactions. Currently SOA Suite on Windows ships with an Oracle Lite database which is suitable for development use only. There is also the option to use a full Oracle Database on Windows, and this is required for non-Windows platforms. Oracle Database XE can be used with the SOA Suite.

Component view

In a previous section, we examined the individual components of the SOA Suite and here we show them in context with the Java EE container and the database.

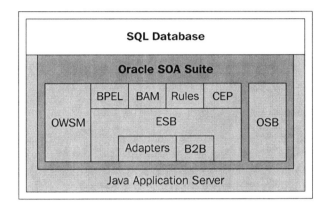

All the services execute within the context of the JEE container (except for BAM which is a Windows application in 10.1.3), although they may use that container in different ways. BPEL listens for events and updates processes based upon those events. Adapters typically make use of the Java EE containers connector architecture (JCA) to provide connectivity and notifications. OWSM acts as a filter when used in embedded mode, and as a separate application when used as a gateway. Note that the Oracle Service Bus (OSB) is only available when the application server is a WebLogic server.

Implementation view

Oracle has put a lot of effort into making SOA Suite consistent in its use of underlying services. A number of lower level services are reused consistently across components.

At the lowest level connectivity services such as adapters, JMS, and Web Service Invocation Framework are shared by higher level components.

A service layer exposes higher level functions. BPEL Process Manager is implemented by a combination of a BPEL engine and access to the Human Workflow engine. Rules is another shared service that is available to BPEL or other components.

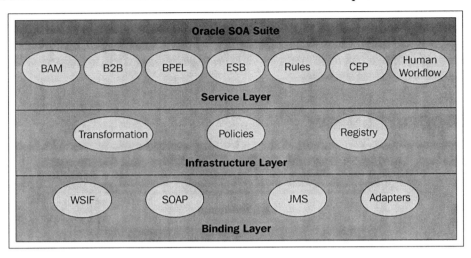

A recursive example

The SOA Suite architecture is a good example of service-oriented design principles being applied. Common services have been identified and extracted to be shared across many components. The high-level services such as BPEL and ESB share some common services such as transformation and adapter services running on a standard Java EE container.

JDeveloper

Everything we have spoken of so far has been related to the executable or runtime environment. Specialist tools are required to take advantage of this environment. It is possible to hand craft the assemblies and descriptors required to build a SOA Suite application but it is not a practical proposition. Fortunately Oracle provide JDeveloper free of charge to allow developers to build SOA Suite applications.

JDeveloper is actually a separate tool but it has been developed in conjunction with SOA Suite so that virtually all facilities of SOA Suite are accessible through JDeveloper. The one exception to this is the Oracle Service Bus which in the current release does not have support in JDeveloper but instead has a different tool, WebLogic Workspace Studio. Although JDeveloper started life as a Java development tool, many users now never touch the Java side of JDeveloper, doing all their work in the SOA Suite components.

JDeveloper may be characterized as a model based, wizard driven development environment. Re-entrant wizards are used to guide the construction of many artifacts of the SOA Suite, including adapters and transformation.

JDeveloper has a consistent view that the code is also the model, so that graphical views are always in synch with the underlying code. It is possible to exercise some functionality of SOA Suite using the Eclipse platform, but to get full value out of SOA Suite it is really necessary to use JDeveloper. However, the Eclipse platform does provide the basis for the Service Bus designer, the Workspace Studio. There are some aspects of development which may be supported in both tools but easier in one than the other; for example, Workspace Studio provides a better WSDL editor than JDeveloper.

Other components

We have now touched on all the major components of the SOA Suite. However, there are a few items that are either of more limited interest or are outside the SOA Suite but closely related to it.

Service repository and registry

Oracle have a service repository and registry product that is integrated with the SOA Suite but separate from it. The repository acts as a central repository for all SOA artifacts and can be used to support both developers and deployers in tracking dependencies betweens components both deployed and in development. The repository can publish SOA artifacts such as service definitions and locations to the service registry. The Oracle Service registry may be used to categorize and index services created. Users may then browse the registry to locate services. The service registry may also be used as a runtime location service for service endpoints.

BPA Suite

The Oracle BPA Suite is targeted at Business Process Analysts who want a powerful repository based tool to model their business processes. BPA Suite is not an easy product to learn, like all modeling tools there is a price to pay for the descriptive power available. Of interest to SOA Suite developers is the ability for the BPA Suite and SOA Suite to exchange process models. Processes created in BPA Suite may be exported to SOA Suite for concrete implementation. Simulation of processes in BPA Suite may be used as a useful guide for process improvement.

Links between BPA Suite and SOA Suite are growing stronger over time and it provides a valuable bridge between business analysts and IT architects.

BPM Suite

Business Process Management Suite is focused on modeling and execution of business processes. As mentioned it includes BPEL Process Manager to provide strong system-centric support for business processes but the primary focus of the suite is on modeling and executing processes in the BPM Designer and BPM Server.

Portals and WebCenter

SOA Suite has no real end user interface outside the Human Workflow service. Front ends may be built using JDeveloper directly or they may be crafted as part of Oracle Portal, Oracle WebCenter or another Portal or front end builder. A number of portlets are provided to expose views of SOA Suite to end users through the portal. These are principally related to human workflow but also include some views onto BPEL process status. Portals can also take advantage of WSDL interfaces to provide a user interface onto services exposed by the SOA Suite.

Enterprise manager SOA management pack

Oracles preferred management framework is Oracle Enterprise Manager. This is provided as a base set of functionality with a large number of management packs which provide additional functionality. The SOA Management Pack extends Enterprise Manager to provide monitoring and management of artifacts within the SOA Suite.

Summary

As we have seen there are a lot of components to SOA Suite and although Oracle has done a lot to provide consistent usage patterns there is still a lot to learn about each component. The rest of this book takes a solution-oriented approach to SOA Suite rather than a component approach. We will examine the individual components in the context of the role they serve and how they are used to enable service-oriented architecture.

2
Writing Your First Service

In this chapter we are going to provide a hands on introduction to the core components of the Oracle SOA Suite, namely the Oracle BPEL Process Manager (or BPEL PM) and the Oracle Service Bus (or OSB). We will do this by implementing an Echo service, a trivial service, which takes a single string as input and then returns the same string as its output.

We will first use JDeveloper to implement and deploy this as a BPEL process. During which, we will take the opportunity to give a high level tour of JDeveloper in order to familiarize you with its overall layout.

Once we have successfully deployed our first BPEL process, we will use the BPEL Console to execute a test instance of our process and examine its audit trail.

Next we will introduce the Service Bus, and look at how we can use its web based console to build and deploy a proxy service on top of our BPEL process. Once deployed, we will use the tooling provided by the Service Bus Console to test our end-to-end service.

Installing SOA Suite

Before creating and running your first service, you will need to download and install the SOA Suite. As of the time of writing, the Oracle SOA Suite 10.1.3.4 deploys on Oracle Application Server 10.1.3.4 (and WebLogic 9.2), apart from the Oracle Service Bus 10gR3 which deploys on WebLogic 10gR3.

This is likely to change in the near future, with all components being certified to deploy on WebLogic 10gR3. Rather than document an installation process which is likely to be out of date almost as soon as the book is published, we have decided to make this available separately from the book.

To download the installation guide, go to the support page of Packt Publishing (www.packtpub.com/support); from here follow the instructions to download a ZIP file containing the code for the book. Included in the ZIP will be a PDF Document named **SoaSuiteInstallation.pdf**.

This document details the quickest and easiest way to get the SOA Suite up and running. It covers the following:

- Where to download the SOA Suite and any other required components

- How to install and configure the SOA Suite

- How to install and run the oBay application, as well as the other code samples that come with this book

Writing our first BPEL process

Ensure that the Oracle SOA Suite has started (as described in the above mentioned installation guide) and start JDeveloper. When you start JDeveloper for the first time, it will be pretty empty as shown in the following screenshot:

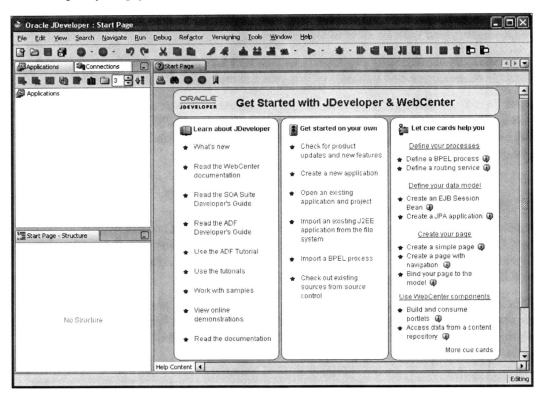

The top left hand window is the **Applications** navigator, which lists all the applications that we are working on (which is currently empty as we have not yet defined any). With JDeveloper an application is a grouping of one or more related projects. A project is a collection of related components that make up a deployable resource (for example a BPEL process, Java Application, web service, and so on).

Within the context of the SOA Suite, each BPEL process is defined within its own project, with an application being a collection of related BPEL Processes.

Next to the **Applications** navigator tab is the **Connections** tab. If we click on this, it will list the types of connections we can define to JDeveloper. A connection allows us to define and manage links to external resources, such as databases, application servers, and rules engines.

Once defined, we can expand a connection to inspect the content of an external resource, which can then be used to create or edit components which utilize the resource. For example, you can use a database connection to create and configure a database adapter to expose a database table as a web service.

Connections also allow us to deploy projects from JDeveloper to the external resource. If you haven't done so already, you will need to define a connection to the integration server (as described in the installation guide); we will need this to deploy our BPEL processes from within JDeveloper.

The main window within JDeveloper is used to edit the artifact we are currently working on (for example BPEL process, Extensible Stylesheet Language Transformations (XSLT), Process, XSLT Transformation, Java code, and so on). The top of this window contains a tab for each resource we have open, allowing you to quickly switch between them.

At the moment, the only artifact that we have opened is the **Start Page**, which provides links to various documents on JDeveloper, and so on.

The bottom left hand corner contains the **Structure** window; the content of this depends on the resource we are currently working on.

Creating an application

Within JDeveloper, an application is the main container for our work; it consists of a directory where all our application projects will be created.

So, before we can create our `Echo` BPEL process we must create the application to which it will belong. Within the **Applications Navigator** tab in JDeveloper right-click on the **Applications** element (circled in the following screenshot) and select **New Application**.

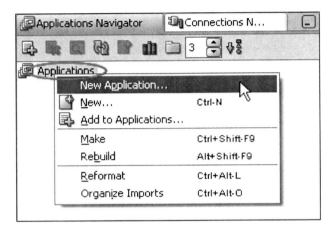

This will launch the **Create Application** dialogue as shown in the following screenshot:

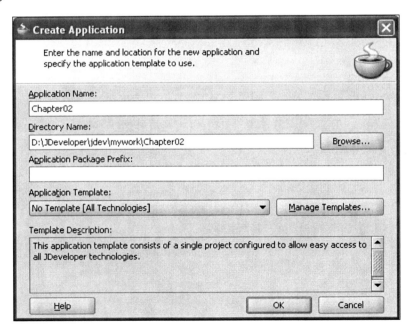

Give the application an appropriate name, such as **Chapter02**.

We can specify the top level directory in which we want to create our applications; by default JDeveloper will set it to:

```
<JDEVELOPER_HOME>\jdev\mywork\<Application Name>
```

Normally, we would specify a directory that's not under JDEVELOPER_HOME, as this makes it simpler to upgrade to future releases of JDeveloper.

In addition you can specify an **Application Template**. This is only applicable if creating a Web or Java Application. For our purposes, always keep the default **No Template [All Technologies]** and click **OK**.

Next JDeveloper will prompt us with the option to create a new empty project; as we don't need this, select **Cancel**.

Creating a BPEL project

The next step is to add a BPEL project to our newly created application. Right-click on the application name and select **New Project**, as shown in the following screenshot:

This will launch the project gallery window, where we can specify the type of project we want to create. Select **BPEL Process Project** as shown in the following screenshot:

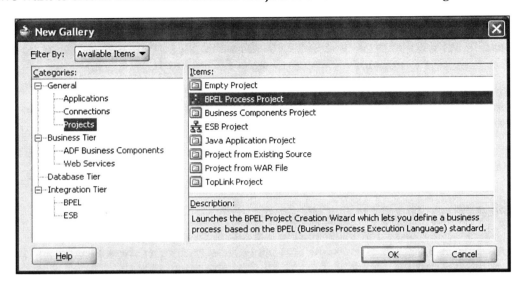

This will launch the **BPEL Project Creation Wizard** as shown in the following screenshot:

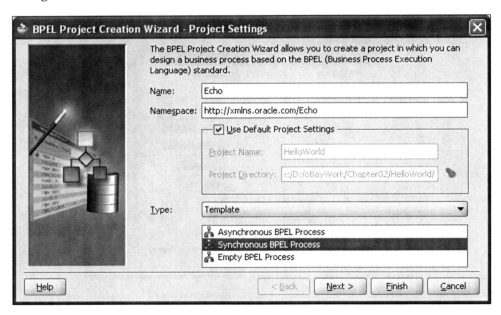

Give the process a name, that is **Echo**, and select a template of type **Synchronous BPEL Process** and click **Finish**. JDeveloper will create a skeleton BPEL process and a corresponding WSDL that describes the web service implemented by our process.

If we look at the process that JDeveloper has created (shown in the following screenshot), we can see in the center is the process itself, which contains the activities to be carried out. At the moment it just contains an initial activity for receiving a request and a corresponding activity for sending a response.

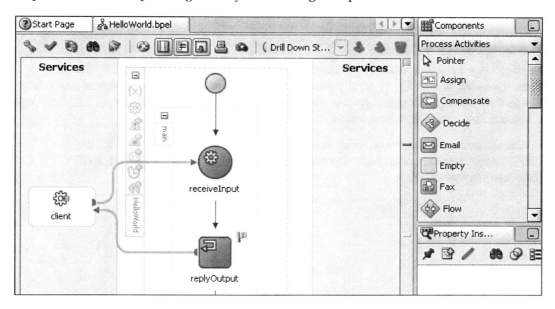

Either side of the process we have a swim lane which contains PartnerLinks that represent either the caller of our process, as is the case with the **client** PartnerLink, or services that our BPEL process calls out to. This at the moment is empty as we haven't defined any.

The **Components** window (to the right of our process window in the previous screenshot) lists all the **Process Activities** that we can use within our process. To use any of these, simply drag-and-drop them onto the appropriate place within our process.

If you click on the **Process Activities** drop down, you also have the option of selecting **Services**, which we use whenever we need to call out to an external system.

Getting back to our skeleton process, we can see it consists of two activities: **receiveInput** and **replyOutput**. In addition it has two variables: inputVariable and outputVariable which were created as part of our skeleton process.

The first activity is used to receive the initial request from the client invoking our BPEL process; on receipt of this request it will populate the variable `inputVariable` with the content of the request.

The last activity is used to send a response back to the client, the content of this response will contain the content of `outputVariable`.

For the purpose of our simple Echo process, we just need to copy the content of the input variable to the output variable.

Assigning values to variables

In BPEL the `<assign>` activity is used to update the values of variables with new data. The assign activity typically consists of one or more copy operations. Each copy consists of a target variable, that is the variable that you wish to assign a value to and a source; this can either be another variable or an XPath expression.

To insert an **Assign** activity, drag one from the **Component** pallet on to our BPEL process at the point just after the **receiveInput** activity, as shown in the following screenshot:

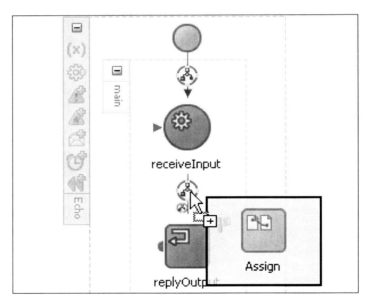

To configure the **Assign** activity, double-click on it to open up its configuration window. Click on the **Create** menu and select **Copy Operation...** as shown in the following screenshot:

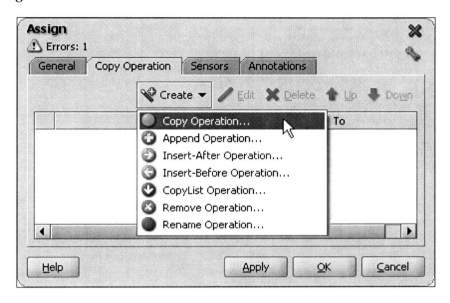

This will present us with the **Create Copy Operation** window as shown:

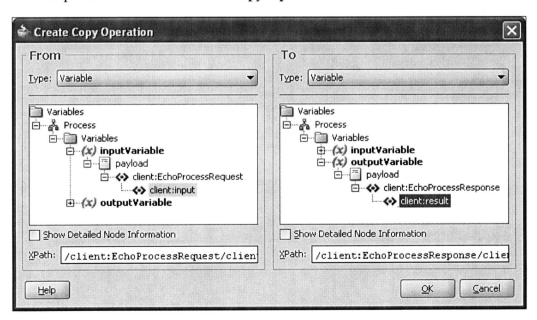

On the left-hand side we specify the **From** variable, that is where we want to copy from. For our process we want to copy the content of our input variable to our output variable. So expand **inputVariable** and select **/client:EchoProcessRequest/client:input** as shown in the previous screenshot.

On the righthand side we specify the **To** variable, that is where we want to copy to. So expand **outputVariable** and select **/client:EchoProcessResponse/client:result**.

Once you've done this click **OK**, and then **OK** again to close the **Assign** window.

Deploying the process

This completes our process, so click on the **Save All** icon (the fourth icon along, in the top left-hand corner of JDeveloper) to save our work.

[As a BPEL project is made up of multiple files, we typically use **Save All** to ensure all modifications are updated at the same time.]

Our process is now ready to be deployed. Before doing this make sure the SOA Suite is running and that within JDeveloper we have defined an **Integration Server** connection (as described in the installation guide).

To deploy the process, right click on our **Echo** project (circled in the next screenshot) and then select: **Deploy | SoaSuite | Deploy to default domain**.

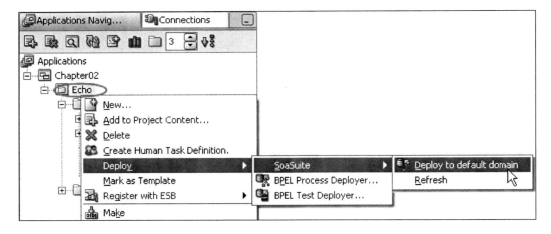

This will start the process of building our process, JDeveloper will open up a window below our process containing three tabs: **Messages**, **BPEL Messages,** and **Apache Ant** to which it outputs the status of the deployment process.

On completion of the build process the **Message** tab will state **Please check Ant log to determine whether the project deployed successfully**. If you click on the **Apache Ant** tab it should show the message **BUILD SUCCESSFUL**, as shown in the following screenshot:.

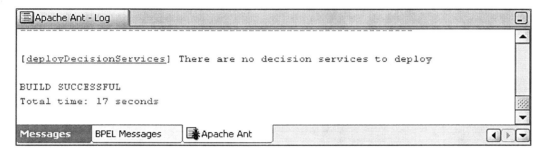

If you don't get this message, check the build log for details of the error and fix it accordingly.

Testing the BPEL process

Now that our process has been deployed, the next step is to run it. A simple way to do this is to initiate a test instance using BPEL Control: the web-based management console for BPEL PM.

To launch BPEL Control, from the programs menu in Windows, select:

All Programs | Oracle - Oracle_Home | Oracle BPEL Process Manager | BPEL Control.

Or alternatively, open up a browser and enter the URL:

```
http://<hostname>:<port>/BPELConsole
```

This will bring up the login screen for BPEL Control; log in as **bpeladmin** (default password **welcome1**). This will take us to the BPEL Control Dashboard as shown in the following screenshot:

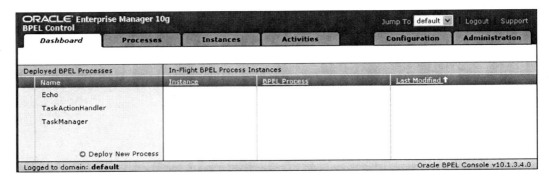

The **Dashboard** provides us with a summary report on a BPEL domain. On the left hand side we have a list of deployed processes, which includes the two default processes created by BPEL as well as the **Echo** process that we have just deployed.

On the right hand-side it lists BPEL processes that are currently executing and the most recently completed processes. At the moment this is empty as we haven't run any yet.

From here click on the process name, that is **Echo**; this will take us to the **Initiate** screen for running a test instance of our process, as we can see in the following screenshot:

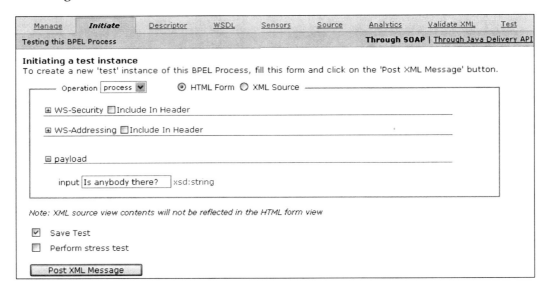

When we created our process, JDeveloper automatically created a WSDL file which contained the single operation (that is **process**). However, it's quite common to define processes that have multiple operations, as we will see later in this book.

The **Operation** drop-down allows us to specify which operation we want to invoke; in our case, it's automatically defaulted to **process**.

When you select the operation to invoke, the console will generate an **HTML Form**, with a field for each element in the message payload of the operation (as defined by the WSDL for the process). Here we can enter into each field the value that we want to submit.

For operations with large message payloads, it can be simpler to just enter the XML source. If you select the **XML Source** radio button, the console will replace the form with a free text area, with a skeleton XML fragment into which we can insert the required values.

You may have noticed that in the previous screenshot we have checked the box **Save Test**; this will cause BPEL PM to save our test values. So next time we initiate a test process, those values will be pre-populated in the form, which we can then modify if required. This can be quite useful if we have several fields as it can save us the hassle of rekeying them every time.

To execute a test instance of our process, enter some text in the **input** field and click **Post XML Message**. This will cause the Console to generate a SOAP message and use it to invoke our Echo process.

Upon successful execution of the process, our test page will be updated to show the response returned by our process. Here we can see that the **result** element contains our original initial **input** string as shown in the following screenshot:

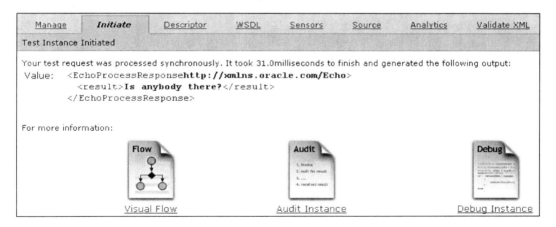

If we click on the **Visual Flow** link, this will display details of the process instance, along with a graphic audit trail showing the activities that have been executed, as shown in the following screenshot:

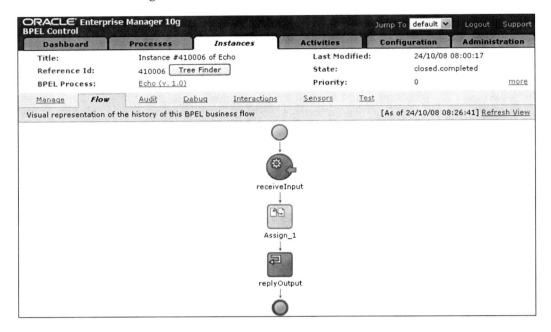

Clicking on any of the activities in the audit trail will pop up a window displaying details of the actions performed by that activity. In the following figure we can see details of the message sent by the **replyOutput** activity.

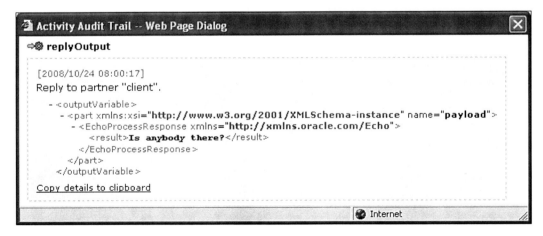

If you close this and return to the **Dashboard** tab in BPEL Control, you will see that our process is listed under the **Recently Completed BPEL Process Instances** section. If you click on the instance ID it will take you back to the process audit trail.

This completes development of our first BPEL process; the next step is to call it via the service bus. In preparation for this, we will need the URL for the WSDL of our process. To obtain this, from the BPEL **Dashboard** click on the **Echo** process, and then the **WSDL** tab; this will display a link for the **WSDL location** and **Endpoint** as shown in the following screenshot:

If you click on this link, the BPEL Console will open a window showing details of the WSDL. Make a note of the WSDL location as we will need this in a moment.

Writing our first proxy service

Rather than allow clients to directly invoke our Echo process, best practice dictates that we provide access to this service via an intermediary or **proxy**, whose role is to route the request to the actual endpoint. This results in a far more loosely coupled solution, which is key if we are to realize many of the benefits of SOA.

In this section, we are going to use the Oracle Service Bus to implement a **proxy Echo service**, which sits between the **Client** and our **Echo BPEL Process** as illustrated in the following figure:

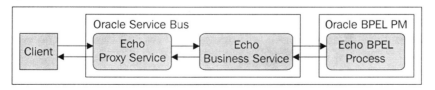

It is useful to examine the above scenario to understand how messages are processed by OSB. The Service Bus defines two types of services:

- A proxy service
- A business service

The **proxy service** is an intermediary service that sits between the client and the actual end service being invoked (that is our BPEL process in the previous example).

On receipt of a request, the proxy service may perform a number of actions on the request, such as validating, transforming, or enriching it before routing it to the appropriate business service.

Within the Oracle Service Bus, a business service is a definition of an external service for which OSB is a client. This defines to OSB how to invoke the external service and includes details such as the service interface, transport, security, and so on.

In the above example we have defined an **Echo Proxy Service**, which routes messages to the **Echo Business Service**, which then invokes our **Echo BPEL Process**. The response from the Echo BPEL Process follows the reverse path, with the proxy service returning the final response to the original client.

Writing the Echo proxy service

Ensure that the Oracle Service Bus has started and then open up the Service Bus Console. Either do this from the programs menu in Windows, using the following path:

Oracle Weblogic | User Projects | OSB | Oracle Service Bus Admin Console

Or alternatively, open up a browser and enter the URL:

```
http://<hostname>:<port>/sbconsole
```

Hostname represents the name of the machine on which OSB is running and port represents the port number. So if OSB is running on your local machine using the default port, enter the following URL in your browser:

```
http://localhost:7001/sbconsole
```

This will bring up the login screen for the Service Bus Console; log in as **weblogic** (default password **weblogic**). By default the OSB Console will display the **Dashboard** view which provides a summary of the overall health of the system.

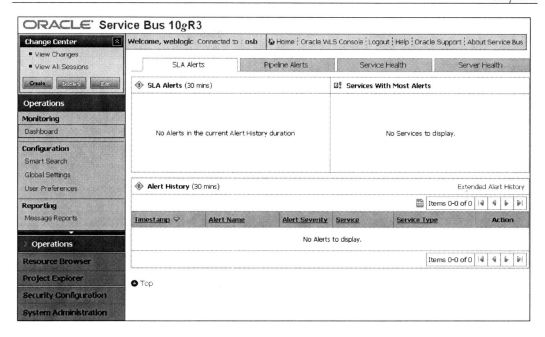

Looking at the console we can see it divides into three distinct areas. In the top left-hand corner is the, the **Change Center**, which we will cover in a moment. Also on the left, below the **Change Center** is the navigation bar which we use to navigate our way round the console.

The navigation bar is divided into the following sections: **Operations**, **Resource Browser**, **Project Explorer**, **Security Configuration,** and **System Administration**. Clicking on the appropriate section will expand that part of the navigation bar, and allow you to access any of its sub-sections and their corresponding menu items.

Clicking on any of the menu items will display the appropriate page within the main window of the console. In the previous screenshot, we are looking at the **Dashboard** view, under **Monitoring** which is part of the **Operations** section.

Creating a change session

Before we can create a new project, or make any configuration changes through the console, we must create a new change session. A **change session** allows us to specify a series of changes as a single unit of work; these changes won't come into effect until we activate a session. At any point we can discard our changes, which will cause OSB to roll back those changes and exit our session.

While making changes through a session, other users can also be making changes under separate sessions. If users create changes that conflict with changes in other sessions then the Service Bus will flag that as a conflict in the **Change Center** and neither user will be able to commit their changes until those conflicts have been resolved.

To create a new change session, click on **Create** in the Change Center; this will update the Change Center to indicate a session and the user who owns that session. As we are logged in as weblogic, it will be updated to show **weblogic session** as shown in the following screenshot:

In addition you will see that the options available to us in the Change Center have changed to **Activate, Discard,** and **Exit.**

Creating a project

Before we can create our Echo proxy service we must create an OSB project in which to place our resources. Typical resources include WSDL, XSD schemas, XSLT, and XQuery as well as Proxy and business services.

Resources can be created directly within our top level project folder, or we can define a folder structure within our project into which we can place our resources.

Note that from within the same OSB domain you can reference any resource regardless of which project it is included in.

The **Project Explorer** is where we create and manage all these artifacts. Click on the **Project Explorer** section within the navigation bar. This will bring up the **Projects** view as shown in the following screenshot:

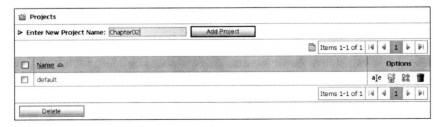

Here we can see a list of all projects defined in OSB, which at this stage just includes the **default** project. From here we can also create a new project; enter a project name, for example **Chapter02** as shown in the screenshot, and then click **Add Project**. This will create a new project and update our list of projects to reflect this.

Creating project folders

Click on the project name; this will take us to the **Project View** as shown in the following screenshot.

We can see that this splits into three sections. The first section provides some basic details about the project including any references to or from artifacts in other projects as well as an optional description.

The second section lists any folders within the current project folder, and provides the option to create additional folders within the project.

The final section lists any resource contained within this folder, and provides the option to create additional resource.

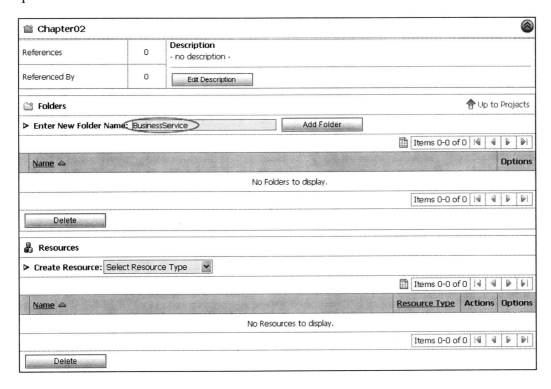

We are going to create the project folders **BusinessService**, **ProxyService,** and **WSDL**, into which we will place our various resources. To create the first of these, in the **Folders** section enter **BusinessService** as the folder name (circled in the previous screenshot) and click **Add Folder**. This will create a new folder and update the list of folders to reflect this.

Once created, follow the same process to create the remaining folders; your list of folders will now look as follows:

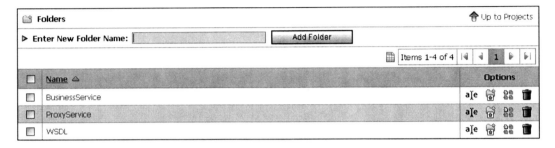

Creating service WSDL

Before we can create either our proxy or business service we need to define the WSDL on which the service will be based. For this we are going to use the WSDL of our Echo BPEL process that we created earlier in this chapter.

Before importing the WSDL, we need to ensure that we are in the right folder within our project; to do this click on the **WSDL** folder in our **Folders** list. On doing this the project view will be updated to show us the content of this folder, which is currently empty. In addition the project summary section of our project view will be updated to show that we are now within the WSDL folder, as circled in the following screenshot:

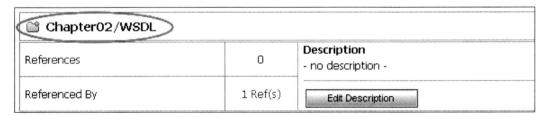

If we look at the **Project Explorer** in the navigation bar, we can see it has been updated to show our location within the projects structure. By clicking on any project or folder in here the console will take us to the project view for that location.

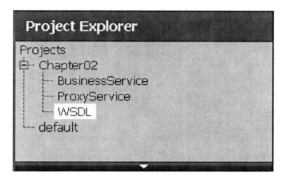

Importing a WSDL

To import the `Echo` WSDL into our project, click on the drop down next to **Create Resource** in the **Resources** section and select **Resources from URL** as shown in the following screenshot:

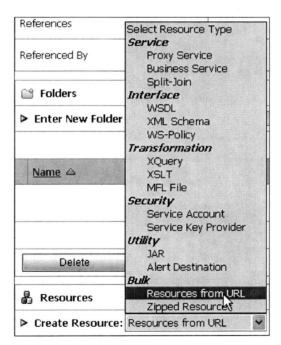

This will bring up the page for loading resources from a URL as shown in the following screenshot:

 A WSDL can also be imported from the file system by selecting the **WSDL** option from the **Create Resource** drop down.

In the **URL/Path** enter the URL for our Echo WSDL. This is the **WSDL Location** we made a note of earlier (in the **WSDL** tab for the Echo process in the BPEL Console) and should look like the following:

```
http://<hostname>:<port>/orabpel/default/Echo/1.0/Echo?wsdl
```

Enter an appropriate value for the **Resource Name** (for example **Echo**), select a **Resource Type** of **WSDL** and click **Next**.

This will bring up the **Load Resources** window, which will list the resources that OSB is ready to import.

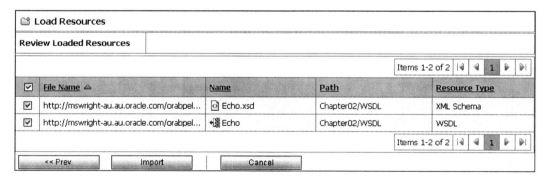

You will notice that in addition to the actual WSDL file, it will also list the `Echo.xsd`. This is because the `Echo.wsdl` contains the following import statement:

```
<types>
  <schema xmlns="http://www.w3.org/2001/XMLSchema">
    <import namespace="http://xmlns.oracle.com/Echo"
            schemaLocation="Echo.xsd"/>
  </schema>
</types>
```

This imports the Echo XML Schema, which defines the input and output message of our Echo service. This schema was automatically generated by JDeveloper when we created our `Echo` process; in order to use our WSDL we will need to import this schema as well.

Click **Import**; the OSB Console will confirm that the resources have been successfully imported, and provide the option to **Load Another** resource, as shown in the following screenshot:

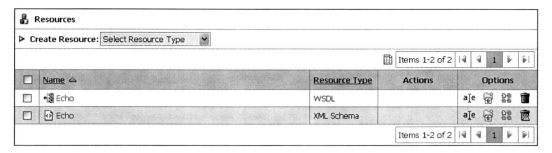

Click on the **WSDL** folder within the **Project Explorer** to return to its project view. This will be updated to include our imported resources, as shown:

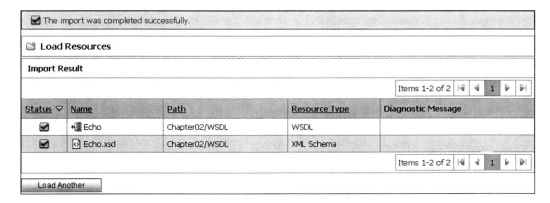

Creating our business service

We are now ready to create our Echo business service. Click on the **Business Service** folder within the **Project Explorer** to go to the project view for this folder.

In the **Resources** section click on the drop down next to **Create Resource** and select **Business Service**. This will bring up the **General Configuration** page for creating a business service as shown in the following screenshot:

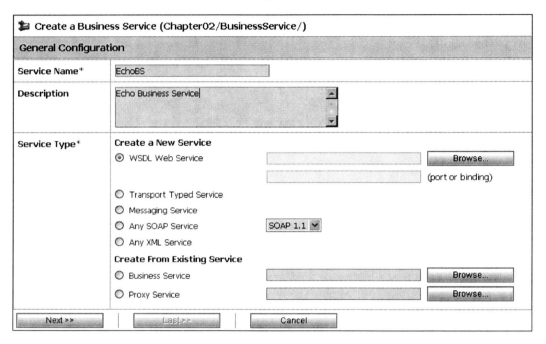

Here we specify the name of our business service (i.e. **EchoBS**) and an optional description. Next we need to specify the **Service Type**. As we are creating our service based on a WSDL select **WSDL Web Service**.

Next click the **Browse** button; this will launch a window from where we can select the WSDL for the business service, as shown in the following screenshot:

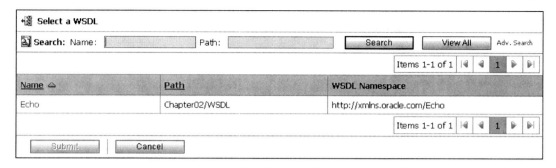

By default, this window will list all WSDL resources defined to the service bus, though you can restrict the list by defining search criteria.

In our case, we have just the Echo WSDL, so click on this. We will now be prompted to select a WSDL definition as shown in the following screenshot:

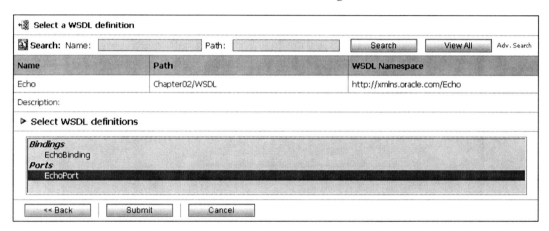

Here we need to select which binding or port definition we wish to use for our Business Service; select **EchoPort** and click **Submit**.

This will return us to the **General Configuration** screen, with the **Service Type** updated to show the details of the selected WSDL and port as shown in the following screenshot:

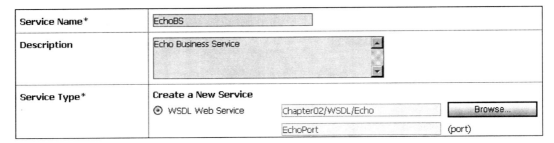

Click **Next**; this will take us to the **Transport Configuration** page shown in the following screenshot. Here we need to specify how the business service is to invoke the external service.

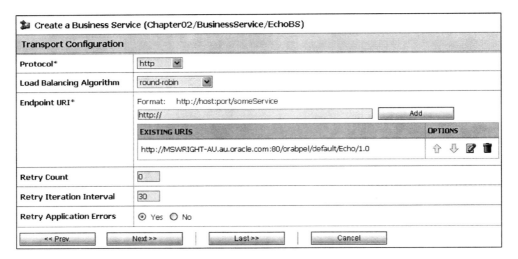

As we based our business service on the **EchoPort** definition, the transport settings are already pre-configured based on the content of our WSDL file.

 If we had based our business service on the **EchoBinding** definition, the transport configuration would still have been pre-populated except for the **Endpoint URI**, which we would need to add manually.

From here click **Last**, this will take us to a summary page of our business service. Click **Save** to create our business service.

This will return us to the project view on the **Business Service** folder, and display the message **The Service EchoBS was created successfully.** If we examine the resources section we should see it now contains our newly created business service.

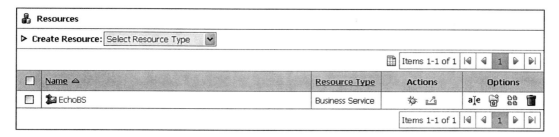

Creating our proxy service

We are now ready to create our Echo proxy service. Click on the **Proxy Service** folder within the **Project Explorer** to go to the project view for this folder.

In the **Resources** section click on the drop down next to **Create Resource** and select **Proxy Service**. This will bring up the **General Configuration** page for creating a proxy service, as shown in the following screenshot:

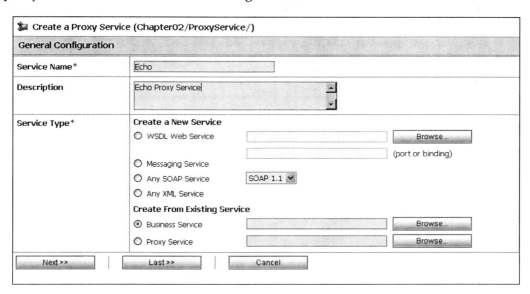

You will notice this looks very similar to the general configuration screen for a business service. So, as before, enter the name of our service (i.e. **Echo**) and an optional description.

Next we need to specify the **Service Type**; we could do this in exactly the same way that we did for our business service and base it on the Echo WSDL. However, this time we are going to base it on our **EchoBS** business service, we will see why in a moment.

For the **Service Type**, select **Business Service** as shown in the previous screenshot and click **Browse**. This will launch the **Select Business Service** window from where we can search for and select the business service that we want to base our proxy service on.

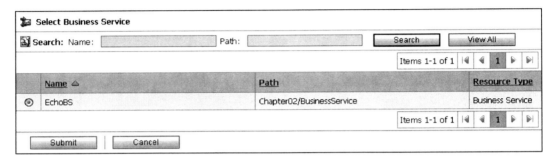

By default, this window will list all business services defined to the Service Bus, though you can restrict the list by defining search criteria.

In our case, we have just the **EchoBS**, so select this and click on **Submit**. This will return us to the **General Configuration** screen, with **Service Type** updated as shown in the following screenshot:

From here click **Last**; this will take us to a summary page of our proxy service. Click **Save** to create out proxy service.

This will return us to the project view on the **Proxy Service** folder, and display the message **The Service Echo was created successfully**.

If we examine the resources section of our project view, we should see it now contains our newly created proxy service.

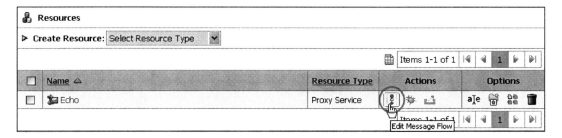

Creating message flow

Once we have created our proxy service, the next step is to specify how it should handle requests; this is defined in the message flow of the proxy service.

The message flow defines the actions that the proxy service should perform on receipt of a request, such as validating the payload, transforming or enriching it before routing it to the appropriate business service.

Within the resource section of our project view, click on the **Edit Message Flow** icon as circled in the previous screenshot. This will take us to the **Edit Message Flow** window, where we can view and edit the message flow of our proxy service, as shown in the following screenshot:

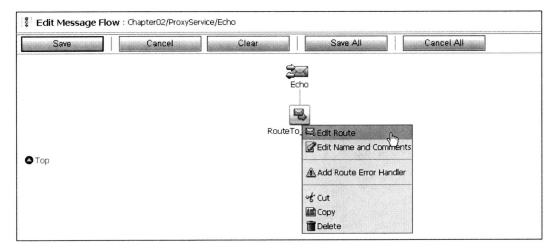

Looking at this, we can see Echo already invokes the route node **RouteTo_EchoBS**.

Click on this and select **Edit Route** (as shown in the previous screenshot). This will take us to the **Edit Stage Configuration** window as shown:

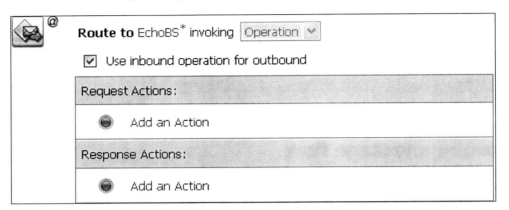

Here we can see it's already configured to route requests to the **EchoBS** business service.

Normally, when we create a proxy service, we have to specify the message flow from scratch. However, when we created our **Echo** proxy service we based it on the **EchoBS** business service (as opposed to a WSDL). Because of this, the service bus has automatically configured the message flow to route requests to **EchoBS**.

As a result, our message flow is already predefined for us, so click **Cancel**, and then **Cancel** again to return to our project view.

Activating the Echo proxy service

We now have a completed proxy service; all that remains is to commit our work. Within the **Change Center** click **Activate**.

This will bring up the **Activate Session** as shown in the following screenshot:

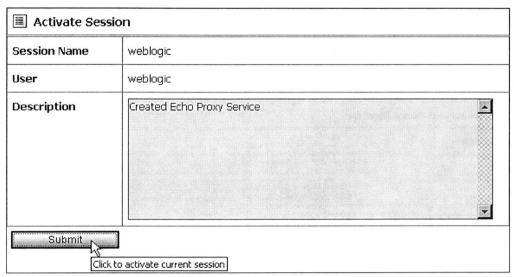

Before activating a session, it's good practice to give a description of the changes that we've made, just in case we need to roll them back later. So enter an appropriate description and then click on **Submit** as shown in the previous screenshot.

Assuming everything is okay, this will activate our changes, and the console will be updated to list our configuration changes as shown in the following screenshot:

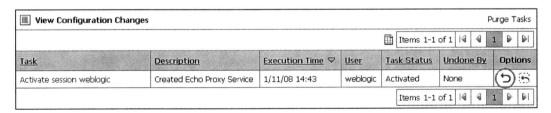

If you make a mistake and want to undo the changes you have activated, you can click on the **undo** icon (circled in the previous screenshot), and if you change your mind you can undo the undo.

OSB allows you to undo any of your previous sessions as long as it doesn't result in an error in the run time configuration of the Service Bus.

Testing our proxy service

All that's left is to test our proxy service; a simple way to do this is to initiate a test instance using the **Service Bus Test Console**.

To do this, we need to navigate back to the definition of our proxy service. Rather than do this via the **Project Explorer**, we will use the **Resource Browser**. This provides a way to view all resources based on their type.

Click on the **Resource Browser** section within the navigation bar, by default it will list all proxy services defined to the Service Bus, as shown in the following screenshot:

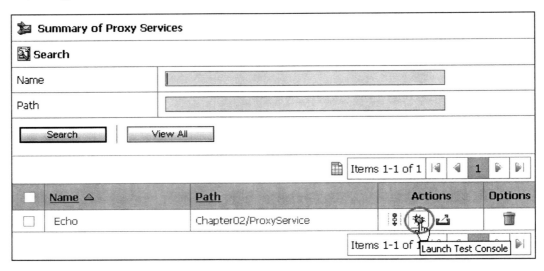

We can then filter this list further by specifying the appropriate search criteria.

Click on the **Launch Test Console** icon for the Echo proxy service (circled in the previous screenshot). This will launch the test console, shown in the following screenshot.

The **Available Operations** drop down allows us to specify which operation we want to invoke; in our case it's automatically defaulted to **process**.

By default, the options **Direct Call** and **Include Tracking** are selected within the **Test Configuration** section; keep these selected as they enable us to trace the state of a message as it passes through the proxy service.

The **Request Document** section allows us to specify the **SOAP Header** and the **Payload** for our service. By default these will contain a skeleton XML fragment based on the WSDL definition of the selected operation, with default values for each field.

To execute a test instance of our service, modify the text in the `<echo:input>` element as we have below and click **Execute**. This will cause the console to generate a request message and use it to invoke our Echo proxy service.

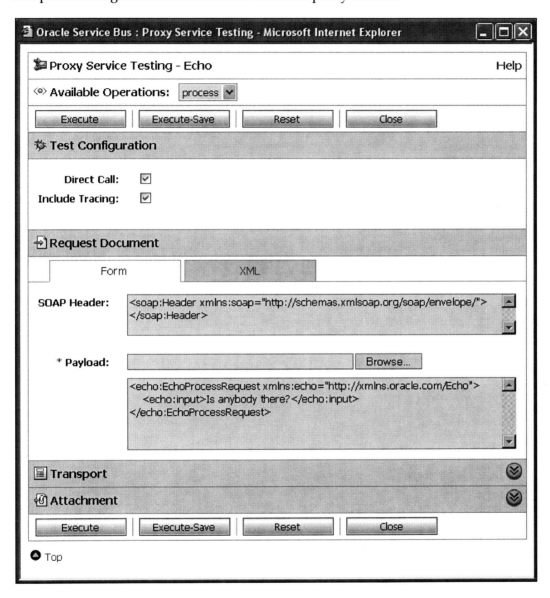

Upon successful execution of the proxy, the test console will be updated to show the response returned. Here we can see that the **result** element contains our original initial **input** string as shown in the following screenshot:

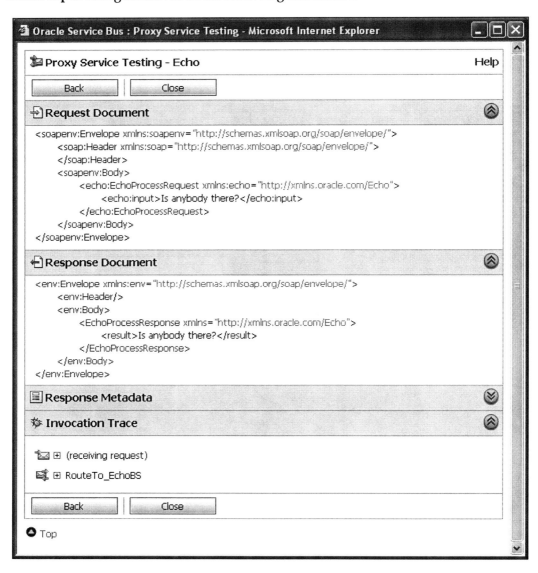

We can examine the state of our message as it passed through the proxy service by expanding the **Invocation Trace**, as we have in the following screenshot.

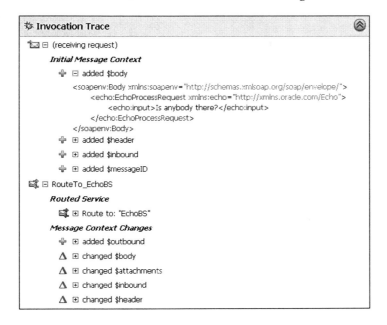

In addition, if you log back into BPEL Control, you should be able to see the process instance that was invoked by the service bus.

Summary

In this section we have implemented our first BPEL process and then built our first proxy service on top of it. While this example is about as trivial as you can get, it has provided us with an initial introduction to both the design time and run time components of Oracle BPEL PM and Oracle Service Bus.

In the next few chapters we will go into more detail on each of these components as well as looking at how we can use adapters to service enable existing systems.

3
Service Enabling Existing Systems

The heart of service-oriented architecture is the creation of processes and applications from existing services. The question arises, where do these services come from? Within a SOA solution some services will need to be written from scratch, but most of the functions required should already exist in some form within the IT assets of the organization. Existing applications within the enterprise already provide many services that simply require exposing to an SOA infrastructure. In this chapter we will examine some ways to create services from existing applications. We refer to this process as service enabling existing systems. After a discussion of some of the different types of systems we will look at the specific functionality provided in the Oracle SOA Suite that makes it easy to convert file and database interfaces into services.

Types of systems

IT systems come in all sorts of shapes and forms, some have existing web service interfaces which can be consumed directly by an SOA infrastructure, others have completely proprietary interfaces and others expose functionality through some well understood but non-web service based interface. In terms of service enabling a system it is useful to classify it by the type of interface it exposes.

Within the SOA Suite, components called adapters provide a mapping between non-web service interfaces and the rest of the SOA Suite. These adapters allow the SOA Suite to treat non-web service interfaces as though they had a web service interface.

Web service interfaces

If an application exposes a web service interface, meaning a SOAP service described by a Web Service Description Language (WSDL) document, it may be consumed directly. Such web services can directly be included as part of a composite application or business process.

The latest versions of many applications expose web services, for example Siebel, Peoplesoft, and E-Business Suite applications provide access to at least some of their functionality through web services.

Technology interfaces

Many applications, such as SAP and Oracle E-Business Suite, currently expose only part of their functionality, or no functionality, through web service interfaces, but they can still participate in service-oriented architecture. Many applications have adopted an interface that is to some extent based on a standard technology.

Examples of standard technology interfaces include:

- Files
- Database Tables and Stored Procedures
- Message Queues

While these interfaces may be based on a standard technology they do not provide a standard data model and generally there must be a mapping between the raw technology interface and the more structured web service style interface that we would like.

The following table shows how these interfaces are supported through technology adapters provided with the SOA Suite.

Technology	Adapter	Notes
Files	File	Reads and writes files mounted directly on the machine. This can be physically attached disks or network mounted devices (Windows shared drives or NFS drives for example).
	FTP	Reads and writes files mounted on an FTP server.
Database	Database	Reads and writes database tables and invokes stored procedures.

Technology	Adapter	Notes
Message Queues	JMS	Reads and posts messages to Java Messaging Service (JMS) queues and topics.
	AQ	Reads and posts messages to Oracle AQ (Advanced Queuing) queues.
	MQ	Reads and posts messages to IBM MQ (Message Queue) Series queues.

In addition to the six technology adapters listed above there are other technology adapters available, such as a CICS adapter to connect to IBM mainframes, and an adapter to connect to systems running Oracle's Tuxedo transaction processing system. There are many other technology adapters that may be purchased to work with the SOA Suite.

Installed adapters are shown in the component palette of JDeveloper when **Services** are selected.

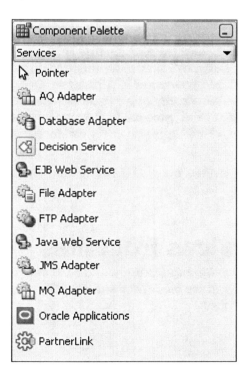

Application interfaces

The technology adapters leave the task of mapping the data structures into XML in the hands of the service enabler. This mapping of data structures is already done when using application adapters such as those for the Oracle E-Business Suite or SAP. These application adapters make life easier for the service enabler by hiding underlying data formats and transport protocols.

Unfortunately the topic of application adapters is too large an area to delve into in this book, but you should always check if an application specific adapter already exists for the system that you want to service enable. This is because application adapters will be easier to use than the technology adapters.

There are hundreds of third party adapters that may be purchased to provide SOA Suite with access to functionality within packaged applications.

Java Connector Architecture

Within the SOA Suite adapters are implemented and accessed using a Java technology known as Java Connector Architecture (JCA). JCA provides a standard packaging and discovery methods for adapter functionality. Most of the time SOA Suite developers will be unaware of JCA because JDeveloper wraps the JCA interfaces in WSDL and automatically deploys them with the appropriate component that is using them, such as a BPEL process. In the current release JCA adapters must be deployed separately to a WebLogic server for use by the service bus.

[At the time of writing, the exact details of this had not been published for Oracle Service Bus.]

Creating services from files

A common mechanism for communicating with an existing application is through a file. File communication is either inbound meaning a file must be read, or outbound meaning a file must be written.

A payroll use case

Consider a company that has a payroll application that produces a file detailing payments. This file must be transformed into a file format accepted by the company's bank and then delivered to the bank through FTP. The company wants to use SOA technologies to perform this transfer because it allows them to perform additional validations or enrichment of the data before sending it to the bank. In addition they want to store the details of what was sent in a database for audit purposes. In this scenario a file adapter could be used to take the data from the file, an FTP adapter to deliver it to the bank and a database adapter could post it into the tables required for audit purposes.

Reading a payroll file

Let's look at how we would read from a payroll file. Normally we will poll to check for the arrival of a file, although it is also possible to read a file without polling. Key points to consider beforehand are:

- How often should we poll for the file?
- Do we need to read the contents of the file?
- Do we need to move it to a different location?
- What do we do with the file when we have read or moved it?
  - Should we delete it?
  - Should we move it to an archive directory?
- How large is the file and its records?
- Does the file have one record or many?

We will consider all these factors as we interact with the File Adapter Wizard.

Starting the wizard

We begin by dragging the file adapter from the component palette in JDeveloper onto either a BPEL process (see Chapter 5) or an ESB interaction (not covered in this book as we use the Oracle Service Bus). We could also create a new adapter by clicking **File** and **New…** in JDeveloper to bring up the **New Gallery** and navigating in the tree to the **Business Tier, Web Services** leaf to display the same list from which we could select the **File Adapter** and click **OK**. We would use this latter route when creating adapters for use with the Oracle Service Bus.

This causes the **File Adapter Configuration Wizard** to start.

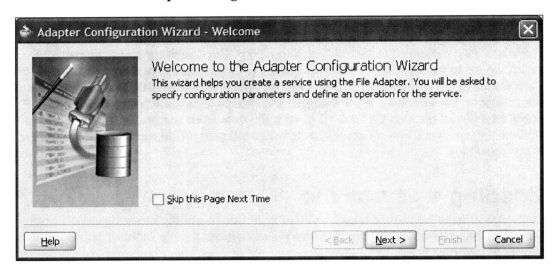

Naming the service

Clicking **Next** allows us to choose a name for the service that we are creating and optionally a description. We will use the service name **PayrollInputFileService**. Any name can be used as long as it has some meaning for the developers.

Identifying the operation

Clicking **Next** allows us to start specifying how we map the files onto a service. It is here that we decide whether we are reading or writing the file. When reading a file we decide if we wish to generate an event when it is available (a normal **Read File** operation that requires an inbound operation to receive the message) or if we want to read it only when requested (a **Synchronous Read File** operation requires an outbound operation).

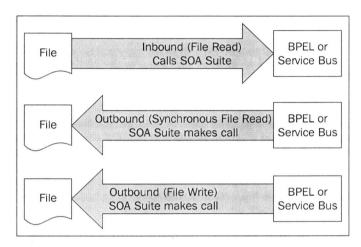

Who calls who?

We usually think of services as something that we call and then get a result. However, in reality services in a service-oriented architecture will often initiate events. These events may be delivered to a BPEL process which is waiting for an event, or routed to another service through the service bus or may even initiate a whole new BPEL process. Under the covers an adapter might need to poll to detect an event, but the service will always be able to generate an event. With a service we either call it to get a result or it generates an event that calls some other service or process.

The file adapter has three types of operation as outlined in the following table. We will explore the read operation to generate events as a file is created.

Operation Type	Direction	Description
Read File	Outbound event from service.	Reads the file and generates one or more events into BPEL or Service Bus when a file appears.
Write File	Inbound call to service with no response.	Writes a file, with one or more calls from BPEL or the Service Bus, causing records to be written to a file.
Synchronous Read File	Inbound call to service returning file contents.	BPEL or Service Bus requests a file to be read, returning nothing if the file doesn't exist.

Why ignore the contents of the file?

The file adapter has an option to not read the file contents. This is used when the file is just a signal for some event. Do not use this feature for the scenario where a file is written and then marked as available by another file being written. This is explicitly handled elsewhere in the file adapter. Instead the feature can be used as a signal of some event that has no relevant data other than the fact that something has happened.

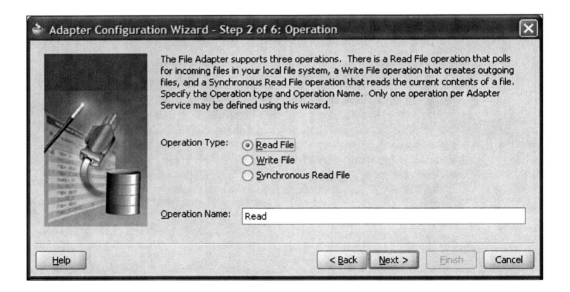

Defining the file location

Clicking **Next** takes us to the screen that allows us to configure the location of the file. Locations can be specified as either physical (mapped directly onto the file system) or logical (an indirection to the real location). The directory for incoming files specifies where the adapter should look to find new files.

A key question is now what to do with the file when it appears. One option is to keep a copy of the file in an archive directory. This is achieved by checking the **Archive processed files** attribute and providing a location for the file archive. In addition to archiving the file we need to decide if we want to delete the original file. This is indicated by the **Delete files after successful retrieval** check box.

Logical versus physical locations

The file adapter allows us to have logical (**Logical Name**) or physical locations (**Physical Path**) for files. Physical locations are easier for developers as we embed the exact file location into the assembly with no more work required. However, this only works if the file locations are the same in the development, test, and production environments, particularly unlikely if development is done on Windows but production is on Linux. Hence for production systems it is best to use logical locations that must be mapped onto physical locations when deployed. Chapter 18 shows how this mapping may be different for each environment.

The screenshot shows a physical file mapping that is really only appropriate in development.

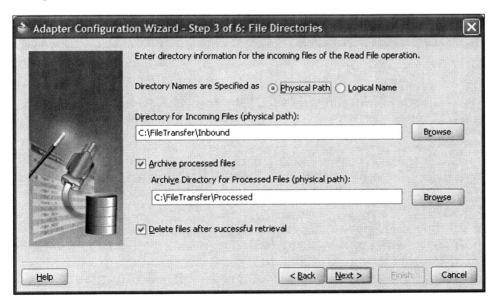

Selecting specific files

Having defined the location where files are found, we can now advance to the next step in the wizard. Here we describe what the filenames look like. We can describe filenames using either wildcards (using '*' to represent a sequence of 0 or more characters) or using Java regular expressions as described in the documentation for the `java.util.regex.Pattern` class. Usually wildcards will be good enough. For example if we want to select all files that start with PR and end with `.txt` then we would use the wildcard string `PR*.txt` or the regular expression `PR.*\.txt`. As can be seen it is generally easier to use wildcards rather than regular expressions.

The final part of this screen in the adapter wizard asks if the file contains a single message or many messages. This is confusing because when the screen refers to messages it really means records.

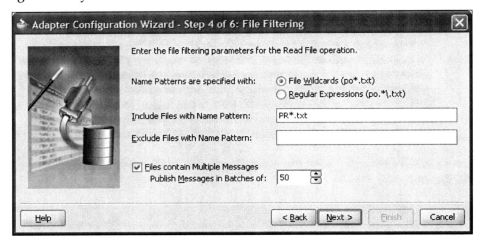

XML files

It is worth remembering that a well formed XML document can only have a single root element, and hence an XML input file will normally only ever have a single input record. In the case of very large XML files it is possible to have the file adapter batch the file up into multiple messages, in which case the root element is replicated in each message, and the 2nd level elements are treated as records. Note that this behavior cannot currently be set using the wizard.

By default a message will contain a single record from the file. Records will be defined in the next step of the wizard. If the file causes a BPEL process to be started then a 1000 record file would result in 1000 BPEL processes being initiated. To improve efficiency, records can be batched and the **Publish Messages in Batches of** attribute controls the maximum number of records in a message.

Message batching

It is common for an incoming file to contain many records. How these records are processed can impact system performance and memory requirements, hence it is important to align the use of the records with their likely impact on system resources.

Detecting that the file is available

The next step in the wizard allows us to configure the frequency of polling for the inbound file. There are two parameters that can be configured here — the **Polling Frequency** and the **Minimum File Age**.

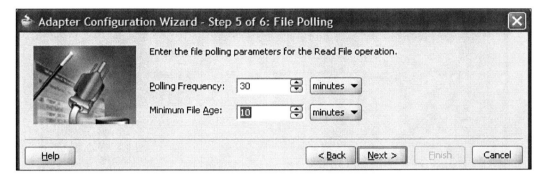

The **Polling Frequency** just means the time delay between checking to see if a file is available for processing. The adapter will check once per interval to see if the file exists. Setting this too low can consume needless CPU resources, setting it too high can make the system appear unresponsive. *Too high* and *too low* are very subjective and will depend on your individual requirements. For example the polling interval for a file that is expected to be written twice a day may be set to 3 hours, while the interval for a file that is expected to be written every hour may be set to 15 minutes.

Minimum File Age specifies how old a file must be before it is processed by the adapter. This setting allows a file to be completely written before it is read. For example a large file may take 5 minutes to write out from the original application. If the file is read 3 minutes after it has been created then it is possible for the adapter to run out of records to read and assume the file has been processed when in reality the application is still writing to the file. Setting a minimum age to 10 minutes would avoid this problem by giving the application at least 10 minutes to write the file.

Message format

The penultimate step in the file adapter is to set up the format of records or messages in the file. This is one of the most critical steps as this defines the format of messages generated by a file.

Messages may be opaque, meaning that they are passed around as black boxes. This may be appropriate with a Microsoft Word file for example that must merely be transported from point A to point B without being examined. This is indicated by the **Native format translation is not required** check box.

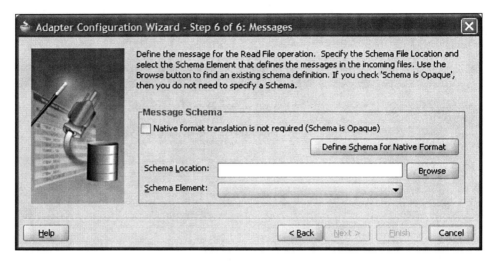

If the document is already in XML format then we can just specify a schema and an expected root element and the job is done. Normally the file is some non-XML format that must be mapped onto an XML Schema generated through the native format builder wizard invoked through the **Define Schema for Native Format** button.

Defining a native format schema

Invoking the **Native Format Builder** wizard brings up an initial start screen that leads on to the first step in the wizard, choosing the type of format as shown in the following screenshot:

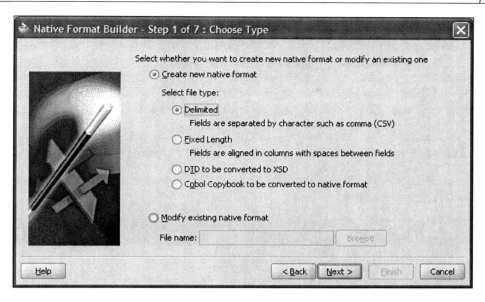

This allows us to identify the overall record structure. If we have an existing schema document that describes the record structure then we can point to that. More usually we will need to determine the type of structure of the file ourselves. The choices available are:

- **Delimited**: Such as CSV files (Comma Separated Values) or records with spaces or '+' signs for separators.
- **Fixed Length**: Files whose records consist of fixed length fields. Be careful not to confuse these with space separated files as if a value does not fill the entire field then it will usually be padded with spaces.
- **DTD**: XML Data Type Definition XML files that will be mapped onto an XML Schema description of the file content.
- **Cobol Copybook**: Files that have usually been produced by a COBOL system, often originating from a mainframe.

We will look at a delimited file as it is one of the most common formats.

Although, we are using the separator file type the steps involved are basically the same for most file types including the fixed length field format, which is also extremely common.

Using a sample file

To make it easier to describe the format of the incoming file the wizard asks us to specify a file to use a sample. If necessary we can skip rows in the file and determine the number of records to read. Obviously reading a very large number of records may take a while and if all the variability on the file is in the first 10 records then there is no point in wasting time reading any more sample records.

Setting the character needs to be done carefully, particularly in international environments where non-ASCII character sets may be common.

After selecting a sample file the wizard will display an initial view of the file with a guess at the field separators.

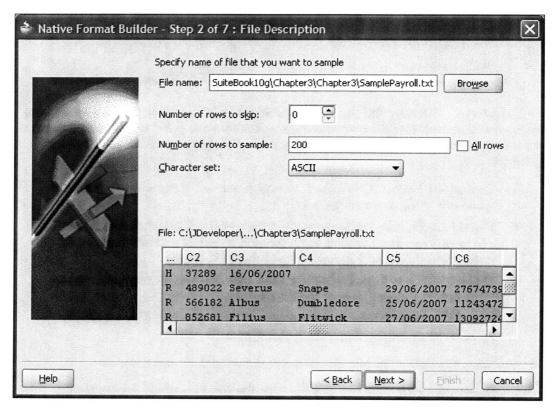

Record structure

The next step of the wizard allows us to describe how the records appear in the file.

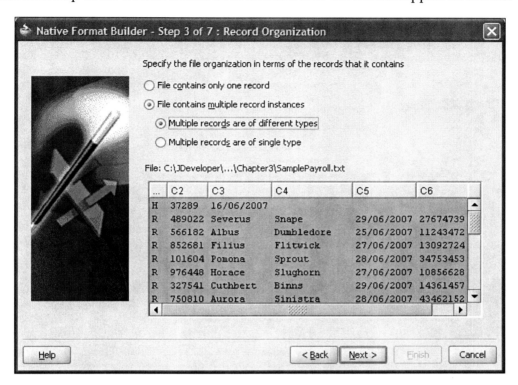

The first option of **File contains only one record** allows us to process the file as a single message. This can be useful when the file has multiple records, all the same format, that we want to read in as single message. Use of this option disables batching.

The next option of **File contains multiple records instances** allows batching to take place. Records are either of the same type or of different types. They can only be marked of different types if they can be distinguished based on the first field in the record. In other words to choose the **Multiple records of different types** the first field in all the records must be a record type identifier. In the example shown the first field is either an **H** for **Header** records or an **R** for **Records**.

Choosing a root element

The next step allows us to define the target namespace and root element of the schema that we are generating.

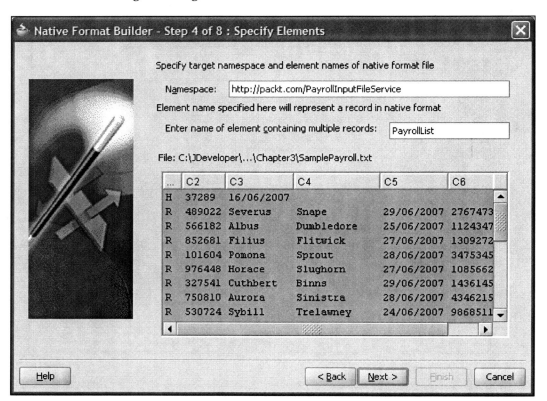

Don't forget that when using the **Native Format Builder** wizard we are just creating an XML Schema document that describes the native (non-XML) format data. Most of the time this schema is transparent to us, but at times the XML constructs have to emerge, such as identifying a name for a root element. The file is described using an XML Schema extension known as NXSD.

As we can see the root element is mandatory. This root element acts as a wrapper for the records in a message. If message batching is set to 1 then each wrapper will have a single sub-element, the record. If message is set to greater than 1 then each wrapper will have at least one and possibly more sub-elements, each sub-element being a record. There can never be more sub-elements than the batch size.

Message delimiters

Having described the overall structure of the file we can now drill down into the individual fields. To do this we first specify the message delimiters.

In addition to field delimiters we can also specify a record delimiter. Usually record delimiters are new lines. If fields may also be wrapped in quotation marks then these can be stripped off by specifying the **Optionally enclosed by** character.

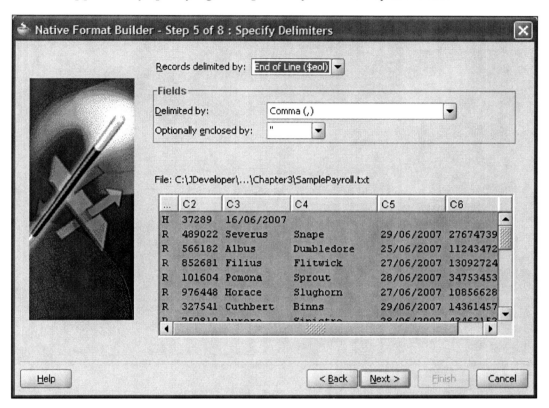

Record type names

The wizard will identify the types of record based on the first field in each record as shown. It is possible to ignore record types by selecting them and clicking **Delete**. If this is done in error then it is possible to add them back by using the **Add** button. Only fields that exist in the sample data can be added in the wizard.

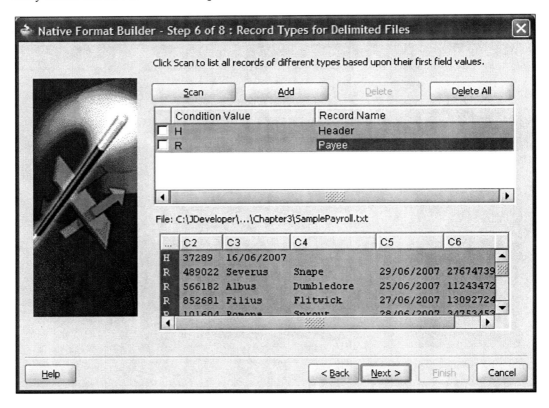

Note that if we want to reset the record types screen then the **Scan** button will re-scan the sample file and look for all the different record types it contains.

The **Record Name** field can be set by double-clicking it and providing a suitable record name. This record name is the XML element name that encapsulates the record content.

Field properties

Now that we have identified record and field boundaries we can drill down into the records and define the data types and names of individual fields. This is done for each record type in turn. We can select which records to define by selecting them from the **Record Name** drop-down box or by clicking the **Next Record Type** button.

It is important to be as liberal as possible when defining field data types because any mismatches will cause errors that will need to be handled. Being liberal in our record definitions will allow us to validate the messages, as described in Chapter 12, without raising system errors.

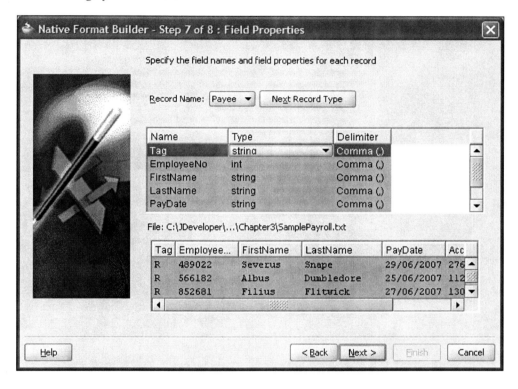

The **Name** column represents the element name of this field. The wizard will attempt to guess the type of the field but it is important to always check this because the sample data you are using may not include all possibilities. A common error is for identification numbers to be tagged as integers when they should really be strings—accept integer types only when they are likely to have arithmetic operations performed on them.

Verifying the result

We have now completed our mapping and can verify what has been done by looking at the generated XML Schema file. Note that the generated schema uses some Oracle extensions to enable a non-XML formatted file to be represented as XML. In particular the `nxsd` namespace prefix is used to identify field separators and record terminators.

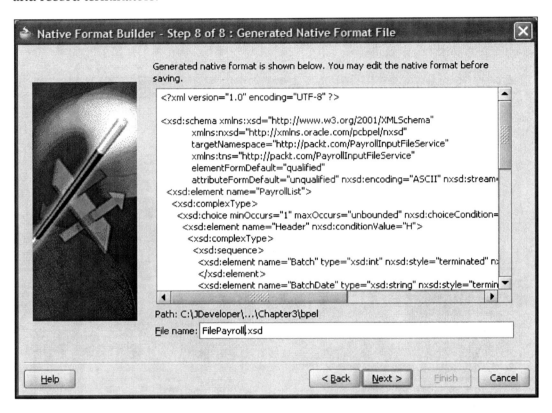

The XML Schema generated can be edited by hand. This is useful to support nested records (records inside other records), such as may be found in a file containing order records with nested detail records (an order record contains multiple line item detail records). In this case it is useful to use the wizard to generate a schema, with order records and detail records at the same level. The schema can then be modified by hand to make the detail records children of the order records.

Clicking **Next** and then **Finish** will cause the generated schema file to be saved.

Finishing the wizards

Up to this point no work has been saved except for the XML Schema mapping the file content onto an XML structure. The rest of the adapter settings are not saved and the endpoint is not set up until the **Finish** button is clicked on the completion screen as shown in the following screenshot. Note that the file generated is a Web Service Description Language (WSDL) file.

Throttling the file and FTP adapter

The file and FTP adapters can consume a lot of resources when processing large files (thousands of records) because they keep sending messages with batches of records until the file is processed, not waiting for the records to be processed. This behavior can be altered by forcing them to wait until a message is processed before sending another message. This is done by making the following changes to the WSDL generated by the wizard. This changes the one-way read operation into a two-way read operation that will not complete until a reply is generated by our code in BPEL or the Service Bus.

Creating a dummy message type

Add a new message definition to the WSDL such as the one shown:

```
<message name="Dummy_msg">
    <part xmlns:xsd="http://www.w3.org/2001/XMLSchema"
          name="Dummy" type="xsd:string"/>
</message>
```

Adding an output message to the read operation

In the `<portType>` add an `<output>` element to the read `<operation>` element.

```
<portType name="Read_ptt">
    <operation name="Read">
        <input message="tns:PayrollList_msg"/>
        <output message="tns:Dummy_msg"/>
    </operation>
</portType>
```

In the `<jca:operation>` element add an empty `<output/>` element.

Using the modified interface

The adapter will now have a two-way interface and will need to receive a reply to a message before it sends the next batch of records, thus throttling the throughput. Note that no data needs to be sent in the reply message. This will limit the number of active operations to the number of threads assigned to the file adapter.

Writing a payroll file

We can now use the FTP adapter to write the payroll file to a remote file system. This requires us to create another adapter within our BPEL process or service bus. Setting up the FTP adapter to write to a remote file system is very similar to reading files with the file adapter.

Selecting the FTP connection

The first difference is that when using the FTP adapter instead of the File adapter we have to specify an FTP connection to use in the underlying application server. This connection is set up in the application server running the adapter. For example, when running SOA Suite on top of Oracle Application Server, this can be done through Application Server Control, or when using WebLogic Application Server then the WebLogic Console can be used. The JNDI location of the connection factory is the location that must be provided to the wizard. The JNDI location must be configured in the application server using the administrative tools provided by the application server, refer to your application server documentation for how to do this as it varies between application servers.

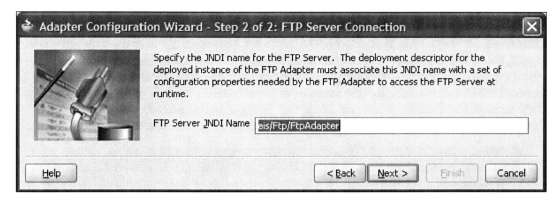

Choosing the operation

When we come to choose the type of operation we again notice that the screen is different to the file adapter, having an additional **File Type** category. This relates to the ASCII and binary settings of an FTP session. ASCII causes the FTP transfer to adapt to changes in character encoding between the two systems. For example converting between EBCDIC and ASCII or altering line feeds between systems. When using text files it is generally a good idea to select the ASCII format. When sending binary files it is vital that the binary file type is used to avoid any unfortunate and unwanted transformations.

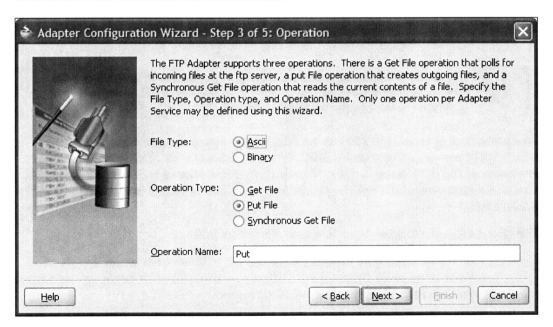

Selecting the file destination

Choosing where the file is created is the same for both the FTP and the File Adapter. Again there is a choice of physical or logical paths. The file naming convention allows us some control over the name of the output file. In addition to the **%SEQ%** symbol that inserts a unique sequence number it is also possible to insert a date or date time string into the filename. Note that in the current release you cannot have both a date time string and a sequence string in the file naming convention.

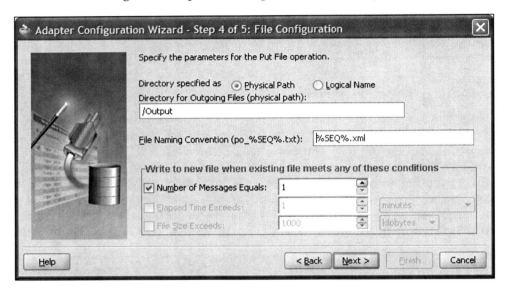

 Note that when using a date time string as part of the filename, files with the same date time string will overwrite each other, if this is the case then consider using a sequence number instead.

When producing an output file we can either keep appending to a single file, which will keep growing without limit, or we can create new files dependant on attributes of the data being written. This is the normal way of working for non-XML files and a new output file will be generated when one or more records are written to the adapter.

The criteria for deciding to write to a new file are as follows:

- **Number of Messages Equals** forces the file to be written when the given number of messages is reached. This can be thought of as batching the output so that we reduce the number of files created.

- **Elapsed Time Exceeds** puts a time limit on how long the adapter will keep the file open. This places an upper time limit on creating an output file.

- **File Size Exceeds** allows us to limit the size of files. As soon as a message causes the file to exceed the given size then no more messages will be appended to this file.

These criteria can all be applied together and as soon as one of them is satisfied a new file will be created.

Writing XML files
When writing XML files care should be taken to have only a single message per file as otherwise there will be multiple XML root elements in the document that will make it an invalid XML document.

Completing the FTP file writer service

The next step in the wizard is to define the actual record formats. This is exactly the same as when creating an input file. If we don't have an existing XML Schema for the output file then we can use the wizard to create one if we have a sample file to use.

Finally, again remember to run through the wizard to the end and click finish rather than cancel or our entire configuration will be lost.

Moving, copying, and deleting files

Sometimes we will just want an adapter to move, copy, or delete a file without reading the file. We will use the ability of the file adapter to move a file in Chapter 14 — *Message Interaction Patterns*, to set up a scheduler service within the SOA suite.

The following steps will configure an outbound file or FTP adapter to move, copy, or delete a file without reading it.

Generate an adapter

Use the file or FTP adapter wizard to generate an outbound adapter, file write or FTP put operation. The data content should be marked as opaque, so that there is no need to understand the content of the file. Once this has been done we will modify the WSDL generated to add additional operations.

Modify the port type

Modify the port type of the adapter to include the additional operations required as shown below. Use the same message type as the Put or Write operations generated by the wizard.

```
<portType name="Write_ptt">
    <operation name="Write">
      <input message="tns:Write_msg"/>
     </operation>
     <operation name="Move">
       <input message="tns:Write_msg"/>
     </operation>
</portType>
```

Note that the following operation names are supported:

- Move
- Copy
- Delete

Modify the binding

Bindings describe how the service description maps onto the physical service implementation. They are covered in more detail in Chapter 17 — *The Importance of Bindings*. For now we will just modify the binding to add the additional operations needed and map them to the appropriate implementation as shown below:

```
<binding name="Write_binding" type="tns:Write_ptt">
  <jca:binding />
  <operation name="Write">
    <jca:operation PhysicalDirectory="C:\FileTransfer\Outbound"
      InteractionSpec="oracle.tip.adapter.file.outbound.
                                  FileInteractionSpec"
      FileNamingConvention="fred_%SEQ%.txt"
      NumberMessages="1"
      OpaqueSchema="true" >
    </jca:operation>
    <input>
      <jca:header message="hdr:OutboundHeader_msg"
                  part="outboundHeader"/>
    </input>
  </operation>
  <operation name="Move">
    <jca:operation
      InteractionSpec="oracle.tip.adapter.file.outbound.
                                  FileIoInteractionSpec"
          SourcePhysicalDirectory="C:\FileTransfer\Inbound"
```

```
      SourceFileName="test.txt"
      TargetPhysicalDirectory="C:\FileTransfer\Outbound"
      TargetFileName="test.txt"
      Type="MOVE">
   </jca:operation>
 <input>
    <jca:header message="hdr:OutboundHeader_msg"
                part="outboundHeader"/>
 </input>
   </operation>
</binding>
```

Note that the following types are supported for use with the equivalent operation names; observe that operation names are mixed case and types are uppercase:

- MOVE
- COPY
- DELETE

For the FTP adapter the `InteractionSpec` property is `oracle.tip.adapter.ftp.` `outbound.FTPIoInteractionSpec`.

Add additional header properties

In order to allow run time configuration of the source and destination locations it is necessary to modify the adapter header file that is provided by the wizard, `ftpAdapterOutboundheader.wsdl` or `fileAdapterOutboundHeader.wsdl`.

We need to add the source destination locations as properties in the header as shown below:

```
<element name="OutboundFileHeaderType">
  <complexType>
    <sequence>
      <element name="fileName" type="string"/>
      <element name="sourceDirectory" type="string"/>
      <element name="sourceFileName" type="string"/>
      <element name="targetDirectory" type="string"/>
      <element name="targetFileName" type="string"/>
    </sequence>
  </complexType>
</element>
```

These elements in the adapter header can be used to dynamically select at run time the locations to be used for the move, copy or delete operation.

With the above modifications the `move`, `copy`, or `delete` operations will appear as additional operations on the service that can be invoked from the service bus or within BPEL.

Adapter headers

In addition to the data associated with the service being provided by the adapter, sometimes referred to as the payload of the service, it is also possible to configure or obtain information about the operation of an adapter through header messages. Adapter header files are generated by the adapter wizard and may be modified to alter the operation of the adapter as was shown in the previous section on moving and copying files with the file adapter.

To use an adapter from within BPEL we first need to create a message variable of the correct type by selecting it from the Project WSDL files in the type chooser. See Chapter 5 for details on creating BPEL variables and using the invoke statement.

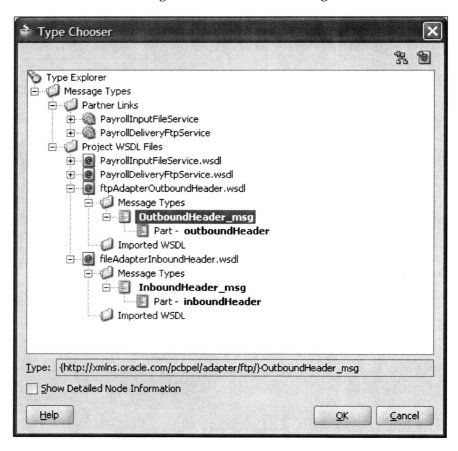

We can then use the header by assigning appropriate values to the fields within the header, such as the filename, before adding it to an invoke statement in BPEL. In JDeveloper the invoke statement property dialog has an **Adapters** tab that can be used to specify the header variable to be used in the invocation.

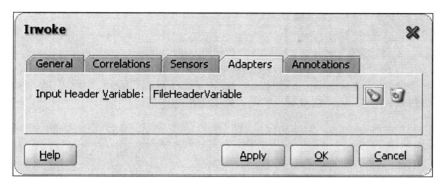

Testing the file adapters

We can test the adapters by using them within a BPEL process such as the one shown in the following screenshot. Building a BPEL process is covered in Chapter 5. This uses the two services we have just described and links them with a copy operation that transforms data from one format to the other.

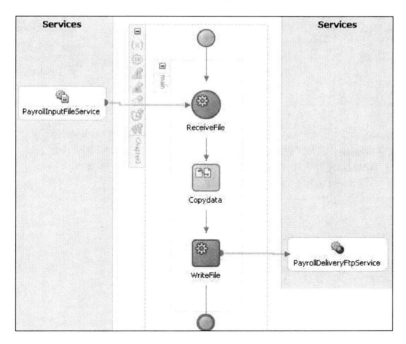

Creating services from databases

In the following sections, we will have a look at how to create services from databases.

Writing to a database

Along with files, databases are one of the most common ways of interfacing with existing applications and providing them with a service interface. Before we configure a database adapter we first need to create a new database connection within JDeveloper. This is done by creating a **Database Connection** from the **New Gallery**.

Choosing a database connection brings up the database connection wizard which allows us to enter the connection details of our database.

Selecting the database schema

With an established database connection we can now create a service based on a database table. We will create a service that updates the database with the payroll details. The model for the database tables is shown in the following screenshot:

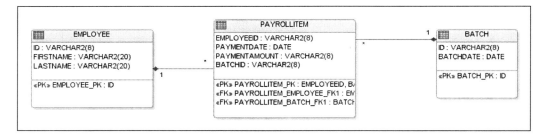

Now we have our database connection. We can run the Database Adapter Wizard by dragging the database adapter icon from the tool palette onto a BPEL process or ESB. This starts the database adapter wizard and after giving the service a name we come to the **Service Connection** screen as shown:

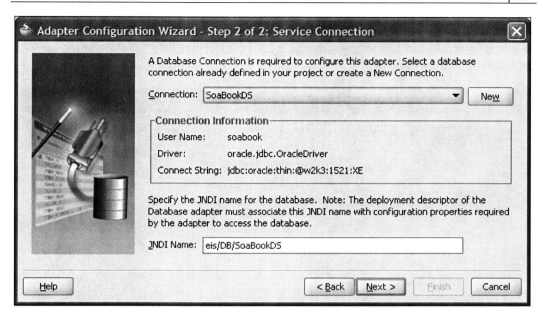

This allows us to choose a local connection in JDeveloper to use and also to select the JNDI location in the run time environment of the database connection. Note that this JNDI connection must be configured as part of the database adapter in the default application in a similar way to configuration of the FTP adapter.

How connections are resolved by the database adapter

When the adapter tries to connect to the database it first tries to use the JNDI name provided, which should map to a JCA connection factory in the application server. If this name does not exist then the adapter will use the database connection details from the JDeveloper database connection that was used in the wizard. This behavior is very convenient for development environments because it means that you can deploy and test the adapters in development without having to configure the JCA connection factories.

Identifying the operation type

The database adapter has many ways in which it can interact with the database to provide a service interface.

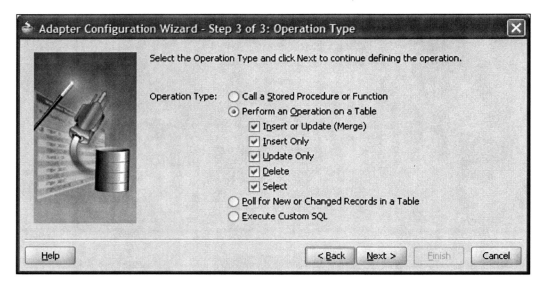

The operation types split into two groups: calls into the database and events generated from the database. Calls into the database cover the following operations:

- Stored procedure or function call to execute a specific piece of code in the database. This could either update the database or retrieve information but in either case it is a synchronous call into the database.

- Perform an `insert`, `update`, `delete`, or `select` operation on the database. Again this is done synchronously as a call into the database.

- Execute custom SQL, this again runs the SQL synchronously against the database.

Poling for new or changed records is the only way for the database adapter to generate messages to be consumed in a BPEL process or the service bus. For this exercise we will select `insert/update` for the operation.

Identifying tables to be operated on

The next step in the wizard asks which table is the root table, or beginning of the query. To select this, we first click the **Import Tables...** button to bring up the **Import Tables** dialog.

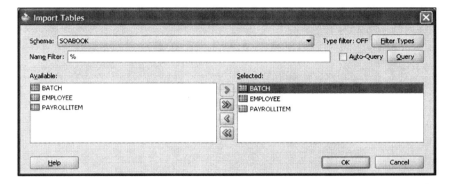

Once we have imported the tables we need, we then select the **PAYROLLITEM** table as the root table. We do this because each record will create a new **PAYROLLITEM** entry. All operations through the database adapter must be done with a root table; any other tables must be referencable from this root table.

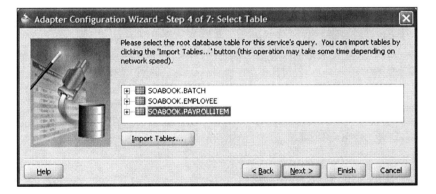

Identifying the relationship between tables

Because we have more than one table involved in this operation, we need to decide which table relationship we want to use. In this case we want to tie a payroll item back to a single employee so we select the one-to-one relation.

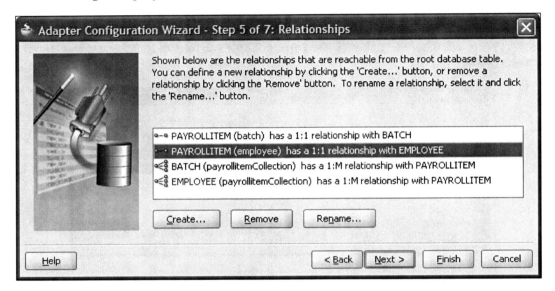

We can now finish the creation of the database adapter and hook it up with the file adapter we created earlier to allow us to read records from a file and place them in a database.

Under the covers

Under the covers a lot has happened. An offline copy of the relevant database schema has been created so that the design time is not reliant on being permanently connected to a database. The actual mapping of a database onto an XML document has also occurred. This is done using Oracle TopLink to create the mapping and a lot of the function of the wizard is implemented using TopLink. The mapping can be further refined using the features of TopLink.

Using keys

Always identify the primary key for any table used by the database adapter. This can be done by applying a primary key constraint in the database; if no such key has been created then TopLink will prompt you to create one. If you have to create one in TopLink, then make sure it is really a primary key. TopLink optimizes its use of the database by maintaining an identity for each row in a table with a primary key. It only reads the primary key on select statements and then checks to see which records it needs to read in from the database. This reduces the amount of work mapping fields that have already been mapped because a record appears multiple times in the selection. If you don't correctly identify a primary key then TopLink may incorrectly identify different records as being the same record and only load the data for the first such record encountered. So if you seem to be getting a lot of identical records in response to a query that should have separate records then check your primary key definitions.

Summary

In this chapter we have looked at how to use the file and database adapters to turn file and database interfaces into services that can be consumed by the rest of the SOA Suite. Note that when using the adapters, the schemas are automatically generated, and changing the way the adapter works may mean a change in the schema. In the next chapter we will look at how to isolate our applications from the actual adapter service details.

4

Loosely Coupling Services

In the previous chapter we explored how we can take functionality in our existing applications and expose them as services. When we do this we often find that the service interface we create is tightly coupled to the underlying implementation. We can make our architecture more robust by reducing this coupling. By defining our interface around our architecture rather than around our existing application interfaces, we can reduce coupling. We can also reduce coupling by using a routing service to avoid physical location dependencies. In this chapter we will explore how service virtualization through the Service Bus of the Oracle SOA Suite can be used to deliver more loosely coupled services.

Coupling

Coupling is a measure of how dependent one service is upon another. The more closely one service depends on another service, the more tightly coupled they are. There have been a number of efforts to formalize metrics for coupling and they all revolve around the same basic items. These are:

- **Number of input data items**: This is basically the number of input parameters of the service.

- **Number of output data items**: It is the output data of the service.

- **Dependencies on other services**: It is the number of services called by this service.

- **Dependencies of other services on this service**: It is the number of services that invoke this service.

- **Use of shared global data**: It is the number of shared data items used by this service. This may include database tables or shared files.

- **Temporal dependencies**: Dependencies on other services being available at specific times.

Let us examine how each of these measures may be applied to our service interface. The principles below are relevant to all services, but widely reused services have a special need for all of the items.

Number of input data items

A service should only accept, as input, the data items required to perform the service being requested. Additional information should not be passed into the service because this creates unnecessary dependencies on the input formats. This economy of input allows the service to focus on only the function it is intended to provide and does not require it to understand unnecessary data formats. The best way to isolate the service from changes in data formats that it does not use is not to require the service to be aware of those data formats.

For example, a credit rating service should only require sufficient information to identify the individual being rated. Additional information such as the amount of credit being requested or the type of goods or services for which a loan is required is not necessary for the credit rating service to perform its job.

[Services should accept only the data required to perform their function and nothing more.]

When talking about reducing the number of data items input or output from a service, we are talking about the service implementation, not a logical service interface that may be implemented using a canonical data model. The canonical data model may have additional attributes not required by a particular service, but these should not be part of the physical service interface.

Number of output data items

In the same way that a service should not accept inputs that are unnecessary for the function it performs, a service should not return data that is related only to its internal operation. Exposing such data as part of the response data will create dependencies on the internal implementation of the service that are not necessary.

Sometimes a service needs to maintain state between requests. **State** implies that state information must be maintained at least in the client of the service, so that it can identify the state required to the service when making further requests, but often the state information in the client is just an index into the state information held in the service. We will return to this subject later in this chapter.

[Services should not return public data that relates to their own internal processing.]

Dependencies on other services

Generally reuse of other services to create a new composite service is a good thing. However dependencies on other services does increase the degree of coupling because there is a risk that changes in those services may impact the composite service and hence any services with dependencies on the composite service. We can reduce the risk that this poses by limiting our use of functionality in other services to just that required by the composite.

[Services should reduce the functionality required of other services to the minimum required for their own functionality.]

For example, a dispatching service may decide to validate the address it receives. If this functionality is not specified as being required, because for example all addresses are validated elsewhere, then the dispatching service has an unnecessary dependency that may cause problems in the future.

Dependencies of other services on this service

Having a widely used service is great for reuse but the greater the number of services that make use of this service then the greater impact a change in this service will have on other services. Extra care must be taken with widely reused services to ensure that their interfaces are as stable as possible. This stability can be provided by following the guidelines in this section.

[Widely reused services should focus their interface on just the functionality needed by clients and avoid exposing any unnecessary functions or data.]

Use of shared global data

Shared global data in the service context is often through dependencies on a shared resource such as data in a database. Such use of shared data structures is subversive to good design because it does not appear in the service definitions and so the owners of the shared data may be unaware of the dependency. Effectively this is an extra interface into the service. If this is not documented then the service is very vulnerable to the shared data structure being changed unknowingly. Even if the shared data structure is well documented, any changes required must still be synchronized across all users of the shared data.

Avoid use of shared global data in services unless absolutely necessary. If it is absolutely necessary then the dependency needs to be clearly documented in all users of the shared data. A services data should only be manipulated through its defined interface.

Temporal dependencies

Not all service requests require an immediate response. Often a service can be requested and the response may be returned later. This is a common model in message based systems and allows for individual services to be unavailable without impacting other services. Use of queuing systems allows temporal or time decoupling of services, so that two communicating services do not have to be available at the same instant in time, the queue allowing messages to be delivered when the service is available rather than when the service is requested.

Use asynchronous message interfaces to reduce dependencies of one service on the availability of another.

Reducing coupling in stateful services

A **stateful service** maintains context for a given client between invocations. When using stateful services, we always need to return some kind of state information to the client. To avoid unnecessary coupling, this state information should always be opaque. By opaque we mean that it should have no meaning to the client other than as a reference that must be returned to the service when requesting follow on operations. We will examine how this may be accomplished later in this section.

A common use of state information in a service is to preserve the position in a search that returns more results than can reasonably be returned in a single response. Another use of state information might be to perform correlation between services that have multiple interactions such as between a bidding service and a bidding client.

Whatever the reason, the first question when confronted with the need for state in a service is to investigate ways to remove the state requirement. If there is definitely a need for state to be maintained then there are two approaches that can followed by the service:

- Externalize all state and return it to the client.
- Maintain state within the service and return a reference to the client.

In the first case it is necessary to package up the required state information and return it to the client. Because the client should be unaware of the format of this data it must be returned as an opaque type. This is best done as an <any> element in the schema for returning the response to the client. An <any> element may be used to hold any type of data from simple strings through to complex structured types.

For example if a listing service returns only twenty items at a time then it must pass back sufficient information to enable it to retrieve the next twenty items in the query.

In the XML Schema example below we have the XML data definitions to support two operations on a listing service. These are:

- `searchItems`
- `nextItems`

The `searchItems` operation will take a `searchItemsRequest` element for input and return a `searchItemsResponse` element. The `searchItemsResponse` has within it a `searchState` element. This element is a sequence that has an unlimited number of arbitrary elements. This can be used by the service to store sufficient state to allow it to deliver the next twenty items in the response. It is important to realize that this state does not have to be understood by the client of the service. The client of the service just has to copy the `searchState` element to the `continueSearchItemsRequest` element to retrieve the next set of 20 results.

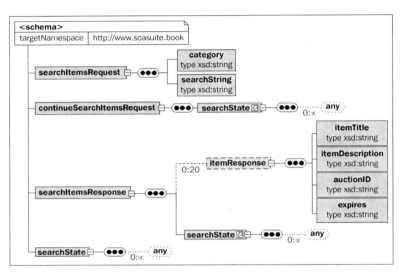

The approach above has the advantage that the service may still be stateless, although it gives the appearance of being stateful. The sample schema shown in the following figure could be used to allow the service to resume the search where it left off without the need for any internal state information in the service. By storing the state information (the original request and the index of the next item to be returned) within the response, the service can retrieve the next set of items without having to maintain any state within itself. Obviously the service for purposes of efficiency could maintain some internal state, such as a database cursor, for a period of time, but this is not necessary.

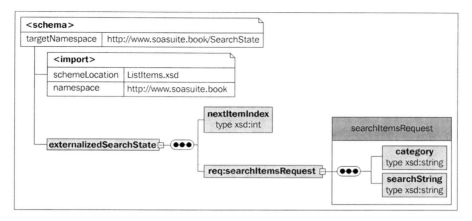

An alternative approach to state management is to keep the state information within the service itself. This still requires some state information to be returned to the client, but only a reference to the internal state information is required. In this case there are a couple of options for dealing with this reference.

One is to take state management outside of the request/response messages and make it part of the wider service contract, either through the use of WS-Correlation or an HTTP cookie for example. This approach has the advantage that the service can generally take advantage of state management functions of the platform, such as support for Java services to use the HTTP session state.

Use of WS-Correlation

It is possible to use a standard correlation mechanism such as WS-Correlation. This is used within SOA Suite by BPEL to correlate process instances with requests. If this approach is used, however, it precludes the use of the externalized state approach discussed earlier. This makes it harder to swap out your service implementation with one that externalizes all its state information. In addition to requiring your service to always internalize state management, no matter how it is implemented, your clients must now support WS-Correlation.

The alternative is to continue to keep the state management in the request/response messages and deal with it within the service. This keeps the client unaware of how state is managed because the interface is exactly the same for a service that maintains internal state and a service that externalizes all state. A sample schema for this is shown in the following figure. Note that unlike the previous schema there is only a service specific reference to its own internal state. The service is responsible for maintaining all the required information internally and using the externalized reference to locate this state information.

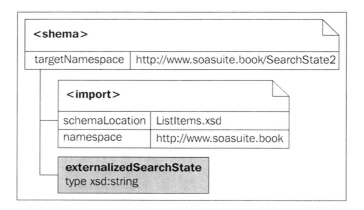

The OSB (Oracle Service Bus) in SOA Suite enables us to have services use their native state management and still expose it as service specific state management that is more abstract and hence less tightly coupled to the way state is handled.

Some web service implementations allow for stateful web services, with state managed in a variety of proprietary fashions. For example, the **Oracle Containers for J2EE (OC4J)** used cookies for native state management, other platforms can use different mechanisms.

We want to use native state management when we internalize session state because it is easier to manage, and the container will do the work for us using mechanisms native to the container. However this means that the client has to be aware that we are using native state management because the client must make use of these mechanisms. We want the client to be unaware of whether the service uses native state management, its own custom state lookup mechanism, or externalizes all session state into the messages flowing between the client and the service. The latter two can look the same to the client and hence make it possible to switch services with different approaches. However, the native state management explicitly requires the client to be aware of how the state is managed.

To avoid this coupling we can use the OSB to wrap the native state management services as shown in the following diagram. The client passes a session state element of unknown contents back to the service façade which is provided by the OSB. The OSB then removes the session state element and maps it onto the native state management used by the service, such as placing the value into a session cookie. Thus we have the benefits of using native state management without the need for coupling the client to a particular implementation of the service. For example, an OC4J service may use cookies to manage session state, by having the OSB move the cookie value to a field in the message we avoid clients of the service having to deal with the specifics of OC4J state management.

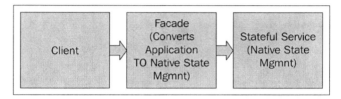

Oracle Service Bus design tools

The Oracle Service Bus can be configured either using the Oracle Workshop for WebLogic or the Oracle Service Bus Console.

Oracle workshop for WebLogic

Oracle Workshop for WebLogic provides tools for creating all the artifacts needed by the Oracle Service Bus. Based on Eclipse, it provides a rich design environment for building service routings and transformations for deployment to the service bus. In future releases it is expected that all the service bus functionality in the Workshop for WebLogic will be provided in JDeveloper. Note that there is some duplication functionality between JDeveloper and Workshop for WebLogic. In some cases, such as WSDL generation, the functionality provided in the Workshop for WebLogic is superior to that provided by JDeveloper. In other cases, such as XSLT generation, the functionality provided by JDeveloper is superior.

Oracle Service Bus Console

Oracle Service Bus Console provides a web-based interface for creating, managing, and monitoring all service bus functions. In this chapter we will focus on using the Service Bus Console. Changes to a service bus configuration are grouped together in a session using the change center. Before any changes are made, it is necessary to **Create** a session from within the change centre. When the changes are complete, they are applied by clicking **Activate**. Clicking **Discard** will cause the changed state to be discarded.

Service Bus overview

The Oracle SOA Suite includes the Oracle Enterprise Service Bus which runs on multiple vendors application servers, and the Oracle Service Bus which in the current release only runs on Oracle WebLogic Server. In the future the Oracle Service Bus may also run on other vendors' applications servers. If you plan on deploying SOA Suite onto non-WebLogic applications servers, then you should use the Oracle Enterprise Service Bus. Most users however run the SOA Suite on Oracle application servers and would be better off using the Oracle Service Bus as it is more functional than the Oracle Enterprise Service Bus and is the stated strategic service bus for Oracle SOA Suite. Because of its additional functionality, we will focus on the Oracle Service Bus in this book.

Service Bus message flow

It is useful to examine how messages are processed by the service bus. Messages normally target an endpoint in the service bus known as a proxy service. Once received by the proxy service, the message is processed through a series of input pipeline stages. These pipeline stages may enrich the data by calling out to other web services, or they may transform the message as well as providing logging and message validation. Finally, the message reaches a routing step where it is routed to a service known as a business service. The response, if any from the service, is then sent through the output pipeline stages which may also enrich the response or transform it before returning a response to the invoker.

Note that there may be no pipeline stages and the router may make a choice between multiple endpoints. Finally note that the business service is a reference to the target service which may be hosted within the service bus or as a standalone service. The proxy service may be thought of as the external service interface and associated transforms required to make use of the actual business service.

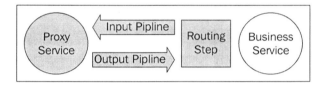

Virtualizing service endpoints

To begin our exploration of the Oracle Service Bus, let us start by looking at how we can use it to virtualize service endpoints. By virtualizing a service endpoint we mean that we can move the location of the service without affecting any of the services' dependents.

We will use an address lookup service as our sample. To begin we create a new **Service Bus Project**. After logging onto the console and before we start making changes in the console we need to create a new session, as described in the previous section. We can then select the **Project Explorer** tab and create a new project by entering a project name and clicking the **Add Project** button. This creates a new Service Bus Project within the console.

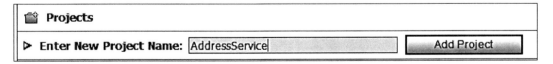

We can now start adding items to our project by clicking on the project name either in the **Project Explorer** tab or in the list of projects under the project creation dialogue. Before adding any items to the project, it is considered good practice to organize the items into folders reflecting their type. So we will use the **Add Folder** dialogue to create folders for the various artifacts we require. We will create a **ProxyService** folder to hold the externally callable service provided by the service bus, a **BusinessService** folder to hold the backend services called by the service bus, and a WSDL folder to hold service definitions (WSDL) files.

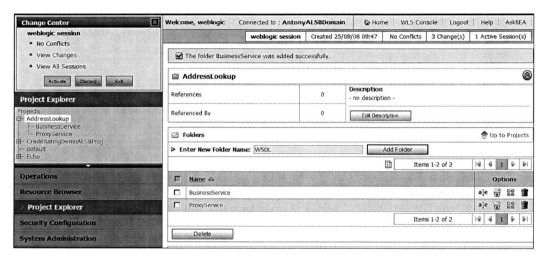

Moving service location

To virtualize the address of our service we first need to add the service definition to the project. In this case we will be adding a web service so we start by adding a service description (WSDL file) to define the service. Before adding the WSDL file, we select the WSDL folder in our project. We then select the appropriate resource type from the **Create Resource** dialogue. We select the **WSDL** resource type from the **Interface** section and are presented with a dialogue enabling us to load the WSDL into the project. We then browse for the WSDL definition and then select **Save** to add it to the project. This registers the WSDL with the internal service bus repository.

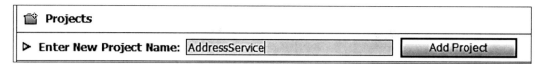

Note that the dialogue requires us to provide a name for the WSDL file and optionally a description. The large blank section in the dialog is used to display the current WSDL file details and is only populated after the WSDL file has been saved.

Endpoint address considerations

When specifying endpoints in the service bus, it is generally not a good idea to use localhost or 127.0.0.1. Because the service bus definitions may be deployed across multiple nodes there is no guarantee that business service will be co-located with the service bus on every node the service bus is deployed upon. Therefore it is best to ensure that all endpoint addresses use actual hostnames.

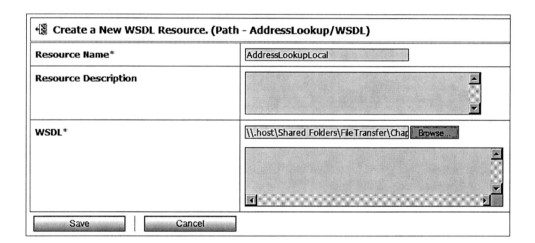

Now that we have a service definition loaded, we can use this to create the business service, or ultimate endpoint of the service. We do this by changing directory to the `BusinessService` directory and creating a resource of type **Business Service**. This brings up a screen allowing us to configure the business service.

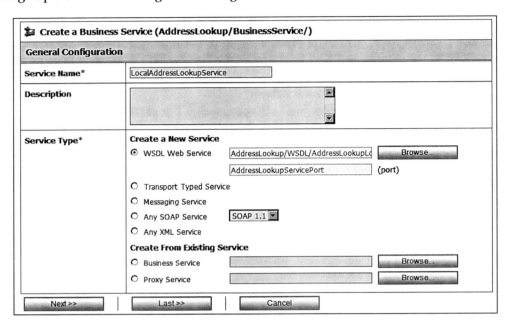

We provide a name for the service and identify the type of service to be accessed. Note that we are not limited to services described by WSDL. In addition to already defined business and proxy services, we can base our service on XML or messaging systems. The easiest to use is the WSDL web service. Browsing for a WSDL web service brings up a dialogue listing all the WSDL documents known to the service bus. We can search this list to select the WSDL document we want to use.

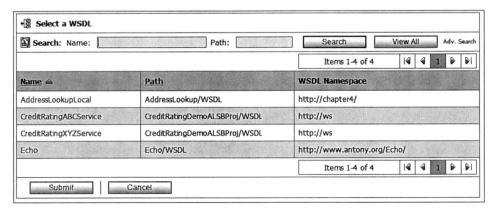

When we select the WSDL name that we want to use, we are taken to another dialogue that introspects the WSDL, identifies any ports or bindings and asks us which one we wish to use. Bindings are mappings of the WSDL service onto a physical transport mechanism such as SOAP over HTTP. Ports are the mapping of the binding onto a physical endpoint such as a specific server. For more information on the makeup of a WSDL file see Chapter 17—*The Importance of Bindings*.

Note that if we choose a port we do not have to provide physical endpoint details later in the definition of the business service, although we may choose to do so. If we choose a binding, because it doesn't include a physical endpoint address, we have to provide the physical endpoint details explicitly. Once we have highlighted the port or binding we want to use we hit the **Submit** button.

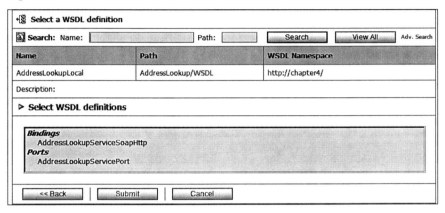

At this point if we have chosen a binding, we can hit last to review the final configuration of the business service. If, however, we chose a port or we wish to change the physical service endpoint, or add additional physical service endpoints, then we hit the **Next** button to allow us to configure the physical endpoints of the service.

This dialogue allows us to do several important things:

- Modify the **Protocol** to support a variety of transports.
- Choose a **Load Balancing Algorithm**. If there is more than one endpoint URI then the service bus will load balance across them according to this algorithm.
- Change, add, or remove **Endpoint URIs** or physical targets.
- Specify retry logic, specifically the **Retry Count**, the **Retry Iteration Interval** and whether or not to **Retry Application Errors** (errors generated by the service called, not the transport).

Note that the ability to change, add, and remove physical endpoint URIs as well as change the protocol used. This allows us to change the target services without impacting any clients of the service, providing us with virtualization of our service location.

Clicking **Last** enables us to review the configuration of this business service and if we are happy with it, then clicking **Save** will create or update our business service.

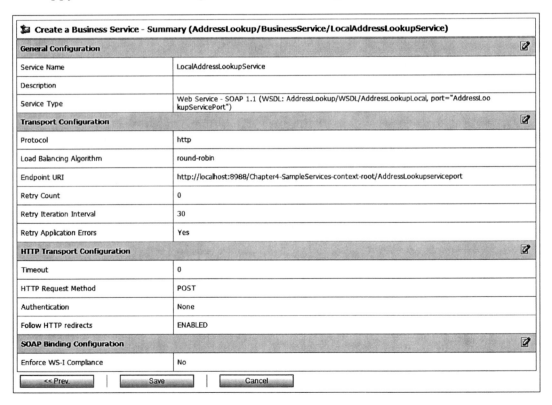

🔁 Create a Business Service - Summary (AddressLookup/BusinessService/LocalAddressLookupService)	
General Configuration	
Service Name	LocalAddressLookupService
Description	
Service Type	Web Service - SOAP 1.1 (WSDL: AddressLookup/WSDL/AddressLookupLocal, port="AddressLookupServicePort")
Transport Configuration	
Protocol	http
Load Balancing Algorithm	round-robin
Endpoint URI	http://localhost:8988/Chapter4-SampleServices-context-root/AddressLookupserviceport
Retry Count	0
Retry Iteration Interval	30
Retry Application Errors	Yes
HTTP Transport Configuration	
Timeout	0
HTTP Request Method	POST
Authentication	None
Follow HTTP redirects	ENABLED
SOAP Binding Configuration	
Enforce WS-I Compliance	No

<< Prev.		Save		Cancel

Now that we have created our business service we need to expose it through the service bus by adding a proxy service. We do this in a similar fashion to creating the business service by creating a resource of type proxy service in the `ProxyService` folder. If we are only virtualizing the location of a service then the proxy service can use the same WSDL definition as the business service. Again we can choose to use either a port or a binding from the WSDL for a service definition. In either case the endpoint URI is determined by the service bus, although we can change its location and transport. Once we have created the new proxy service we then need to link the proxy service to the business service.

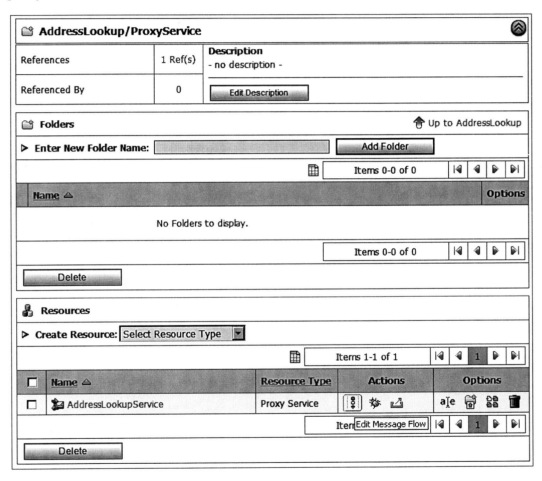

We link the proxy service to business services by selecting the newly created proxy service and clicking on the message flow icon to activate the message flow editor. Within the message flow editor we want to create a routing to the business service so we click on **Add Route**. This creates a new route entry in the message flow.

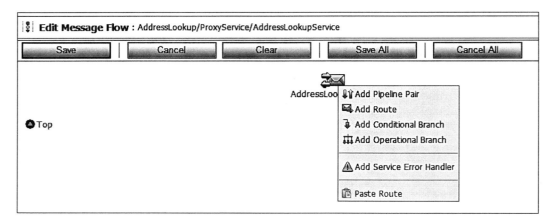

Having created the new route node we can now edit it by clicking on it. We can choose to edit the name of the node and, more interestingly, we can choose to edit the routing details.

Selecting **Edit Route** brings up the route node editor which allows us to configure the routing details. Clicking on **Add an Action** allows us to choose the type of **Communication** we want to add. **Flow Control** allows us to add If ... Then ... logic to our routing decision. However in most cases the **Communication** items will provide all the flexibility we need in our routing decisions. This gives us three types of routing to apply:

- **Dynamic Routing**: It allows us route to the result of an XQuery. This is useful if the endpoint address is part of the input message.

- **Routing**: It allows us to select a single static endpoint.

- **Routing Table**: It allows us to use an XQuery to route between several endpoints. This is useful when we want to route to different services based on a particular attribute of the input message.

For simple service endpoint virtualization we only require the **Routing** option.

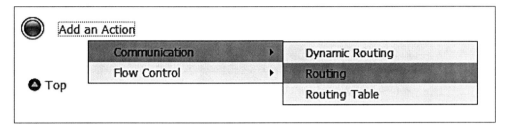

Selecting the **Routing** option then enables us to configure the route by first selecting a service by clicking on the **<Service>** label. This brings up a dialog from which we can select out target endpoint, usually a previously defined business service.

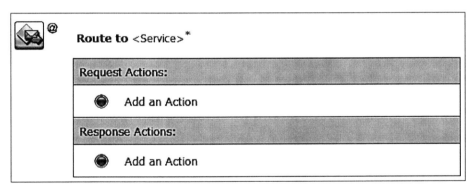

Having selected a target endpoint, we can then configure how we use that endpoint. In the case of simple location virtualization then the proxy service and the business service endpoint are the same and so we can just pass on the input message directly to the business service. Later on we will look at how to transform data to allow virtualization of the service interface.

To provide a simple pass through function we can check the **Use inbound operation for outbound** checkbox. This means that the operation that is requested on the proxy service, the inbound operation, will be invoked on the business service, the outbound operation. Because there is no need to transform the data or perform additional operations we can now save our message flow and activate our changes by clicking **activate** in the session dialog.

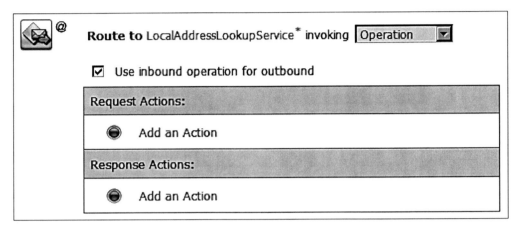

Selecting a service to call

We can further virtualize our endpoint by routing different requests to different services, based upon the values of the input message. For example, we may use one address lookup service for addresses in our own country and another service for all other addresses. In this case, we would use the routing table option on the add action to provide a list of possible service destinations.

The routing table enables us to have a number of different destinations and the message will be routed based the value of an expression. When using a routing table all the services must be selected based on the same expression, the comparison operators may vary but the actual value being tested against will always be the same. If this is not the case then it may be better to use if ... then ... else routing. The routing table may be thought of as a switch statement and as with all switch statements, it is good practice to add a default case.

In the routing table we can create additional cases, each of which will have a test associated with it. Note that we can also add the default case.

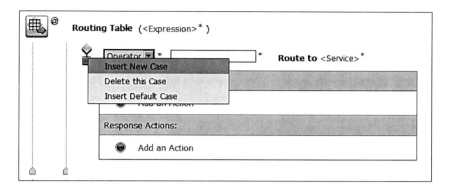

We need to specify the expression to be used for testing against. Clicking on the **<Expression>** link takes us to the **XQuery /XSLT Expression Editor**. By selecting the **Variable Structures** tab and selecting a new structure we can find the input body of the message which enables us to select the field we wish to use as the comparison expression in our routing table.

When selecting in the tab on the left of the screen the appropriate xpath expression should appear in the **Property Inspector** window. We can then click on the **XQuery Text** area of the screen prior to clicking on the **Copy Property** to transfer the property xpath expression from the property inspector to the **XQuery Text** area. We then complete our selection of the expression by clicking the **Save** button.

In the example we are going to route our service based on the country of the address. In addition to the data in the body of the message, we could also route based on other information from the request, or by using a message pipeline, we could base our lookup on data external to the request.

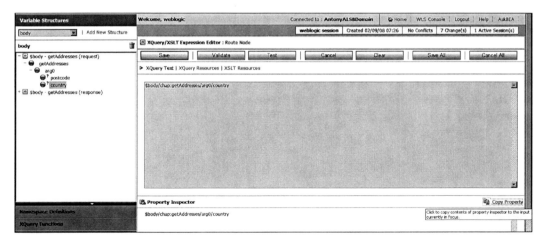

Once we have created an expression to use as the basis of comparison for routing then we select an operator and a value to use for the actual routing comparison. In the example below, if the country value from the expression matches the string **uk** (include the quotes) then the local address lookup service will be invoked. Any other value will cause the default service to be invoked, as yet undefined in the following example:

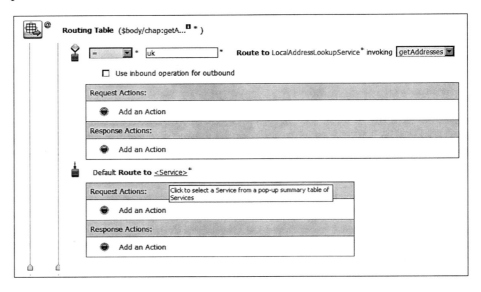

Once the routing has been defined then it can be saved as shown earlier in this chapter.

Note that we have shown a very simple routing example. The service bus is capable of doing much more sophisticated routing decisions. A common pattern is to use a pipeline to enrich the inbound data and then route based on the inbound data. For example a pricing proxy service may use the inbound pipeline to look up the status of a customer, adding that status to the data available as part of the request. The routing service could then route high value customers to one service and low value customers to another service, based on the looked up status. In this case the routing is done based on a derived value rather than on a value already available in the message.

In summary, a request can be routed to different references based on the content of the request message. This allows messages to be routed based on geography or pecuniary value for example. This routing, because it takes place in the composite, is transparent to clients of the composite and so aids us in reducing coupling in the system.

Virtualizing service interfaces

We have looked at how to virtualize a service endpoint. Now let us look at how we can further virtualize the service by abstracting its interface into a common format, known as canonical form. This will provide us further flexibility by allowing us to change the implementation of the service with one that has a different interface but performs the same function. The native format is the way the data format service actually uses, the canonical format is an idealized format that we wish to develop against.

Physical versus logical interfaces

Best practice for integration projects was to have a canonical form for all messages exchanged between systems. The canonical form was a common format for all messages. If a system wanted to send a message then it first needed to transform it to canonical form before it could be forwarded to the receiving system who would then transform it from canonical form to its own representation. This same good practice is still valid in a service-oriented world and the Service Bus is the mechanism SOA Suite provides for us to do this.

The benefits of a canonical form are that:

- Transformations are only necessary to and from canonical form, reducing the number of different transformations required to be created.
- Decouples format of data from services, allowing a service to be replaced by one providing the same function but a different format of data.

This is illustrated graphically by a system where two different clients make requests for one of four services, all providing the same function but different implementations. Without canonical form we would need a transformation of data between the client format and the server format inbound and again outbound. For four services this yields eight transformations, and for two clients this doubles to sixteen transformations.

Using canonical format gives us two transformations for each client, inbound and outbound to canonical form; with two clients this gives us four transformations. To this we add the server transformations to and from canonical form, of which there are two per server giving us eight transformations. This gives us a total of twelve transformations that must be coded up rather than sixteen if we were using native to native transformation.

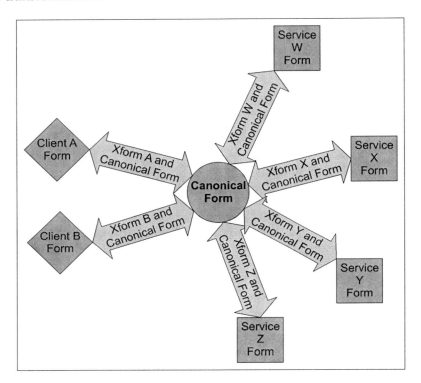

The benefits of canonical form are most clearly seen when we deploy a new client. Without canonical form we would need to develop eight transformations to allow the client to work with the four different possible service implementations. With canonical form we only need two transformations, to and from canonical form.

Let us look at how we implement canonical form in Oracle Service Bus.

Mapping service interfaces

In order to take advantage of canonical form in our service interfaces, we must have an abstract service interface that provides the functionality we need without being specific to any particular service implementation. Once we have this we can then use it as the canonical service form.

We set up the initial project in the same way as we did in the previous section on virtualizing service endpoints. The proxy should provide the canonical interface, the business service providing the native service interface. Because the proxy and business services are not the same interface we need to do some more work in the route configuration.

We need to map the canonical form of the address list interface onto the native service form of the interface. In the example, we are mapping our canonical interface to the interface provided by a web-based address solution provided by Harte-Hanks Global Address (`http://www.qudox.com`). To do this we create a new service bus project and add the Harte-Hanks WSDL (`http://webservices.globaladdress. net/globaladdress.asmx?WSDL`). We use this to define the business service. We also add the canonical interface WSDL that we have defined and create a new proxy with this interface. We then need to map the proxy service onto the Harte-Hanks service by editing the message flow associated with the proxy, as we did in the previous section.

Our mapping needs to do two things:

- Map the method name on the interface to the correct method in the business service.
- Map the parameters in the canonical request onto the parameters needed in the business service request.

For each method on the canonical interface we must map it onto a method in the physical interface. We do this by selecting the appropriate method from the business service operation drop-down box. We need to do this because the methods provided in the external service do not match the method names in our canonical service. In the example we have mapped onto the **SearchAddress** method.

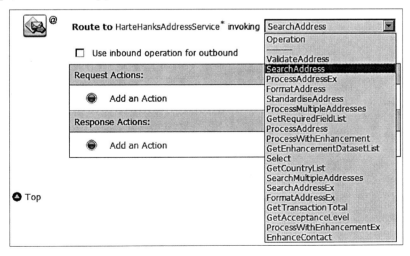

Having selected an operation we now need to transform the input data from the format provided by the canonical interface into the format required by the external service. We need to map the request and response messages if it is a two-way method, or just the request message for one-way methods. The actual mapping may be done either by XQuery or XSLT. In our example we will use the XSLT transformation.

To perform the transformation we add a messaging processing action to our message flow, in this case a replace operation. The variable body always holds the message in the service bus flow; this receives the message through the proxy interface and is also used to deliver the message to the business service interface. This behavior differs from BPEL and most programming languages where we typically have separate variables for the input and output messages. We need to transform this message from the proxy input canonical format to the business service native output format.

Be aware that there are really two flows associated with the proxy service. The **request flow** is used to receive the inbound message and perform any processing before invoking the target business service. The **response flow** takes the response from the business service and performs any necessary processing before replying to the invoker of the proxy service.

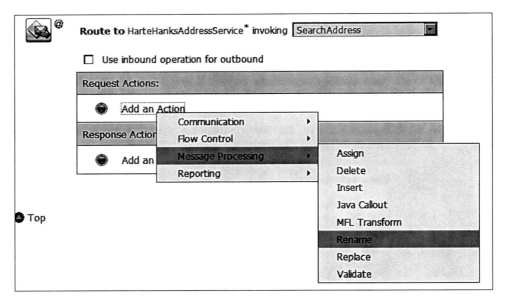

On selecting replace we can fill in the details in the replace action dialogue. The message is held in the body variable and so we can fill this (body) in as the target variable name. We then need to select which part of the body we want to replace.

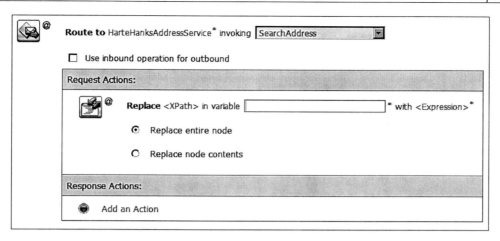

Clicking on the **XPath** link brings up the **XPath Expression Editor** where we can enter the portion of the target variable that we wish to replace. In this case we wish to replace all the elements so we enter `./*` which selects the top level element and all elements beneath it. Clicking **Save** causes the expression to be saved in the replace action dialogue.

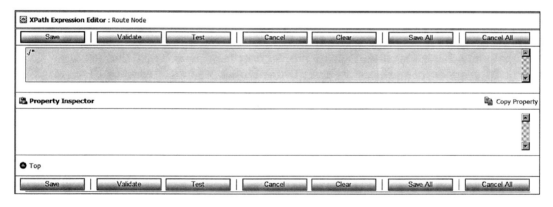

Having identified the portion of the message we wish to replace, all of it, we now need to specify what we will replace it with. In this case we wish to transform the whole input message, so we click on the **Expression** link and select the **XSLT Resources** tab. Clicking on **Browse** enables us to choose a previously registered XSLT transformation file. After selecting the file we need to identify the input to the transformation. In this case the input message is in the body variable and so we select all the elements in the body by using the expression **$body/***. We then save our transformation expression.

Having providing the source data, the target, and the transformation we can then save the repeat the whole process for the response message, in this case converting from native to canonical form.

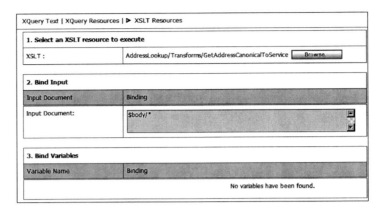

We can use JDeveloper to build an XSLT transformation and then upload it into the service bus; a future release will add support for XQuery in JDeveloper similar to that provided in Oracle Workshop for WebLogic. XSLT is an XML language that describes how to transform one XML document into another. Fortunately most XSLT can be created using the graphical mapping tool in JDeveloper, and so SOA Suite developers don't have to be experts in XSLT, although it is very useful to know how it works. Note that in our transform we may need to enhance the message with additional information, for example the Global Address methods all require a username and password to be provided to allow accounting of the requests to take place. This information has no place in the canonical request format but must be added in the transform. A sample transform is shown that does just this.

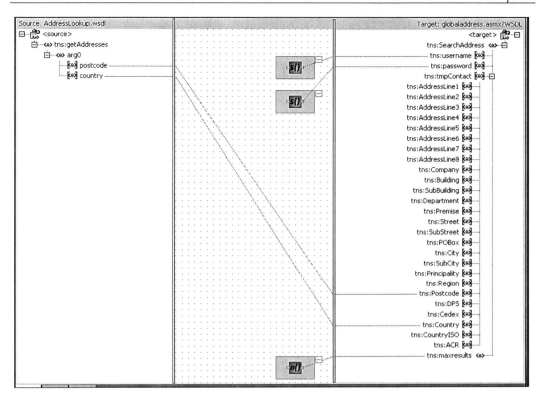

Note that we use XPath string functions to set the username and password fields. It would be better to set these from properties or an external file as usually we would want to use them in a number of calls to the physical service. XPath functions are available to allow access to composite properties. We actually only need to set five fields in the request, a country, postcode, username, password, and maximum number of results to return. All the other fields are not necessary for the service we are using and so are hidden from end users because they do not appear in the canonical form of the service.

Applying canonical form in the service bus

When we think about canonical form and routing, we have several different operations that may need to be performed. These are:

- Conversion to/from native business service form and canonical proxy form.
- Conversion to/from native client form to canonical proxy form.
- Routing between multiple native services, each potentially with its own message format.

The following diagram represents these different potential interactions as distinct proxy implementations in the service. To reduce coupling and make maintenance easier, each native service has a corresponding canonical proxy service, which isolates the rest of the system from the actual native formats. This is shown in the following figure in the Local-Harte-Hanks-Proxy and Local-LocalAddress-Proxy services that transform the native service to/from canonical form. This approach allows us to change the native address lookup implementations without impacting anything other than the Local-*-Proxy service.

The Canonical-Address-Proxy has the job of hiding the fact that the address lookup service is actually provided by a number of different service providers each with their own message formats. By providing this service we can easily add additional address providers without impacting the clients of the address lookup service.

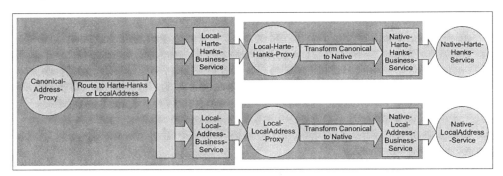

In addition to the services shown in the figure we may have clients that are not written to use the canonical address lookup. In this case we need to provide a proxy that transforms the native input request to/from the canonical form. This allows us to be isolated from the requirements of the clients of the service. If a client requires its own interface to the address lookup service we can easily provide that through a proxy without the need to impact the rest of the system, again reducing coupling.

An important optimization

The above approach provides a very robust way of isolating service consumers and service requestors from the native formats and locations of their partners. However there must be a concern about the overhead of all these additional proxy services and also about the possibility of a client accessing a native service directly. To avoid these problems the service bus provides a **local** transport mechanism that can be specified as part of the binding of the proxy service. The local transport provides two things for us:

- It makes services only consumable by other services in the service bus; they cannot be accessed externally.

- It provides a highly optimized messaging transport between proxy services, providing in-memory speed to avoid unnecessary overhead in service hand-offs between proxy services.

These optimizations mean that it is very efficient to use canonical form, and so the service bus not only allows us great flexibility in how we decouple our services from each other but it also provides a very efficient mechanism for us to implement that decoupling. Note though that there is a cost involved in performing XSLT or XQuery transformations; this cost may be viewed as the price of loose coupling.

Summary

In this chapter we have explored how we can use the Oracle Service Bus in the SOA Suite to reduce the degree of coupling. By reducing coupling, or the dependencies between services, our architectures become more resilient to change. In particular, we looked at how to use the Service Bus to reduce coupling by abstracting endpoint interface locations and formats. Crucial to this is the concept of canonical or common data formats that reduce the amount of data transformation that is required, particularly in bringing new services into our architecture. Finally we considered how this abstraction can go as far as hiding the fact that we are using multiple services concurrently by allowing us to make routing decisions at run time.

All these features are there to help us build service-oriented architectures that are resilient to change and can easily absorb new functionality and services.

5

Using BPEL to Build Composite Services and Business Processes

In the previous two chapters, we've looked at how we can service enable functionality embedded within existing systems. The next challenge is how to assemble these services to build "composite" applications or business processes. This is the role of the Web Service **Business Process Execution Language** or **BPEL** as it's commonly referred to.

BPEL is a rich XML based language for describing the assembly of a set of existing web services into either a composite service or a business process. Once deployed, a BPEL process itself is actually invoked as a web service.

Thus anything that can call a web service, can also call a BPEL process, including of course other BPEL processes. This allows you to take a nested approach to writing BPEL processes, giving you a lot of flexibility.

In this chapter we first introduce the basic structure of a BPEL process, its key constructs, and the difference between a synchronous and asynchronous service.

We then demonstrate through the building and refinement of two example BPEL processes, one synchronous the other asynchronous, how to use BPEL to invoke external web services (including other BPEL processes) to build composite services. During this procedure we also take the opportunity to introduce the reader to many of the key BPEL activities in more detail.

Basic structure of a BPEL process

The following diagram shows the core structure of a BPEL process, and how it interacts with components external to it; either web services that the BPEL process invokes (Service A and Service B in this case) or external clients that invoke the BPEL process as a web service.

From this we can see that the BPEL process divides into two distinct parts; the **Partner Links**, with associated **WSDL** files which describe the interactions between the BPEL process and the outside world; and the **core BPEL process** itself, which describes the process to be executed at run time.

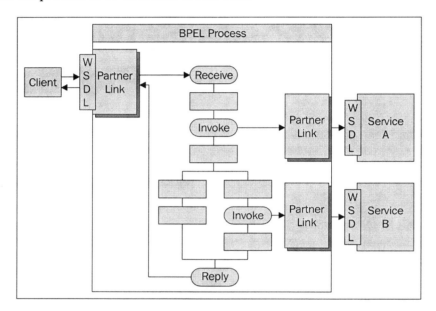

Core BPEL process

The core BPEL process consists of a number of steps, or activities as they are called in BPEL. These consist of simple activities, including:

- Assign: It is used to manipulate variables.
- Transform: It is a specialised assign activity that uses XSLT to map data from a source format to a target format.
- Wait: It is used to pause the process for a period of time.
- Empty: It does nothing. It is used in branches of your process where syntactically an activity is required, but you don't want to perform an activity.

The structured activities which control the flow through the process. These include:

- `While`: It is used for implementing loops.
- `Switch`: It is a construct for implementing conditional branches.
- `Flow`: It is used for implementing branches which execute in parallel.
- `FlowN`: It is used for implementing a dynamic number of parallel branches.

There are messaging activities as well (for example `Receive`, `Invoke`, `Reply`, and `Pick`).

The activities within a BPEL process can be sub-divided into logical groups of activities, using the `Scope` activity. As well as providing a useful way to structure and organize your process, it also enables you to define attributes such as variables, fault handlers, and compensation handlers that just apply to the scope.

Variables

In addition each BPEL process also defines variables, which are used to hold the state of the process as well as messages that are sent and received by the process. They can be defined at the process level, in which case they are considered global and visible to all parts of the process. Or it can be declared within a `Scope` in which case they are only visible to activities contained within that `Scope` (and scopes nested within the scope to which the variable belongs).

Variables can be one of the following types:

- **Simple Type**: It can hold any simple data type defined by XML Schema (for example string, integer, boolean, and float).
- **WSDL Message Type**: It is used to hold the content of a WSDL Message sent to or received from partners.
- **Element**: It can hold either a complex or simple XML Schema element defined in either a WSDL file or a separate XML Schema.

Variables are manipulated using the `<assign>` activity, which can be used to copy data from one variable to another, as well as create new data using XPath Expressions or XSLT.

For variables which are WSDL Messages or Complex Elements we can work with it at the sub-component level by specifying the part of the variable we would like to work with using an XPath expression.

Partner Links

All interaction between a process and other parties (or partners) is via web services as defined by their corresponding WSDL files. Even though each service is fully described by its WSDL, it fails to define the relationship between the process and the partner, that is who the consumer of a service is and who the provider is. On first appearance, the relationship may seem implicit; however, this is not always the case so BPEL uses Partner Links to explicitly define this relationship.

Partner Links are defined using the `<partnerLinkType>` which is an extension to WSDL (defined by the BPEL standard). Whenever you reference a web service whose WSDL doesn't contain a `<partnerLinkType>`, JDeveloper will automatically ask you whether you want it to create one for you. Assuming you answer yes it will create this as a separate WSDL document, which then imports the original WSDL.

Messaging activities

BPEL defines three messaging activities `<receive>`, `<reply>`, and `<invoke>`. How you use these depends on whether the message interaction is either synchronous or asynchronous and whether the BPEL process is either a consumer or provider of the service.

Synchronous messaging

With synchronous messaging, the caller will block until it has received a reply (or times out); that is the BPEL process will wait for a reply before moving onto the next activity.

As we can see in the diagram below, Process A uses the `<invoke>` activity to call a synchronous web service (Process B in this case); once it has sent the initial request, it blocks and waits for a corresponding reply from Process B.

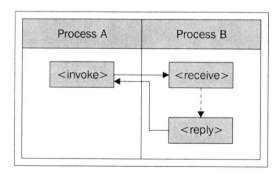

Process B, uses the <receive> activity to receive the request; once it has processed the request it uses the <reply> activity to send a response back to Process A.

Theoretically Process B could take as long as it wants before sending a reply, but typically Process A will only wait a short time (for example 30 seconds) before it times out the <invoke> operation under the assumption that something has gone wrong. Thus if Process B is going to take a substantial period of time before replying, then you should model the exchange as an Asynchronous Send-Receive (see next section).

Asynchronous messaging

With asynchronous messaging, the key difference is that once the caller has sent the request, the send operation will return immediately, and the BPEL process may then continue with additional activities until it is ready to receive the reply, at which point the process will block until it receives the reply (which may already be there).

If we look at the following diagram, you will notice that just like the synchronous request Process A uses the <invoke> activity to call an asynchronous web service. However, the difference is that it doesn't block waiting for a response, rather it continues processing until it is ready to process the response. It then receives this using the <receive> activity.

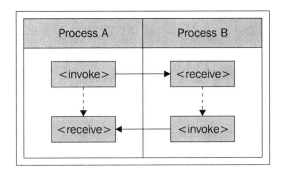

Conversely, Process B uses a <receive> activity to receive the initial request and an <invoke> activity to send back the corresponding response.

While at a logical level there is little difference between synchronous and asynchronous messaging (especially if there are no activities between the <invoke> and <receive> activity in Process A), at a technical level there is a key difference.

This is because with asynchronous messaging, we have two <invoke>, <receive> pairs, each corresponding to a separate web service operation; one for the request, the other for the reply.

From a decision perspective a key driver as to which to choose is the length of time it takes for Process B to service the request, since asynchronous messaging supports far longer processing times. In general once the time it takes for Process B to return a response goes above 30 seconds you should consider switching to asynchronous messaging.

 With potentially many instances of Process A and Process B running at the same time, BPEL needs to ensure that each reply is matched (or correlated) to the appropriate request. By default BPEL uses WS-Addressing to achieve this. We look at this in more detail in Chapter 14—*Message Interaction Patterns*.

One way messaging

A variation of asynchronous messaging is one way messaging (also known as **fire and forget**). This involves a single message being sent from the calling process, with no response being returned.

If we look at the following diagram, you will notice that just like the asynchronous request Process A uses the <invoke> activity to send a message to Process B.

Once Process A has sent the message, it continues processing until it completes, that is it never stops to wait for a response from Process B. Likewise Process B, upon receipt of the message, continues processing until it has completed and never sends any response back to Process A.

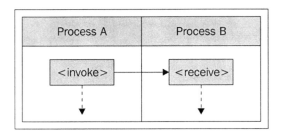

A simple composite service

Despite the fact that BPEL is intended primarily for writing long running processes, it also provides an excellent way to build a composite service, that is a service that is assembled from other services.

Let's takes a simple example: say I have a service that gives me the stock quote for a specified company, and that I also have a service that gives me the exchange rate between two currencies. I can use BPEL to combine these two services and provide a service that gives the stock quote for a company in the currency of my choice.

So let's create our stock quote service; we will create a simple synchronous BPEL process which takes two parameters, the stock ticker and the required currency. This will then call two external services.

Creating our Stock Quote service

Before we begin, we will create a **StockService** application, which we will use for all our samples in this chapter. To do this follow the same process we used to create our first application in Chapter 2.

Next add a BPEL project to our **StockService** application. Specify a name of **StockQuote** and select a synchronous BPEL process. However, at this stage **DO NOT** click **Finish**.

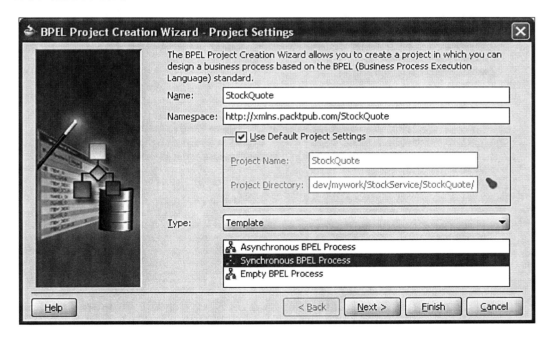

You may remember when we created our `Echo` service back in Chapter 2; JDeveloper automatically created a simple WSDL file for our service, with a single input and output field for our service. For our stock quote service we need to pass in multiple fields (that is Stock Ticker and Currency). So to define the input and output messages for our BPEL process we are going to make use of a predefined schema `StockService.xsd`, shown below (for brevity only the parts which are relevant to this example are shown; however, the complete schema is provided in the downloadable samples file for this book).

```xml
<?xml version="1.0" encoding="windows-1252"?>
<xsd:schema xmlns:xsd="http://www.w3.org/2001/XMLSchema"
            xmlns="http://xmlns.packtpub.com/StockService"
            targetNamespace="http://xmlns.packtpub.com/StockService"
            elementFormDefault="qualified" >

  <xsd:element name="getQuote"         type=" tGetQuote"/>
  <xsd:element name="getQuoteResponse" type=" tGetQuoteResponse"/>

  <xsd:complexType name="tGetQuote">
    <xsd:sequence>
      <xsd:element name="currency" type="xsd:string"/>
      <xsd:element name="stockSymbol" type="xsd:string"/>
    </xsd:sequence>
  </xsd:complexType>

  <xsd:complexType name="tGetQuoteResponse">
    <xsd:sequence>
      <xsd:element name="stockSymbol" type="xsd:string"/>
      <xsd:element name="currency" type="xsd:string"/>
      <xsd:element name="amount" type="xsd:decimal"/>
    </xsd:sequence>
  </xsd:complexType>

  ...

</xsd:schema>
```

Import StockService schema

Within the **Create BPEL Process** dialogue, click on **Next**, this will show you the input and output elements for your process, as shown in the following screenshot:

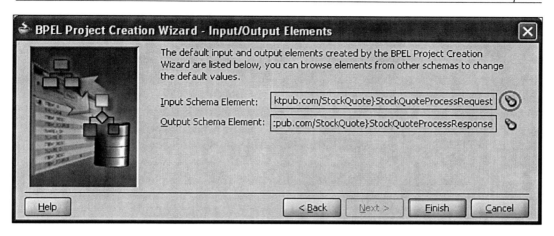

To override the default input and output schema elements generated by JDeveloper, click on the **flashlight** (circled above). This will bring up a dialogue that allows you to browse all schemas imported by the BPEL process and select an element from them. In our case, as we have yet to import any schemas it will automatically launch the **Select Schema** window in file mode which will allow us to search our file system for an appropriate schema.

Find the `StockService.xsd` located in the samples folder for Chapter 5 and select this. It will now open the schema browser dialogue. Browse this and select the **getQuote** element as illustrated in the following screenshot:

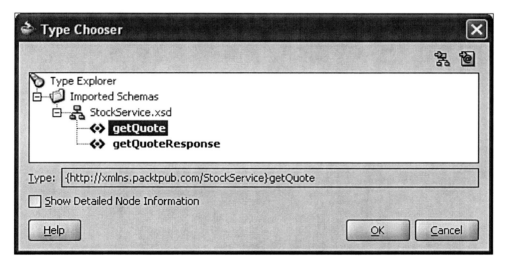

Repeat this step for the **Output Schema Element**, but this time, select the **getQuoteResponse** element. Click **Finish** and this will create our **StockQuote** process.

You will see that by default JDeveloper has created a skeleton BPEL process, which contains an initial `<receive>` activity to receive the stock quote request, followed by a `<reply>` activity to send back the result (as we discussed in the earlier section—*Synchronous messaging*). In addition it will have created two variables: `inputVariable` which contains the initial stock quote request and `outputVariable` in which we will place the result to return to the requestor.

If you look in the **Projects** section of the **Application** navigator you will see it contains the file `StockQuote.wsdl`. This contains the WSDL description (including Partner Link extensions) for our process. If you examine this, you will see we have a single operation: `process`, which is used to call the BPEL process.

Calling the external web services

The next step is to call our external web services; for our stock quote service we are going to use Xignite's Quotes web service which delivers delayed equity price quotes from all U.S. stock exchanges (NYSE, NASDAQ, AMEX, NASDAQ OTC bulletin board, and Pink Sheets).

Before you can use this service you will need to register with Xignite; to do this or for more information on this and other services provided by Xignite go to www.xignite.com.

To call a web service in BPEL we first need to create a Partner Link (as discussed at the start of this chapter). So from the component pallet, select the **Services** drop down and drag a **PartnerLink** into the **Services** swim lane in your BPEL process. This will pop up the following screen:

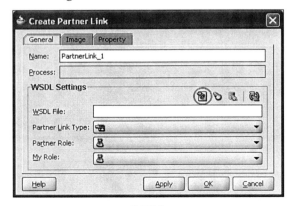

First enter a name for the Partner Link, for example `XigniteQuotes`. Next we need to specify the WSDL file for the Partner Link. JDeveloper provides the following ways to do this:

- **Browse WSDL File**: This allows us to browse the file system for WSDL files that define the service.

- **Service Explorer**: This allows us to browse services that are already defined within the composite application (for example other BPEL processes or ESB services).

- **Define Adapter Service**: This enables us to define adapter services (as covered in Chapter 3) directly within the context of a BPEL process.

- **Enter URL**: Directly enter the URL for the WSDL File into the corresponding field.

For our purposes, we have a local copy of the WSDL for Xignite's Quotes service, called `XigniteQuotes.wsdl`, which is included with the samples for Chapter 5. Click on the **Browse WSDL File ...** icon (highlighted in previous screenshot) then browse to and select this file (select **Yes** if prompted to create a local copy of the file).

JDeveloper will parse the WSDL and, assuming it is successful, will pop up a window saying there are no Partner Link types defined in the current WSDL, and will ask if you want to create partner links for the file: click **Yes**. JDeveloper will then create one **Partner Link Type** for each Port Type defined in the WSDL.

In cases where we have multiple Partner Link types, we will need to specify which one to use within our process. To do this, click on the drop down next to **Partner Link Type** and select the appropriate one. In our case we have selected **XigniteQuotesSoap_PL**, as shown in the following screenshot:

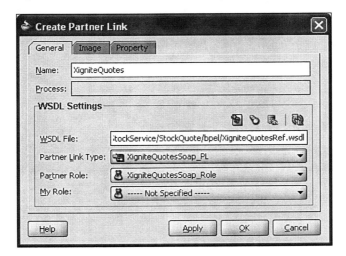

Finally we need to specify the **Partner Role** and **My Role**. When invoking a synchronous service, there will only be a **single** role defined in the WSDL, which represents the provider of the service. So specify this for the **Partner Role** and leave **My Role** as ----- **Not Specified** -----.

[Best practice would dictate that rather than call the Stock Quote service directly from within BPEL, we would invoke it via the service bus.]

Calling the web service

Once we have defined a Partner Link for the web service, the next step is to call it. As this is a synchronous service we will need to use an <invoke> activity to call it, as we described earlier in this chapter.

On the component palette, ensure the submenu of **Process Activities** is selected, and then from it drag an **Invoke** activity on to your BPEL process.

Next, place your mouse over the arrow next to the **Invoke** activity; click and hold your mouse button and then drag the arrow over your Partner Link, then release. This is shown in the following screenshot:

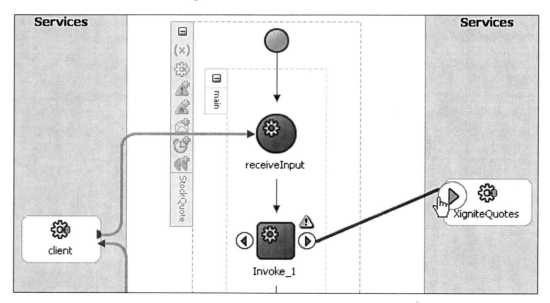

This will then pop up the **Edit Invoke** activity window as shown in the following screenshot:

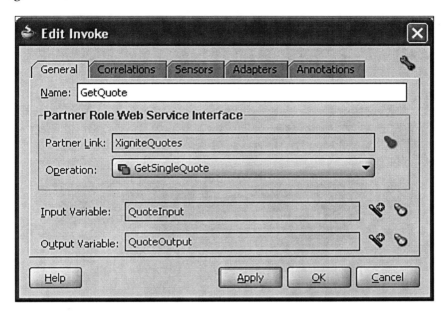

We need to specify a number of values to configure the invoke activity, namely:

- **Name**: This is the name we want to assign to the invoke activity, and can be any value. So just assign a meaningful value such as GetQuote.

- **Partner Link**: This is the Partner Link whose service we want to invoke; it should already be set to use XigniteQuotes, as we have already linked this activity to that Partner Link. An alternative approach would be to click on the corresponding spotlight icon which would allow us to select from any Partner Link already defined to the process.

- **Operation**: Once we've specified a Partner Link, we need to specify which of its operations we wish to invoke. This presents us with a drop down, listing all the operations that are available; for our purpose select GetSingleQuote.

- **Input Variable**: Here we must specify the variable which contains the data to be passed to the web service that's being invoked. It is important that the variable is of type Message, and that it is of the same message type expected by the **Operation** (that is as defined in the WSDL file for the web service).

The simplest way to ensure this is to get JDeveloper to create the variable for you; to do this, click on the **magic wand** to the right of the input variable field. This will bring up the **Create Variable** window as shown below. You will notice that JDeveloper creates a default name for the variable (based on the name you gave the invoke operation and the operation that you are calling), you can override this with something more meaningful (for example `QuoteInput`).

- **Output Variable**: Finally, we must specify the variable into which the value returned by the web service will be placed. As with the input variable, this should be of type `Message`, and corresponds to the output message defined in the WSDL file for the selected operation. Again the simplest way to ensure this is to get JDeveloper to create the variable for you.

Once you've specified values for all these fields, as illustrated above, click **OK**.

Assigning values to variables

In our previous step, we created the variable `QuoteInput`, which we pass to our invocation of `GetSingleQuote`. However, we have yet to initialize the variable or assign any value to it.

To do this BPEL provides the `<assign>` activity, which is used to update the values of variables with new data. The assign activity typically consists of one or more copy operations. Each copy consists of a target variable, that is the variable that you wish to assign a value to and a source; this can either be another variable or an XPath expression.

For our purpose, we want to assign the stock symbol passed into our BPEL process to our `QuoteInput` variable.

To do this drag an assign activity from the component pallet on to your BPEL process at the point just before our invoke activity. Then double click on it to open up the **Assign** configuration window. Click on the **Create** menu and select **Copy Operation...**

This will present us with the **Create Copy Operation** window shown in the following screenshot:

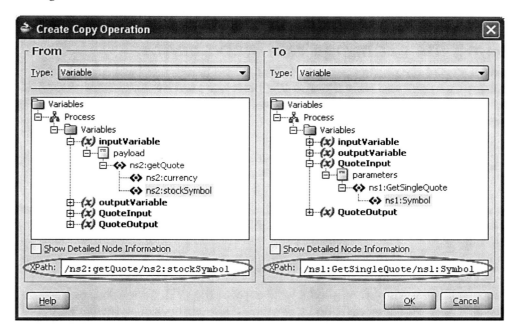

On the left-hand side we specify the **From** variable (that is the source). Here we want to specify the stock symbol passed in as part of the input variable to the BPEL process, so expand the **inputVariable** tree and select **/ns2:getQuote/ns2:stockSymbol**.

For the target expand **QuoteInput** and select **/ns1:GetSingleQuote/ns1:Symbol**.

You will notice that for both the source and target, JDeveloper has created the equivalent XPath expression (circled in the previous screenshot).

 The source and target can either be a simple type (for example `xsd:int`, `xsd:date`, or `xsd:string`), as in the above example. Or a complex type (for example `ns2:getQuote`), but make sure the source and target are either of the same type, or at least compatible.

Testing the process

At this stage, even though the process isn't complete, we can still save, deploy, and run our process. Do this in the same way as previously covered in Chapter 2. When you run the process from the BPEL console you will notice that it doesn't return anything (as we haven't specified this yet). But if you look at the audit trail you should successfully see the GetSingleQuote operation being invoked. Assuming this is the case, we know we have implemented that part of the process correctly.

Calling the exchange rate web service

The next step of the process is to determine the exchange rate between the requested currency and the US dollar (the currency used by the GetSingleQuote operation). For this we are going to use the currency convertor service provided by webserviceX.NET.

 For more information on this and other services provided by webserviceX.NET go to www.webservicex.net.

This service provides a single operation ConversionRate, which gets the conversion rate from one currency to another. The WSDL file for this service can be found at the following URL:

    http://www.webservicex.net/CurrencyConvertor.asmx?wsdl

For convenience we have included a local copy of the WSDL for webserviceX.NET's Currency Convertor service, called CurrencyConvertor.wsdl, which is included with the samples for Chapter 5.

To invoke the ConversionRate operation, we will follow the same basic steps that we did in the previous section to invoke the GetQuickQuote operation. For the sake of brevity we won't repeat them here, but will allow the reader to do this.

 For the purpose of following the examples below, name the input variable for the exchange rate web service ExchangeRateInput and the output variable ExchangeRateOutput.

Assigning constant values to variables

The operation ConversionRate takes two input values:

- FromCurrency, which should be set to USD
- ToCurrency, which should be set to the currency field contained within the inputVariable for the BPEL process

To set the `FromCurrency`, create another copy operation. However for the **From** value select **Expression** as the **Type** (circled in the following screenshot).

This will replace the Variable browser with a free format text box. In here you can specify any value, within quotes, that you wish to assign to your target variable. For our purpose we have entered **'USD'**, as shown in the following screenshot:

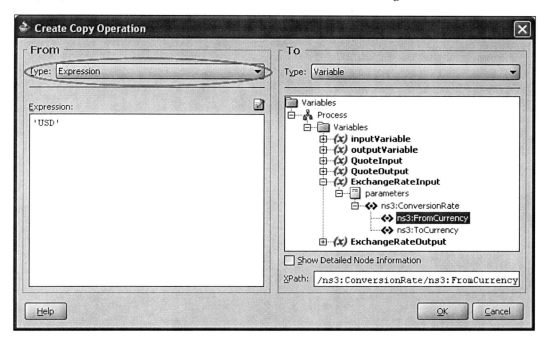

To set the value of **ToCurrency**, create another copy operation and copy in the value of the `currency` field contained within the **inputVariable**.

Again at this stage, save, deploy, and run the process to validate that we are calling the exchange rate service correctly.

Using the Expression builder

The final part of the process is now to combine the exchange rate returned by one service with the stock price returned by the other in order to determine the stock price in the requested currency and return that to the caller of the BPEL process.

To do this, we will again use an assign activity; so drag another assign activity onto the process, just after our second invoke activity. Now in our previous use of the assign activity, we have just used it to copy a value from one variable to another.

Here, it is slightly different, in that we want to combine multiple values into a single value, and to do that we will need to write the appropriate piece of XPath. Create a copy operation as before, but for the source type, select **Expression** from the drop down as shown in the following screenshot:

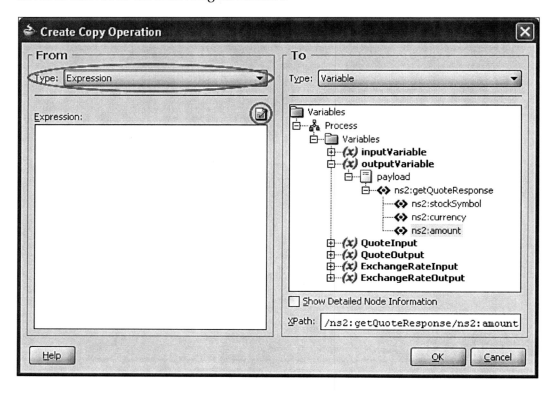

Now if you want, you can type in the XPath expression manually (into the **Expression** area), but it's far easier and less error prone to use the expression builder. To do this click on the **XPath expression builder** icon, circled in the previous figure. This will pop up the expression builder (shown in the following screenshot).

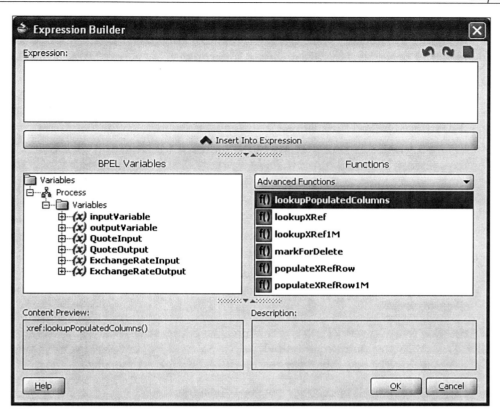

The expression builder provides a graphical tool for writing XPath expressions which are executed as part of the copy operation. It consists of the following areas:

- **Expression**: The top text box contains the XPath expression, which you are working on. You can either type data directly in here or use the Expression Builder to insert XPath fragments in here to build up the XPath required.

- **BPEL Variables**: This part of the expression builder lets you browse the variables defined within your BPEL process. Once you've located the variable that you wish to use click the **Insert Into Expression** button and this will insert the appropriate code fragment into the XPath Expression.

 The code fragment is inserted at the point within the expression that the cursor is currently positioned.

- **Functions**: This shows you all the different types of XPath functions that are available to build up your XPath expression. To make it easier to locate the required function, they are grouped into categories such as String Functions, Mathematical Functions.

  The drop-down list lets you select the category that you are interested in (for example **Advanced Functions** as illustrated in the previous figure), and then the window below that lists all the functions available with that group.

  To use a particular function, select the required function and click **Insert into Expression**. This will insert the appropriate XPath fragment into the XPath Expression (again at the point that the cursor is currently positioned).

- **Content Preview**: This box displays a preview of the content that would be inserted into the XPath Expression if you clicked the **Insert into Expression** button. For example, if you had currently selected a particular BPEL variable, it would show you the XPath to access that variable.

- **Description**: If you've currently selected a function, this box provides a brief description of the function, as well as the expected usage and number of parameters.

So let's use this to build our XPath expression. The expression we want to build is a relatively simple one, namely, the stock price returned by the stock quote service multiplied by the exchange rate returned by the exchange rate service.

To build our XPath expression, carry out the following steps:

1. First, within the **BPEL Variables** area, in the variable **QuoteOutput** locate the element **ns1:GetSingleQuoteResult/ns1:Last** as shown:

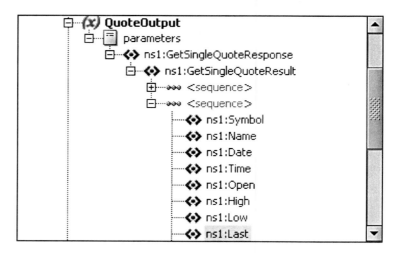

2. Then click **Insert into Expression** to insert this into the XPath Expression.

3. Next, within the **Functions** area, select the **Mathematical Functions** category and select the **multiply** function (notice the description in the **Description** box as shown in the following screenshot) and insert this into the XPath Expression.

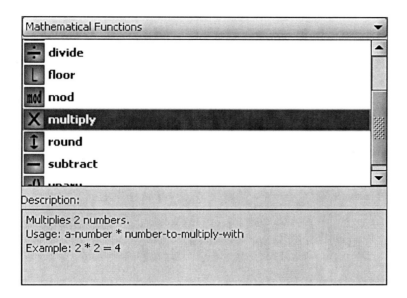

4. Finally, back in the the **BPEL Variables** area, locate the element `ConversionRateResult` within the variable `ExchangeRateOutput` and insert that into the XPath Expression.

You should now have an XPath Expression similar to the one illustrated below; once you are happy with this click **OK**.

```
bpws:getVariableData('QuoteOutput','parameters','/ns1:GetSingleQuoteResponse
/ns1:GetSingleQuoteResult/ns1:Last') * bpws:getVariableData('ExchangeRateOutput'
,'parameters','/ns3:ConversionRateResponse/ns3:ConversionRateResult')
```

Finally make sure you specify the target part of the `Copy` operation, which should be the `amount` element within the `outputVariable`.

In order to complete the assign activity, you will need to create two more copy operations to copy the `Currency` and `StockSymbol` specified in the `inputVariable` into the equivalent values in the `outputVariable`.

Once done, your BPEL process should be complete, so deploy it to the BPEL engine and run the process.

Asynchronous service

Following our stock quote service; another service would be a stock order service, which would enable us to buy or sell a particular stock. For this service a client would need to specify the stock, whether they wanted to buy or sell, the quantity and the price.

It makes sense to make this an asynchronous service, since once the order had been placed it may take seconds, minutes, hours, or even days for the order to be matched.

Now, I'm not aware of any trade services that are free to try (probably for good reason!). However, there is no reason why we can't simulate one. To do this we will write a simple asynchronous process.

To do this add another BPEL project to our StockService application and give it the name of StockOrder, but specify that it is an asynchronous BPEL process.

As with the StockQuote process we also want to specify predefined elements for its input and output. The elements we are going to use are placeOrder for the input and placeOrderResponse for the output, the definitions for which are shown:

```
<xsd:element name="placeOrder"         type="tPlaceOrder"/>
<xsd:element name="placeOrderResponse" type="tPlaceOrderResponse"/>
<xsd:complexType name="tPlaceOrder">
  <xsd:sequence>
    <xsd:element name="currency"     type="xsd:string"/>
    <xsd:element name="stockSymbol"  type="xsd:string"/>
    <xsd:element name="buySell"      type="xsd:string"/>
    <xsd:element name="quantity"     type="xsd:integer"/>
    <xsd:element name="bidPrice"     type="xsd:decimal"/>
  </xsd:sequence>
</xsd:complexType>

<xsd:complexType name="tPlaceOrderResponse">
  <xsd:sequence>
    <xsd:element name="currency"     type="xsd:string"/>
    <xsd:element name="stockSymbol"  type="xsd:string"/>
    <xsd:element name="buySell"      type="xsd:string"/>
    <xsd:element name="quantity"     type="xsd:integer"/>
    <xsd:element name="actualPrice"  type="xsd:decimal"/>
  </xsd:sequence>
</xsd:complexType>
```

These are also defined in the `StockService.xsd` that we imported for the `StockQuote` process; we will also need to import it into our `StockOrder` process, so that we can use it here (in Chapter 10 we will look at how we can share a schema across multiple processes).

As we did when creating our `StockQuote` process, click on **Next** within the **Create BPEL Process** dialogue to display the input and output elements from the process. Then in turn for each field click on the flashlight to import the schema, bring up the type chooser and select the appropriate element definitions. Then click **Finish** to create the process.

You will see that by default JDeveloper has created a skeleton asynchronous BPEL process, which contains an initial `<receive>` activity to receive the stock order request, but this time followed by an `<invoke>` activity to send the result back (as opposed to a `<reply>` activity used by the synchronous process).

If you look at the WSDL for the process, you will see that it defines two operations; `initiate` to call the process, and `onResult` which will be called by the process to send back the result. Thus the client that calls the `initiate` operation will need to provide the `onResult` callback in order to receive the result (this is something we will look at in more detail in Chapter 14—*Message Interaction Patterns*).

Now for the purpose of our simulation we will assume that the `StockOrder` request is successful and the `actualPrice` achieved is always the bid price. So to do this, create an assign operation, that copies all the original input values to their corresponding output values. Deploy the process and run it from the console.

This time you will notice that no result is returned to the console, rather it displays a message to indicate that the process is being processed asynchronously, as shown in the following screenshot:

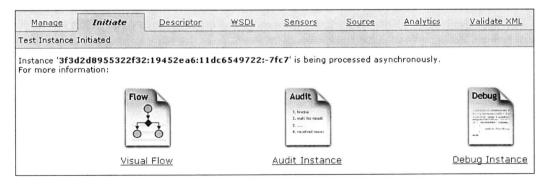

Click on the **Visual Flow** link to bring up the audit trail for the process and then click on the **callbackClient** activity at the end of the audit trail. This will pop up a window showing the details of the response sent by our process, as shown in the following screenshot:

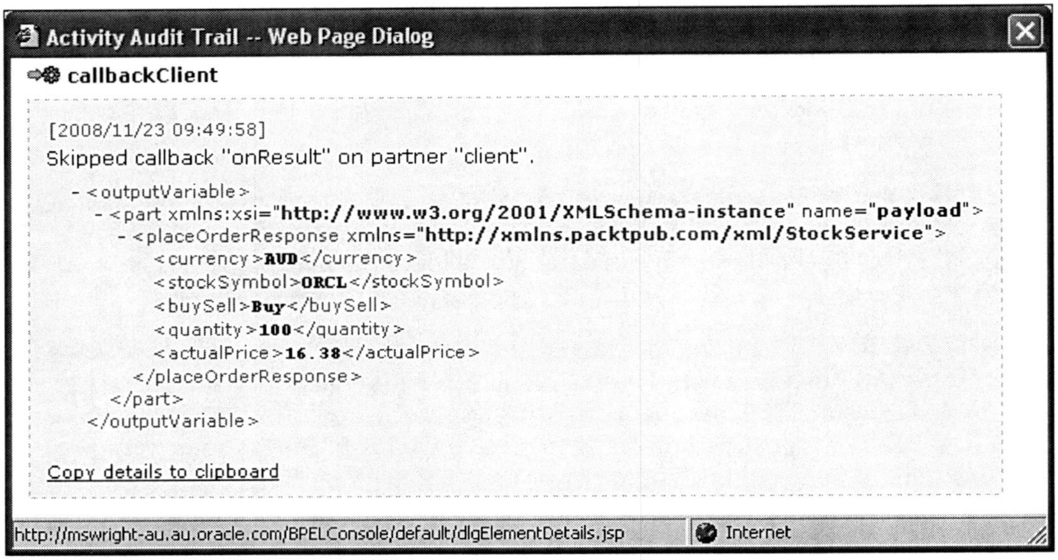

```
Activity Audit Trail -- Web Page Dialog                                    X

callbackClient

    [2008/11/23 09:49:58]
    Skipped callback "onResult" on partner "client".

     - <outputVariable>
       - <part xmlns:xsi="http://www.w3.org/2001/XMLSchema-instance" name="payload">
         - <placeOrderResponse xmlns="http://xmlns.packtpub.com/xml/StockService">
             <currency>AUD</currency>
             <stockSymbol>ORCL</stockSymbol>
             <buySell>Buy</buySell>
             <quantity>100</quantity>
             <actualPrice>16.38</actualPrice>
           </placeOrderResponse>
         </part>
       </outputVariable>

    Copy details to clipboard

http://mswright-au.au.oracle.com/BPELConsole/default/dlgElementDetails.jsp        Internet
```

Using the Wait activity

Now you've probably spotted the most obvious flaw with this simulation, in that the process returns a response almost immediately, which negates the whole point of making it asynchronous.

To make it more realistic we will use the `<wait>` activity to wait for a period of time. To do this drag the **Wait** activity from the component pallet onto your BPEL process just before the assign activity, and then double click on it to open the **Wait** activity window as shown on the next page.

The **Wait** activity allows you to specify that the process waits **For** a specified duration of time or **Until** a specified deadline. In either case you specify a fixed value or choose to specify an XPath Expression to evaluate the value at run time.

If you specify **Expression**, then if you click the icon to the right of it, this will launch the Expression builder that we introduced earlier in the chapter. The result of the expression must evaluate to a valid value of xsd:duration for periods and xsd:dateTime for deadlines.

The format of xsd:duration is PnYnMnDTnHnMnS; for example P1M would be a duration of 1 month and P10DT1H25M would be 10 days, 1 hour, and 25 minutes.

For deadlines the expression should evaluate to a valid value of xsd:date.

The structure of xsd:dateTime is YYYY-MM-DDThh:mm:ss+hh:mm, where the +hh:mm is optional and is the time period offset from UTC (or GMT if you prefer), obviously the offset can be negative or positive.

For example 2008-08-19T17:37:47-05:00 is the time 17:37:47 on August 19th 2008, 5 hours behind UTC (that is Eastern Standard Time in the US).

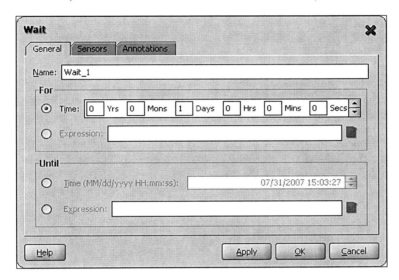

For our purposes we just need to wait for a relatively short period of time, so set it to wait for one minute.

By default, Wait will wait for a period of **one day**. So after you've changed the **Mins** field to 1, ensure that **Days** field is set to 0. I've often had people complaining that the BPEL process has been waiting more than a minute and something has gone wrong!

Now save, deploy and run the process. If you now look at the audit trail of the process you will see it has paused on the Wait activity (which will be highlighted in orange).

Improving the stock trade service

We have a very trivial trade service, which always results in a successful trade after 1 minute. Let's see if we can make it a bit more "realistic".

We will modify the process to call the **StockQuote** service and compare the actual price against the requested price. If the quote we get back matches or is better than the price specified, then we will return a successful trade (at the quoted price). Otherwise we will wait a minute and loop back round and try again.

Creating the while loop

The bulk of this process will now be contained within a while loop, so from the **Process Activities** list of the **Component Pallet** drag a **while** activity into the process.

Click on the plus symbol to expand the **while** activity; it will now display an area where you can drop a sequence of one or more activities that will be executed every time the process iterates through the loop.

We want to iterate through the loop until the trade has been fulfilled, so let's create a variable of type `xsd:Boolean` called `tradeFullfilled` and use an assign statement before the while loop to set its value to `false`.

The first step is to create a variable of type `xsd:Boolean`. Up to now we've used JDeveloper to automatically create the variables we've required, typically as part of the process of defining an `invoke` activity. However, that's not an option here.

If you look at the diagram of your BPEL process you will see that it is surrounded by a light grey dashed box, and on the top left hand side are a number of icons. If you click on the top one of these icons **(x)** (as shown in the following screenshot), this will open a window which lists all the variables defined to the process.

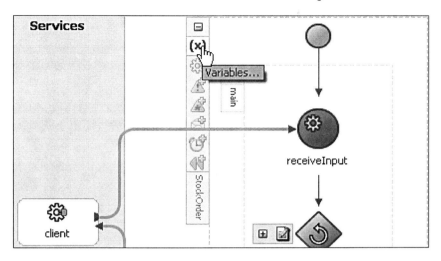

At this stage it will list just the default `inputVariable` and `outputVariable` which were automatically created with the process. Click on the **Create** button; this will bring up the **Create Variable** window, as shown in the following screenshot:

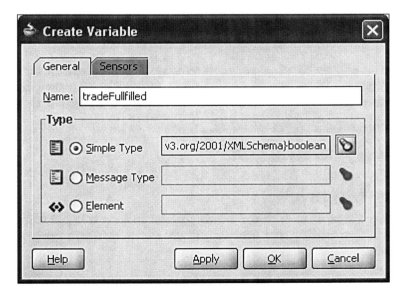

Here we simply specify the **Name** of the variable (for example `tradeFullfilled`) and its type. In our case we want an `xsd:Boolean`, so select **Simple Type** and click the flashlight to the right of it.

This will bring up the **Type Chooser**, which will list all the simple built in data types defined by XML Schema. Select **Boolean** and then click **OK**.

We need to initialize the variable to false, so drag an assign statement on to your process just before the while loop. Use the function `false()`, under the category **Logical Function** to achieve this.

Next we need to set the condition on the while loop, so that it will execute only while `tradeFulfilled` equals `false`. Double click on the **while** loop; this will open the **While** activity window, as shown in the following screenshot:

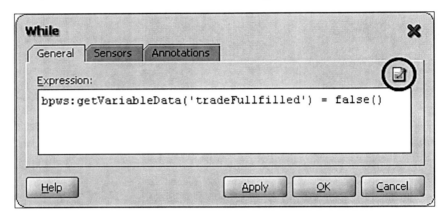

We must now specify an XPath expression which will evaluate to either `true` or `false`. If you click on the expression builder icon (circled in the previous screenshot), this will launch the Expression builder. Use this to build the following expression:

```
bpws:getVariableData('tradeFullfilled') = false()
```

Once we are happy with this click **OK**.

Checking the price

The first activity we need to perform within the `while` loop is to get a quote for the stock that we are trading. For this we will use the stock quote process we created earlier.

The approach is very similar to the one used when calling an external web service (as we did when implementing the StockQuote process). Create a Partner Link as before, but this time click on the **Service Explorer** icon, circled in the following diagram:

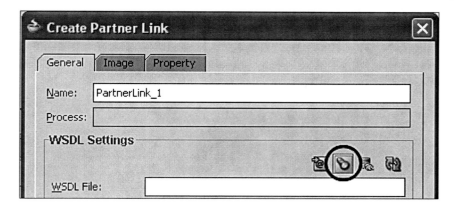

This will launh the **Service Explorer** window, which allows us to browse all the services defined to the SOA Suite. Expand the **BPEL Services** node and locate the **StockQuote** process as shown below in the following screenshot. Select this and click **OK**.

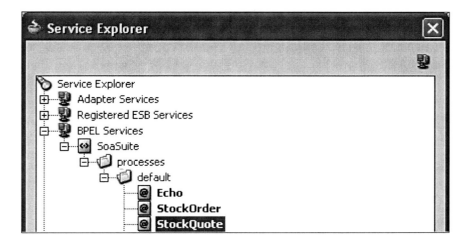

From here implement the required steps to invoke the **process** operation of the **StockQuote** process, making sure that they are included within the `while` loop.

Using the Switch activity

Remember our requirement is that we return success if the price matches or is better than the one specified in the order. Obviously whether the price is better depends on whether we are selling or buying. If we are selling we need the price to be equal to or greater than the asking price; whereas if we are buying we need the price to be equal to or less than the asking price.

So for this we will introduce the `<switch>` activity. Drag a `<switch>` activity from the **Process Activities** list of the **Component Pallet** on to your process, and then click on the plus symbol to expand the `<switch>` activity. By default it will have two branches as illustrated in the following screenshot:

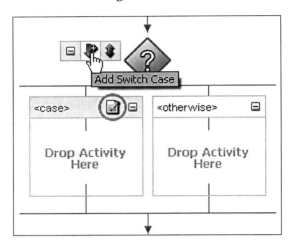

The first branch contains a `<case>` condition, with a corresponding area where you can drop a sequence of one or more activities that will be executed if the condition evaluates to `true`.

The second branch contains an `<otherwise>` sub-activity, with a corresponding area for activities. The activities in this branch will only be executed if all case conditions evaluate to `false`.

We want to cater for two separate tests (one for buying, the other for selling), so click on the **Add Switch Case** arrow (highlighted in the previous diagram) to add another `<case>` branch.

Next we need to define the test condition for each `<case>`. To do this, click on the corresponding **ExpressionBuilder** icon to launch the expression builder (circled in the previous screenshot). For the first one use the expression builder to create the following:

```
bpws:getVariableData ( 'inputVariable','payload',
                       '/ns1:PlaceOrder/ns1:BuySell') = 'Buy' and
bpws:getVariableData ( 'inputVariable', 'payload',
                       '/ns1:PlaceOrder/ns1:BidPrice') >=
bpws:getVariableData ( 'StockQuoteOutput', 'payload',
                       '/ns3:GetQuoteResult/ns3:Amount')
```

For the second branch, use the expression builder to define the following:

```
bpws:getVariableData ( 'inputVariable','payload',
                        '/ns1:PlaceOrder/ns1:BuySell') = 'Sell' and
bpws:getVariableData ( 'inputVariable', 'payload',
                        '/ns1:PlaceOrder/ns1:BidPrice') <=
bpws:getVariableData ( 'StockQuoteOutput', 'payload',
                        '/ns3:GetQuoteResult/ns3:Amount')
```

Once we have defined the condition for each case, we just need to create a single <assign> activity in each branch. This needs to set all the values in the outputVariable to the corresponding values in the inputVariable, except for the ActualPrice element, which we should set to the value returned by the StockQuote process. Finally we also need to set tradeFullfilled to true, so that we exit the while loop.

The simplest way to do this is drag the original <assign> we created in the first version of this process and drag it onto the first branch and then modify it as appropriate. Then create a similar assign activity in the second.

You've probably noticed that you could actually combine the two tests into a single test; however we took this approach to illustrate how you can add multiple branches to a switch.

If we don't have a match, then we want to wait a minute and then circle back round the while loop and try again. As we've already defined a <wait> activity, simply drag this from its current position within the process, into the Activity area for the <otherwise> activity.

That completes the process, so try deploying it and running it from the console.

The other obvious thing is that this process could potentially run forever if we don't get a stock quote in our favor. One way to solve this would be to put the while activity in a scope and then set a timeout period on the scope so that it would only run for so long.

Summary

In this chapter we've gone beyond individual services and looked at how we can use BPEL to quickly assemble these services into composite services. Using this same approach we can also implement end-to-end business processes or complete composite applications (something we will do in the second section of this book).

You may have also noticed that although BPEL provides a rich set of constructs for describing the assembly of a set of existing services, it doesn't try to reinvent the wheel where functionality is already provided by existing SOA standards. Rather it has been designed to fit naturally with and leverage the existing XML and web services specifications, such as XML Schema, XPath, XSLT, and of course WSDL and SOAP.

This chapter should have given you a solid introduction into the basic structure of a BPEL process, its key constructs, and the difference between a synchronous and asynchronous service. Building the examples will help to re-enforce this as well as give you an excellent grasp of how to use JDeveloper to build BPEL processes.

Even though this chapter will have given you a good introduction to BPEL, we haven't yet looked at much of its advanced functionality, such as its ability to handle long-running processes, its fault and exception management, and how it uses compensation to undo events in the case of failures. These are areas we will cover in more detail within later chapters of this book.

6
Adding in Human Workflow

Many business processes require an element of human activity; common tasks include approving an expense item or purchase order. But even fully automated processes can require human involvement especially when things go wrong.

In this chapter we will introduce you to the various parts of the Human Workflow component of the Oracle SOA Suite, and take you through a practical example to create and run your first *simple* workflow. Once we've done that, we will examine how to carry out other basic workflow activities, such as how to:

- Dynamically assign a task to a user or group based on the content of the task
- How to cancel or change a workflow task while it's still in process
- How to enable the workflow user to request additional detail about a task
- How to reassign, delegate or escalate a task, either manually or through the use of user-defined business rules

Workflow overview

The following diagram illustrates the three core participants in any workflow:

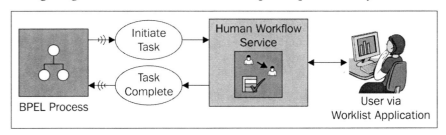

On the left hand side we have the BPEL Process that creates the task and submits it to the Human Workflow Service. Once it's initiated the task, the process itself will pause until the completed task is returned.

On the right hand side we have the user who carries out the task. Tasks can either be directly assigned to a user, or to a group to which the user belongs; in which case they need to claim the task before they can work on it. When working on a task, a user typically does this via the Worklist Application, a web-based application that is included as part of the SOA Suite.

Sitting between the BPEL process and the Worklist Application is the Human Workflow Service; this is responsible for routing the task to the appropriate user or group, managing the lifecycle of a task until it completes and returning the result to the initiator (that is the BPEL process in the previous diagram).

Leave approval workflow

For our first workflow, we will create a very simple BPEL process which takes a leave request, creates a simple approval task for the individual's manager who can then either approve or reject the request.

Note, during installation of the SOA Suite, a sample user community is installed for use with the identity service, which we will use for the workflow examples within this book (see the BPEL Process Managers Administrators Guide for details of the sample user community). In a production deployment you would typically configure the identity service to use an LDAP Repository such as Oracle Internet Directory or Active Directory.

Creating our workflow process

The first step is to create a simple asynchronous leave approval BPEL process. The input and output schema elements for the process are defined in LeaveRequest.xsd, as shown (note the schema is also provided in the sample folder for Chapter 6).

```
<?xml version="1.0" encoding="windows-1252"?>
<xsd:schema xmlns:xsd="http://www.w3.org/2001/XMLSchema"
          xmlns="http://schemas.packtpub.com/LeaveRequest"
          targetNamespace="http://schemas.packtpub.com/LeaveRequest"
          elementFormDefault="qualified" >

  <xsd:element name="leaveRequest" type="tLeaveRequest"/>

  <xsd:complexType name="tLeaveRequest">
    <xsd:sequence>
      <xsd:element name="employeeId" type="xsd:string"/>
      <xsd:element name="fullName" type="xsd:string" />
      <xsd:element name="startDate" type="xsd:date" />
      <xsd:element name="endDate" type="xsd:date" />
      <xsd:element name="leaveType" type="xsd:string" />
```

```
        <xsd:element name="leaveReason" type="xsd:string"/>
        <xsd:element name="requestStatus" type="xsd:string"/>
      </xsd:sequence>
    </xsd:complexType>

  </xsd:schema>
```

Make sure you import this file as part of the process of creating the BPEL process and set the input and output schema elements to `leaveRequest`.

Defining the workflow task

Once you've created your outline process, drag a **Human Task** from the **Process Activities** palette into your BPEL process, as shown in the following diagram:

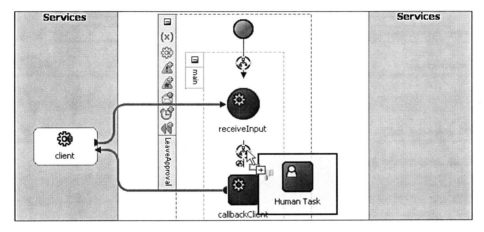

This will pop up the following screen:

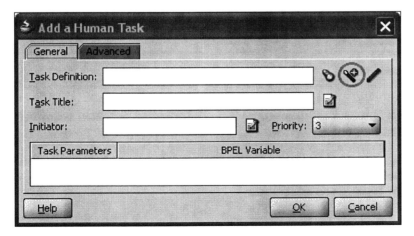

Press the **Magic Wand** button (circled in the previous screenshot) to create a new task (if coming back to edit a previously created workflow, then press the **pencil** button to edit the task details).

This will bring up **Add Human Task Wizard**. Give the task a meaningful name (for example **LeaveRequest**) and click **OK**.

This will open up the task definition form as a new tab within JDeveloper (shown in the following figure) where you can configure the task.

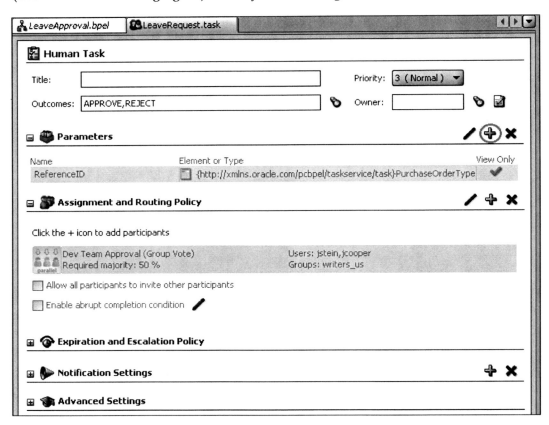

At first glance it may look quite complicated; however, for what we want to do it's pretty straightforward.

The key things we need to define for the task are its title, what its possible outcomes are (that is **Leave Request Approved** or **Rejected**), the parameters (or payload) of the task, and who to route or assign it to.

So let's give the task a **Title**, such as **Approval required for Leave Request**. Note, this is what a user will see in their work queue if they are allocated the task. For the time being we can leave the other values (**Priority**, **Outcomes**, and **Owner**) with their default values.

Specifying task parameters

Next we need to define the task parameters; that is the content of the task that we want the approver to base their decision upon. For our purposes we simply want to pass in the leave request received by the BPEL Process. To do this click on the **+** symbol (circled in the previous screenshot) to add a parameter. This will pop up the following window:

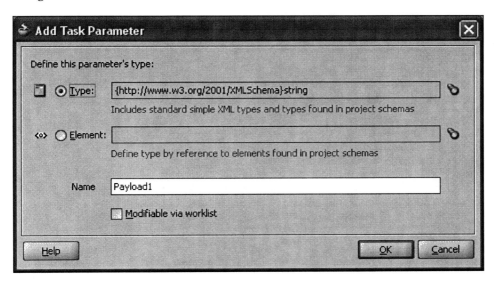

Here we can specify any standard XML type, such as string, integer, and so on as well as any types defined in any of our imported XML Schemas. Alternatively we can use any elements defined in any of our imported XML Schemas.

We want to use the same leaveRequest element specified in the schema we imported at the start, so select **Element** as the parameter type and then click on the corresponding flashlight to bring up the standard type chooser. From here just browse the **LeaveRequest** schema file that we imported at the start and select the leaveRequest element.

If we check **Modifiable via worklist** anyone who works on the task will be able to update the content of that parameter. In our case we will leave it unchecked.

Click **OK** and we now should have defined a LeaveRequest Parameter for your task.

Specifying task assignment and routing policy

Finally we need to specify who is going to approve the task; we do this by creating an **Assignment and Routing Policy**. In the **Human Task Definition** window, shown previously (see the section *Defining the workflow task*), click on the **+** symbol to the right of the **Assignment and Routing Policy** section. This should bring up the following window:

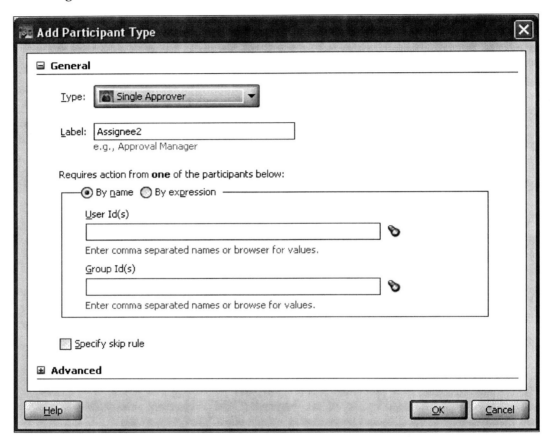

By default **Single Approver** is selected as the default routing type which is fine for our purpose (we will examine the other types in more detail in Chapter 15). Labels are used to provide a meaningful description of the routing rules, and are also useful if we specify multiple participants for a task. So for our purpose, just enter a meaningful value (for example **Manager Approval**).

We now need to specify who the task is going to be assigned to. We can either assign a task to a specific user or a group. For our purpose we are going to assume that the CEO of the company is required to approve every holiday, so we will always assign it to **cdickens**. Probably not ideal! But we will re-visit this later in the chapter to look at how we can make it more realistic.

You can type this value in directly to the userID's field or press the flash light to bring up the identity look-up dialog. This allows you to search and browse the users and groups defined to the identity service.

Once you've specified the assignment, the task definition should have been updated to contain a routing policy. Select **Save** on JDeveloper to make sure you save the task definition, as they are not saved as part of your BPEL Process.

If you look at your project structure, you will see a new folder has been added to it, in our case **LeaveRequest** (ringed in the following screenshot). This folder contains the task metadata file which we've just defined and the schema for the task payload which is based on the parameters we specified for the task.

Anytime we want to edit the task definition, just double click on the **LeaveRequest.task** file to open it in JDeveloper.

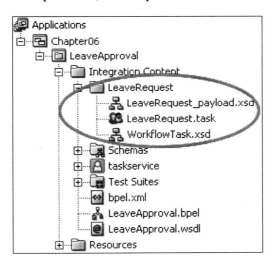

Initializing the workflow parameter

So far we have defined our task and integrated it into our BPEL process; however we still need to specify the actual content of the workflow parameter. To do this, go back to the BPEL process and double click on the **Human Task**. This will re-open the **BPEL Human Task configuration** window (shown in screenshot) which is where we bind the task definition that we've defined to the BPEL process.

You will notice now that we have a **Task Parameter** defined for the Human Task which we need to map to a BPEL variable. Click on the **spotlight** for the **LeaveRequest** parameter and this will bring up the **Task Parameters** window, which allows you to browse the variables defined to the BPEL process; select the **LeaveRequest** element passed in as part of the `inputVariable` for the BPEL process.

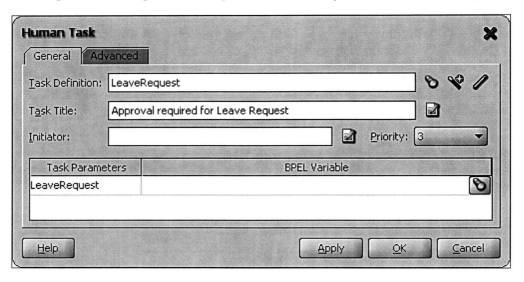

You may also have noticed that the **Task Title** has defaulted to the value we specified earlier as part of the task definition. We want to make the task title a bit friendlier, first type in (without the quotes):

```
'Leave Request for '
```

Then click on the icon to the right of the **Task Title** field. This will launch the now familiar expression builder. Here, from the `inputVariable` just select the element:

```
/ns1:LeaveRequest/ns1:fullName
```

This expression will be appended to the end of our title text embedded between `<%` and `%>`, to give the following:

```
Leave Request for <%bpws:getVariableData('inputVariable', 'payload',
                              '/ns1:LeaveRequest/ns1:fullName')%>
```

At run time the BPEL process will evaluate the expression between `<%` and `%>`, substituting the result. For now we won't specify a task initiator as this is optional, and we will leave the priority set to three.

Creating the user interface to process the task

So far we have defined the task that needs to be carried out and plugged it into a simple BPEL process. What we need to do next is implement the part of the user interface that allows someone to view the details of our specific task and then either approve or reject the leave request.

Out of the box the SOA Suite provides the worklist application, which provides all the main workflow user interface screens and provides a framework in which to plug your task specific interface component. This can be developed from scratch if you want, but the simplest way is to get JDeveloper to generate it automatically for you based on the schema definition of the payload.

To do this go back to the **Application** navigator in JDeveloper to browse the content of your project, and locate the new **LeaveRequest** folder that was added when we defined the task, right-click on it and select **Auto Generate Simple Task Form**.

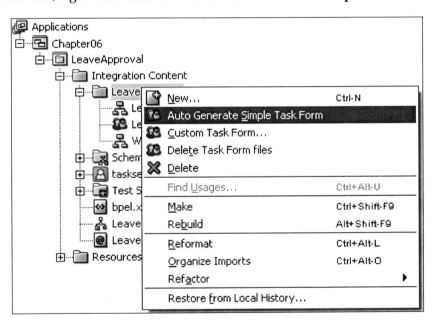

This will generate a web-based form, which JDeveloper will place in the **Web Content** folder of the **LeaveApproval** project, just below the **Resources** folder. The web-based form is generated as a JSP (Java Server Page), which we can customize in JDeveloper as required to give a better look and feel.

Your process is now complete, so deploy it to the server in the normal way.

Running the workflow process

Log into the BPEL Console and launch the process; ensure you specify a valid employee ID (such as **jcooper**). This will launch the BPEL process, which in turn will create the Leave Request task.

If you browse the audit trail for the process, you will see the process is paused at the **LeaveRequest** activity, as shown in the following screenshot:

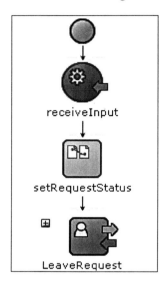

If click on the **LeaveRequest** activity this bring up the **Activity Audit Trail** for the workflow task showing that it is assigned to **cdickens** as shown in the following screenshot:

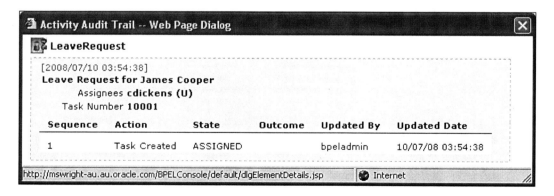

At the moment the process will wait forever, until the task is either approved or rejected; to do that we need to log in to the worklist application to process the task.

Processing tasks with the worklist application

Launch the worklist application (**Oracle BPEL Process Manager | WorkList Application**) and login as **cdickens** (password **welcome1**). This will bring you into the **My Tasks** tab, which provides access to your various work queues. By default it displays our inbox, which lists all the tasks currently allocated to us (or any groups that we belong to). We can then filter this based on keywords, task status, and priority.

The application also provides a number of other views, known as work queues, onto our tasks, which enable us to quickly identify high priority tasks, tasks due soon, or new tasks. In addition, we can also define our own views.

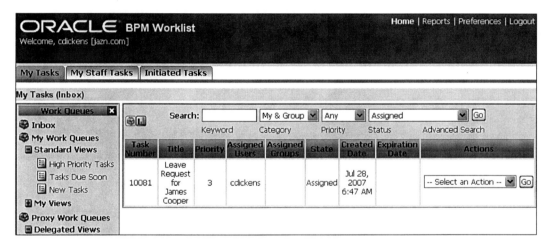

Here you should see the leave request task created by our process; click on the **task number** and it will open up a **Task Details** page, like the one shown in the following screenshot:

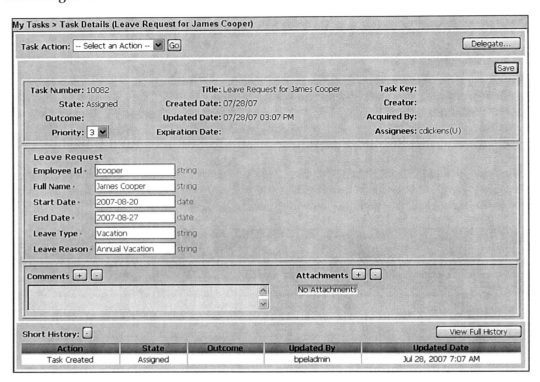

If we study this, we can see it is made up of the following five areas:

- **Task Action**: Contains the actions that can be performed on a task. This is split into two sets. The first contains the outcomes that we defined in the task definition (that is approve or reject). The second defines standard actions available for tasks such as escalate and delegate, which we will examine later.

- **Task Header**: Contains the standard header information about the task, a summary of which was in our work queue.

- **Task Payload**: This contains the task specific payload, in our case details of the leave request. This may be editable, depending on how we configure the task.

- **Task Comments**: Here we can add comments or attach documents to the task. This can be useful especially when a task is exchanged between multiple participants.

- **Task History**: Provides a history of when the task was created, who it's been assigned to and so on. This is useful as it provides a complete audit trail of the task. Note, this is also available in the BPEL Console.

For our purpose, we just want to approve or reject the task, so select the appropriate action from the drop down and select **Go**. This will action the task and take you back to the **Worklist application** homepage. You will see the task has now disappeared from your work queue.

However, change the search filter at the top to show tasks with a completed status and you will see that the task is still there. If you select the task it will take you back into the task pane, where you can view the task details but no longer perform any actions as the task is now complete.

If you go back to the BPEL Console and look at the audit trail for the process, you will see that it has now completed. The other thing to note is that within the BPEL process a switch statement has been automatically added, so that the process will take a different path depending on the outcome of the task. For the purpose of this example we don't need to do anything, but in a real system we might update the HR system with details of the leave if it was approved.

Improving the workflow

At this point we have a simple workflow up and running. However, we have the following issues with it:

- At the moment all requests go to the CEO, it would be better if requests went to the applicant's manager.

- Also what happens if the requester makes a mistake with his/her request, or changes their mind? How do we let the original requester amend or cancel their request?

- What if the approver needs additional information about a task, is there a simple way to enable that?

Dynamic task assignment

There are two approaches here. One is to assign the task to a specific group which may contain one or more individuals, a classic example would be to assign a support request to the customer support group.

The other is to dynamically specify the user to assign to a task at run-time, based on the value of some parameter; which is roughly what we want to do. Actually we want to look up the manager of the employee requesting the task and assign it to them.

If we go back to the **Human Task Definition** form (see the section *Defining the workflow task*), and double-click on the routing policy we defined, this will re-open the edit participant type form. Specify that you want to select the participant **By expression** and the click on the icon to the right of **Dynamic User XPath** field (circled in the following screenshot).

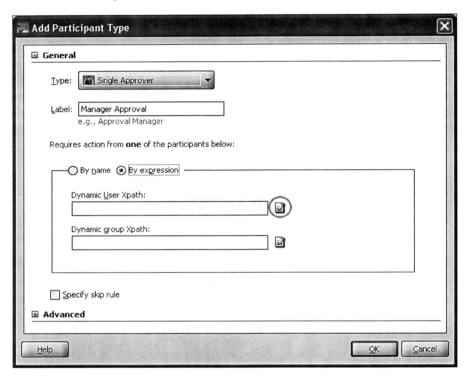

This will open up the expression builder introduced in Chapter 5. However the key thing to notice here is that we only have access to the content of the task we are working on (not the full content of the BPEL Process).

We need to create an expression that evaluates to the userID of the employee's manager. Fortunately one of the services that come with workflow is the identity service, which provides us with a simple way of querying the underlying identity layer to find out details about a user. In our case we can use the **getManager** function to get the ID of the manager.

So within the **Expression builder** select the **Identity Services Functions** and from within here select the **getManager** function and insert it into the expression. We now need to pass it the employee ID of whoever is requesting the leave. Expand the task payload; you will find it contains the content of the leave request. Select the **employeeId** and insert that as the parameter as shown in the following screenshot:

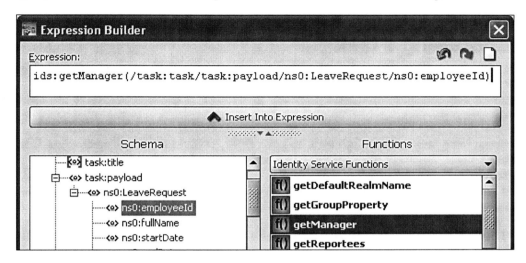

You can now save the task, redeploy it and run the process. Assuming you specify that the request is for **jcooper**, you will need to log in as **jstein** to approve the task.

Assigning tasks to multiple users or groups

So far we have only looked at scenarios where we assign a task to a single user. However workflow enables you to either assign a task to multiple users or to one or more groups (or a combination of the two).

In this case, every user who is a member of the group or has the task assigned to them will be able to see the task on their queue. However, before anyone can work on the task, they must first claim it. Once claimed, other users will still be able to see the task, but only the user who has claimed the task will be able to perform any operations on it.

Although group assignments are more likely to be static, you can also specify them dynamically in the same way we have for the user.

Cancelling or modifying a task

Another common requirement is to cancel or modify a task before it has completed the workflow. If we take our example, suppose that having submitted the leave request we changed our mind, ideally we would like to be able to withdraw the task or modify it before someone goes to the effort of approving it.

Withdrawing a task

You may remember when we first added the task to the BPEL process, we had a field where we could specify a task initiator, that at the time we left blank. Well if you specify a task initiator, they are effectively the creator of the task and have the ability to withdraw the task.

To specify the task initiator, go back to your BPEL process and double-click on the **Human Task**. This will re-open the **Human Task configuration** window (see the section *Initializing the workflow parameter*), click the icon to the right of the **initiator field** and this will launch the **Expression Builder**. Use this to specify the employeeId as the task initiator.

Now save the process, redeploy it and run the process. Again specify that the request is for **jcooper**, then log into the Worklist Application as **jstein**. You should notice that the task creator is **jcooper**. Don't approve the task, rather log out and log back into the Worklist application as **jcooper**.

This will take you into the **My Tasks** tab which is probably empty, but if you click the **Initiated Tasks** tab, then this will list all the tasks that you have initiated. If you look at the task you will see that you can perform a single action on the task, which is to withdraw it.

Modifying a task

When we defined the task parameters on the task definition form we had the option to specify if the parameters are **Modifiable via Worklist**; at the time we didn't select this option. If this option is selected, then anyone who works on the task has the ability to modify the task payload, including the task initiator.

Difference between task owner and initiator

Now you may have noticed while specifying the various task details that as well as being able to specify the task initiator we can also specify the task owner. At this point you may be asking what the difference is between these two roles.

The simple answer is the **task owner** has more administrative privileges when it comes to a task. The *task initiator* is the person who creates a particular instance of a task, for example in our case **jcooper** and **jstein** may both request leave. In this case they are both initiators and can each withdraw the task they requested (but not each other's).

On the other hand the task owner may be the holiday administrator. They are responsible for administering **all** leave requests. This enables them to perform operations on behalf of any of the assigned task participants, additionally they can also reassign or escalate tasks.

The task owner can either be specified as part of the task definition, or on the **Advanced** tab of the BPEL Human Task configuration window.

 If no task owner is specified it defaults to the system user `bpeladmin`.

When the task owner logs into the worklist application, they will see an additional tab, **Administration Tasks,** which will list all the tasks for which they are the task owner.

Requesting additional information about a task

Once assigned a task, sometimes you need additional information about it before you can complete it. In our example, the manager may need more information about the reason for the leave request.

If a task initiator has been specified, then on the task details form we have the option of selecting **Request Info**. If we select this option, we are presented with the **Request More Information** form, where we can select who we want more information from and enter details of the information required which will be added as a comment to the task.

This will then assign the task to the initiator. The task will then appear on the task creators work queue, with a state of **Info Requested**. The task creator can either update the details of the task (if allowed) or add their own comment to provide the additional information. Once done, they can choose the action **Submit Info** and the task will be reassigned back to whoever requested the additional information.

This feature is automatically enabled when the task is opened. You can disable this feature if you want by overriding the default system actions in the **Advance Settings** section of the **Task Configuration**.

We can request additional information, not just from the person who created the task, but anyone else who has already worked on the task.

Managing the assignment of tasks

Often there is a requirement to reassign tasks. Maybe the task approver is about to go on leave themselves and before they go they may want to reassign all uncompleted tasks so they can be dealt with by someone else while they are away.

Alternatively, the individual may have already gone on leave (or be indisposed for some other reason) with a series of tasks already in their queue, which their manager may need to reassign to someone else.

Depending on a user's privileges and whether they are a manager, the worklist application provides a number of methods for either reassigning, delegating or escalating tasks. We will examine these in detail below.

Reassigning reportee tasks

If a user has any direct reports, then the worklist application will treat them as a manager. This will give them additional privileges to work on tasks that are either assigned to any of their direct reports or groups that they own.

Within the work list application, managers have the additional tab, **My Staff Tasks**. If they select this it will list all tasks currently assigned to any of their reports.

The list can be further filtered by selecting **Advanced Search** and specifying an appropriate query. For example you could just show tasks assigned to a particular user or high priority tasks about to expire.

The manager has two basic options when it comes to staff tasks, they can either work on the task directly themselves, where they can carry out the same sets of actions as the assignee. Alternatively, they can choose to reassign the task to another of their direct reports or to any of the groups that they own.

To see how we do this, log in as **wfaulk** (**jstein**'s manager) and click on **My Staff Tasks**. Then open one of the listed tasks; this will open up the familiar task form. In the task action area of the form there will be a **Reassign** button, circled in the following screenshot:

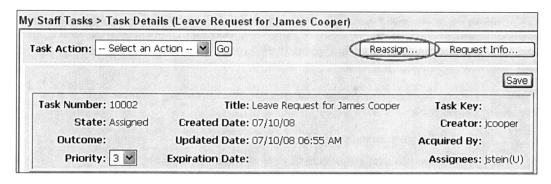

Click this and the worklist application will open **Assignees** form under the **Task Details** as shown:

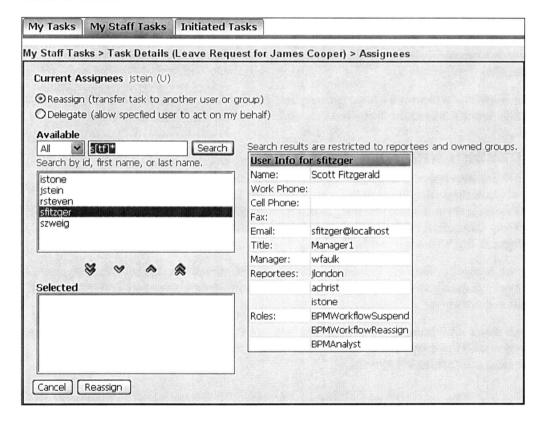

You will see you have the option to either **Reassign** or **Delegate** the task. Stick with the **Reassign** option for the time being as we will look at delegation shortly.

The remainder of the screen allows us to search for the users and or groups that we want to reassign the task to. You can choose to search just **Users**, **Groups**, or **All**. In addition you can further filter the list on the ID of the user or group, as well as the first name or last name of the user.

When specifying the search criteria you can use the following pattern matching characters:

.   Matches any single character

*   Matches any sequence of zero or more character

[]   Matches any of the single characters specified between the square brackets

For example, the pattern s[tf]* will bring back the list of users whose userID, first or last name begins with either st or sf.

You will also notice that if you select a user, the panel to the right will display basic information about the user, including their Manager, Reportees, and any roles they have.

Use the arrows to move users/groups that you wish to reassign the task to from the search results box to the **Selected** box and then click the **Reassign** button.

Reassigning your own task

In addition to reassigning staff tasks, **any user** can also reassign their own tasks. To do this they simply open the task from their task list as normal and click the **Reassign** button (note if the user is not a manager, that is, they have no direct reports, they must click the **Delegate** button). This will bring up the task details assignees form that we just looked at.

An important point here is that the same restrictions on who a user can assign a task to apply regardless of whether it's the users own task or a task belonging to one of their reportees.

Thus users who have no direct reports will not be able to reassign their task to any other user. However, if they are a group owner they will still have the ability to reassign the task to the group.

 If a user has the role *BPMWorkflowReassign*, then they are allowed to reassign a task to anyone.

Delegating tasks

The other option we have when reassigning a task is to delegate it. This is very similar to reassigning a task but with a number of key differences:

- You can only delegate a task to a single user
- You cannot delegate a task to a group
- You can delegate a task to anyone regardless of where they are in the organizational hierarchy

When you delegate a task it's assigned to a new user, but it also remains on your work queue; so that either you or the delegated user can work on the task.

Escalating tasks

There will often be cases where a user needs to reassign a task to their manager, which a user typically can't do (remember you can only reassign tasks to direct reports). To do this, a user may choose to escalate a task; this is similar to reassigning a task. The key difference being is that it is assigned to a reportee's manager.

 Tasks can also be automatically escalated, usually if not handled within a specified period of time. This is specified in **Expiration and Escalation Policy**, which forms part of the task definition.

Using rules to automatically manage tasks

Even though it's possible to manually reassign tasks, this can be inefficient and time consuming; an alternative approach is to automate this using workflow rules.

You can either define a rule to be applied to a particular task type (for example our Leave Request) or to all tasks. Optionally you can specify a time period for which the rule is active; otherwise it will be active all the time.

You can specify various filter criteria which are applied to the task attributes (e.g. priority, initiator, acquired by) to further restrict which tasks the rule applies to.

Once you've specified the matching criteria for a rule, you can then specify whether you want to reassign or delegate the task. Essentially the same criteria applies to who you are allowed to reassign a task to if you were to do it manually as covered in the previous section, with the added caveat that you can only reassign a task to a single user or group.

For rules defined for a particular task type, we have the option of being able to automatically set the task outcome. In the case of our Leave Request task, we can write a rule to automatically approve all leave requests that are 1 day in duration.

The final option is to take no action, which may seem a bit strange. However, this serves a couple of useful purposes. Often you only want a rule to be active at certain periods of time; one way to do this is to just specify a date range, the alternative is to use this to turn the rule on and off as required over time.

The other use comes in when you define multiple rules. Rules are evaluated in order against a task until a rule is found that matches a particular task.

For example, to create a rule that reassigned all tasks, except say an expense approval task, then we could define two rules, a generic rule to reassign any task and a specific rule that matched the expense approval task that did nothing. We would then order the rules so that the expense approval rule triggered first. This way the generic rule to reassign task would be triggered for all tasks except the expense approval task.

Setting up a sample rule

For example, let's say Robert Stevenson (userID **rsteven**) is John Steinbeck's deputy, and we want to create a rule that reassigns all leave requests assigned to **jstein**, to **rsteven** except for any leave request made by **rsteven**.

To do this log onto the worklist application as **jstein** and click on the **Preferences** link in the top right hand corner of the **Worklist** title bar. This will take you to the preferences homepage.

In the preferences frame (on the left hand side), select **My Rules**. This will show you a list of all rules the user currently has defined (which is probably empty at the moment). Click on the **Create** button, this will bring up the **Create new rule** screen shown as follows:

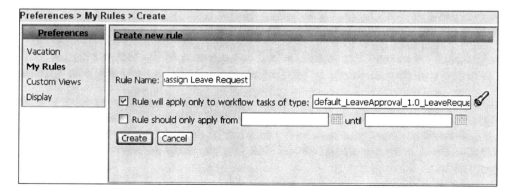

Enter a suitable name for the rule, and select the check box to specify that the rule will only apply to workflow tasks of a specific type. Then click on the torch icon to the right and this will pop up a window listing all specified task types. Select the **LeaveRequest** for the **LeaveApproval** process.

We will not specify a time period for the rule as we want it to be active all the time. So click on the **Create** button and this will bring up the **Rule Detail** window, as shown:

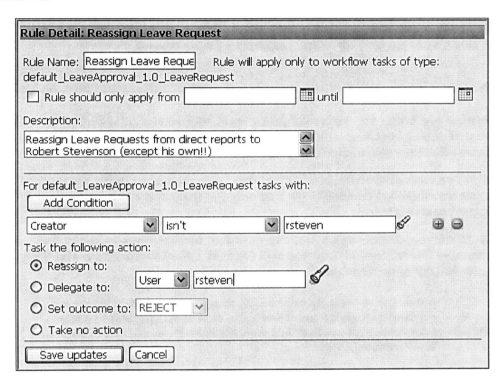

Here you specify the conditions that apply to the rule and the appropriate action to take.

First let's add the condition to prevent the rule reassigning leave request made by **rsteven**. Then click on the **Add Condition** button and this will insert a condition line into the rule.

From the first drop down select the task attribute to which we want to apply the rule, which is in our case the **Creator** (that is the task initiator). In the second drop down select the test to be applied to the attribute, so in our case **isn't** and finally specify the user (**rsteven**). You can either type the userID straight in or click the flash light to search for the user, using the user search facility we introduced earlier.

Then specify the task action which is to reassign the task to **rsteven**. Your rule description should now look like the one shown in the previous figure.

Finally click **Save Updates** to create the rule. This will return you to the rule list window, as shown in the following screenshot, which should now list the rule you've just defined.

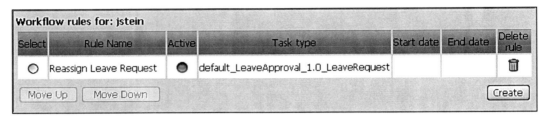

The traffic light under the **Active** column should be green to indicate that the rule is active. If you've specified a date period for the rule, then this may well be gray indicating that the rule isn't currently active.

Once you've created the rule, try creating two leave requests, one for **jcooper** and the other for **rsteven**. You should see that only the request created for **jcooper** is reassigned to **rsteven**.

Log in as **rsteven**, and select the leave request that has been reassigned to that user. If you examine the full task history you will see that it shows which rule was triggered to cause the task to be reassigned.

 A user can also specify rule conditions against the content of the task payload through the use of flex fields, as well as being able to define rules for any groups that they own. We examine flex fields in Chapter 15 — *Workflow Patterns*.

Summary

Human workflow is a key requirement for many projects; in this chapter we saw how easy it is to insert a human task in to a BPEL process, as well as implement the corresponding user interface to process the task.

We also looked at how business users can use the Worklist Application to process their tasks as well as manage the routing of them, including reassigning, delegating, and escalating tasks. We also looked at how business users could automate much of the management of tasks by defining business rules to automatically delegate, reassign, or complete a task.

7
Using Business Rules to Define Decision Points

At run time there may be many potential paths through a BPEL process, controlled by conditional statements such as `switch` or `while` activities. Typically the business rules that govern which path to take at any given point are written as XPath expressions embedded within the appropriate activity.

Although this in an acceptable approach, we often find that while the process itself may be relatively static, the business rules embedded within the activities may change on a more frequent basis. This will require us to update the BPEL process and redeploy it even though the process flow itself hasn't changed.

In addition, by embedding the rule directly within the decision point, we often end up having to re-implement the same rule every time it is used, either within the same process or across multiple processes. Apart from being inefficient, this can lead to inconsistent implementations of the rules as well as requiring us to update the rule in multiple places every time it changes.

In this chapter we will look at how we can use the Business Rules engine to externalize rules from a BPEL process into a separate decision service, and then once we've done this, we will know how to invoke the rule from a BPEL process.

The advantage of separating out decision points as external rules is that we not only ensure that each rule is used in a consistent fashion, but in addition make it simpler and quicker to modify; that is we only have to modify a rule once and can do this with almost immediate effect, thus increasing the agility of our solution.

Business Rule concepts

Before we implement our first rule, let's briefly introduce the key components which make up a **Business Rule**. These are:

- **Facts**: Represent the data or business objects that rules are applied to.
- **Rules**: A rule consists of two parts, an IF part which consists of one or more tests to be applied to fact(s), and a THEN part, which lists the actions to be carried out should the test to evaluate to true.
- **Rule Set**: As the name implies, it is just a set of one or more related rules that are designed to work together.
- **Dictionary**: A dictionary is the container of all components that make up a business rule, it holds all the facts, rule sets, and rules for a business rule.

In addition, a dictionary may also contain functions, variables, and constraints. We will introduce these in more detail later in this chapter.

To execute a business rule, you submit one or more facts to the rules engine. It will apply the rules to the facts, that is each fact will be tested against the IF part of the rule and if it evaluates to true, then it will perform the specified actions for that fact. This may result in the creation of new facts or the modification of existing facts (which may result in further rule evaluation).

Leave approval rule

For our first rule we are going to build on our leave request example from the previous chapter. If you remember we implemented a simple process requiring every leave request to go to an individual's manager for approval. However, what we would like is a rule that automatically approves a request as long as it meets certain company guidelines.

To begin with we will write a simple rule to automatically approve a leave request that is of type Vacation and only for 1 day's duration. A pretty trivial example, but once we've done this we will look at how to extend this rule to handle more complex examples.

Using the Rule Author

In SOA Suite 10.1.3 you use the **Rule Author**, which is a browser based interface for defining your business rules. To launch the Rule Author within your browser go to the following URL:

```
http://<host name>:<port number>/ruleauthor/
```

This will bring up the **Rule Author Log In** screen. Here you need to log in as user that belongs to the `rule-administrators` role. You can either log in as the user **oc4jadmin** (default password **Welcome1**), which automatically belongs to this group, or define your own user.

Creating a Rule Repository

Within Oracle Business Rules, all of our definitions (that is facts, constraints, variables, and functions) and rule sets are defined within a **dictionary**. A dictionary is held within a **Repository**.

A repository can contain multiple dictionaries and can also contain multiple versions of a dictionary. So, before we can write any rules, we need to either connect to an existing repository, or create a new one.

Oracle Business Rules supports two types of repository—File based and WebDAV. For simplicity we will use a File based repository, though typically in production you want to use a WebDAV based repository as this makes it simpler to share rules between multiple BPEL Processes.

 WebDAV is short for Web-based Distributed Authoring and Versioning. It is an extension to HTTP that allows users to collaboratively edit and manage files (that is business rules in our case) over the Web.

To create a File based repository click on the **Repository** tab within the **Rule Author**, this will display the **Repository Connect** screen as shown in the following screenshot:

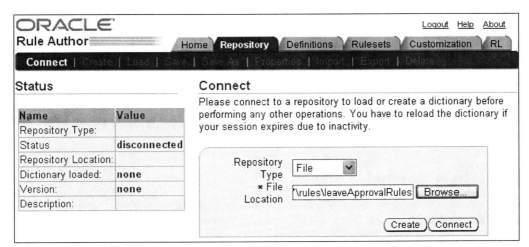

From here we can either connect to an existing repository (WebDAV or File based) or create and connect to a new file-based repository. For our purposes, select a **Repository Type** of **File**, and specify the full path name of where you want to create the repository and then click **Create**.

To use a WebDAV repository, you will first need to create this externally from the Rule Author. Details on how to do this can be found in Appendix B of the Oracle Business Rules User Guide (`http://download.oracle.com/docs/cd/B25221_04/web.1013/b15986/toc.htm`).

From a development perspective it can often be more convenient to develop your initial business rules in a file repository. Once complete, you can then export the rules from the file repository and import them into a WebDAV repository.

Creating a dictionary

Once we have connected to a repository, the next step is to create a dictionary. Click on the **Create** tab, circled in the following screenshot, and this will bring up the **Create Dictionary** screen. Enter a **New Dictionary Name** (for example **LeaveApproval**) and click **Create**.

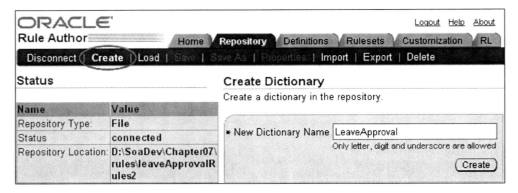

This will create and load the dictionary so it's ready to use. Once you have created a dictionary, then next time you connect to the repository you will select the **Load** tab (next to the **Create** tab) to load it.

Defining facts

Before we can define any rules, we first need to define the facts that the rules will be applied to. Click on the **Definitions** tab, this will bring up the page which summarizes all the facts defined within the current dictionary.

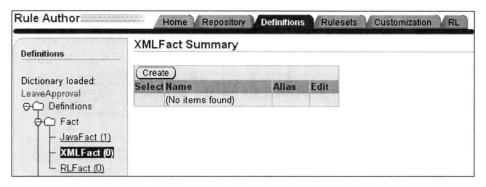

You will see from this that the rule engine supports three types of facts: Java Facts, XML Facts, and RL Facts. The type of fact that you want to use really depends on the context in which you will be using the rules engine.

For example, if you are calling the rule engine from Java, then you would work with Java Facts as this provides a more integrated way of combining the two components. As we are using the rule engine with BPEL then it makes sense to use XML Facts.

Creating XML Facts

The Rule Author uses XML Schemas to generate JAXB 1.0 classes, which are then imported to generate the corresponding XML Facts. For our example we will use the same Leave Request schema that we used in Chapter 6, shown as follows for convenience:

```xml
<?xml version="1.0" encoding="windows-1252"?>
<xsd:schema xmlns:xsd="http://www.w3.org/2001/XMLSchema"
            xmlns="http://schemas.packtpub.com/LeaveRequest"
            targetNamespace="http://schemas.packtpub.com/LeaveRequest"
            elementFormDefault="qualified" >

  <xsd:element name="leaveRequest" type="tLeaveRequest"/>

  <xsd:complexType name="tLeaveRequest">
    <xsd:sequence>
      <xsd:element name="employeeId" type="xsd:string"/>
      <xsd:element name="fullName" type="xsd:string" />
      <xsd:element name="startDate" type="xsd:date" />
      <xsd:element name="endDate" type="xsd:date" />
      <xsd:element name="leaveType" type="xsd:string" />
      <xsd:element name="leaveReason" type="xsd:string"/>
      <xsd:element name="requestStatus" type="xsd:string"/>
    </xsd:sequence>
  </xsd:complexType>

</xsd:schema>
```

Using JAXB, particularly when used in conjunction with BPEL, places a number of constraints on how we define our XML Schemas, including:

- When defining rules, the Rule Author can only work with globally defined **types**. This is because it's unable to introspect the properties (i.e. attributes and elements) of global elements.

- Within BPEL you can only define variables based on globally defined **elements**.

The net result is that any facts we want to pass from BPEL to the rules engine (or vice versa) must be defined as **global elements** for BPEL and have a corresponding **global type** definition so that we can define rules against it.

The simplest way to achieve this is to define a global type (for example `tLeaveRequest` in the above schema) and then define a corresponding global element based on that type (for example `leaveRequest` in the above schema).

Even though it is perfectly acceptable with XML Schemas to use the same name for both elements and types, it presents problems for JAXB, hence the approach taken above where we have prefixed every type definition with t as in `tLeaveRequest`.

Fortunately this approach corresponds to best practice for XML Schema design, something we cover in more detail in Chapter 10 — *Designing the Service Contract*.

The final point you need to be aware of is that when creating XML facts the JAXB processor maps the type `xsd:decimal` to `java.lang.BigDecimal` and `xsd:integer` to `java.lang.BigInteger`. This means you can't use the standard operators (for example >, >=, <=, and <) within your rules to compare properties of these types. To simplify your rules, within your XML Schemas use `xsd:double` in place of `xsd:decimal` and `xsd:int` in place of `xsd:integer`.

To generate XML facts, from the **XML Fact Summary** screen (shown previously), click **Create**, this will display the **XML Schema Selector** page as shown:

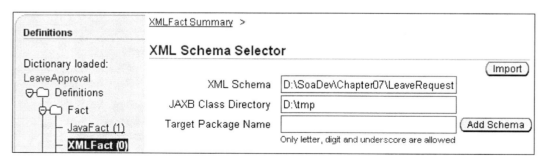

Here we need to specify the location of the **XML Schema**, this can either be an absolute path to an `xsd` file containing the schema or can be a URL.

Next we need to specify a temporary **JAXB Class Directory** in which the generated JAXB classes are to be created.

Finally for the **Target Package Name** we can optionally specify a unique name that will be used as the Java package name for the generated classes. If we leave this blank, the package name will be automatically generated based on the target namespace of the XML Schema using the JAXB XML-to-Java mapping rules. For example, our leave request schema has a target namespace of `http://schemas.packtpub.com/LeaveRequest`; this will result in a package name of `com.packtpub.schemas.leaverequest`.

Next click on **Add Schema**; this will cause the Rule Author to generate the JAXB classes for our schema in the specified directory. This will update the **XML Fact Summary** screen to show details of the generated classes; expand the class navigation tree until you can see the list of all the generated classes, as shown in the following screenshot:

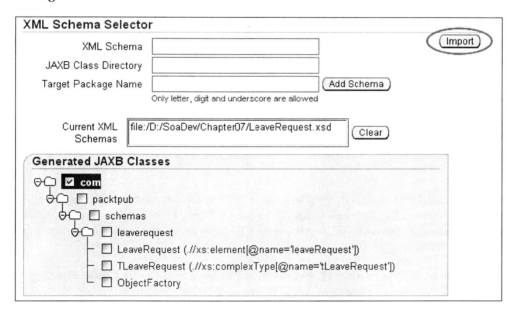

Select the top level node (that is **com**) to specify that we want to import all the generated classes. We need to import the `TLeaveRequest` class as this is the one we will use to implement rules and the `LeaveRequest` class as we need this to pass this in as a fact from BPEL to the rules engine.

The `ObjectFactory` class is optional, but we will need this if we need to generate new `LeaveRequest` facts within our rule sets. Although we don't need to do this at the moment it makes sense to import it now in case we do need it in the future.

Once we have selected the classes to be imported, click **Import** (circled in previous screenshot) to load them into the dictionary. The Rule Author will display a message to confirm that the classes have been successfully imported. If you check the list of generated JAXB classes, you will see that the imported classes are shown in bold.

In the process of importing your facts, the Rule Author will assign default aliases to each fact and a default alias to all properties that make up a fact, where a property corresponds to either an element or an attribute in the XML Schema.

Using aliases

Oracle Business Rules allows you to specify your own aliases for facts and properties in order to define more business friendly names which can then be used when writing rules.

For XML facts if you have followed standard naming conventions when defining your XML Schemas, we typically find that the default aliases are clear enough and that if you start defining aliases it can actually cause more confusion unless applied consistently across all facts.

Hiding facts and properties

The Rule Author lets you hide facts and properties so that they don't appear in the drop downs within the Rule Author. For facts which have a large number of properties, hiding some of these can be worth while as it can simplify the creation of rules.

Another obvious use of this might be to hide all the facts based on elements, since we won't be implementing any rules directly against these. However any facts you hide will also be hidden from BPEL, so you won't be able to pass facts of these types from BPEL to the rules engine (or vice versa).

In reality, the only fact you will typically want to hide will be the **ObjectFactory** (as you will have one of these per XML Schema that you import).

Saving the rule dictionary

As you define your business rules, it makes sense to save your work at regular intervals. To save the dictionary, click on the **Save Dictionary** link in the top right hand corner of the Rule Author page.

This will bring up the **Save Dictionary** page. Here either click on the **Save** button to update the current version of the dictionary with your changes or, if you want to save the dictionary as a new version or under a new dictionary name, then click on the **Save As** link and amend the dictionary name and version as appropriate.

Creating a rule set

Once we have defined our facts, we are ready to implement our first rule set. Click on the **Rulesets** tab within the Rule Author, which will bring up the **RuleSet Summary** page. This will initially be empty, as shown in the following screenshot:

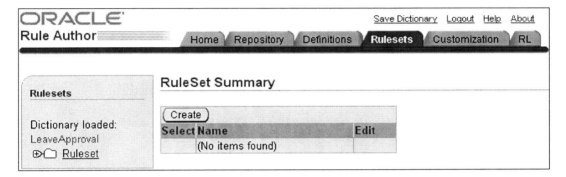

Click on **Create** and this will bring up the **Ruleset** page, as shown in the following screenshot:

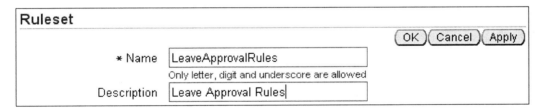

Enter a name, for example **LeaveApprovalRules**, and an optional description and then click **Apply**.

This will update the **RuleSet Summary** page (shown in the following screenshot), showing you details of the newly created rule set, plus a list of its rules which is currently empty.

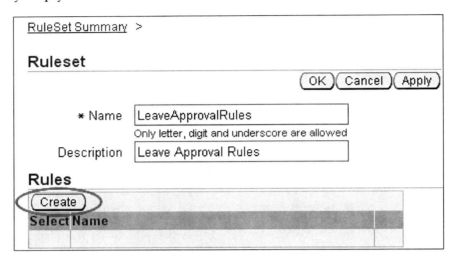

Adding a rule to our rule set

To create a rule, click on the **Create** button (circled in the previous screenshot); this will bring up the **Rule** page where we can give the rule a meaningful name (for example **OneDayVacation**) and optionally provide a **Description** for the rule as well.

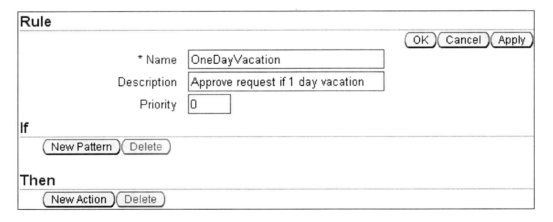

From this we can see a rule consists of two parts, an **If** part which consists of one or more tests (or patterns) to be applied to a fact or facts, and a **Then** part, which specifies the actions to be carried out should the test to evaluate to true.

Creating the If clause

To create the `If` clause we need to define one or more patterns to be applied. To define a pattern click on **New Pattern**, this will open the **Pattern Definition** window, as shown in the following screenshot:

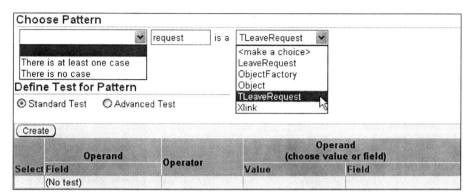

A **Pattern** consists of two parts, the first is the type of pattern that we wish to test for, and the second is the tests we want to apply to the pattern.

Choosing the pattern

The first drop down is used to specify the type of pattern that we want to test for; this can take one of the following three values:

1. **Blank**: This is the default pattern, and is used to specify that the rule should be applied to each fact, where the test evaluates to `true`. So, for example, if we submitted multiple leave requests in one go, we would the trigger the rule for each leave request that is of type `Vacation` and only 1 day in duration.

2. **There is at least one case**: With this option, the rules will only be triggered once, as long as there is at least one match.

3. **There is no case**: With this option, the rule will be fired once if there are no matches.

With the second drop down we specify the type of fact that we wish to apply the rule to. In our case we want to test facts of type **TLeaveRequest**. The text area before this is used to assign a temporary alias to the fact being tested, i.e. **request** in our case. This alias is useful when testing multiple facts of the same type (we will cover this in more detail in Chapter 16 — *Using Business Rules to Implement Services*).

Defining the test for the pattern

For our leave approval rule we need to define **two** tests, one to check that the request is only for 1 day in duration, which we can do by checking that the start date equals the end date, the second to check that the request is of type `Vacation`.

To define the first test, click the **Create** button; this will add a row to our **Define Test for Pattern** table where we can define the test conditions (as shown in the following screenshot).

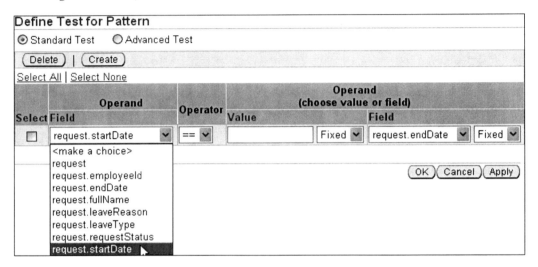

In the first **Operand** drop down, select the value to be tested, for example **request.StartDate** in our case. Next from the **Operator** drop down select the test to be applied to the first operand (**==** in our case). Next we can either choose to compare it to a specified value or a second **Operand**. For our purpose we want to check that the **request.startDate** equals the **request.endDate**.

To create our second test, we follow pretty much the same process. This time we want to test the operand **leaveRequest.leaveType** is equal to the value **Vacation.**

You may have noticed when specifying the second operand for each test that there is another drop down containing the values **Fixed** (as selected in the previous screenshot) or **Any**. Oracle Rules refers to these values as constraints. If an operand is set to **Any**, this specifies that non-technical users of the Rule Author can use the customization tab to modify the value of the operand.

Once we've defined both our tests, then click **OK**; this will take us back to the **Rule** page, which will now be updated with details of the **If** clause, as shown in the following screenshot:

Creating the Then clause

Now that we have defined our test, we need to define the action to take if the test evaluates to `true`. Click on **New Action**. This will pop up the **Add Action** window where you need to specify the **Action Type** you wish to carry out.

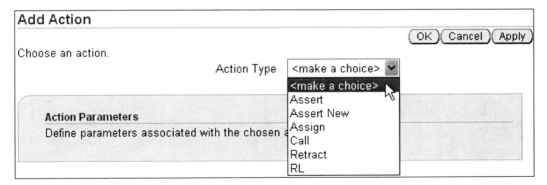

The Rule Engine supports the action types listed below:

- **Assert**: Used to reassert any facts matched in a pattern (for example request). When a fact is altered, if we want the rule engine to be aware of the change and re-evaluate the modified fact against the rule set, we must assert it.

- **Assert New**: If we create a new fact, for example a new **LeaveRequest**, then we must assert the new fact to make the rule engine aware of it, so that it can evaluate the new fact against the rule set.

- **Assign**: We can use this to either assign a value to a variable or a fact property; in our case we want to assign a status of **Approved** to the **request. requestStatus** property.

- **Call**: This allows you to call a function to perform one or more actions.

- **Retract**: This enables you to retract any of the facts matched in the pattern (for example **request**) so that it will no longer be evaluated as part of the rule set.

- **RL**: Allows you to enter RL text directly to perform one or more actions.

The actions **Assert**, **Assert New**, and **Retract**, are important when we are dealing with rule sets which deal with multiple interdependent facts, as this allows us to control which facts are being evaluated by the rule engine at any one time. Here, we only are dealing with a single fact, so don't examine these constructs in this chapter, leaving them for Chapter 16— *Using Business Rules to Implement Services*.

For our purpose we want to update the status of leave request to approved, so select **Assign** as the **Action Type**. This will update the **Add Action** screen shown as follows:

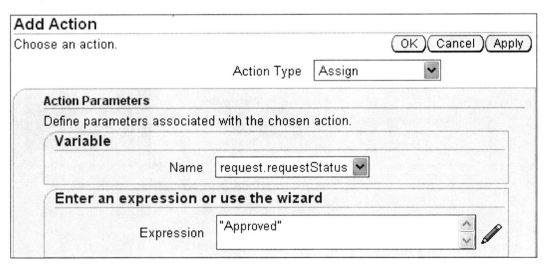

From the drop down select **request.requestStatus** as the variable that we wish to assign a value to. Then in the **Expression** field enter the value of **Approved**.

To calculate the value based on a more complicated formula, we can use the **Expression Wizard** to build this; the wizard is launched by clicking on the pencil icon.

Once we have completed our assign action, then click **OK**, this will take us back to the **Rule** page, which will now be updated with details of the **Then** clause, as shown in the following screenshot:

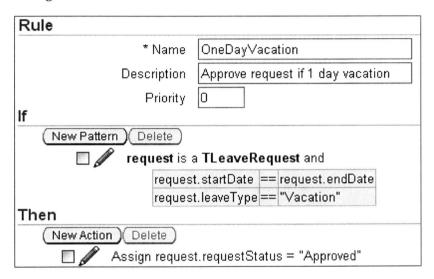

At this point make sure you save the dictionary. This completes the definition of our **LeaveApproval** rule set. The next step is to wire it into our BPEL process.

Creating a Decision Service

To invoke a rule we need to go through a number of steps. First we must create a session with the rules engine, then we can assert one or more facts, before executing the rule set and finally we can retrieve the results.

We do this in BPEL via a **Decision Service**; this is essentially a web service wrapper around a rules dictionary, which takes cares of managing the session with the rules engine as well as governing which rule set we wish to apply.

The wrapper allows a BPEL process to assert one or more facts, execute a rule set against the asserted facts, retrieve the results and then reset the session. This can be done within a single invocation of an operation, or over multiple operations.

Creating a Rule Engine Connection

Before you can create a Decision Service you need to create a connection to the repository in which the required rule set is stored. In the **Connections** panel within JDeveloper, right-click on the **Rule Engines** folder and select **New Rule Engine Connection…** as shown in the following screenshot:

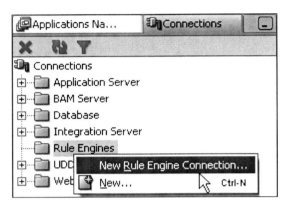

This will launch the **Create Rule Engine Connection** dialogue; first you need to specify whether the connection is for a file repository or WebDAV repository.

Using a file based repository

If you are using a file repository, all we need to specify is the location of the actual file. Once the connection has been created, we can use this to create a decision service for any of the rule sets contained within that repository.

However it is important to realize that when you create a decision service based on this connection, JDeveloper will take a copy of the repository and copy this into the BPEL project.

When you deploy the BPEL process, then the copy of this repository will be deployed with the BPEL process. This has a number of implications; first if you want to modify the rule set used by the BPEL Process you need to modify the copy of the repository deployed with the BPEL Process.

To modify the rule set deployed with a BPEL Process, log onto the BPEL console, from here click on the **BPEL Processes** tab, and then select the process that uses the decision service. Next click on the **Descriptor** tab; this will list all the Partner Links for that process, including the Decision Service (for example **LeaveApprovalDecisionServicePL**) as shown in the following screenshot:

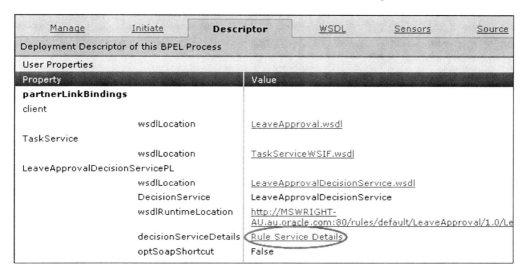

This PartnerLink will have the property **decisionServiceDetails**, with the link **Rule Service Details** (circled in the previous screenshot); click on this and the console will display details of the decision service. From here click on the link **Open Rule Author**; this will open the Rule Author complete with a connection to the file based rule repository.

The second implication is that if you use the same rule set within multiple BPEL Processes, each process will have its own copy of the rule set. You can work round this by either wrapping each rule set with a single BPEL process, which is then invoked by any other process wishing to use that rule set. Or once you have deployed the rule set for one process, then you can access it directly via the WSDL for the deployed rule set, for example **LeaveApprovalDecisionService.wsdl** in the above screenshot.

Using a WebDAV repository

For the reasons mentioned above, it often makes sense to use a WebDAV based repository to hold your rules. This makes it far simpler to share a rule set between multiple clients, such as BPEL and Java.

Before you can create a Rule Engine Connection to a WebDAV repository, you must first define a WebDAV connection to JDeveloper, which is also created from the **Connections** palette.

Creating a Decision Service

To create a decision service within our BPEL process, select the **Services** page from the **Component Palette** and drag a **Decision Service** onto your process, as shown in the following screenshot:

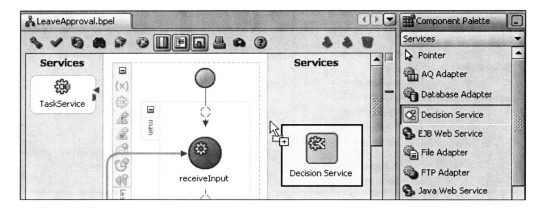

This will launch the **Decision Service Wizard** dialogue, as shown:

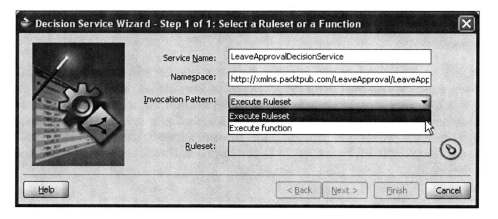

Give the service a name, and then select **Execute Ruleset** as the invocation pattern. Next click on the flashlight next to **Ruleset** to launch the **Rule Explorer**. This allows us to browse any previously defined rule engine connection and select the rule set we wish to invoke via the decision service.

For our purposes, select the **LeaveApprovalRules** as shown below, and click **OK**.

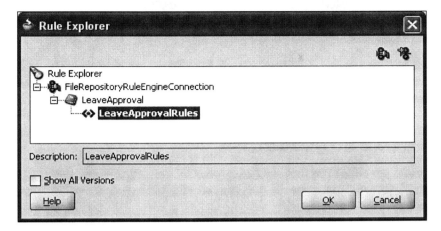

This will bring us back to the **Decision Service Wizard** which will be updated to list the facts that we can exchange with the Rule Engine, as shown in the following screenshot:

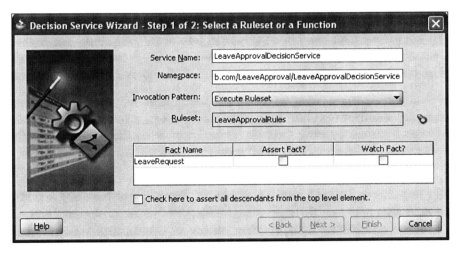

This dialogue will only list XML Facts that map to global elements in the XML Schema. Here we need to define which facts we want to assert, that is which facts we pass as inputs to the rule engine from BPEL, and which facts we want to watch, that is which facts we want to return in the output from the rules engine back to our BPEL process.

For our example we will pass in a single leave request. The rule engine will then apply the rule set we defined earlier and update the status of the request to **Approved** if appropriate. So we need to specify that Assert and Watch facts of type **LeaveRequest**.

Finally, you will notice the checkbox **Check here to assert all descendants from the top level element**; this is important when an element contains nested elements (or facts) to ensure that nested facts are also evaluated by the rules engine. For example if we had a fact of type **LeaveRequestList** which contained a list of multiple **LeaveRequests**, if we wanted to ensure the rules engine evaluated these nested facts, then we would need to check this checkbox.

Once you have specified the facts to **Assert** and **Watch**, click **Next** and complete the dialogue; this will then create a decision service partner link within your BPEL process.

Adding a Decide activity

We are now ready to invoke our rule set from within our BPEL process. From the **Component Palette**, drag a **Decide** activity onto our BPEL process (at the point before we execute the **LeaveRequest** Human Task).

This will open up the **Edit Decide** window (shown in the following screenshot). Here we need to specify a **Name** for the activity, and select the **Decision Service** we want to invoke (that is the **LeaveApprovalDecisionService** that we just created).

Once we've specified the service, we need to specify how we want to interact with it. For example, whether we want to incrementally assert a number of facts over a period of time, before executing the rule set and retrieving the result or whether we want to assert all the facts, execute the rule set and get the result within a single invocation.

We specify this through the **Operation** attribute. For our purpose we just need to assert a single fact and run the rule set, so select the value of **Assert facts, execute rule set, retrieve results** (we look at other modes of operation in more detail in Chapter 16 — *Using Business Rules to Implement Services*).

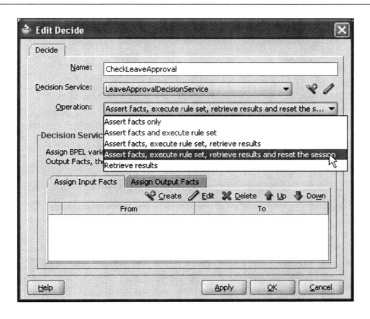

Once we have selected the operation to invoke on the decision service, the **Decsion Service Facts** will be updated to allow you to assign input and output facts as appropriate.

Assigning facts

The final step to invoke our business rules is to assign BPEL variables to the input and output facts. Click on **Create**, which will launch the **Decision Fact Map** window, as shown in the following screenshot:

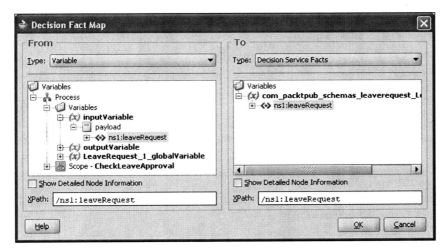

At first glance this will look like the standard **Create Copy Operation** window that we use when carrying out assigns within BPEL (which in reality is exactly what it is).

The key difference is that we are using this to assign values to the input facts to be submitted to the rules engines, so the **Type** on the **To** side of the copy operation is a **Decision Service Facts**.

The reverse is true for an output fact, where we use this dialog to map the output from the decision service back into a corresponding BPEL variable.

For our purpose we just want to map the initial `leaveRequest` in the process `inputVariable` into the corresponding fact as shown in the above screenshot, and then map the output fact which will contain our updated `leaveRequest` back into our `inputVariable`.

We have now wired the invocation of the rule into our BPEL process. Before finally running our process we need to modify our process to only invoke the workflow if the leave request hasn't been automatically approved.

To do this just drag a `switch` activity onto your process, then drag your workflow task into the first branch in the switch and define a test to check that the `leaveRequest` hasn't been approved. You are now ready to deploy and run your modified process.

Using functions

Our current rule only approves vacations of 1 day in duration, requiring all other leave requests to be manually approved. Ideally we would like to approve holidays, of varying duration, as long as sufficient notice has been given, for example:

- Approve vacations if 1 day in duration and its start date is two weeks or more in the future
- Approve if for 2-3 days and more than 30 days in the future
- Approve if 5 days or less and more than 60 days in the future
- Approve if 10 days or less and more than 120 days in the future

To write these rules, we will need to calculate the duration of the leave period as well as calculate how long it is before the start date. Out of the box the rule engine doesn't provide functionality for this, but the Rule Author allows us to write our own functions to do exactly this. For our purpose we want to create two functions:

- `leaveDuration`: It returns the number of days between the start and end date, excluding weekends
- `startsIn`: It returns the number of days before the specified `startDate`

These functions are very similar in nature, so we will actually write a base function, `durationInDays`, which takes 3 parameters. The `startDate` and `endDate` of the period to be calculated, as well a Boolean `includeWeekends`, to control whether weekends are to be counted.

Importing Java classes as facts

Each of the functions will take arguments which hold dates, if you examine the `TLeaveRequest` fact that the Rule Author created when we imported out XML Schema, you will see that those elements of type `xsd:Date` are mapped to properties of type `java.util.Calendar`. So our functions should take arguments of this type.

Rules Author allows you to create facts based on Java objects; however before you can do this you need to import them as Java Facts. The process for this is similar to the one we followed earlier to import XML Facts.

Select the **Definitions** tab within Rule Author and then under the **Fact** folder click on the **JavaFact** branch. This will list all Java facts currently defined. If you click on **Create**, it will take you to the class selector page, listing the top level hierarchy of all the classes on the class path, as shown in the following screenshot:

Click on the **+** symbol to expand the relevant nodes; for our example, expand the **java** node, then the **util** node and then select the **Calendar** class. Once selected, click **Import** and this class will be added to your list of Java facts. Once imported, the classes and their methods will be available to the Rule Author as facts.

By default the Rule Author has visibility of classes in the **java**, **javax**, and **org** packages; if you need a class that is not included within those packages then enter the `classpath` for the required classes in the **User Classpath** field and click **Add**.

Creating a function

We are now ready to create our first function, `durationInDays`. Within the **Definitions** tab, select the **RLFunctions** folder, as highlighted in the following screenshot. This will bring up the **RLFunction Summary** which lists all the functions currently defined.

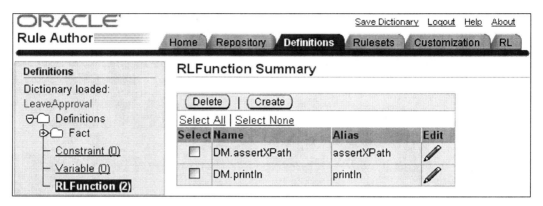

Click **Create** to bring up the **RLFunction** editor page as shown:

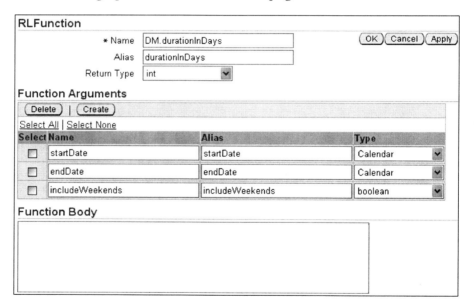

First give the function a name, for example **DM.durationInDays**, plus a corresponding alias and from the drop-down list select the **Return Type** of the function, which is **int** in our case.

Next we need to specify the arguments we wish to pass to our function; select **Create** and this will add an argument to our list. Here we can specify the argument name (for example **startDate**), a corresponding alias for it and from the drop down the argument type. At the top of this list will be the **Calendar** fact that we just imported.

We can then add parameters for **endDate**, and **includeWeekends** as shown in the previous screenshot.

The final step is to implement the business logic of our function; we enter this in the **Function Body** text box. Defining the function here is painful, since the Rule Author doesn't validate the body of the function. A consequence of this is you won't know if the function is valid until you try to execute it at run time, which if it contains an error will typically result in the rule engine throwing an exception, which is not always easy to debug.

However when implementing a function you are effectively writing a static Java method. Therefore it is more effective to write this using JDeveloper, where we can then use the development tools to compile, run, and test our function. Once we are satisfied that the function performs as expected we can cut and paste the function body from JDeveloper into the Rule Author.

When using this approach you need to allow for the restriction that you can't use the Java `import` statement within an RLFunction (in the same way you can't import within the body of a Java method). This means whenever you reference a Java Class you need to prefix it with its package name, for example when we use the `Calendar` class within our function we always have to specify `java.util.Calendar`.

So the `durationInDays` function implemented in Java looks as follows:

```
public static int durationInDays(java.util.Calendar startDate, java.util.Calendar endDate, boolean includeWeekends)
{
    int duration = 0;
    java.util.Calendar currentDate = (java.util.Calendar) startDate.clone();

    while ( (currentDate.get(java.util.Calendar.YEAR) <  endDate.get(java.util.Calendar.YEAR)) ||
          ((currentDate.get(java.util.Calendar.YEAR) == endDate.get(java.util.Calendar.YEAR)) &&
           (currentDate.get(java.util.Calendar.DAY_OF_YEAR) <= endDate.get(java.util.Calendar.DAY_OF_YEAR)))) {

        if ( (includeWeekends == true) ||
            (currentDate.get(java.util.Calendar.DAY_OF_WEEK) != java.util.Calendar.SATURDAY &&
             currentDate.get(java.util.Calendar.DAY_OF_WEEK) != java.util.Calendar.SUNDAY       )) {
            duration++;
        }
        currentDate.add(java.util.Calendar.DAY_OF_YEAR, 1);
    }
    return duration;
}
```

We can then just cut and paste this straight from JDeveloper into the Rule Author and click **OK** to create our function.

To implement the other two functions `leaveDuration` and `startsIn` we follow the same approach.

Invoking a function from within a rule

The final step is to invoke the functions as required from our rule set. Before writing the additional rules for vacation of less than 3, 5, and 10 days respectively, we will update our first rule **OneDayVacation** to use these new functions.

Go back to the **Rulesets** tab and click on the **OneDayVacation** branch within the **LeaveApprovalRules** and then click on the pencil icon for the **If** part of the rule. This will bring us back to the **Pattern Definition** window for the rule.

Previously, when we defined our test for a pattern we defined a **Standard Test**. With this approach the Rule Author lets us define one or more simple tests. Each simple test allows us to compare one variable with either another variable or a fixed value, and for the pattern to evaluate to true all simple tests must evaluate to `true`.

However, if we want to define more complex expressions or use functions, then we need to define this as an **Advanced Test**. When **Advanced Test** is selected, rather than enter every test as a single row within the pattern, Rule Author presents a single free format text entry box where we can directly enter the test pattern.

If when selecting **Advanced Test** we already have a simple test defined, Rule Author will automatically convert its free format equivalent, as shown in the following screenshot:

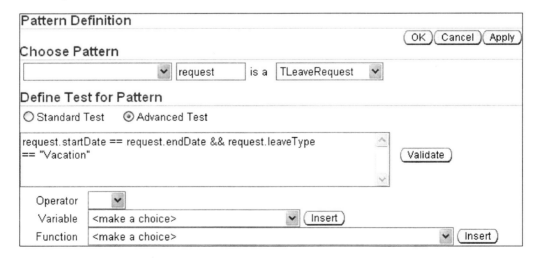

Below the **Advanced Test** text entry box are three drop downs: **Operator**, **Variable**, and **Function**, which we can use to help build the expression. For example, to modify our test, first of all delete the comparison `request.startDate == request.endDate`. Next from the **Function** drop select the `leaveDuration` function and click **Insert**, as shown in the following screenshot:

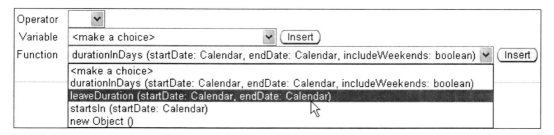

This will insert `leaveDuration (startDate: Calendar, endDate: Calendar)` at the current cursor location within the test text box. We then need to modify the parameters to pass in the actual `request.startDate` and `request.endDate`.

We can either enter this manually, or use the **Variable** drop down to insert the required variables in a similar fashion to the **Function** drop down.

We can then repeat these steps to apply the `startsIn` function to test that the start date for the leave request is two or more weeks away. Once completed our test pattern for approving a 1 day vacation should look as follows:

Define Test for Pattern

○ Standard Test ⦿ Advanced Test

```
leaveDuration (request.startDate, request.endDate) == 1 &&
startsIn (request.startDate) >= 14 &&
request.leaveType == "Vacation"
```

(Validate)

Once we have completed our test pattern, we can click **Validate** just to check that its syntax is correct.

Having completed this test, we can define similar approval rules for vacations of less than 3, 5, and 10 days respectively.

When completed, save your dictionary and rerun the leave approval process; you should now see that vacations which match our leave approval rules are automatically approved.

Summary

Business rules are a key component of any application. Traditionally these rules are buried deep within the code of an application, making them very difficult to change.

Yet in a typical application it is the business rules which change most frequently; by separating these out as a specialized service it allows us to change these rules without having to modify the overall application.

In this chapter we have looked at how we can use the Oracle Business Rules engine to implement such rules, and how we can invoke these from within BPEL as a decision service.

It's worth noting that you are not restricted to calling these rules from just BPEL, the rules engine comes with a Java API that allows it to be easily invoked from any Java application or alternatively you can expose the rules as web services which can then be invoked from any web service client.

Finally, while in this chapter we have only looked at very simple rules, the Oracle Business Rules Engine implements the industry standard Rete Algorithm, making it ideal for evaluating a large number of interdependent rules and facts. We will examine some of these capabilities in more detail in Chapter 16— *Using Business Rules to Implement Services*.

8
Building Real-time Dashboards

The key objective driving service-oriented architecture is to move the IT organization closer to the business. Creation of services and their assembly into composite applications and processes is the mechanism by which IT can move to be more responsive to the business. However, it is the provision of real-time business information via dashboards that really gives business the confidence that IT can deliver. In this chapter we will examine how to use **Business Activity Monitoring (BAM)** to provide real-time dashboards that give the business an insight into what is happening with their processes currently, not what happened yesterday or last week.

How BAM differs from traditional business intelligence

The Oracle SOA Suite stores the state of all processes in a database in documented schemas so why do we need yet another reporting tool to provide insight into our processes and services? In other words how does BAM differ from traditional BI (Business Intelligence)? In traditional BI, reports are generated and delivered either on a scheduled basis or in response to a user request. Any changes to the information will not be reflected until the next scheduled run or until a user requests the report to be rerun. BAM is an event-driven reporting tool that generates alerts and reports in real time, based on a continuously changing data stream, some of whose data may not be in the database. As events occur in the Services and Processes, the business has defined they are captured by BAM and reports and views are updated in real time. Where necessary these updated reports are delivered to users. This delivery to users can take several forms. The best known is the dashboard on users' desktops that will automatically update without any need for the user to refresh the screen. There are also other means to deliver reports to the end user, including sending them via a text message or an email.

Traditional reporting tools such as Oracle Reports and Oracle Discoverer as well as Oracles latest Business Intelligence Suite can be used to provide some real-time reporting needs but they do not provide the event driven reporting that gives the business a continuously updating view of the current business situation.

Event Driven Architecture

Event Driven Architecture (EDA) is about building business solutions around responsiveness to events. Events may be simple triggers such as a stock out event or they may be more complex triggers such as the calculations to realize that a stock out will occur in three days. An Event Driven Architecture will often take a number of simple events and then combine them through a complex event processing sequence to generate complex events that could not have been raised without aggregation of several simpler events.

Oracle BAM scenarios

Oracle Business Activity Monitoring is typically used to monitor two distinct types of real-time data. Firstly it may be used to monitor the overall state of processes in the business. For example it may be used to track how many auctions are currently running, how many have bids on them, and how many have completed in the last 24 hours (or other time periods). Secondly it may be used to track in real-time **Key Performance Indicators** or **KPIS**. For example it may be used to provide a real-time updating dashboard to a seller to show the current total value of all the sellers' auctions and to track this against an expected target.

In the first case, we are interested in how business processes are progressing and are using BAM to identify bottlenecks and failure points within those processes. Bottlenecks can be identified by too much time being spent on given steps in the process. BAM allows us to compute the time taken between two points in a process, such as the time between order placement and shipping, and provide real-time feedback on those times. Similarly BAM can be used to track the percentage drop-out rate between steps in a sales process, allowing the business to take appropriate action.

In the second case, our interest is on some aggregate number, such as our total liabilities should we win all the auctions we are bidding on. This requires us to aggregate results from many events, possibly performing some kind of calculation on them to provide us with a single KPI that gives an indication to the business of how things are going. BAM allows us to continuously update this number in real on a dashboard without the need for continued polling. It also allows us to trigger alerts, perhaps through email or SMS, to notify an individual, when a threshold is breached.

In both cases reports delivered can be customized based on the individual receiving the report.

BAM architecture

It may seem odd to have a section on architecture in the middle of a chapter about how to effectively use BAM, but key to successful utilization of BAM is an understanding of how the different tiers relate to each other.

Logical view

The following diagram represents a logical view of how BAM operates. Events are acquired from one or more sources through event acquisition and then normalized, correlated, and stored in event storage (generally a memory area in BAM that is backed up to disc). The report cache generates reports based on events in storage and then delivers those reports, together with real-time updates through the report delivery layer. Event processing is also performed on events in storage, and when defined conditions are met, alerts will be delivered through the alert delivery service.

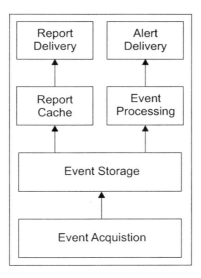

Physical view

To better understand the physical view of the architecture of BAM, we have divided this section into four parts. Let us discuss these in detail.

Capture

This logical view maps onto the physical BAM components shown in the following diagram. Data acquisition in the SOA Suite is handled by sensors in BPEL and ESB. BAM can also receive events from JMS message queues and access data in databases (useful for historical comparison). For complex data formats or for other data sources then **Oracle Data Integrator** (ODI is a separate product to the SOA Suite) is recommended by Oracle. Although potentially less efficient and more work than running ODI, it is also possible to use adapters to acquire data from multiple sources and feed it into BAM through ESB or BPEL.

At the data capture level we need to think of the data items that we can provide to feed the reports and alerts that we desire to generate. We must consider the sources of that data and the best way to load it into BAM.

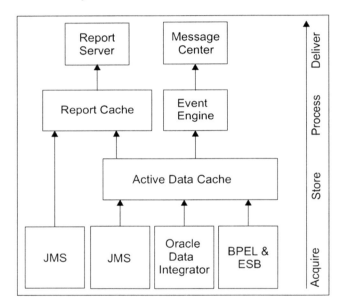

Store

Once the data is captured, it is then stored in a normalized form in the **Active Data Cache (ADC)**. This storage facility has the ability to do simple correlation based on fields within the data, and multiple data items received from the acquisition layer may update just a single object in the data cache. For example the state of a given BPEL process instance may be represented by a single object in the ADC and all updates to that process state will just update that single data item rather than creating multiple data items.

Process

Reports are run based on user demand. Once a report is run it will update the user's screen on a real time basis. Where multiple users are accessing the same report only one instance of the report is maintained by the report server. As events are captured and stored in real time the report engine will continuously monitor them for any changes that need to be made to those reports which are currently active. When changes are detected that impact active reports, then the appropriate report will be updated in memory and the updates sent to the user screen.

In addition to the event processing required to correctly insert and update items in the ADC, there is also a requirement to monitor items in the ADC for events that require some sort of action to be taken. This is the job of the event processor. This will monitor data in the ADC to see if registered thresholds on values have been exceeded or if certain time-outs have expired. The event processor will often need to perform calculations across multiple data items to do this.

Deliver

Delivery of reports takes place in two ways. First, users request reports to be delivered to their desktop by selecting views within BAM. These reports are delivered as HTML pages within a browser and are updated whenever the underlying data used in the report changes. The second approach is that reports are sent out as a result of events being triggered by the Event Processing Engine. In the latter case, the report may be delivered by email, SMS, or voice messaging using the notifications service. A final option available for these event generated reports is to invoke a web service to take some sort of automated action.

Closing the loop

While monitoring what is happening is all very laudable, it is only of benefit if we actually do something about what we are monitoring. BAM provides the real-time monitoring ability very well but it also provides the facility to invoke other services to respond to undesirable events such as stock outs. The ability to invoke external services is crucial to the concept of a closed loop control environment where as a result of monitoring we are able to reach back into the processes and either alter their execution or start new ones. For example when a stock out or low stock event is raised then the message centre could invoke a web service requesting a supplier to send more stock to replenish inventory. Placing this kind of feedback mechanism in BAM allows us to trigger events across multiple applications and locations in a way that may not be possible within a single application or process. For example, in response to a stock out, instead of requesting our supplier to provide more stock, we may be monitoring stock levels in independent systems and, based on stock levels elsewhere, may redirect stock from one location to another.

BAM platform anomaly

In 10g SOA Suite, BAM runs only as a Windows application. Unlike the rest of SOA Suite, it does not run on a JEE Application Server and it can only run on the Windows platform. In the next release, 11g, BAM will be provided as a JEE application that can run on a number of application servers and operating systems.

User interface

Development in Oracle BAM is done through a web-based user interface.

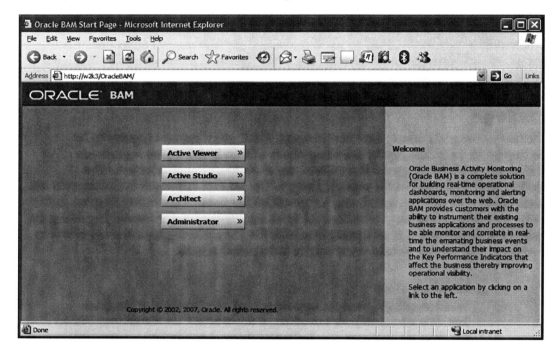

This user interface gives access to four different applications that allow you to interact with different parts of BAM. These are:

- **Active Viewer** for giving access to reports; this relates to the deliver stage for user requested reports.

- **Active Studio** for building reports; this relates to the 'process' stage for creating reports.

- **Architect** for setting up both inbound and outbound events. Data elements are defined here as data sources. Alerts are also configured here. This covers setting up, acquire and store stages as well as the deliver stage for alerts.

- **Administrator** for managing users and roles as well as defining the types of message sources.

We will not examine the applications individually but will take a task-focused look at how to use them as part of providing some specific reports.

Monitoring process state

Now that we have examined how BAM is constructed, let us use this knowledge to construct some simple dashboards that track the state of a business process. We will instrument a simple version of an auction process. The process is shown in the following figure:

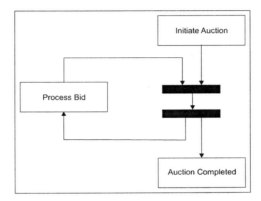

An auction is started and then bids are placed until the time runs out — at which point the auction is completed. This is modelled in BPEL. This process has three distinct states:

- Started
- Bid received
- Completed

We are interested in the number of auctions in each state as well as the total value of auctions in progress. We will follow a middle out approach to build our dashboard. We will take the following steps:

- Define our data within the Active Data Cache
- Create sensors in BPEL and map to data in the ADC
- Create suitable reports
- Run the reports

Defining data objects

Data in BAM is stored in data objects. Individual data objects contain the information that is reported in BAM dashboards and may be updated by multiple events. Generally BAM will report against aggregations of objects, but there is also the ability for reports to drill down into individual data objects.

Before defining our data objects let's group them into an **Auction** folder so they are easy to find. To do this we use the **BAM Architect** application and select **Data Objects** which gives us the following screen.

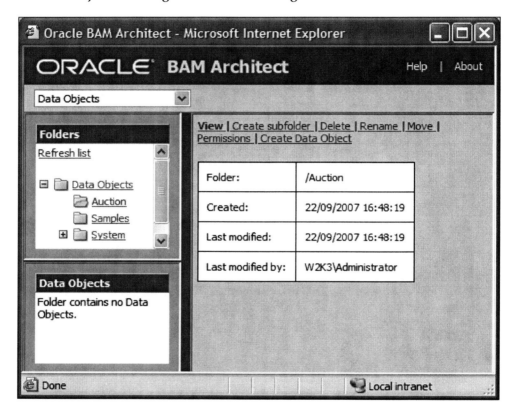

We select **Create subfolder** to create the folder and give it a name **Auction**.

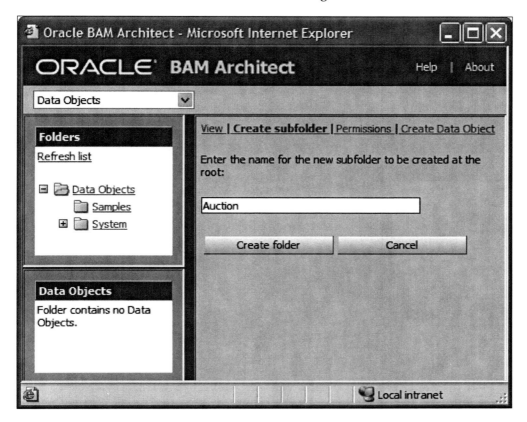

We then select **Create folder** to actually create the folder and we get a confirmation message to tell us that the folder was created. Notice that once created, the folder also appears in the **Folders** window on the left-hand side of the screen.

Now we have our folder we can create a data object. Again we select **Data Objects** from the drop-down menu. To define the data objects that are to be stored in our Active Data Cache, we open the **Auction** folder if it is not already open and select **Create Data Object**. If we don't select the **Auction** folder then we pick it later when filling in the details of the data object.

We need to give our object a unique name within the folder and optionally provide it with a tip text that helps explain what the object does when the mouse is moved over it in object listings. Having named our object we can now create the data fields by selecting **Add a field**. When adding fields we need to provide a name and type as well as indicating if they must contain data; the default **Nullable** does not require a field to be populated. We may also optionally indicate if a field should be public—available for display—and what if any tool tip text it should have.

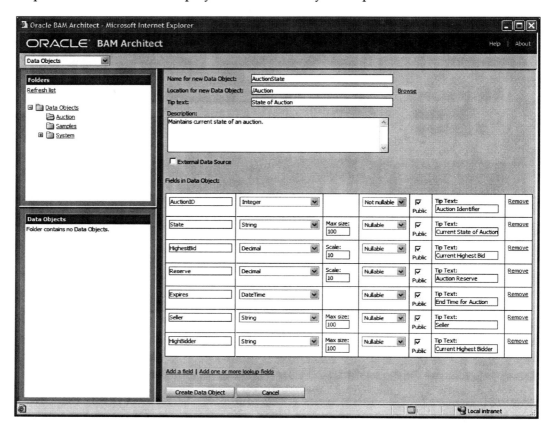

Once all the data fields have been defined then we can click **Create Data Object** to actually create the object as we have defined it. We are then presented with a confirmation screen that the object has been created.

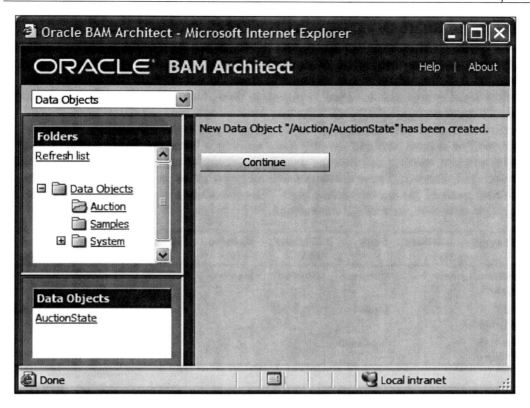

Grouping data into hierarchies

When creating a data object it is possible to specify *Dimensions* for the object. A dimension is based on one or more fields within the object. A given field can only participate in one dimension. This gives the ability to group the object by the fields in the given dimension. If multiple fields are selected for a single dimension then they can be layered into a hierarchy, for example to allow analysis by country, region, and city. In this case all three elements would be selected into a single dimension, perhaps called geography. Within geography a hierarchy could be set up with country at the top, region next, and finally city at the bottom, allowing drill down to occur in views. Just as a data object can have multiple dimensions, a dimension can also have multiple hierarchies.

A digression on populating data object fields

In the previous discussion we mentioned the **Nullable** attribute that can be attached to fields. This is very important as we do not expect to populate all or even most of the fields in a data object at one moment in time. Do not confuse data objects with the low level events that are used to populate them. Data objects in BAM do not have a one-to-one correspondence with the low level events that populate them. In our auction example there will be just one `auction` object for every auction. However there will be at least two and usually more messages for every auction; one message for the auction starting, another for the auction completing, and additional messages for each bid received. These messages will all populate or in some cases overwrite different parts of the auction data object. The table shows how the three messages populate different parts of the data object.

Message	Auction ID	State	Highest bid	Reserve	Expires	Seller	Highest bidder
Auction Started	Inserted	Inserted	Inserted	Inserted	Inserted	Inserted	
Bid Received		Updated	Updated				Updated
Auction Finished		Updated					

Instrumenting BPEL

Having defined the data we wish to capture in BAM we now need to make our BPEL auction process generate appropriate events. To do this we use **Sensors**. Sensors are not part of the normal BPEL executable flow; they can be thought of as event generators. They are attached to almost any kind of activity in BPEL, including partner link operations (invoke, receive, reply) and assigns. They can also be attached to variables and will fire whenever the variable is modified.

To create a new sensor for an activity, edit the activity and select the **Sensors** tab. We can then click the **Create** link to start creating the sensor.

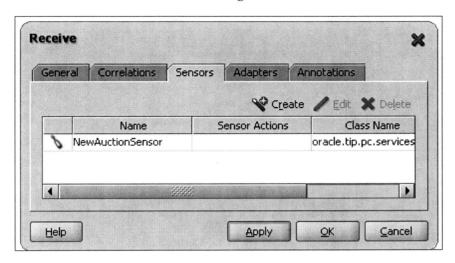

When creating a new sensor we need to provide it with a name and indicate when it should fire. The options are:

- **Activation** for when the activity is started
- **Completion** for when the activity is completed
- **Fault** for when the activity raises a fault
- **Compensation** for when compensation is invoked on a surrounding scope
- **Retry** for when the activity is retried, such as retrying an invoke
- **All** for all of the above

We must also provide a variable that contains the data we want to be part of the sensor generated event. This variable must be an element variable, not a simple type or a message type.

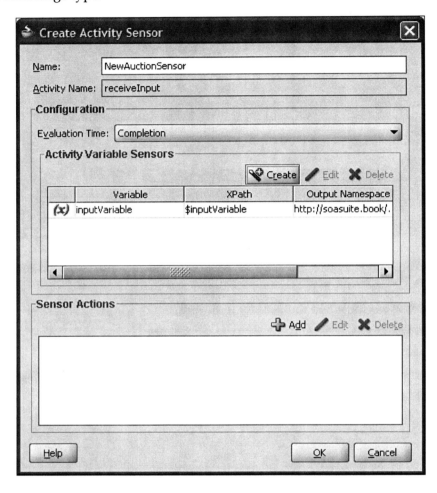

Sensors can have a number of sensor actions associated with them. Sensor actions can be thought of as the targets for the sensor event. One option is to send the events into the BPEL repository which is useful for testing purposes. Another option is to send them to BAM.

Unfortunately we cannot add a BAM sensor from the **Create Activity Sensor** dialog. They can only be created by using the structure pane for the BPEL process. To do this we navigate to **Sensor Actions** in the structure pane, right-click, and select **Bam Sensor Action**. This brings up the **Create Sensor Action** dialog.

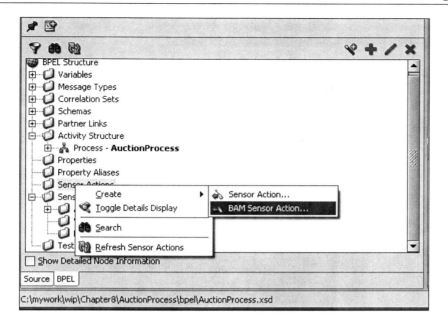

We provide a name for the sensor action and then select an eligible sensor from the drop-down list. There is a one-to-one relationship between BAM Sensor Actions and Sensors. This is not the case for other types of sensor. The reason for the one-to-one relationship is that the BAM Sensor actions transform the variable associated with the action into the relevant fields for the BAM Data Object. This is done through an XSLT transform.

Having selected our sensor we then click the torch next to the **Data Object** so that we can choose the BAM Data Object that we will map the sensor variable onto.

Having selected the BAM Data Object we need to select the operation to be performed on the data object. The drop-down box gives us four options:

- Insert
- Update
- Delete
- Upsert

The **Insert** operation creates a new instance of the BAM Data Object. This may result in multiple data objects having the same field values.

The **Insert** operation does not use a key as it always creates a new data object. The remaining three operations require a key because they may operate on an existing data object. The key must uniquely identify a data object and may consist of one or more data object fields.

The **Update** operation will update an existing data object, overwriting some or all of the fields as desired. If the object cannot be found from the key then no data is updated in the ADC.

The **Delete** operation will remove a data object from the ADC. If the key does not identify an object then no object will be deleted.

The **Upsert** operation behaves as an update operation if the key identifies an existing data object in the ADC. If the key does not identify an existing object in the ADC, then it behaves as an Insert operation.

Generally we use the Insert operation when we know we are creating an object for the first time and the Update operation when we know that the object already exists. We use the Upsert operation when we are unsure if an object exists.

For example, we may use an Insert to create an instance of a process status object and then use an Update to change the status value of the object as the process progresses. When tracking process state it is a good idea to use the process instance identifier as a key field in the data object.

Having chosen our operation, an insert for example, we then need to map the fields in the sensor variable defined in BPEL to the BAM data object. We do this by creating a new XSLT transformation by clicking the green cross next to the **Map File** field.

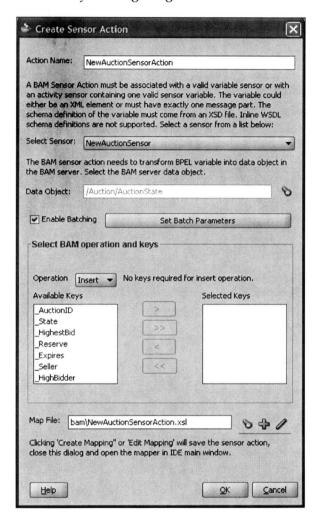

Within the XSLT transformation editor we can map the BPEL variable to the BAM data object. In addition to the variable itself there is a host of other information available to us in the BPEL variable source document. This can be categorized as follows:

- Header Information: This relates to the process instance and the specific sensor that is firing.
- Payload: This contains not only the sensor variable contents but also information about the activity and any fault associated with it.

Useful data includes the instance ID of the process and also the time the sensor fired as well as elapsed times for actions. Once we have wired up the variable data we can save the transform file.

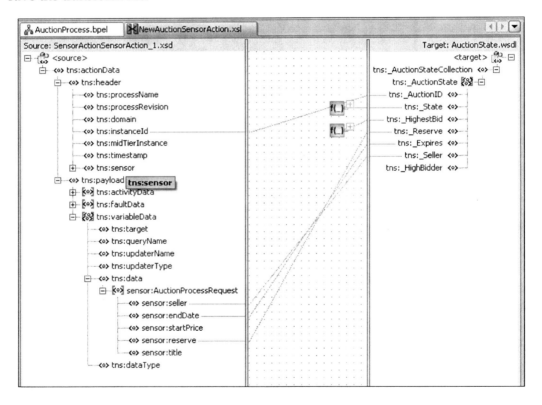

Before completing the **BAM Sensor Action** dialog, it is worth investigating the use of the batching parameters.

It is possible that many sensor updates will be taking place in quick succession. To reduce the number of calls that the BPEL Process Manager makes to BAM it is possible to batch the data. The batch parameters can be interpreted as "while the **Batch timeout** has not expired, data will be sent in batches of at least **Batch size lower limit** and no bigger than **Batch size upper limit**".

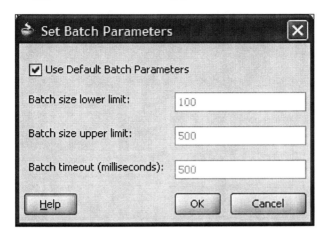

Generally it is safe to leave the batch parameters at the default values. When we have finished creating the Sensor action, then we can deploy it to the BPEL Server and events will be fired to populate the BAM active data cache.

Testing the events

After creating our BAM sensors we can test them by executing a process in BPEL and ensuring that the events appear in the Active Data Cache. We can find the actual event data by selecting the object in BAM Architect and then clicking **Contents** which will then list the actual data object instances.

Creating a simple dashboard

Now that our sensors are in place and working, we can use the **BAM Active Studio** application to create a report based on the sensor information. To help organize our reports it is possible to create folders to hold reports in a similar fashion to the way we created folders to hold data objects.

Let's create a report that shows the status of auctions in the system and also shows the value of all currently open auctions. We will start by creating the report itself. The report is just a holder for views and we create it by selecting the **CREATE A NEW REPORT** button.

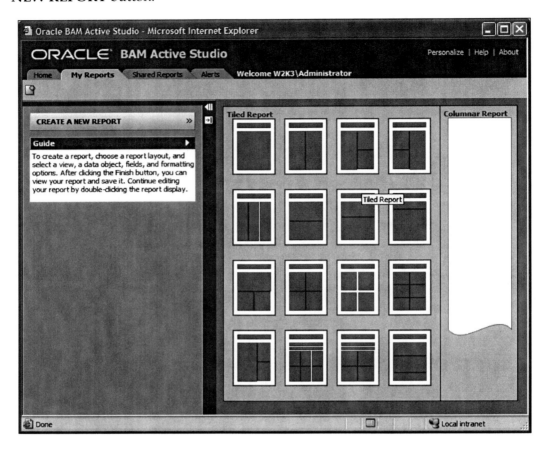

We can select a report that has the right number of panes for the number of views we want. Note that it is possible to change the number of panes on the report, so if we get it wrong it does not matter. For now, we will choose a simple split screen report with two panes, one above the other.

We can provide a title for a report by editing the title section directly. Having updated the title we can then proceed to create the views.

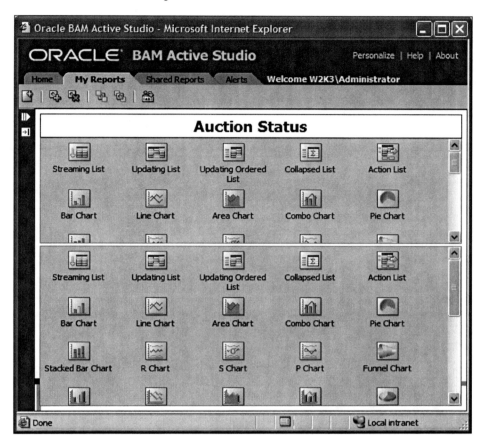

Monitoring process status

For our first view let us monitor how many auctions are at particular states. We are interested in a count of the number of auctions with a given state value. This would be well represented with a histogram style chart, so we select a 3-D bar chart from the view pane.

A wizard appears at the bottom of the screen which gives us the opportunity to select a data object to be used as the basis of the view. We navigate to the **Auction** folder and select the **AuctionState** object. Note that it is possible to have multiple data objects in a view, but additional data objects are added later.

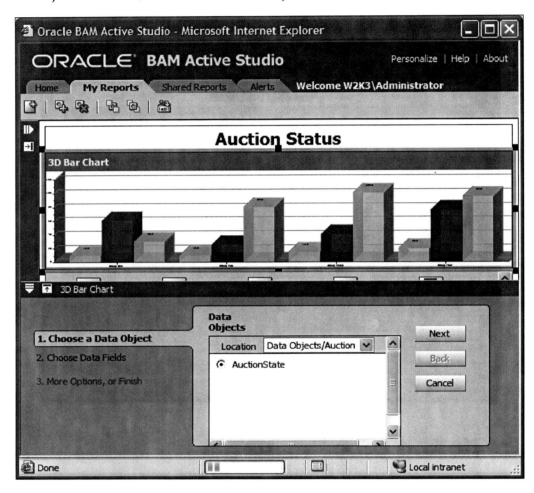

Having selected the data object we select the fields from the data object that we will need to present the current state an auction is in. We choose the state field as a value we want to use in our report by selecting it from the **Chart Values** column. We can choose to group the data by particular fields, in this case the state of the auction. By default, date and string fields can be grouped, but by selecting **Include Value Fields** it is possible to group by any field by selecting it in the **Group By** column. By selecting a summary function (**Count**) for our state field we can count the number of auctions in a given state.

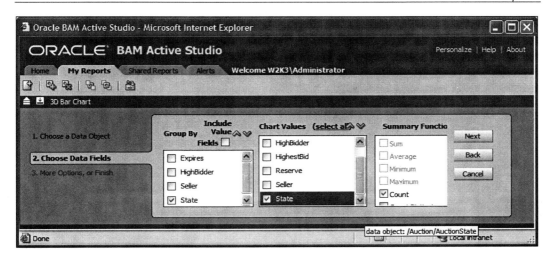

Finally the wizard gives us the opportunity to further modify the view by:

- Creating a filter to restrict the range of data objects included in the view
- Adding additional calculated fields to the view
- Adding additional data objects to the view to be displayed alongside the existing data object
- Changing the visual properties of the view

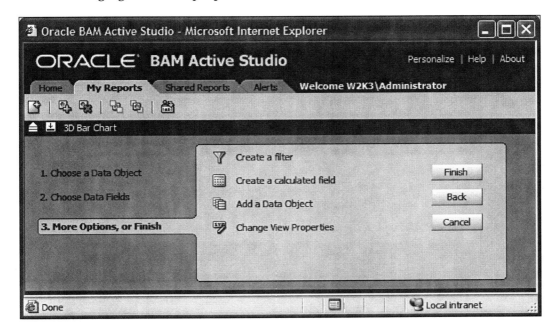

We will create a filter to restrict the display to those processes that are either currently running or have completed in the last 7 days. To do this, after selecting the filter link, add a new entry to the filter. Headers in this context are a mechanism for building Boolean expressions between filter elements. A single **AT LEAST ONE** header is sufficient for our needs.

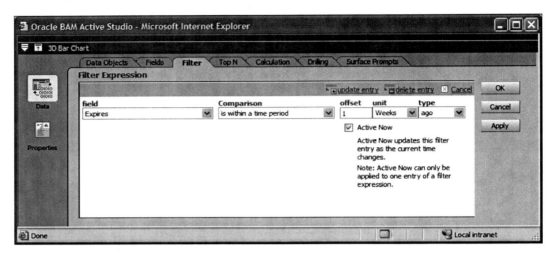

We can now select a date field (expires) and select that we want to include all data object whose expires field **is within a time period** of 1 week ago. This will prevent us from having an ever-increasing number of completed processes. When the filter expression is completed we click **update entry** to add the entry to the filter.

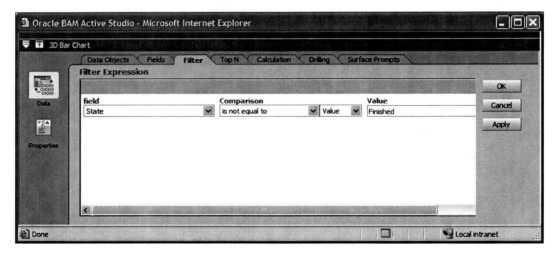

We can then add a second value based filter. In this case we want to include all data objects whose auction has not yet finished. We do this by selecting the state field as our filter field and then choosing all data objects whose **State** field **is not equal to** the value **Finished**.

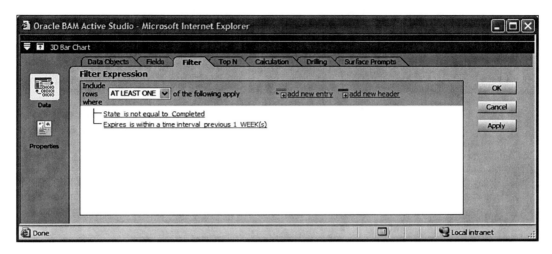

When we have clicked update entry then we can review the filter and select apply. This will update the underlying view and we can verify that the data is as we expect it to look.

Monitoring KPIs

In the previous section we looked at monitoring the state of a process. In this section we will use BAM to give a real-time view of our KPIs. For example we may be interested in monitoring the current value of all open auctions. This can be done by creating a view using a gauge or arrow control. The gauge will give us a measure of a value in the context of acceptable and unacceptable bounds. The arrow control will show us direction of movement. Creating the view is done in a similar fashion to previously and again we may make use of filters to restrict the range of data objects that is included in the view.

When we have completed the views in our report and saved the report then we may view the report though the **Active Viewer** application and watch the values change in real time.

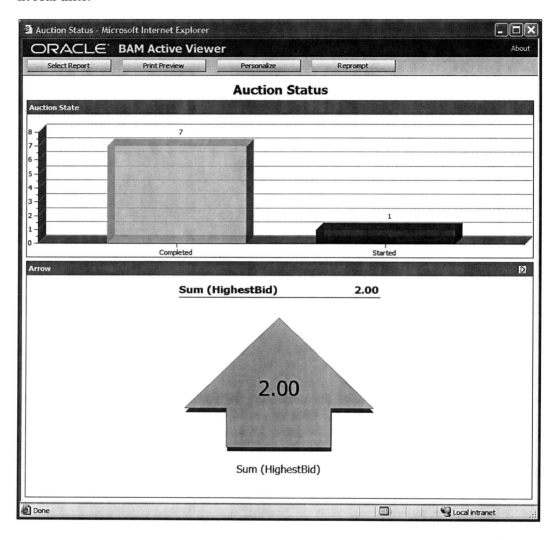

Note that we can drill down into the reports to gain additional information. This only gives a list of individual data objects with the same values displayed as on the top level view. To gain more control over drill down it is necessary to use the **Drilling** tab in the view editor to specify the drill-down parameters.

Summary

In this chapter we have explored how Business Activity Monitoring differs from and is complementary to more traditional Business Intelligence solutions such as Oracle Reports and Business Objects. We have explored how BAM can allow the business to monitor the state of business targets and Key Performance Indicators, such as the current most popular products in a retail environment or the current time taken to serve customers in a service environment. We also looked at how BAM can be used to allow the business to monitor the current state of processes, both in aggregate and also drilling down to individual process instances.

9

oBay Introduction

By now you should have a good initial understanding of all the key components which make up the Oracle SOA Suite. Typically, we will find that once someone has an initial grasp of the various components, one of the next questions we get is:

What is the best way to combine/use all of these different components to implement a real world SOA solution?

Answering this question is very much the focus of this section. To do this we have built a complete, all be it relatively small, SOA solution designed for an online auction site, for a fictional company called **oBay** (the o stands for Oracle by the way).

Each chapter in this section tackles specific areas that need to be considered when developing a SOA based solution, such as the design of the service contract, validation, error handling, message interaction patterns, and so on. To highlight and demonstrate key design considerations, each chapter uses examples based on key parts of the oBay application to illustrate what it is talking about.

This chapter introduces oBay and details the overall business requirements of the online auction site. Before looking at the overall design of the oBay application we take a step back and consider some of the key goals of a SOA based approach, such as interoperability, reusability, and agility.

Next we present you with our outline of a typical SOA architecture, and in particular pay attention to how we might want to layer our services, as well as highlight some of the key design considerations behind this.

Only when we have our blueprint for SOA, we apply it to the business requirements of oBay, and present you with its overall architecture.

oBay requirements

oBay is a new start-up company that provides a web-based auction site for users to buy and sell items online.

User registration

Before someone can either sell or bid on items, they must first register as a user on oBay. When registering, a user will be required to provide the following information:

- Name (First Name and Last Name)
- Date of Birth
- Address (Line 1, Line 2, City, State, Zip, Country)
- Email Address
- UserID
- Password
- Credit Card (Card Type, Number, Expiry Date)

They will also be required to accept oBay's standard terms and conditions.

As part of the registration process, the system will perform the following checks:

- That the UserID is not already in use
- That the user is at least 18 years of age
- That the password falls within the required constraints
- That for US and UK addresses, the supplied Zip Code is valid and that it matches the other details provided
- That the email address is valid; this will be checked by sending the user a confirmation email to the supplied address, with a link for them to activate their account
- That the credit card details provided are valid

User login

Once a user has successfully registered and activated their account, they can log into oBay. This will take them to their homepage from where they can choose to start selling or bidding on items.

Selling items

When a user goes to their seller's page, it will list all the items they have put up for auction. By default it will be filtered to show just those items where the auction is still in progress, or the sale has yet to complete (for example, still awaiting payment or shipping).

However, the user can further refine this filter in a number of ways, for example, to show all listings in a particular state (such as awaiting payment) or all listings regardless of state.

The filter can be further qualified by specifying a time period, for example , to just show the user's listings for the last day, week, month, 90 days, 180 days, or a year.

From here they can choose to view the details of any of these items, as well as:

- Cancel a listing
- Update the status of the item where the sale is still in process (for example, payment received, shipped)

In addition the user may choose to list a new item, or view the status of their account.

List a new item

Once a user has successfully registered with oBay, they are ready to start selling. The first step is to create a listing for the item that they want to sell. To do this, the user will need to enter the following details about the item:

- Category and sub-category
- Title
- Description
- Condition (new or used)
- Confirm accepted payment methods (for example, cheque, cash, credit card, or bank transfer)
- Starting price, plus an optional reserve price
- Auction duration, which can be 1, 3, 7, or 10 days
- An optional start time; if not specified this defaults to an immediate start
- Postage description and cost

Once submitted the system will perform a number of validations on the listing, including a check that:

- Values are specified for all mandatory fields
- The starting price is positive and less than the reserve price (if specified)
- The reserve price is above a pre-determined amount (for example $50)
- The start time, if specified, is in the future

The final part of the validation is to check whether the item being listed meets the criteria for what constitutes an acceptable item; for example the item isn't one that is prohibited by law.

In addition oBay may also decide that certain items do not fit within the morals, beliefs, or spirit of oBay and therefore are also not acceptable; for example tickets for a charity rock concert.

Ideally the system is required to do an initial automated check on the listing to identify potential suspect items. If an item is flagged as suspect then a task will need to be created for an oBay administrator to check whether the item is suitable for sale.

 A key requirement is that the list of prohibited items is likely to be changing continually, and change may be required at very short notice so the solution must be able to cater for this.

Whether an item is acceptable is not always black and white. The solution will need to allow for questionable items to be submitted to a panel who will vote on whether to accept it or not (assuming there is a majority vote then the item will be deemed acceptable).

For valid non-questionable items, the system will calculate the listing fee and return this to the user, who can then confirm whether they wish to proceed with the listing or not. Upon confirmation, the item will be listed immediately, unless a start time has been specified, in which case the item will be held in a queue until the specified start time.

Listing fees are calculated according to the starting price (or reserve price if specified), as shown in the following table:

Starting or reserve price	Listing fee
$0.01 - $0.99	$0.15
$1.00 - $4.99	$0.25
$5.00 - $14.99	$0.40

Starting or reserve price	Listing fee
$15.00 - $29.99	$0.75
$30.00 - $99.99	$1.50
$100.00 or more	$2.00

If the item is suspect, the user will be informed that the listing requires manual vetting before it can be approved for listing. Upon completion of the manual vetting, the user will be informed of the result by email. If the item has been approved, the user will be informed of the listing fee and can then choose whether to proceed with the listing.

Cancel listing

For various reasons a user may want to cancel a listing. However, whether they are permitted to do this will depend on the listing's current status. If the auction has not yet begun, either because it is still waiting approval (due to it being flagged as a suspect item) or it is a scheduled listing, then it can be cancelled and any paid fee will be refunded.

[If the listing was awaiting approval then any outstanding tasks will need to be cancelled automatically.]

However, if the auction has begun, then it can be cancelled up to 12 hours before the end of the auction; unless it has no bids against it. In this case, it can be cancelled any time and the listing fee will not be refunded.

Completing the sale

The auction will end automatically after the specified duration. The user with the highest bid (subject to it meeting the reserve price if specified) will be declared the winner.

Once completed, the listing will proceed through the following steps to complete the sale:

- **Specify shipping details**: The winning bidder will be notified by email and requested to provide details of where the item is to be delivered to as well as any preferences for postage. An email will be sent to the seller containing the shipping details.
- **Invoice buyer**: The seller will invoice the buyer for the winning amount, plus postage. An email will be sent to the buyer containing details of the invoice.

- **Make payment**: The buyer will then be required to pay the seller via a method accepted by the seller (note that this is done outside of oBay). Once done the buyer will update the status of the item to indicate that they have made the payment. An email will be sent to the seller to inform them that the payment has been made.

- **Confirm receipt of payment**: The seller, on receipt of the payment, will update the status of the item accordingly. An email will be sent to the buyer to inform them that the seller has received the payment.

- **Ship item**: After receiving payment the seller will pack and ship the item to the buyer; again they will update the status of the item to indicate that it has been shipped. An email will be sent to the buyer to inform them that the item has been dispatched.

- **Receive item**: Upon receipt of the item, the buyer will record the fact that they have received the item. An email will be sent to the seller to inform them that it has been received.

Upon successful completion of the sale, a seller's fee, based on the final price as set out in the following table, will be charged to the seller's account.

Sale price	Seller's fee
$0.01 - $50.00	5% of the sale price
$50.01 - $1000.00	$1.00 plus 3% of the sale price
More than $1000.00	$16.00 plus 1.5% of the sale price

If there are no bids or the reserve price isn't met, the auction will just finish without a winner. In this case a seller's fee will not be charged to the seller's account.

View account

Whenever a user lists an item they will be charged a listing fee. Upon successful sale of an item, they will be charged a seller's fee, based on the actual sale price.

Each of these charges will be billed against the user's oBay account, then on a monthly basis oBay will automatically charge the user's credit card for the outstanding amount.

Buying items

When a user goes to their buyer's page, it will list all the items on which they have placed a bid. By default it will be filtered to show just those items where the auction is still in progress, but they will be able to view items on which they bid but lost.

From here the user can choose to view the details of the item, as well as place a bid if the auction is still in progress.

In addition, it will show those items that they have successfully won. By default it will only show those items where the sale is still in progress (for example, still awaiting payment or shipping). The user can further refine this by listing all items in a particular state (for example, awaiting payment) or all items regardless of state.

The filter can be further qualified by specifying a time period, for example, to just show the user's listings for the last week, month, 90 days, 180 days, or a year.

From here they can choose to view the details of any of these items, as well as perform outstanding tasks on open items (for example, specify shipping details, confirm receipt of item).

In addition, the user may choose to search for a new item on which to bid.

Search for items

The first step in bidding for an item is to find something that you're interested in. oBay will provide buyers with the ability to search for items listed on oBay. The user will be able to search on a combination of Category, Sub-category, Title, and Condition.

The search will return all items that match the criteria, which will be displayed 10 items at a time.

Bidding on items

Once a user has found an item of interest, they can view all details of it, including existing bids. They can then choose whether to place a bid.

 The system will also ensure that a user can't bid on their own items.

oBay uses an auction format which lets a user bid the maximum amount they currently want to go up to. However, their bid will only be increased by a sufficient amount required to beat the current winning bid.

When the first bid is placed, it must be at least equal to the starting price set by the seller. However, regardless of the amount actually bid, the current winning bid will be equal to the starting price of the item.

After this, any future bids must be at least equal to the current winning bid plus one bidding increment, where the bidding increment is determined by the amount of the current winning bid as shown in the following table:

Current winning bid	Bidding increment
$0.00 to $1.00	$0.05
$1.01 to $5.00	$0.25
$5.01 to $10.00	$0.50
$10.01 to $50.00	$2.50
$50.01 to $100.00	$5.00
$100.01 to $500.00	$25.00
$500.01 to $1000.00	$50.00
and so on	

When a new bid is placed, oBay determines the winning bid by comparing the **maximum amount** of the current winning bid with the new bid; whichever is highest is determined to be the winner. However, the amount of the winning bid is determined by adding one bidding increment to the maximum amount of the losing bid.

If the calculated winning bid is greater than the maximum bid of the winning bid, then the winning bid is set equal to the maximum bid.

In the event of a tie, whoever placed the bid first is deemed to have the winning bid and the winning bid is set to their maximum bid amount.

At first glance this might sound quite complicated, so let's look at an example to clarify. If the minimum amount set by the seller is $1.00, then the winning bid would be worked out as follows:

1. If Bidder A places a bid of $7.00, then they would currently have a winning bid of $1.00.

2. If Bidder B then bids $3.00, Bidder A would still have the winning bid, but it would now be $3.25 (Bidder B's maximum bid plus one bidding increment).

3. If Bidder B then bids $6.99, Bidder A would still have the winning bid, but now it would be $7.00.

If it had have gone up by a full bidding increment it would now be $7.49, but the maximum bid of Bidder A is $7.00.

4. Finally, if Bidder B bids $10.00 then they would now be the winning bidder, with a winning bid of $7.50.

Upon placing a bid the user will be informed if they have been successful or not and the amount of the current winning bid. If successful, the previous highest bidder will be emailed to inform them that they have been outbid.

On completion of the auction, the winning bidder will be notified by email and requested to provide shipping details and any preferences on postage. Once provided they will subsequently receive an invoice from the seller, confirming the amount to pay (that is the winning price plus shipping and packing costs) and instructions on how to pay it.

Once paid, the buyer should notify the seller that they have made the payment. Once the seller has received the payments, they will then ship the item to the buyer.

Upon receipt of the item, the buyer should then notify that they have received the item.

Defining our blueprint for SOA

Before we leap in and start building our service-oriented solution, let's take a moment to understand why we would want to do this. After all, we could build this application using a standard web-based architecture using tools such as Java or .NET.

We will use this section to remind ourselves of the goals we are trying to achieve, as well as to discuss the basic concepts of SOA. We then look at how we can bring this together to define a blueprint for a typical SOA architecture which we can use to architect our oBay application.

Architecture goals

The core goals of SOA can typically be summarized as:

- **Improved interoperability**: A major cost of any project is the effort required to integrate an application with existing applications both inside and outside the enterprise.

The use of standards-based communication frameworks (for example, web services); a standard representation for the exchange of data and common design standards can greatly simplify the integration between disparate systems, greatly reducing the cost of cross application integration.

- **Improved reuse**: Designing and building services to be intrinsically reusable enables you to not just meet initial requirements but also leverage them in future applications. Similarly, you can service enable existing systems which enables you to further leverage existing investments.

  This not only saves you the time and effort of rebuilding similar functionality, but can also help consolidate your IT estate, as now you only need to implement a piece of functionality once, as opposed to having similar functionality buried in multiple systems. This can help reduce the cost of administering and maintaining your existing systems (on which approximately 80% of today's IT budget is spent).

- **Improved agility**: One of the key design principals behind SOA is that systems are no longer built to last, but rather built to change.

  Following SOA principals, not only allows you to more rapidly implement new solutions through reusing existing functionality, but also enables you to reduce the time it takes to modify and adapt existing SOA based solutions in response to ever changing business requirements.

Using SOA standards and technologies will take you **part of the way** towards achieving some of these goals, but as the A in SOA indicates, a key component of this is architecture.

Typical SOA architecture

Up to now we've been throwing around the term "SOA" without really spending much time looking at what a service is, or at least what a well-designed service looks like or how we should go about assembling them into an overall solution, that is the architecture of our application.

The simple reality is that services come in all shapes and sizes, each of which have some bearing on how you design, build and use them within your overall architecture. So it makes sense to further define the different types of services that we will need, how they should be used, how they should be organized into different layers, and so on.

Taking this approach enables us to ensure services are designed, built and used in a consistent fashion, improving the overall interoperability and reusability of a service as well as ensuring the overall implementation is architected in such a way to address key non-functional requirements such as performance, fault tolerance, and security, as well as providing a solution that addresses our other goal of agility.

Now before we do this we should add a **health warning**. There is no single definition as to how you should compose your SOA architecture, but there are many opinions. It is also a pretty big topic in its own right, so we could quite easily dedicate an entire book to this subject alone.

Hence, we offer this up really as an introductory opinion on how you might want to design your overall SOA architecture. Feel free to agree or disagree with parts of it as you see fit. However, what we would stress is that you need to go through the process of defining your architectural approach to SOA and that you continue the process of refining it over time based on the experience and requirements of your organization.

With that caveat out the way, the following diagram illustrates one way of organizing our services into distinct layers within our overall architecture.

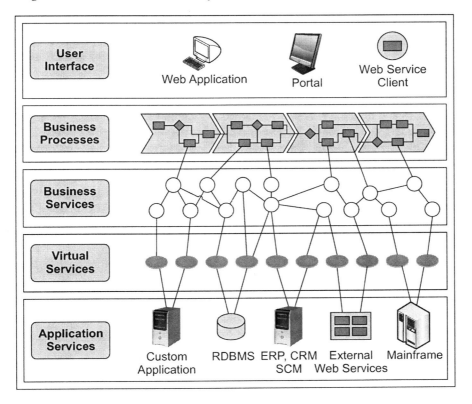

We can see that this breaks into five layers. It should also be apparent that all layers, except the top layer, actually provide a set of services to the layer above and typically do this by building on the layer beneath.

Like most architecture diagrams this is over simplified. For example, it implies here that the **User Interface** layer will always have to go via the **Business Processes** layer to access a **Business Service**. In many circumstances to mandate this as an architecture requirement would be over burdensome, and as a result impair our key goals of reusability and agility.

While we've labelled the top layer **User Interface**, it could potentially be any consumer of our services which sits outside our domain of control, whether internal or external to our organization.

Let's examine these layers one by one, starting at the bottom and working our way up.

Application services layer

When we look at the various layers within a service-oriented architecture, each layer typically builds on the layer below. However, at some point we need to hit the bottom. This is the layer we have termed the **Application Services Layer**. The layer is typically where the core service is actually implemented, or if you like where the *real* work happens.

We refer to it as the application service layer since most services are typically provided by existing applications. These could be packaged applications, such as Oracle e-Business Suite, Siebel, Peoplesoft, SAP, or custom applications developed in-house using technologies such as Java, C#, Oracle Forms, PL/SQL, and so on.

Many modern day applications are web service enabled, meaning that they provide web services out of the box. For those that aren't then adapters can be used to service enable them (as we have already discussed in Chapter 3 — *Service Enabling Existing Systems*).

The key here is that from our perspective this is the lowest level of granularity that we can go down to, and also the actual control we have over the interface of services at this level is limited or non-existent. This tends to be the case regardless of whether or not we have control of the application that provides the service, as the actual interface provided is often a reflection of the underlying application.

It's for this reason (i.e. lack of control over the service interface) that we also include in this category native web services provided by other third parties, for example services provided by partners, suppliers, customers, and so on as well as **software as a service (SaaS)**.

Virtual services layer

This is a relatively thin layer that provides a façade on top of the Application Services layer. The key driver here is to achieve our goal of de-coupling the services provided by the underlying applications (over which we have varying degrees of control) from any consumers of that service.

The simplest way to illustrate the **criticality** of this layer is to demonstrate the potential impacts of trying to bypass it, which during the pressure of a development lifecycle can be easily done (and often is).

A typical scenario is where a developer or architect will argue that it's only used in one place, and it's unlikely to change for a long time anyway, or we need to do it this way for performance reasons, and so on. And often it is the case that the **FIRST** time you use something it is only being used in one place. The trouble is that before long you may find it being used in many places (and often you don't always know where).

Then change happens. It may initially be a simple change, for example it may be just moving the application to a bigger box (as the amount of requests it is now processing has increased). Or the actual application itself may be changing. Maybe it's being upgraded to a new version, or maybe it's being replaced with a completely new application.

Either way the WSDL for the service is likely to change, requiring every caller of that service to be modified, tested and redeployed, and of course this needs to be coordinated across all users of that service.

This becomes even more complicated when you have multiple changes in the same time frame. You could very quickly end up with 100's of 1000's of changes to implement and coordinate. Suddenly change becomes very complicated and our systems far from agile.

As we mentioned earlier, the job of this layer is to provide a virtual service layer to decouple consumers of services from the underlying application and thus minimize the impact of change. It achieves this in two ways—first it provides a virtual endpoint for the client to call. Upon receipt of a request it then routes it to the underlying application service.

Secondly, it allows us to define an abstract description of the service, that is the operations provided by the service and its corresponding input and output messages, so that these are no longer dictated by the underlying application. This layer is then responsible for transforming an incoming input message from the format of our service contract to the one expected by the application service and vice versa for any response.

Business services layer

As the name suggests, this is a fairly generic term used to describe encapsulated business logic that is made available through a **designed** service contract. The keyword here is "designed". In particular, when it comes to exchanging data models, as each service will typically share a common data model defined in one or more XML Schemas. This is often referred to as the canonical model and is something we will look at in a lot more detail in the next chapter (Chapter 10 — *Designing the Service Contract*).

One of the implications of this is a virtual service, as discussed in the previous layer, which is in reality a specialized type of business service. As we will see in a moment that a business process is also a specialized type of business service. However, each of these has a specific role, and tends to gravitate towards a specific layer.

This still leaves us with a rather large category for all our remaining services, so from a design perspective it makes sense to break these down further into specific sub-categories.

There are many ways and many opinions on how exactly business services should be categorized. From a personal standpoint, we believe that there are two key perspectives to consider, the first being to look at the **type of functionality** contained within the service as this will guide how we may wish to implement the service. The second is to consider who is going to call or **consume the service**, in particular where they sit within our layered architecture as this will often drive other considerations such as granularity, security, and so on.

Functional type

Our first category is the type of functionality provided by a service. We've split this into three groups: Entity, Functional, and Task based service. Let's examine each of these in more detail:

- **Entity services**: It is also known as data services, emulate business objects within an enterprise. For example User, Account, and Listing are all entities within oBay. Entity services often represent data entities held in a relational database and provide the corresponding lifecycle (i.e. create, read, update, and delete) and query operations.

  Entity services can often be used within multiple contexts, making them excellent candidates for reuse. To further promote this, it is considered good practice to minimize any business specific logic (such as validation) that you place within the service.

The one draw back here is that you wouldn't want to expose an Entity service directly to the presentation layer or any external third party service; rather you would use it within a task based service or business process.

- **Functional services**: These are used to implement raw business logic, for example business rules, pricing algorithms, and so on. It is quite common to embed rules directly within task based (or even entity) services, often leading to the same rule being implemented in multiple locations and not always consistently.

  By separating out this logic as a standalone service, you not only ensure it's used in a consistent fashion, but also make it simpler to modify (i.e. you only have to do it once), thus increasing the agility of your solution.

  Functional services typically don't use entity services (except maybe to look-up reference values used by the algorithm). If you have a functional service that does, then in reality you have a task based service with functional logic embedded within it.

  In many cases this may be fine. However, it will limit how reusable the service is and could result in the same functionality being reimplemented in other task based services.

- **Task based services**: These are modeled to carry out a specific set of related activities, often within the context of a business process. By their nature they will often act across one or more entity services, and may also make use of other task based or functional services.

  For example, if we look at the operation `submitBid`, this would very much form part of a task based `Auction` service as it supports the task of placing a bid. However, it is likely to use an Entity Service to store the received bid in the underlying database and it may use a Functional Service (i.e. `AuctionEngine`) to calculate the result of placing the bid.

Service consumer

A key design point that needs considering is who will be consuming our business services? It could be other business services, business processes, or an external consumer such as the user interface layer, partners, or other parts of the organization, though a service could potentially be called by all types of consumers.

Knowing who will call a service will impact areas such as service granularity, validation, and security.

Granularity is a key consideration in service design. Current industry wisdom tends to encourage the use of more coarse grained services, but it's important to understand why when considering the granularity of an individual service.

Granularity is essentially the number of operations we need to call on a service in order to achieve the desired result. The more fine grained a service is, the more operations you will typically need to call, the more coarse grained the less.

The key driver for coarse grained services is the performance impact of going across a network. Thus, if you can achieve the desired result by calling a coarse grained service, as opposed to calling for example four fine grained services, then it is likely to be approximately four times faster. Because the actual processing time of the service is likely to be insignificant in comparison to the cost of going across the network.

However, using coarse grained services often come at a price; if you combine multiple functions into a single operation, it may becomes less useable as requestors may be required to provide additional data to use the service, or the service could result in unwanted side effects. Additionally, it may impose redundant processing on the server side which could adversely impact performance. For example, it may cause the service to make unnecessary reads to a database, or make calls to additional services across the network, each with resultant implications on overall performance.

The other consideration is that if a service is calling another service within the same environment (for example, with the same deployment of the SOA Suite), then the call is likely to be optimized and to not require a network hop.

Understanding where the service consumer lives in relation to the service is a key design consideration. So when deciding on service granularity it's worth bearing the following guidelines in mind:

- For business services that are only going to be consumed by either business processes or other business services (for example, Entity Services and Functional Services), then you can afford to use finer grained services.

- If a service is to be used outside the domain of control, then coarse grained services are more appropriate, though you should consider the downstream performance implications of any redundant processing.

- When providing coarse grained services, if there are potential impacts on either performance or reuse then consider providing a number of redundant fine grained services in addition to the coarse grained services. Effectively by de-normalizing the service contract, it gives the consumer the ability to choose the appropriate service.

In addition, depending on the nature of the service consumer, you may need to place other requirements on a service, such as:

- **Security**: As with all IT systems security is key, but more so if you start using SOA to expose your systems via web services to external third party consumers.
- **Management**: Many third party consumers will want to agree some sort of service level agreement; you need to ensure you have sufficient infrastructure in place to manage your services appropriately.
- **Support**: When exposing services to third parties you need to consider how they are going to build systems that use them, i.e. what level of documentation you are going to provide, who do they call when something goes wrong, and so on.
- **Change management**: When services change, how are you going to manage that? Depending on who the consumer is, you may be able to coordinate any upgrades with them; however, that won't always be the case.
- **Validation**: The less control you have over the consumer of a service, then generally the less assumptions you can make about the quality of data you will receive and the more validation that will be required.

Typically service management and security is not something you build into individual services, rather it tends to be provided by the underlying infrastructure in which you host the service (something we look at in more detail in Chapter 20—*Defining Security and Management Policies*).

Support is more of an organizational issue, as is change management to a certain extent. However, design of the service contract is key to making change more manageable and something we look at in detail in the next chapter (Chapter 10—*Designing the Service Contract*).

Finally validation is an important consideration in design, and something we look at in more detail in Chapter 12—*Building Validation into Services*.

Business process

As we've already mentioned, you could argue that a business process is no more than just a specialized Business Service, especially when viewed through the eyes of the service consumer. However, it has a number of key differences that make it worth considering as a separate layer in its own right.

Before we look at why, lets take a step back. If we look at the traditional application architecture which splits out an application into its presentation layer, business logic and database layer, within that business logic, it is the business process that is more likely to change.

A business process is more likely to span multiple systems, which has led to the proliferation of point-to-point integration solutions, aimed at tying those bits of process together into an end-to-end business process. This can further obfuscate the business process, as a result making it more resistant to change.

Abstracting out business process into a separate layer gives us a number of advantages. Firstly, rather than having the process logic buried across multiple applications, we can now define a single end-to-end process with a far higher level of visibility and clarity than would normally be achievable. This makes it far simpler to monitor the end-to-end process, as well as to modify it in the future.

It also simplifies our underlying business services, since by extracting the business process specific logic from them, they naturally become more generic and therefore more reusable.

Another by-product is that since processes are long running in nature, whether for minutes, hours, days, months, or even years, they are inherently stateful. Thus, it often removes the need for other services to manage state, again simplifying them as well as making them more reusable.

It is currently deemed best practice to make services stateless, since stateless architectures are typically more scalable (or at least easier to scale) than stateful ones. In addition stateless services tend to be simpler to build and use, making them more reusable.

While to a certain extent this is true, you could argue that up until recently many of the WS-* standards and corresponding vendor tools have not had the required completeness of functionality to support stateful services. This is now starting to change, so going forward there is likely to be more of a mix of stateless and stateful services within SOA.

User Interface layer

As the top layer within our architecture, this is the layer which consumes the services provided by the Business Processes and Business Services layers. We have labelled this the User Interface layer, mainly because we are using our SOA architecture as the blueprint for building a composite application and this is the layer where the GUI (either web-based or thick client) would sit.

For the purpose of this book, we will not spend much time looking at this layer, as it falls outside the boundary of what is provided by the Oracle SOA Suite. Though for the purpose of delivering a fully working application we have provided a simple web-based user interface developed using JDeveloper.

The reality is that many users of the SOA Suite continue to develop the GUI component of an application using their technology of choice, as in most cases it dovetails very nicely with a SOA based approach.

> Many user interfaces are based on variations of the **Model-View-Controller (MVC)** design pattern. The Model represents the business logic and data of an application and defines a set of operations that can be performed against it.
>
> The **View** is the user interface (for example, web page); it presents information from the Model to the user, and then captures actions taken by the user against the view. The Controller maps actions performed on the View (for example, clicking a **Submit** button) to operations on the Model (for example, placing a bid). After the Model is updated, the **View** is refreshed and the user can perform more actions.
>
> This approach fits extremely well within the context of SOA, where the Model is effectively provided by the Business Process and Business Service layers. The View and Controller can then be implemented using your GUI framework of choice (for example Oracle ADF, Spring, or Struts). The Controller would then provide the integration between the two, with it invoking the appropriate operations on the underlying services.

One additional layer

While we have focused on the user interface being the top layer within our architecture, the reality is that these services could be consumed by applications built by other parts of the organization, or those of our partners or customers.

If these consumers are using the same architecture as us, they would view our services in the same way as we are viewing external web services within the Application Services layer of our architecture.

This implies the need to have an additional Virtual Services layer in our model, between the User Interface and Business Process layer. We could rely on the consumer of our services to build this layer, but it actually makes a lot of sense for us to provide it.

Remember that the goal of our original Virtual Services layer was to de-couple our composite application from the underlying services provided by the Application Services layer, so that we can insulate ourselves from changes to the underlying applications.

Here is the reverse. We want to de-couple the services we are providing from the consumers of those services, as this gives us greater flexibility to change our services without being constrained by the consumer of our services.

This layer also provides a suitable point of control for managing access to our services enabling us to define, enforce, and monitor polices for security and service level agreements.

With this additional layer, our SOA architecture now looks as follows:

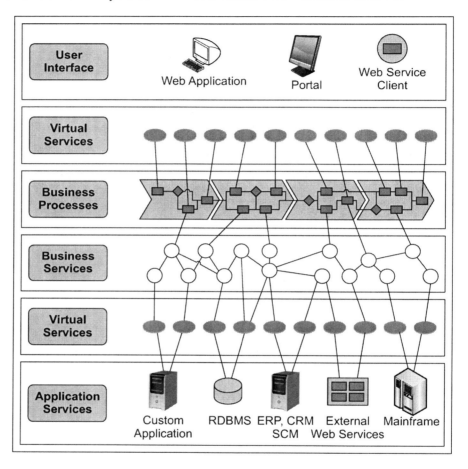

Where the SOA Suite fits

You may have noticed, we have deliberately stayed clear of saying which parts of the Oracle SOA Suite are used for which areas within our architecture, and there is a good reason for this. Firstly, we wanted to produce a meaningful architecture that clearly demonstrated the key objectives and consideration of each layer, rather than just a piece of marketecture.

Secondly, it's not a simple one-to-one mapping, as many of the components can be used within multiple layers within the architecture and within most layers you have the luxury of choosing between multiple components. The following is a guide as to which technologies can be used where within our architecture:

- **Application Services layer**: This layer is pretty straightforward, in that if the application doesn't provide in-built support for web services, then it is the case of using the appropriate adapter to hook into the underlying application.

- **Virtual Services layer**: The Service Bus should be your default starting point for this layer, as it has been designed to address the specific challenges tackled by this layer of our architecture.

  BPEL PM provides an alternative to the Service Bus. While not as optimized for this layer, it does provide a valid substitute in some scenarios. For example, the implementation of two-way asynchronous services.

- **Business Services layer**: BPEL is typically used for task based services, as it provides a rich language for building composite services, with human workflow being used for manual tasks. However, the Service Bus is also a good choice for building light weight synchronous services.

  Business Rules provide an excellent tool for implementing functional services, as well as the validation within task based services.

- **Business Processes layer**: This layer, as you've no doubt already realized, is the natural domain for BPEL. However, Business Rules also plays an important role in allowing you to externalize the logic behind decision points within your process.

Business Activity Monitoring is then used to instrument your business processes and any other relevant services, in order to provide you with a holistic view across your application.

Finally Web Services Manager is used to define, enforce, and monitor polices across your services around security, service level agreements, logging, and so on.

Oracle Service Bus has the concepts of Proxy service and Business service. Within our terminology, a Proxy Service maps to a Virtual Service. However, an OSB Business service maps to what we have termed an Application service.

We realize this could be confusing and did consider changing our terminology to match. However, we have tried to base our architecture on accepted industry practice and terminology. So believed it was better to keep with this terminology rather than modify if to fit with the naming of specific products.

oBay high-level architecture

Now that we have our blueprint for SOA, let's apply it to the business requirements of oBay. Doing this we come up with the following high-level architecture.

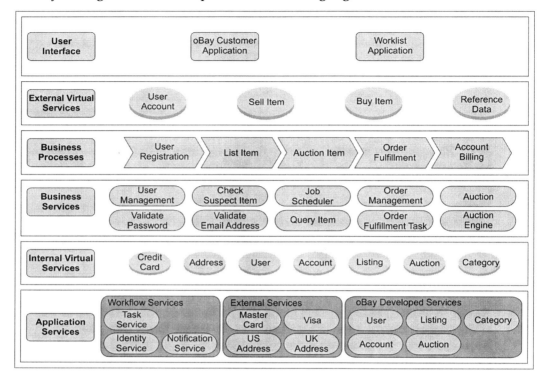

We won't go into this in detail at this point (as we do that in the remainder of this section), but it's worth looking at each layer and highlighting a few significant features.

oBay Application services

As you will see from the above diagram, we have broken out our Application Services into three categories:

- oBay Developed Services
- External Web Services
- Workflow Services

Each of these raises some interesting points, which we will examine in further sections.

Workflow services

The Task, Identity, and Notification services are a subset of the services provided out of the box by the Oracle SOA Suite. Because we typically access these services via the **Human Task** activity within BPEL, it is easy to overlook their very existence.

The workflow services have documented API's, so can be invoked just like any other web service. We take advantage of these APIs to build the Order Management business service and look at how to do this as part of Chapter 15 — *Workflow Patterns*.

External web services

oBay makes use of a number of real world web services; we look at how to include these within our overall solution in Chapter 11 — *Building Business Services*.

Another key consideration when using external web services is what happens if they fail. We look at this as part of Chapter 13 — *Error Handling*.

oBay developed services

As oBay is a start-up, it has rather limited applications in-house, so we are going to build most of these services from scratch. The great thing about SOA is that we can actually build these application services using whichever technology is appropriate to our organization.

To demonstrate this we've examined how these services could be implemented using a number of alternative technologies, namely Java and PL/SQL. We will cover this in detail in Chapter 11 — *Building Business Services*.

oBay internal virtual services

All of our oBay developed application services have a straight one-to-one mapping with a corresponding virtual service. This is quite common when developing the underlying application services as part of the overall implementation.

When exposing functionality from existing systems, this won't always be the case. For example, you may have multiple systems performing the same function. In this scenario multiple application services would map to a single virtual service, which would be responsible for routing requests to the appropriate system. This is the case for our external services, where we have multiple services for address and credit card services.

In Chapter 11 — *Building Business Services*, we cover both use cases, as we look at how to build business services either from scratch or by reusing existing logic.

oBay business services

At first glance this looks pretty unremarkable; however, there are a few areas worth further scrutiny. Many of the task based services, such as `UserManagement`, are built using one or more entity services and do little more than layer validation on top. We examine this approach in Chapter 12—*Building Validation into Services*.

A number of the task based services (for example `check Suspect Item` and `Order Fulfillment Task`) are manual in nature and therefore predominately built using the Workflow Service provided by the SOA Suite. In Chapter 15—*Workflow Patterns*, we look at why we have separated them out as separate business services, rather than embedding them directly within the core business processes.

Finally the Auction Engine is an interesting example of a functional service. One way to implement this would be to write it using a standard programming language such as Java or C#. However, an alternative is to use Business Rules. We will look at this in Chapter 16—*Using Business Rules to Implement Services* and examine some of the advantages and disadvantages to this approach.

oBay business processes

Effectively within oBay there are two key business processes: registering a customer and the end-to-end process of listing an item and selling it through auction. The, second of which we've split up into three sub-processes (for the purpose of reusability and agility should oBay change or extend its core business model at any point in the future).

It is also worth examining the `Account Billing` process; all our other processes are initiated to handle a specific request (for example, register a user, list an item for auction), while this is a scheduled process, which we will run nightly to settle the account of all users with outstanding monies. We examine how we do this in Chapter 14—*Message Interaction Patterns*.

oBay user interface

Here we've defined two user interfaces, where one is for oBay customers which we've built using JDeveloper and the other is for oBay employees who need to perform human workflow tasks.

Both sets of users will be performing human workflow tasks, one via the out-of-the-box worklist application, the other through our own hand cranked GUI. We will look at how to do this in Chapter 15—*Workflow Patterns*.

Downloading and installing oBay application

To download this application, go to the support page of Packt Publishing (www.packtpub.com/support), and from here, follow the instructions to download the code for this book, which includes the oBay application.

Included with the code will be a PDF with detailed instructions on how to install and run the oBay application.

Summary

In this chapter, we've provided you with a detailed introduction as to the business requirements of oBay, our fictional online auction site, as well as presenting you with the architecture for our composite application.

Before we developed our solution, we took you through the process of defining our high level SOA blueprint, outlining some of the objectives and considerations you should take into account when developing a SOA based architecture.

Along the way we've also thrown up a number of questions or issues that need to be addressed, as well as highlighting particular areas of interest in our overall design.

In the remainder of this section, each chapter will focus on addressing a particular subset of those issues raised, using various parts of the oBay application to illustrate each answer. This is so that by the end of this section we will have tackled all the matters that we've raised including the key question:

> *What is the best way to combine/use all of these different components to implement a real world SOA solution?*

As you are no doubt already realizing from this chapter, there isn't a single simple answer, but rather you have many choices, each with their own set of advantages and disadvantages. By the end of this section you should at least be in a position to better understand those choices and which ones are more applicable to you and that of your own development.

10
Designing the Service Contract

Service contracts provide the glue that enable us to assemble together disparate pieces of software or services into complete composite applications. If we are to build a sustainable solution, that is, one that will achieve our goals of improved agility, reuse, and interoperability then careful design of the service contract is crucial.

The contract of a web service is made up of the following technical components:

- WSDL definition: This defines the various operations which constitute a service, their input and output parameters, and the protocols (bindings) it supports.

- XML Schema Definition (XSD): Either embedded within the WSDL definition or referenced as a standalone component, this defines the XML elements and types which constitute the input and output parameters.

- WS-Policy definition: An optional component, which describes the service's security constraints, quality of service, and so on.

Additionally the service contract may be supported by a number of non-technical documents, which define areas such as Service-level agreements and Support.

From a contract design perspective, we are primarily interested in defining the XML Schema and the WSDL definition of the service. This chapter gives guidance on best practice in the design of these components as well as providing strategies for managing change when it occurs. We leave the discussion on defining security and management policies until Chapter 20.

Using XML Schema to define business objects

Each business service acts upon one or more business objects. Within SOA the data that makes up these objects is represented as XML, with the structure of the XML being defined by one or more XML Schemas. Thus the definition of these schemas forms a key part in defining the overall service contract.

To better facilitate the exchange of data between services, as well as achieve better reusability, it is good practice to define a common data model, often referred to as the *canonical data model* which is used by all services.

As well as defining the structure of data exchanged between components, XML is also used in all components of the SOA Suite. For example it defines the structure of variables in BPEL, provides the vocabulary for writing business rules and transforming data via XSLT. So it is important that our XML model is well thought out and designed.

Modelling data in XML

When designing your XML data model, a typical starting point is to base it on an existing data model, such as a database schema, UML model, or EDI document.

While this is a perfectly legitimate way to identify your data elements, the crucial point in this approach is how you make the transition from your existing model to an XML model. Too often the structure of the existing model is directly replicated in the XML model, often resulting in poor design.

Data decomposition

To produce an effective model for XML, it's worth taking a step back to examine the core components which make up an XML document. Consider the following XML fragment:

```
<order>
  <orderNo>123456</orderNo>
  ...
    <shipTo>
       <name>
       <title>Mr</title>
       <firstName>James</firstName>
       <lastName>Elliot</lastName>
       </name>
       <address>
```

```
        <addressLine1>7 Pine Drive</addressLine1>
        <addressLine2></addressLine2>
    <city>Eltham<city>
    <state>VIC</state>
        <zip>3088</zip>
        <country>Australia</country>
    </address>
  </shipTo>
</order>
```

If we pull out the raw data from this we would end up with:

```
123456 Mr, James, Elliot, 7 Pine Drive, , Eltham, VIC, 3088.
Australia.
```

By doing this we have greatly reduced our understanding of the data. XML, through the use of tags, gives meaning to the data, with each tag describing the content of the data it contains. Now this may seem an obvious point, but too often by failing to sufficiently decompose our data model we are doing exactly this, albeit within an XML wrapper. For example, another way of modelling the above piece of XML is as follows:

```
<order>
  <orderNo>123456</orderNo>
  ...
  <shipTo>
      <name>Mr James Elliot</name>
      <address>7 Pine Drive, Eltham, VIC, 3088, Australia</address>
  </shipTo>
</order>
```

With this approach, we have again reduced our understanding of the data. So you should always look to decompose your data to the appropriate level of granularity; and if in doubt go for the more granular model as it's a lot simpler to convert data held in a granular model to a less granular model than the other way round.

Data hierarchy

Another key component of our data model is the relationship between the different elements of data, which is defined by the composition or hierarchy of the data. If from our example fragment we take the element `<city>Eltham<city>`, on its own it does not signify much, as we have provided insufficient context to the data.

However, when we take it in the context of `<order><shipTo><address><city>`, we have a far clearer understanding of the data.

A common mistake is to use a flat structure, and then name the elements to compensate for this, for example changing the name to `<order_shipTo_address_city>`. While this provides more context than just `<city>`, it introduces a whole set of other problems including:

- It makes your XML far harder to read, as well as more bloated.
- The relationships are no longer visible to your XML parser. This makes XPath manipulation, XSLT mappings, and so on a lot more complex and onerous.
- It reduces the opportunity for reuse, for example each address element will have to be redefined for every single context in which it is used. This is likely to lead to inconsistent definitions as well as make change harder to manage.

If you see elements named in this fashion, e.g. `<a_b_c>`, `<a_b_d>`, it's a pretty good clue that the schema has been poorly designed.

Data semantics

Another key of our data model is the semantics of our data. Looking at the above example, it is obvious what the `<state>` element contains, but not as obvious as to the exact format of that data, that is it could be Victoria, VIC, Vic, 0, and so on.

While different target systems will have different requirements, it is important that a set of semantics are agreed for the canonical model, so that these differences can be isolated in the Virtual Services layer.

While semantics can be enforced within our XML Schema through the use of facets such as `enumeration`, `length`, `pattern`, this is not always the best approach. This is an area that we will examine in more detail in Chapter 12—*Building Validation into Services*.

Use attributes for metadata

A common debate is when to model XML data using elements and when to use attributes, or whether attributes should be used at all.

Elements are more flexible than attributes, particularly when it comes to writing extensible schemas, since you can always add additional elements (or attributes) to an element; however once an attribute has been defined it can't be extended any further.

One approach is to use attributes for metadata and elements for data. For example, on some of our query based operations (for example `getSellerItems`, `getBuyerItems`) we have defined two attributes `startRow` and `endRow` which are used to control which portion of the result set is returned by the query.

Schema guidelines

It is important to have a clear set of guidelines for schema design, this not only warrants that best practices is followed, but it also ensures schemas are created consistently making them more reusable, easier to combine, simpler to understand, as well as easier to maintain.

Element naming

Consistent naming of elements within an XML Schema will ensure that schemas are easier to understand, as well as reducing the likelihood of error due to names being misspelt (or spelt differently) within a different context.

Name length

While there is no theoretical limit on the length of an element or attribute name, you should try to limit them to a manageable length. This is because overly long names can reduce the readability of a document as well as making them overly bloated, which in extreme cases could have performance implications.

We tend to try to limit names to a maximum of 15 characters; this may not always be possible but there are a number of simple strategies that can be adopted to help achieve this.

Compound names

For element and attribute names that are made up of multiple words, we follow the practice of capitalizing the first letter of each word (often called *camel* case). For example, we would write the name 'shipping address' as `shippingAddress`.

Another approach is to use a separator, that is a hyphen or an underscore between words; personally we don't find this as readable as well as resulting in marginally longer names. Whichever approach you use, you should ensure that you do so consistently.

For types (that is, `complexType` and `simpleType`), we follow the same convention but prefix the name with a `'t'` in order that we can easily distinguish it from elements and attributes.

Naming standards

We also recommend the use of a defined dictionary for commonly used words, abbreviations, and so on to ensure that they are used in a consistent fashion. Areas that should be considered include:

- **Synonyms**: For names that have multiple potential options, for example Order and Purchase Order, the dictionary should define the standard term to be used.

- **Abbreviations**: For words that are used commonly, it makes sense to define standard abbreviations, for example we may use `address` on its own but when combined with another word (for example, shipping), we use its abbreviation to get `shippingAddr`.

- **Context based names**: When a name is used in context, don't repeat the context in the name itself. For example, rather than use `addressLine1`, when used inside an `address` element we would use `line1`.

  Note, in some cases this is not always pragmatic, in particular if it reduces clarity in the meaning of the element. For example, if within the context of name you have the element `family`, then this is not as clear as using `familyName`. So a degree of common sense should be used.

- **Generic names**: As far as reasonable, use generic names, for example, avoid using specific company or product names; this will result in more reusable models and also reduce the likelihood of change.

A sample of the oBay dictionary is shown as follows:

Standard term	Abbreviaton	Synonyms
address	addr	
amount	amt	cost, price, fee
description	desc	
end	end	finish, stop
id	id	number, identifier
item	item	product
max	max	ceiling, maximum, top
min	min	least, lowest, minimum
order	ord	purchase order
start	start	effective, begin
status	status	state
user	usr	client, customer

Namespace considerations

Namespaces are one of the biggest areas of confusion with XML Schemas, yet in reality they are very straightforward. The purpose of a namespace is just to provide a unique name for an element, type or attribute, allowing us to define components with the same name.

For example the element `Glass`, will have a different definition to a company that sells windows as opposed to one that runs a bar. The namespace allows us to uniquely identify each definition, so that we can use both definitions within the same instance of an XML document, as well as understand the context in which each element is being used.

 If you're familiar with Java, then a namespace is a bit like a package, name, that is, you can have multiple classes with the same name, but each one would be defined in a separate package.

One feature of namespaces is that they have a degree of flexibility in how you apply them, which then impacts how you construct and interpret an instance of an XML document. This is often the cause of confusion, especially when they are used inconsistently across multiple schemas.

So it's critical that you define a standard approach to namespaces before defining your canonical model.

Always specify a target namespace

Unless you are defining a chameleon schema (see next section) always specify a target namespace.

Default namespace

When defining a schema you have the option of defining a default namespace. If you do, we would recommend setting the default namespace to be equal to the target namespace. The advantage of this approach is that you only prefix elements, types, and attributes which are defined externally to the schema (that is anything that is not pre-fixed is defined locally).

 An alternative approach is not use to use a default namespace, so that all elements require a prefix. This can often be clearer when combining many schemas from multiple namespaces, especially if you have similarly named elements.

Qualified or unqualified element names

When constructing an XML instance based on an XML Schema we have the option as the schema designer to decide whether each element should be qualified, that is, have a prefix which identifies the namespace of where the element is defined. Or have no prefix, that is, it is unqualified and the origin of the namespace is hidden within the instance.

The approach you take is often a question of style; however, each has its own advantages and disadvantages, particularly when you create XML instances that are defined across multiple namespaces. Take the schema definition for the element `<address>`, shown as follows:

```
<xsd:schema xmlns:xsd="http://www.w3.org/2001/XMLSchema"
            xmlns="http://xmlns.packtpub.com/obay/cmn"
            targetNamespace="http://xmlns.packtpub.com/obay/cmn"
            elementFormDefault="qualified or unqualified" >

    <xsd:element name="address" type="tAddress"/>

    <xsd:complexType name="tAddress">
        <xsd:sequence>
            <xsd:element name="addressLine1"  type="xsd:string"/>
            <xsd:element name="addressLine2"  type="xsd:string"/>
            <xsd:element name="city"          type="xsd:string"/>
            <xsd:element name="state"         type="xsd:string"/>
            <xsd:element name="zip"           type="xsd:string"/>
            <xsd:element name="country"       type="xsd:string"/>
        </xsd:sequence>
    </xsd:complexType>

</xsd:schema>
```

If we chose **unqualified** elements, then an instance of this schema would look like:

```
<cmn:address xmlns:cmn="http://xmlns.packtpub.com/obay/core">
    <addressLine1>7 Pine Drive</addressLine1>
    <addressLine2></addressLine2>
    <city>Eltham<city>
    <state>VIC</state>
    <zip>3088</zip>
    <country>Australia</country>
</cmn:address>
```

However if we chose to use **qualified** elements, our XML instance would now appear as follows:

```
<cmn:address xmlns:cmn="http://xmlns.packtpub.com/obay/core">
    <cmn:addressLine1>7 Pine Drive</cmn:addressLine1>
    <cmn:addressLine2></cmn:addressLine2>
    <cmn:city>Eltham<cmn:city>
    <cmn:state>VIC</cmn:state>
    <cmn:zip>3088</cmn:zip>
    <cmn:country>Australia</cmn:country>
</cmn:address>
```

With unqualified namespaces, the XML instance loses most of its namespace declarations and prefixes, resulting in a slimmed down and simpler XML instance hiding the complexities of how the overall schema is assembled.

The advantage of using qualified namespaces is that you can quickly see what namespace an element belongs to. As well as removing any ambiguity, it also provides the context in which an element is defined giving a clearer understanding of its meaning.

Whichever approach you use, it's important to be consistent, since mixing qualified and unqualified schemas will produce instance documents where some elements have a namespace prefix and others don't. This makes it a lot harder to **manually** create or validate an instance document as the author needs to understand all the subtleties of the schemas involved, making this approach more error prone.

Another consideration over which approach to use, is whether you are using local or global element declarations, because unqualified namespaces only apply to local elements. Having a mixture of global elements and local unqualified elements in your schema definition will again produce instance documents where some elements have a namespace prefix and others don't with the same issues mentioned above.

A final consideration is whether you are using default namespaces. If you are, then you should use qualified names as unqualified names and default namespaces don't mix.

As we recommend using both global elements (see next section for why) and default namespaces we would also recommend using qualified namespaces.

Qualified or unqualified attributes

Like elements, XML Schema allows us to choose whether an attribute is qualified or not. Unless an attribute is global, that is declared a child of `schema`, and thus can be used in multiple elements, there is no point in qualifying it.

The simplest way to achieve this is to not specify the `form` and `attributeFormDefault` attributes; this will result in globally declared attributes being prefixed with a namespace and locally declared attributes will have unqualified names.

Namespace prefixes

As part of your naming standards you should also define standard namespace prefixes for each namespace.

Global versus local

A component (element, simple type, or complex type) is considered global if it is defined as a child of the schema element, otherwise, if defined within another component, it's considered local. Consider the following fragment of XML.

```
<shipTo>
<name>
      <title>Mr</title>
      <firstName>James</firstName>
      <lastName>Elliot</lastName>
</name>
<address>
  <addressLine1>7 Pine Drive</addressLine1>
    <addressLine2></addressLine2>
    <city>Eltham<city>
      <state>VIC</state>
    <zip>3088</zip>
  <country>Australia</country>
  </address>
</shipTo>
```

One way of implementing its corresponding schema would be to design it to mirror the XML, for example:

```
<xsd:element name="shipTo">
   <xsd:complexType>
      <xsd:sequence>
         <xsd:element name="name">
            <xsd:complexType>
               <xsd:sequence>
                  <xsd:element name="title"     type="xsd:string"/>
                  <xsd:element name="firstName" type="xsd:string"/>
                  <xsd:element name="lastName"  type="xsd:string"/>
               </xsd:sequence>
            </xsd:complexType>
         </xsd:element>
         <xsd:element name="address">
            <xsd:complexType>
               <xsd:sequence>
                  <xsd:element name="line1"     type="xsd:string"/>
```

```
                        <xsd:element name="line2"     type="xsd:string"/>
                        <xsd:element name="city"      type="xsd:string"/>
                        <xsd:element name="state"     type="xsd:string"/>
                        <xsd:element name="zip"       type="xsd:string"/>
                        <xsd:element name="country"   type="xsd:string"/>
                    </xsd:sequence>
                </xsd:complexType>
            </xsd:element>
        </xsd:sequence>
    </xsd:complexType>
</xsd:element>
```

Using this approach only the shipTo element is declared globally, and thus reusable, that is no other elements or types either within this schema or other schema can make use of the elements or types declared inside the shipTo element.

Another way of defining the schema would be as follows:

```
<xsd:element name="shipTo">
    <xsd:complexType>
        <xsd:sequence>
            <xsd:element ref="name"/>
            <xsd:element ref="address/>
        </xsd:sequence>
    </xsd:complexType>
</xsd:element>

<xsd:element name="name">
    <xsd:complexType>
        <xsd:sequence>
            <xsd:element name="title"     type="xsd:string"/>
            <xsd:element name="firstName" type="xsd:string"/>
            <xsd:element name="lastName"  type="xsd:string"/>
        </xsd:sequence>
    </xsd:complexType>
</xsd:element>

<xsd:element name="address">
    <xsd:complexType>
        <xsd:sequence>
            <xsd:element name="line1"     type="xsd:string"/>
            <xsd:element name="line2"     type="xsd:string"/>
            <xsd:element name="city"      type="xsd:string"/>
            <xsd:element name="state"     type="xsd:string"/>
            <xsd:element name="zip"       type="xsd:string"/>
```

```
            <xsd:element name="country"    type="xsd:string"/>
        </xsd:sequence>
    </xsd:complexType>
</xsd:element>
```

With this approach `shipTo`, `name`, and `address` are globally declared, therefore the elements `name` and `address` are now also reusable.

 You could always go a step further and separately define all the simple types such as title, first name as global elements.

The temptation is may be to define elements you wish to reuse within your schema as global, and have the rest as local definitions. However, you should consider the following points:

- Any element you may wish to use as a parameter for a web service operation must be globally defined.
- BPEL variables can only be declared for global elements not local elements.

Because at the point of schema definition it's not always easy to determine where an element may need to be reused, we would recommend always declaring your components as global.

Elements versus types

A common dilemma is whether to use elements or types to define global components. Types tend to be more flexible, in that once you've defined the type it can be reused to define multiple elements of the same type.

Also once you have defined a type, you can easily use it to define an element. In the example below, we have remodelled the above schema to separately define the types and have then used them to define the elements. As a result we have slightly less lines of XML as well as a more flexible model.

```
<xsd:element name="shipTo" type="tShipTo">

<xsd:complexType name="tShipTo">
    <xsd:sequence>
        <xsd:element ref="name"/>
        <xsd:element ref="address/>
    </xsd:sequence>
</xsd:complexType>

<xsd:element name="name" type="tName">
<xsd:complexType name="tName">
```

```
    <xsd:sequence>
        <xsd:element name="title"     type="xsd:string"/>
        <xsd:element name="firstName" type="xsd:string"/>
        <xsd:element name="lastName"  type="xsd:string"/>
    </xsd:sequence>
</xsd:complexType>

<xsd:element name="address" type="tAddress">

<xsd:complexType name="tAddress">
    <xsd:sequence>
        <xsd:element name="line1"   type="xsd:string"/>
        <xsd:element name="line2"   type="xsd:string"/>
        <xsd:element name="city"    type="xsd:string"/>
        <xsd:element name="state"   type="xsd:string"/>
        <xsd:element name="zip"     type="xsd:string"/>
        <xsd:element name="country" type="xsd:string"/>
    </xsd:sequence>
</xsd:complexType>
```

 With BPEL 1.1, you can only create variables based on global elements, NOT global types.

When reusing components from other namespaces, reference the **element** that is defined against the type (as highlighted above), rather than use the type directly. Otherwise the namespace of the top element will take on the namespace of the schema that is reusing the type.

Finally, we recommend that you use different names for elements and complex types. Although, the XML Schema specification allows for an element and a type to have the same name, this can cause issues for some tools.

For example, the JAXB class generator, which is used by the Rules engine doesn't support elements and types with the same name. For our purposes, we prefix all types with a lower case `t` to indicate that it's a type.

Partitioning the canonical model

When building your first SOA application it's very easy to fall into the trap of defining a single schema that meets the specific needs of your current set of services. However, as each project develops its own schema it will often redesign its own version of common elements. This not only reduces the opportunity for reuse, but makes interoperability between applications more complicated as well as increasing the maintenance burden.

The other common pitfall is to design a single all-encompassing schema that defines all your business objects within an organisation. There are two issues with this approach, first you could end up *boiling the ocean*; that is, as you set out to define every single business object the project never starts because it is waiting for the model to be completed.

Even if you take a more iterative approach, only defining what's required upfront and extending this schema as new applications come online, you very quickly end up with the situation where every application will become dependent on this single schema; change often becomes very protracted as a simple change could potentially impact many applications. The end result is strict change control being required often resulting in protracted time frames for changes to be implemented, not exactly an agile solution.

The approach of course lies somewhere in the middle, and that is to partition your data model into a set of reusable modules, where each module is based on a logical domain. For example in oBay we have defined the following schemas:

- `Account.xsd`: Defines all the business objects specific to a financial account, i.e. a record of all debit and credit activities related to a specific user.
- `Auction.xsd`: Defines all business objects specific to an auction.
- `Listing.xsd`: Defines all business objects specific to the listing of an item.
- `Order.xsd`: Defines all business objects specific to order fulfilment, i.e. from the placement of an order through to its final shipment and delivery.
- `User.xsd`: Defines all business objects specific to a user.
- `Common.xsd`: This schema is used to define common objects, such as name, address, credit card that is used by multiple domains, but where there is no obvious owner.
- `Base.xsd`: This is used to define common simple types that can be re-used within all other schemas, such as currency and country codes.

Once we have partitioned our data model, we need to decide on our strategy for namespaces. There are a number of potential approaches which we cover in the following sections.

Single namespace

With this approach we have a single target namespace which is used by all schema definitions. Using this approach we typically have a single master document which uses the `xsd:include` element to combine the various schemas documents into a single schema.

This approach is taken below, where we have a master oBay schema that includes all our other schemas.

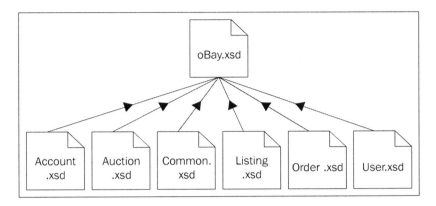

The advantage of this approach is that it keeps it simple, as we only have a single namespace and corresponding prefix to worry about.

The disadvantage is that we have taken a single schema and just broken it up into multiple but more manageable files, but apart from this we still have all the other disadvantages that we outlined above when creating a single master model.

The major disadvantage being that if we make a change to any single document, we would have changed the entire model. This would result in a new version of the entire model, and thus would potentially mean that we update every single service implemented to date.

Multiple namespaces

The other approach of course is to define a namespace for each individual domain; each schema can then reference definition in other schemas by making use of the `xsd:import` element. This is the approach we have taken for oBay and is illustrated here.

With this approach we have no master schema, thus services only need to import the parts of the canonical model which are relevant to them, whereas with the single namespace approach you will typically end up being required to import the entire schema.

Another advantage of this approach is it allows different groups to be responsible for each namespace, and for each namespace to evolve to a certain extent independently of others.

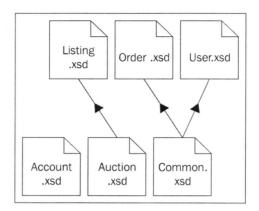

The drawback with this approach is that instance documents become more complex, as they will need to reference multiple namespaces. To prevent this becoming a problem it is important to partition your data model into sensible domains and also resist the urge to over partition it and end up with too many namespaces.

Separate common objects into their own namespace

Common objects which are used across multiple namespaces should be created in their own namespace. For example the address element is used across multiple domains; if we were to create it in the order namespace, we would be forcing the User schema to import the Order schema, which would unnecessarily complicate our XML instances. The issue would become more acute if common object definitions were sprinkled across multiple namespaces.

Chameleon namespaces

With this approach, as the name suggests, the namespace for a schema can change based on the environment in which it is used. This can be quite a useful trick if not over used.

For oBay we have defined the schema `base.xsd`, which we have used to define our base elements, such as `countryCode`, `currencyCode`, and `emailAddress` which will be reused by multiple schemas.

To use this technique, we don't specify a target namespace in the chameleon schema, so the definition of `base.xsd` looks like:

```
<xsd:schema xmlns:xsd="http://www.w3.org/2001/XMLSchema"
           elementFormDefault="qualified" >

  <xsd:element name="countryCode" type="tCountryCode">

  <xsd:simpleType name="tCountryCode">
    <xsd:restriction base="xsd:string">
      <xsd:length value="2"/>
      </xsd:restriction>
  </xsd:simpleType>

   <xsd:element name="currencyCode" type="tCurrencyCode">

   <xsd:simpleType name="tCurrencyCode">
     <xsd:restriction base="xsd:string">
       <xsd:length value="2"/>
     </xsd:restriction>
  </xsd:simpleType>
    ...

</xsd:schema>
```

We can then incorporate this into any of our other schemas using the `xsd:include` command. The elements defined in our base schema will then assume the namespace of the schema that's including them.

To look at the advantage of this approach, let us consider the disadvantages of the alternative approach, which would be to define all base elements in our common schema. Consider the following fragment of XML, which makes up an order.

```
<ord:order>
  <ord:orderNo>123456</ord:orderNo>
   <cmn:countryCode>IR<cmn:countryCode>
  <ord:cost>
    <cmn:currencyCode>EU<cmn:currencyCode>
    <ord:subTotal>12.45</ord:subTotal>
    <ord:tax>1.15</ord:tax>
      <ord:total>13.60</ord:total>
  </ord:cost>
    ...
</ord:order>
```

Here we can see that fragment contains two namespaces, which are interleaved with one another. However, using the chameleon approach, we would end up with the following:

```
<ord:order>
  <ord:orderNo>123456</ord:orderNo>
    <ord:countryCode>IR<ord:countryCode>
  <ord:cost>
    <ord:currencyCode>EU<ord:currencyCode>
    <ord:subTotal>12.45</ord:subTotal>
    <ord:tax>1.15</ord:tax>
    <ord:total>13.60</ord:total>
  </ord:cost>
  ...
</ord:order>
```

We are now only dealing with a single namespace, which makes our XML instance a lot cleaner and simpler to understand.

Disadvantages of chameleon namespace

However this approach does have some disadvantages, particularly if used to define complex elements. Consider the `address` element; if we define it in our chameleon namespace, the address within the context of `<user>` would look like:

```
<usr:user>
    ...
    <usr:address>
        <usr:addressLine1>7 Pine Drive</usr:addressLine1>
        <usr:addressLine2></usr:addressLine2>
    <usr:city>Eltham<usr:city>
        <usr:state>VIC</usr:state>
        <usr:zip>3088</usr:zip>
        <usr:country>Australia</usr:country>
    </usr:address>
</usr:user>
```

While if it is used in the context of `<order>` it would look like the following:

```
<ord:shipTo>
    ...
    <ord:address>
        <ord:addressLine1>7 Pine Drive</ord:addressLine1>
        <ord:addressLine2></ord:addressLine2>
        <ord:city>Eltham<ord:city>
        <ord:state>VIC</ord:state>
```

```
        <ord:zip>3088</ord:zip>
        <ord:country>Australia</ord:country>
    </ord:address>
</ord:shipTo>
```

Now this is exactly the behavior that we expect. However, the issue would come if we used XPath, for example within a BPEL assign activity to map the user address to the shipping address for the order as illustrated in the code snippet as shown:

```
<assign name="SetShippingAddress">
    <copy>
        <from variable="customer" query="/cus:customer/cus:address"/>
        <to    variable="order"    query="/ord:shipTo/ord:address"/>
    </copy>
</assign>
```

Performing this mapping would give us the following result shown below, which is clearly invalid.

```
<ord:shipTo>
    ...
  <ord:address>
    <usr:addressLine1>7 Pine Drive</usr:addressLine1>
    <usr:addressLine2></usr:addressLine2>
    <usr:city>Eltham<usr:city>
    <usr:state>VIC</usr:state>
    <usr:zip>3088</usr:zip>
    <usr:country>Australia</usr:country>
  </ord:address>
</ord:shipTo>
```

The reason we have ended up with the address containing elements in the wrong namespace, is that the XPath in the `from` clause is selecting all the nodes in the `<usr:address>` element and copying them to the `<ord:address>` element specified in the `to` clause.

To ensure that each element ended up in the correct namespace we would have to copy each node on an individual basis. While this is a completely valid approach it does rely on the developer to pick up on this nuance, or otherwise introduce a bug into the system. We have chosen to err on the side of caution and so only use chameleon namespaces for simple types so that we don't have to worry about this issue.

The other drawback with this approach is the risk of namespace collisions, that is where we have a type defined in the chameleon schema that shares a name with a type in the schema document that is including it.

Using WSDL to define business services

A service as defined by a WSDL document is made up of two parts. First is the abstract part which defines the individual operations that make up a service, the messages that define the parameters for the operations and the types which define our XML data types used by our messages.

The second part of the WSDL document defines the binding, that is, how to physically encode the messages on the wire (for example SOAP), the transport protocol on the wire (for example HTTP) and also the physical location or endpoint of the service (for example its URL).

Ideally we should only be concerned with designing the abstract part of the WSDL document as the run-time binding should be more of a deployment detail. However, the reality is that the style of binding has implications on how we design the abstract components if we want to ensure interoperability between services, providers and consumers.

By far the most common binding for a web service is SOAP over HTTP; however, this comes in a number of different varieties as we can specify whether the invocation method adopts a **Remote Procedure Call** (**RPC**) style or a document style binding (that is, a more message-oriented approach). We also have a choice as to whether the SOAP message is encoded or literal. This gives us four basic combinations, that is RPC/ encoded, RPC/literal, Document/encoded, and Document/literal.

It is generally accepted that for the purpose of interoperability, that document/literal is best practice. However, the document literal style has some drawbacks.

Firstly not all document literal services are WS-I compliant, because WS-I recommends that the SOAP body contains only a single child element within the SOAP body. However, document/literal allows you to define WSDL messages containing multiple parts, where each part is manifested as a child element within the SOAP body.

Another minor issue with document/literal is that it doesn't contain the operation name in the SOAP message, which can make dispatching of messages difficult in some scenarios and can also make debugging complicated when monitoring SOAP traffic, particularly when multiple operations contain the same parameters.

Use document (literal) wrapped

Document wrapped is a particular style or use of document literal which addresses these issues. With this approach, the request and response parameters for an operation are 'wrapped' within a single request and response element.

The request wrapper must have the same name as the corresponding operation, whereas the name of the response wrapper is derived by appending the string `Response` to the operation name.

This ensures that the SOAP body only contains a single nested element whose name matches that of the operation.

These wrapping elements must be defined as elements not complex types. While WSDL allows either, the use of `complexTypes` is not WS-I compliant.

Following this approach ensures that you have WS-I compliant messages.

 A document wrapped web service looks very similar to a RPC/literal style since they both produce a SOAP message containing a single nested element matching the name of the operation within the `soap:Body`.

Building your abstract WSDL document

Once we have standardized on the document wrapped pattern, we can define the abstract part our WSDL contract without at this stage having to worry about the actual binding.

WSDL namespace

As with our schema definitions, we need to define a namespace for our business service; here we would recommend defining a different namespace for each service, which should also be different from the namespaces used within your canonical model.

Defining the 'wrapper' elements

Wrapper elements should either be defined directly inline within your WSDL document or in a separate standalone schema which is imported into your WSDL document.

If you follow the latter approach it is advisable to define your wrapper schema within the same namespace as your WSDL document (as another namespace doesn't provide any additional value here).

Whichever approach you follow resist the temptation to define your wrapper elements within your canonical model, doing so will pollute your model as well as make change harder to manage.

Importing canonical model

When defining your wrapper elements make sure that you first import the relevant parts of your canonical model.

For example, the `OrderFulfilment` service needs to import the `Order.xsd` schema, which is defined in the namespace `http://schema.packtpub.com/obay/ord`.

So within the `types` section of our WSDL, we have included the following `import` statement.

```
<types>

  <xsd:import namespace="http://schema.packtpub.com/obay/ord"
              schemaLocation="order_v1_0.xsd" />
   <!-- Wrapper Elements Defined Here -->
   ...

<types>
```

Before we can reference elements contained within this schema, we must also declare its namespace and corresponding prefix within the `definitions` element of the WSDL, as highlighted:

```
<definitions name="OrderFulfillment"
    targetNamespace="http://xmlns.packtpub.com/obay/OrderFulfillment"
    xmlns:tns="http://xmlns.oracle.com/OrderFulfillment
    xmlns="http://schemas.xmlsoap.org/wsdl/"
    xmlns:xsd="http://www.w3.org/2001/XMLSchema"
    xmlns:ord="http://schema.packtpub.com/obay/ord"
    xmlns:plnk="http://schemas.xmlsoap.org/ws/2003/05/partner-link/">
```

Next we can define our wrapper elements, so for the `setShippingInstruction` operation within the `OrderFulfilment` service we have defined the following:

```
<xsd:element name="setShippingInstruction"
             type="tSetShippingInstruction"/>

<xsd:element name="setShippingInstructionResponse"
             type="tSetShippingInstructionResponse"/>

<xsd:complexType name="tSetShippingInstruction">
   <xsd:sequence>
      <xsd:element ref="ord:orderNo"/>
      <xsd:element ref="ord:shippingDetail" />
   </xsd:sequence>
</xsd:complexType>
```

```
<xsd:complexType name="tSetShippingInstructionResponse">
    <xsd:sequence>
        <xsd:element ref="ord:order"/>
    </xsd:sequence>
</xsd:complexType>
```

Defining the 'message' elements

Once we have defined our wrapper elements it's pretty straightforward to define our message elements; we should have one message element per wrapper element. From a naming perspective we use the same name for the message element as we did for our wrapper elements. So for our setShippingInstruction operation we have defined the following message elements:

```
<message name="setShippingInstruction">
    <part name="payload" element="setShippingInstruction"/>
</message>

<message name="setShippingInstructionResponse">
    <part name="payload" element="setShippingInstructionResponse"/>
</message>
```

Defining the 'portType' element

The final component of abstract WSDL document is to define the portType and its corresponding operations. For our OrderFulfilment service we have defined the following:

```
<portType name="orderFulfilment">
    <operation name="setShippingInstruction">
        <input message="setShippingInstruction"/>
        <output message="setShippingInstructionResponse"/>
    </operation>

    <operation name="submitInvoice">
        <input message="submitInvoice"/>
        <output message="submitInvoiceResponse"/>
    </operation>
    ...
</portType>
```

Note for the sake of brevity we have only listed two operations, for the full set please refer to OrderFulfilment.wsdl contained within the sample application.

Using XML Schema and the WSDL within BPEL PM

Once we have defined the abstract WSDL and corresponding XML Schemas, we are ready to implement the services they define within the SOA Suite. These services will typically be implemented as BPEL processes or proxy services within the service bus.

Sharing XML Schemas across BPEL processes

As we've seen in earlier chapters, the simplest way to use a pre-defined schema within BPEL is to import the schema from the file system into our BPEL Project.

When we do this, JDeveloper does two things. First it will add a **copy** of the schema file to the project of our BPEL Process. Second it will add an import statement into the WSDL of your BPEL Process, for example:

```
<types>
    <schema xmlns="http://www.w3.org/2001/XMLSchema">
        <import  namespace="http://schema.packtpub.com/obay/ord"
                 schemaLocation="Order_v1_0.xsd" />
    </schema>
</types>
```

Where schemaLocation is a relative URL which references the imported file. In many scenarios this is fine. However, if you have several processes, each referencing their own local copy of the same XML Schema, which is likely to be the case with our canonical model, then when you need to change the schema you will be required to update every copy.

One way is to just have a master copy of your XML Schema and use build scripts to update each of the copies every time you create a build. However, this isn't ideal; a better approach is to have a single copy of the schema that is referenced by all processes.

Deploying schemas to the BPEL server

BPEL PM allows you to deploy XML Schemas directly to the server; to do this simply place the schema under the directory structure:

```
<SOA_HOME>\bpel\system\xmllib
```

The schema will then be made available at the following URL:

```
http://server:port/orabpel/xmllib/<schema name>
```

For example if we created the sub-directory `obay` and dropped the `order_v1_0.xsd` in there, we would just need to modify our `schemaLocation` attribute to point to this URL, so in the above example it would now be:

```
schemaLocation="http://host:port/orabpel/xmllib/obay/order_v1_0.xsd"
```

Importing schemas

Once we have deployed the schema to the BPEL server, the next step is to create a reference to it within the appropriate WSDL document.

We can either do this by manually editing the WSDL, or we can import the schema in a similar fashion to when we import the file directly into the BPEL project. But instead of specifying the file location of the XML Schema, we just enter the schema URL, as shown in the following screenshot:

When we import a schema in this fashion, JDeveloper will import it as an **Inline Schemas**, meaning it doesn't actually make a copy of the schema, rather it just adds an import statement into your WSDL where the `schemaLocation` attribute is set to the specified URL.

Updating the schema URL

One minor issue with this approach is that the specified URL is an absolute one, so the host name and port is fixed within it. Thus when you move your process from one environment to another (for example, development to test) then you need to update the URL as appropriate.

However this is relatively straightforward to automate by creating a deployment plan for the BPEL Process; details on how to do this are described in Chapter 18 — *Packaging and Deployment.*

Importing the WSDL document into BPEL PM

For those services which we are going to implement as a business process, we need to create a BPEL process that implements the abstract WSDL contract that we have designed.

Essentially there are two approaches to this; the first is to create a BPEL process in the normal way, using the appropriate template, either synchronous or asynchronous. When you do this JDeveloper will create a basic WSDL file for the process. You can then modify this WSDL to conform to the abstract WSDL that you have already defined.

The alternative is to import the abstract WSDL document into the process itself. With this approach you create your BPEL process using the template for an **Empty BPEL Process**, as shown in the following screenshot:

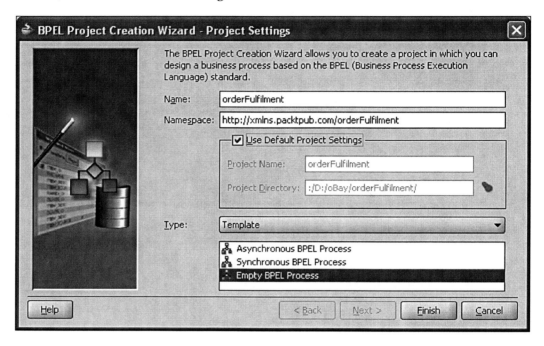

This will create a completely empty business process, containing no activities or partner links as shown.

When we create a BPEL process based on either the asynchronous or synchronous template, JDeveloper does a number of things.

First it will create a WSDL which describes the service provided by the process, it will create a default process containing a single PartnerLink (named **client**) which references the WSDL for the process. It will also create an initial receive and reply/invoke activity for the process.

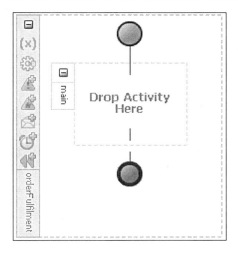

As we have created an empty process, we will need to create these components. The first step is to create the **client** partner link that implements our abstract service; we do this by dragging a `PartnerLink` onto our process in the normal way and then pointing it at the WSDL file that we've just defined.

Adding the PartnerLink definition to the abstract WSDL

Before importing an abstract WSDL, we need to create a modified version of the WSDL which includes the `partnerLinkType` extension required by BPEL, so for our Order Fulfillment service that we defined above we would need to add the following:

```
<plnk:partnerLinkType name="OrderFulfillment">
    <plnk:role name="OrderFulfillmentProvider">
        <plnk:portType name="client:orderFulfilment "/>
    </plnk:role>
</plnk:partnerLinkType>
```

Make sure that you set **My Role** within the PartnerLink to be the service provider (that is, `OrderFulfillmentProvider` in the above case). Once you have done this you can implement your BPEL process as normal.

We will also need to create the initial receive and corresponding reply/invoke activity for our process. When doing this make sure you check the box **Create Instance** on the initial receive activity.

Sharing XML Schemas in the service bus

As with BPEL PM, it is possible within the Service Bus to create multiple projects each with their own local copy of the schema. However, as before it's considered best practice to only have a single copy of each schema.

This is easily achieved by having a single project that defines your schemas, which is then shared across other projects. To be consistent with BPEL, we have defined the project xmllib which corresponds with the xmllib in the BPEL system directory, and under this created an identical folder structure into which we have imported our schemas.

For example, to mirror how we have deployed the order schema to the BPEL server we have created the folder obay within the xmllib project and into which we have imported the order_v1_0.xsd schema.

Importing the WSDL document into the service bus

Before we create a proxy service that implements our abstract WSDL, we need to define the bindings for the service, which in our case will be document/literal. We can either modify the WSDL file to include the bindings before we import it, or add in the bindings after we have imported the WSDL into the service bus.

Defining the SOAP bindings for our service and each of its corresponding operations is pretty straightforward, as we have already settled on document/literal for this.

For example, the bindings for our orderFulfillment service are as follows:

```
<binding name="orderFulfillmentBinding" type="tns:orderFulfillment">
    <soap:binding style="document"
                  transport="http://schemas.xmlsoap.org/soap/http"/>
    <operation name=" setShippingInstruction">
        <soap:operation style="document"
                        soapAction="setShippingInstruction"/>
        <input>
           <soap:body use="literal"/>
        </input>
        <output>
            <soap:body use="literal"/>
        </output>
    </operation>
    <operation name="submitInvoice">
        <soap:operation style="document" soapAction="submitInvoice"/>
```

```
    <input>
       <soap:body use="literal"/>
    </input>
    <output>
       <soap:body use="literal"/>
    </output>
  </operation>
  ...
</binding>
```

When we import our WSDL, if it imports any schemas, then the Service Bus will present us with a warning message, similar to the one shown as follows, indicating that there were validation errors with the WSDL.

⚠ The WSDL "orderFullfilment" was successfully created with validation errors. View the WSDL/Conflicts to see detailed diagnostic messages.

If you look at the list of resources in the browser it will also have an **X** next to the WSDL we just imported.

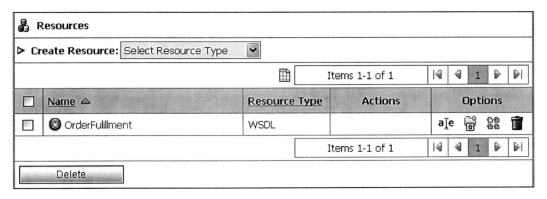

If you click on the WSDL name to edit it, the Service Bus will display the WSDL details, with the error **One of the WSDL dependencies is invalid**.

This is because if a WSDL references any external resources (i.e. the order schema in this case), we must first import that resource into the Service Bus and then update the WSDL reference to point to the imported resource.

To do this, click on the button **Edit References**, the Service Bus will display a window listing all the references included in the WSDL, with a section listing all the schema references as shown in the following screenshot:

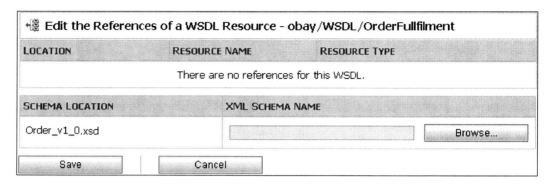

Clicking on the **Browse** button will launch a window from where you can select the corresponding XML Schema that the WSDL is referring to, shown as follows:

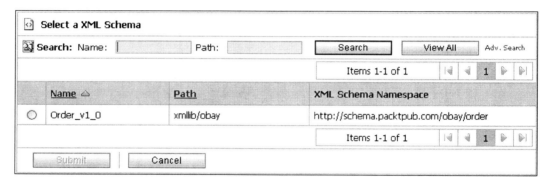

By default, the window will list all the schemas defined to the Service Bus, though you can restrict the list by defining search criteria. In the case or our orderFulfilment service, just select the schema order_v1_0.xsd and click **Submit**.

This will return you to the **Edit References** screen, click **Save**, this will return you to the **View/Edit WSDL** screen, which should display the confirmation **The References for the WSDL "orderFulfillment" were successfully updated.**

Your WSDL can now be used to define a proxy service in the normal way.

 If you import a schema into the Service Bus which references other schemas, then you will need to go through a similar process to define all its dependencies.

Strategies for managing change

One of the key design principals behind SOA is that systems should be designed and built to accommodate future change in response to ever changing business requirements.

So far we have looked at how to design and build the initial system, so that when change does occur it can be isolated through the use of service contracts to particular parts of the overall system.

While allowing us to restrict the impact of change, it doesn't completely mitigate all the complexities, especially when you consider the consumer and provider of a service may be in completely separate organizations.

Major and minor versions

When we upgrade the version of a service, e.g. from version 1 to version 2, then from the perspective of the consumer there are two possible outcomes. Either the version 1 consumer can continue to successfully use version 2 of the service, in which case the service is said to be backward compatible or the change will break the existing contract.

To be explicit, a service is said to be backwards compatible if **ALL** messages that would have been successfully processed by version 1 of the service will be successfully processed by version 2 of the service.

It is good practice to assign a version number to each service which indicates the level of backward compatibility. A typical approach is to assign a major and minor version of the format `<major>.<minor>` (e.g. 1.0, 1.1, 2.0), where:

- A minor change signifies a change that is backward compatible with previous versions of the service that share the same major number. These types of changes typically contain small new features, bug fixes, and so on.

- A major change signifies a change that is incompatible with previous deployment of the service. Major changes typically indicate significant new features or major revisions to the existing services.

 You also have the concept of forward compatibility, whereby the consumer is upgraded to use a future version of the service, before the actual provider of the service is upgraded.

If we examine the anatomy of a web service, it is essentially made up of three components. Namely its WSDL contract, referenced data types from our canonical model and the actual implementation of the service.

From a versioning standpoint we need to consider how a change to any of these components is reflected in the version of the overall service.

Service implementation versioning

This may seem a strange topic to cover. After all surely one of the key concepts of SOA is to isolate change. For example, if I change the implementation of a service, but the consumer sees no change to the contract, has it really changed at all?

At first the answer may seem obvious; however, if we revisit our earlier definition of backward compatible, we can see some issues:

> *A service is said to be backwards compatible if ALL messages that would have been successfully processed by version 1 of the service will be successfully processed by version 2 of the service.*

Under this definition if we add some extra validation to version 2 of the service (such as we check that a date is in the future) then it would mean some messages valid under the original version are no longer valid. The same sort of scenario could again occur if we were to fix a bug (or even introduce one).

Another more surreptitious change is one whereby we change the processing of the data, so that ALL messages are still processed successfully, but the result is different. For example, if we had a service which returned the price of an item, we could change it so that instead of returning the price in dollars and cents, it now returned the price in cents.

With each of these scenarios there is no hard and fast rule. However, when you implement these types of changes, you need to consider whether it requires the release of a new version of a service and whether that should be a minor or major version.

 Another way of handling this type of change is not to modify the version of the service, but rather provide a means of notifying the consumer that there has been a change to the service. One mechanism for doing this is though a UDDI registry.

Schema versioning

When we modify a schema, we follow the same core principals for major and minor versions that we outlined above. Namely a minor change to a schema indicates that an instance document created against a previous version of the schema is still valid against the new version of the schema as long as the schemas share the same major version number. Minor changes include:

- The definition of new elements, attributes and types
- Adding optional attributes and elements to existing elements and types
- Make existing mandatory attributes and elements optional
- Convert an element into a choice group
- Make simple types less restrictive

Change schema location

Encode the schema version in the file name of the schema, for example we have named our auction schema `auction_1_0.xsd`. Whenever we import a schema either in another schema or within a WSDL document the `schemaLocation` attribute will contain the version of the schema being used.

This has two advantages; first, we can immediately see what version of a schema a web service is based on, simply by looking at what files we are importing within the WSDL. Second, it allows us to have multiple versions of a schema deployed side by side allowing each service to upgrade to a newer version of a schema as it suites them.

When we upgrade a service to use the new version of a schema, then of course we will have a corresponding new version of the service.

Update schema version attribute

Use the schema `version` attribute to document the version of the schema. Note this is purely for documentation as there is no processing of this attribute by the parser. This ensures that if the schema is renamed so as to remove the encoding of the schema version from the file name, we still know the version of that schema.

Resist changing the schema namespace

One common practice is to embed the version of the schema within its namespace, and update the namespace for new versions of the schema. However, this has the potential to cause major change to both consumers and providers of a service so it is strongly recommended that you use this approach with care if at all.

Firstly when you change the namespace of a schema, it is no longer backward compatible with previous versions of the schema. So by definition changing the namespace is a major change in its own right. Therefore never change the namespace for a minor change.

For major changes, changing the namespace would appear a very valid approach as apart from being a clear indication to the client that we have introduced a service that is not backward compatible, it will prevent you from successfully calling any of the operations provided by the new version of the service.

However, it is important to understand the magnitude of this change as it will typically break a number of components on both the client and service provider. For example all your XPath assignments, XSLT transformations will have to be updated to use the new namespace. Therefore, implementing the change will be more time consuming.

In some ways you may want to consider how significant a major change is. For example the change might often impact one operation. Do you really want your clients to have to reimplement every call to every single operation because one operation (which they might not be using) has changed?

WSDL versioning

When we modify our WSDL contract, we again follow the same core principals for major and minor versions that we outlined above. From a service perspective a minor change includes:

- Addition of an operation; this merely extends the WSDL and thus on its own is backwards compatible.
- Addition of a new optional parameter within the element wrapper used by an input message.
- Make existing mandatory parameters within the element wrapper optional for input messages.

While major changes would include:

- Deletion or renaming of an operation.
- Changes to the input and output parameters of an operation that don't fall under the category of minor change, that is, adding a new parameter whether optional or mandatory to the response wrapper.

Incorporating changes to the canonical model

If we upgrade our service to use a new **minor** version of the canonical model, then our initial reaction might be that this only results in a minor change to the service, since our new version will still be able to process all requests from consumers using a service definition based on an earlier version of the schema.

While this is true, the response generated by our service may no longer be compatible with an earlier version of the schema. So the consumer may not be able to successfully process the response. In this scenario you need to create a new major version of the service.

Changes to the physical contract

From a versioning perspective, we don't generally consider changes to either the `<binding>` or `<service>` element. With regards to the `<binding>` element, we find it helpful to consider it as part of the service implementation and thus follow the same guidelines discussed above to decide whether it warrants a new version of a service.

Changes to the service endpoint presented by a composite merely indicates the relocation of a service, as is typically required when moving a composite from development into test and finally into production. As such this is more of a deployment consideration and is covered in detail in Chapter 18.

Updating the service endpoint

A simple way to record the version of a service is to encode it within its endpoint. BPEL PM does this for you already, for example whenever you deploy a process (that is, service) you specify its version.

For example when deploying version `1.0` of the `orderFulfillment` process to the `obay` domain, its endpoint will be:

```
http://host:port/orabpel/obay/OrderFulfillment/1.0
```

With the WSDL for the service being available at the URL:

```
http://host:port/orabpel/obay/OrderFulfillment/1.0?WSDL
```

With the Service Bus you have even more flexibility over the endpoint of a proxy service as you can specify this as part of the Transport Configuration. We recommend following a similar naming strategy to that used by BPEL PM in order to maintain consistency.

This has two advantages; first we can immediately see from the URI what version of a service we are looking at. Second, it provides a simple mechanism for us to have multiple versions of a service deployed side by side, which is important when we consider the lifecycle of a service.

Managing the service lifecycle

When we release a new version of a service, we need to consider how we wish to manage previous releases of that service.

A typical first step is to set the status of the previous version to deprecated, this indicates to existing users that the service has been updated with a newer version and therefore will be retired at some point in the future.

This signals to existing users that they need to start the process of migrating to the newer version of the service as well as indicating to new users that there is a newer version of the service they should use. The final step is to retire the service; at this point the service is removed from production, so that it is no longer available for use.

When we make a minor release of the service, because it is backward compatible with the previous version, it should be straightforward to migrate to the newer version, because the only change that the consumer will be required to make is to call the service at a new endpoint (and even this may not have changed). In this case, the previous version of the service can be retired relatively quickly.

However, with a major release, changes will be required to be made to the consumer before they can move to the new version; in this case, the deprecated service will need to be maintained for a longer period of time and may require even minor releases of its own to fix bugs, and so on.

With both of these scenarios, a lot will depend on the number of consumers, how easy or difficult they are to identify and coordinate change across, as well as the nature of the change.

One way to handle change is to create a façade that would map the old interface to the new service interface. This maintains support for existing consumers (without modification), but means that there is only a single instance of the implementation of the service.

A key to simplify this is also to keep the consumers of services informed of planned future versions of services, as well as those under development, as this will allow them to plan for future releases and thus shorten the required life span of deprecated services.

Summary

Design of the service contract and the underpinning canonical model are fundamental steps in the overall implementation of a SOA based solution. The keyword here is **design**, as it's all too easy with the tools we have at our disposal to knock out a model in order that the "real work" of implementation can begin.

In this chapter, we have given you an overview of how to go about structuring your XML canonical model, both in terms of modelling your data in a tree like structure as well as how to partition it across multiple namespaces.

We've also given some guidance on best practice for the implementation of those schemas, whether you follow ours or define your own, the key is to put in place some standard guidelines in order to ensure consistency as this will result in schemas which better interoperate, are easier to reuse and maintain.

The canonical model provides the foundation for our service contracts, and with this in place we have defined best practice around how we define our service contract, paying particular attention to using the document literal wrapped pattern in order to conform to WS-Interoperability guidelines.

As stated earlier, a core tenet of SOA is that systems should be designed to accommodate change; with this in mind we have also examined how we can manage change both in our schemas and our actual service contract, and outlined a versioning approach to support this.

Lastly, we looked at how the SOA Suite supports the running of deprecated services along side most recent release in order to enable consumers to upgrade to the newer version of a service in its own time.

11
Building Business Services

In the previous chapter, we discussed the principles involved in designing a good service abstraction. In this chapter, we will look at how to actually implement these strategies to build business services. The focus of this chapter is on building new business services either from scratch or by reusing existing logic. Within the Oracle SOA Suite the most natural languages to use to build new functionality are Java and PL/SQL and we will focus on it. It should be remembered, however, that it is also possible to create new services from scratch in other languages and consume them within the SOA Suite.

Build versus reuse

Earlier we looked at how to reuse existing application functionality by exposing it as a service. When comparing our existing application functionality with our list of desired services we find that our desired services fall into three distinct groups:

- Services that can be built by reusing existing functionality directly
- Services that can be built by modifying existing functionality
- Services that must be built from scratch

Each of the above cases causes us to work in a slightly different way. The first two cases use existing functionality, but differ in how they expose it. In the first case we are able to take the functionality already provided and expose it directly as a web service because it already complies with how we wish our service to perform. In the second case the functionality exists but is not readily exposed in the form we require for our services. Hence, we must first perform a re-factoring of the functionality to better fit it into our architecture. Finally, there are always services that we need that do not already exist, or exist at such a low level that there is a significant amount of development required to create them.

Let us examine how we deal with each of these service scenarios.

Adapters and web service wrappers

In Chapter 3, we looked at the use of adapters to expose service functionality. In this chapter, we use service wrappers to provide a web service interface onto existing code. Adapters support both event driven and request/response services. Service wrappers generally provide just a request/response interaction.

Adapters

Following are the characteristics of adapters:

- Support request/response interaction
- Support event notification (the service initiates the call)
- Support a wide range of technologies and packaged applications
- By default are co-located with core SOA Suite components
- Configuration often deployed with clients
- May support XA transactions—for example the database adapter
- By default don't use SOAP bindings (JCA binding is used by default)

Service wrappers

Following are the characteristics of service wrappers:

- Support request/response interaction
- SOA Suite and JDeveloper support wrapping Java and PL/SQL only
- Must be deployed and run as services in their own right
- All configuration is held in the service description
- Any transactional support is handled through SOAP headers
- By default use SOAP bindings

It should also be noted that applications such as Peoplesoft and Siebel support definition of their own services using the tools provided with the applications.

Reusing existing functionality directly

In this case we are either using existing services exposed by the application or exposing existing functionality directly as services as we did in Chapter 3. If the application already exposes a WSDL interface then we can use it directly and no further work is required on our part other than adapting the interface to support the canonical data model as explained in Chapter 4. If the application does not expose a WSDL interface, then we need to expose the required functionality through a WSDL interface by providing a service wrapper that maps directly onto the functionality. Normally this is achieved by taking existing Java or PL/SQL code and providing a service wrapper directly around it using a JDeveloper wizard. The format of data and the operations supported are determined by the existing application functionality rather than an idealized service design.

Exposing a PL/SQL stored procedure as a service

Often business logic is captured inside a PL/SQL stored procedure. The following PL/SQL code is used to create a new auction. It uses a database sequence to generate a unique auction ID, inserts the auction details into a table and then returns the new auction ID as an out parameter.

```
PROCEDURE CREATEAUCTION
  ( userID IN NUMBER
  , Title IN VARCHAR2
  , Description IN VARCHAR2
  , Reserve IN NUMBER
  , AuctionID OUT NUMBER
  ) IS
BEGIN
  INSERT
    INTO Listing
      (Id, Name, Description, Reserve, SellerID)
    VALUES
      (AuctionIdSeq.nextval, Title, Description, Reserve, userID);
  SELECT AuctionIdSeq.currval INTO AuctionID FROM dual;
  COMMIT;
END CREATEAUCTION;
```

When creating a new auction we need to assign it a unique ID and the use of a sequence guarantees that this occurs correctly. Because we want to use the sequence every time we create an auction it is convenient to wrap up the use of the sequence into a stored procedure.

Launching the PL/SQL web service wizard

To turn this stored procedure into a service we can call from elsewhere in the SOA Suite we use the JDeveloper PL/SQL web service wizard. To invoke this, we select **New...** from within an existing project. Then under **Business Tier**, select the **Web Services** group to find the **PL/SQL Web Service** wizard as shown.

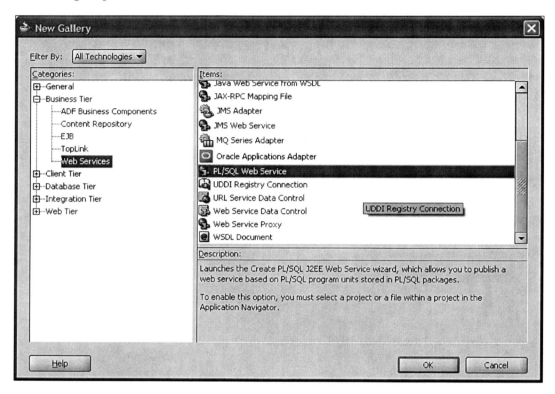

Choosing the level of Java Enterprise Edition support

The service we create will need to be deployed to a J2EE container to execute. The wizard wants to know what version of the specification to generate code for. Choose **J2EE 1.4 (JAX-RPC) Web Service** unless you are deploying to a pre-10.1.3 Oracle Application Server.

Selecting a database connection and defining service bindings

Having chosen the level of Java support required, we select a database connection that will be introspected to find appropriate candidate stored procedures. When deployed, the database connection will be looked up at JNDI location `java:comp/env/jdbc/<ConnectionName>` where `<ConnectionName>` is the name of the connection in JDeveloper. This setting must be configured to point to the correct database in the target Java container.

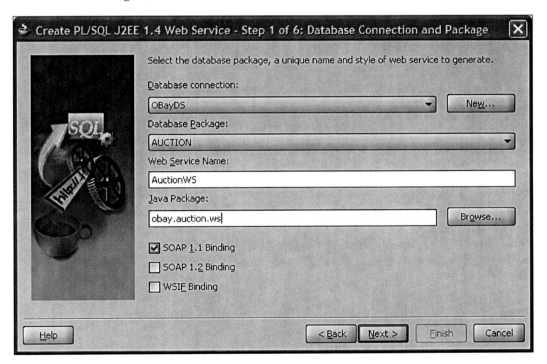

Once a **Database connection** in JDeveloper is selected, we can choose the **Database Package** containing the procedures we want to expose as a service. We also set the name of the service at this point using the **Web Service Name** field.

The **Java Package** is the package used by the wizard when generating Java code.

The final section of this screen allows us to define the service bindings. These define how the services maps onto message protocols. The Oracle SOA Suite components will work with any of the available bindings. However, for maximum interoperability it is probably wise to choose **SOAP 1.1** support; this will ensure interoperability with older web services implementations. For more information on these settings see Chapter 17 — *The Importance of Bindings*.

Determine message style

The wizard now requires us to select the type of message format. Again for maximum interoperability use Document/Wrapped message format.

Select stored procedures and functions to expose

The wizard will now introspect the database to determine the functions and procedures available to be added to the service. Any procedures that cannot be turned into web services will be greyed out. To discover why a service cannot be exposed as a web service, select the greyed out service and click **Why Not?**

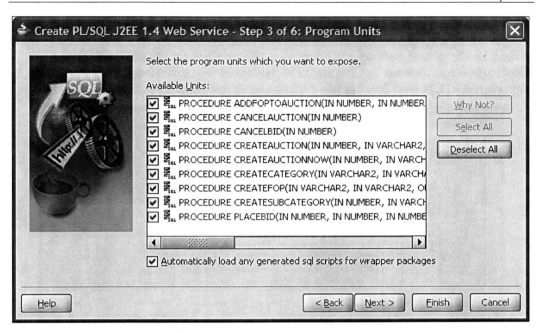

Each procedure or function selected in the wizard will appear as an operation on the generated service interface. The wizard will then ask how the PL/SQL types should be mapped onto XML. The defaults are usually sufficient.

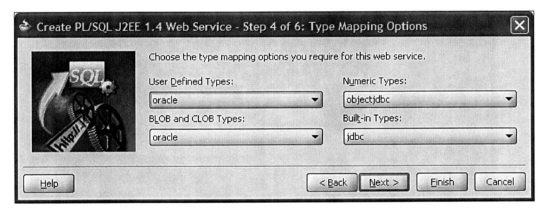

Once the desired procedures and functions have been selected, the wizard may be completed by clicking on **Finish**. Additional steps on the wizard allow customization of data bindings and setting of web service policy. Custom data mappings and serialization are covered in Chapter 17 — *The Importance of Bindings*. Policy settings are covered in Chapter 20 — *Defining Management and Security Policies*.

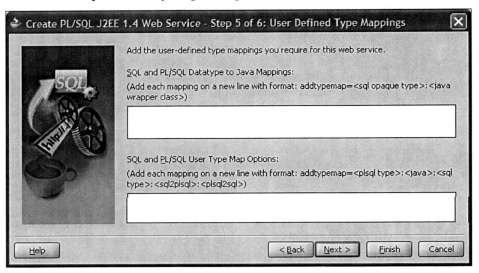

Finally it is possible to add additional header fields to the service, allowing customization of the headers using JAX-RPC.

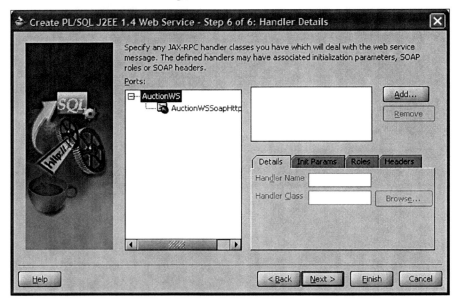

Modifying existing functionality using service bus

In Chapter 4, we discussed the importance of a canonical form for data. We typically want all our interactions to be in canonical form. This may require us to wrap or modify existing services to convert their data representation to canonical form.

If the functionality we require is already exposed as a service, we can choose to modify it through transformation in the Service Bus. Complicated transformations, where there is a significant mismatch between canonical form and actual service, may require the use of BPEL or more complex request/response pipelines in the Service Bus. In the worst case, we may need to combine several services into a single canonical service. This approach may be characterized as using the SOA Suite to adapt the exposed functionality to our needs.

If the function we need is not already exposed as a service, then we may choose to provide a native language wrapper around the functionality. This wrapper is intended to make it easier to transform the resultant service to canonical form.

We can avoid the need to transform to canonical form by generating a service stub from the canonical form and then implementing it by using our existing functionality. This is similar to creating a new service from scratch except that we don't have to provide the functionality of the service. We just need to provide some code to call the functionality. This approach may be characterized as extending the existing code base before exposing it to the SOA Suite to provide the functionality we need.

Converting an existing service to canonical form

Often we have existing services available but they are not in canonical form. Hence, these services are relatively brittle and enforce their structure on the rest of the infrastructure. To avoid this, we can provide a more flexible interface in the Service Bus that performs the transformation of an existing web service from a service implementation specific interface to the canonical interface.

Create a new service interface

To do this, we first create a new session in the service bus console, and then create a new project as shown:

We give the project a meaningful name. Note that this could also be done in the Oracle WebLogic Workshop.

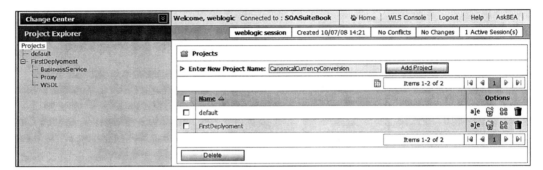

After selecting the project in the **Project Explorer**, we can start adding the resources that we need. We start by defining the canonical service interface as described by a WSDL definition. Before importing a WSDL, it is best to ensure that any external references within the WSDL, such as references to XML Schema files, are already loaded. If the schema files are unique to this project, they can be loaded into this project; if they are not, they can be placed in a shared common project to ensure that the same resource is used consistently across projects. Note that, in the examples, we have created sub-folders under the project to hold different types of resource. This is not necessary and is done only to make it easier to manage the resources.

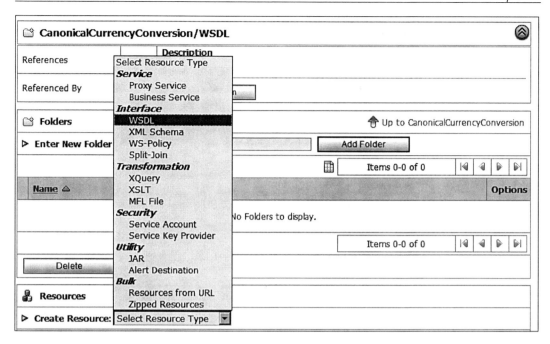

We are able to browse the file system for WSDL to upload to the project. The WSDL for our canonical interface generally does not need any port or binding details because these will be provided by our wrapper, in this case by the Service Bus.

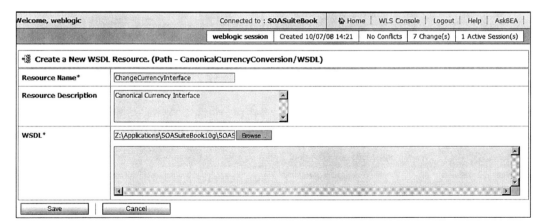

After loading the WSDL, we can verify that it has correctly resolved any external resource references such as XML Schemas by clicking on the newly loaded WSDL and looking at the WSDL definitions. Note that because the referenced XML Schema was pre-loaded into the Service Bus, it has automatically been resolved correctly. If the schema had not been pre-loaded, it would now be necessary to load the schema and manually set the reference between the WSDL and the schema.

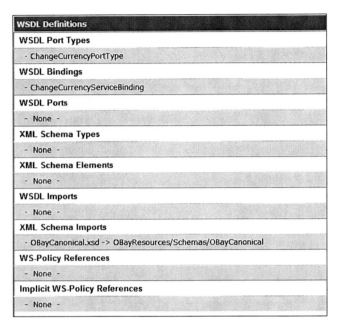

Now that we have loaded the interface WSDL, then we can create a proxy that will implement this interface. After choosing to create a Proxy resource, we can browse for a pre-loaded WSDL and select it.

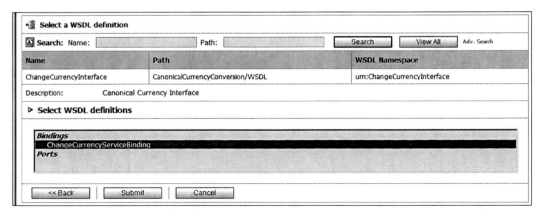

If the WSDL contains multiple port types or services, then we need to select the appropriate port type or service. We also need to provide a service name. Note that in addition to WSDL, we can also define the proxy service provided in other ways. We would generally want to use these to adapt existing clients to our web service based infrastructure. Note that we have chosen not to stream the content because this service is a simple request/response service with small amounts of data. If large amounts of data were involved, we may have wanted to buffer the data to avoid overwhelming the business endpoint.

Create a Proxy Service (CanonicalCurrencyConversion/Proxy/)	
General Configuration	
Service Name*	CurrencyConversionSvc
Description	
Service Type*	**Create a New Service** ⦿ WSDL Web Service CanonicalCurrencyConversion/WSDL/Cha [Browse...] ChangeCurrencyServiceBinding (binding) ○ Messaging Service ○ Any SOAP Service [SOAP 1.1 ▾] ○ Any XML Service **Create From Existing Service** ○ Business Service [Browse...] ○ Proxy Service [Browse...]
Content Streaming	☐ Enabled ⦿ Memory Buffer ○ Disk Buffer

[Next >>] | [Last >>] | [Cancel]

Having selected the interface to our WSDL, we can skip to the last screen, which is a summary of the proxy service that we are about to create. Note that the summary screen details the options that we have skipped. We have elected to use HTTP as a transport Protocol, but we could have selected another transport such as JMS. We have also chosen to keep the default endpoint identifier or Endpoint URI. Other options we have ignored include the ability to add headers into the message, provide secure socket support (HTTPS) or require HTTP authentication.

Enforce compliance to standards for external services

If a proxy is intended to be used by a consumer external to the company, it is a good idea to enforce WS-I compliance. WS-I is the Web Services Interoperability standard and defines which subsets of the various web service standards can be reliably used to guarantee interoperability between different vendors SOA stacks.

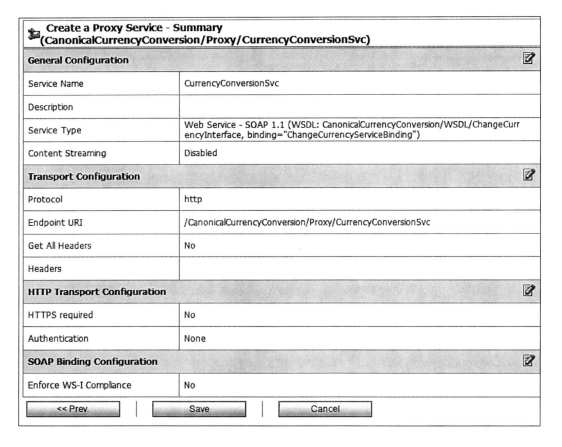

**Create a Proxy Service - Summary
(CanonicalCurrencyConversion/Proxy/CurrencyConversionSvc)**

General Configuration	
Service Name	CurrencyConversionSvc
Description	
Service Type	Web Service - SOAP 1.1 (WSDL: CanonicalCurrencyConversion/WSDL/ChangeCurrencyInterface, binding="ChangeCurrencyServiceBinding")
Content Streaming	Disabled

Transport Configuration	
Protocol	http
Endpoint URI	/CanonicalCurrencyConversion/Proxy/CurrencyConversionSvc
Get All Headers	No
Headers	

HTTP Transport Configuration	
HTTPS required	No
Authentication	None

SOAP Binding Configuration	
Enforce WS-I Compliance	No

<< Prev. | Save | Cancel

Selecting **Save** completes the initial creation of the proxy.

Adding the non-canonical service

We now need to add the non-canonical web service into the assembly which we do by loading the WSDL of the service into our project. We then create a **Business Service** resource in our project. We select the target WSDL for this in a similar way in which we selected the WSDL for the proxy service. However, when we are creating a business service, it usually is a concrete WSDL that has specific endpoint locations or ports within it. When selecting the binding or port type it is generally a good idea to select the port rather than the binding, as the port includes a physical endpoint for the service. This is shown in the following screenshot. Note that we could just choose a binding, but this would require us to provide the physical port later in the business service definition.

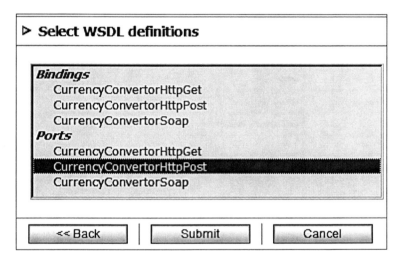

Once the appropriate port has been selected, the business service summary can be viewed by clicking **Last**. Note that the summary for the business service includes details such as the type of **Load Balancing Algorithm** to use, although this is only useful if more than one **Endpoint URI** is specified. Note that it is also possible to specify the retry logic (**Retry Count** and **Retry Iteration Interval**) for the business service.

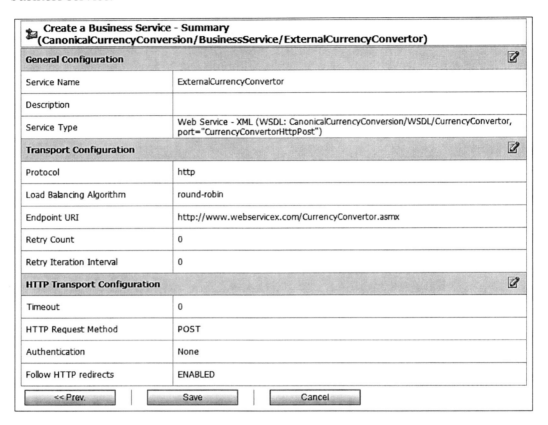

We have now created all the components that we require in the Service Bus and can now wire the proxy to make use of the external business service. Within the Service Bus we now need to map the inbound data from the exposed service onto the input of the external reference and the same for the return from the external reference. We can do this using either an XSL transform or an XQuery operation.

More complex conversions

If the conversion between canonical and actual service is too complicated to do within a mediator, we can use a BPEL process in its place. The principle is the same as using a mediator except now we can access all the power of BPEL to assist us in the conversion. This is usually necessary when there are semantic differences between the services rather than purely syntactic differences.

Exposing a Java class as a service

Although we could expose existing Java classes directly as web services it is generally better to create a thin wrapper class around them to better align the resulting web service with the required canonical formats. This allows us to remove Java specific types from an interface, simplifying the task of mapping the interface onto the canonical form.

Wrapping the Java code

For example, take a Java class that performs encryption and decryption of credit card details. It has three operations—to retrieve a key, encrypt a card using the key, and decrypt a card using the key.

```
public class EncryptionService {
    public SealedObject encryptCard(Key key, CreditCard card) …
    public CreditCard decryptCard(Key key,
                                  SealedObject encryptedCard) …
    public Key getKey(String passPhrase) …
}
```

There are two problems with this Java API as a service interface:

- It is too granular, requiring two calls for every encryption and decryption
- It uses Java classes that cannot be easily mapped onto XML types

The `java.security.Key` interface and `javax.crypto.SealedObject` class cannot be readily mapped to XML types in any way other than as an opaque series of bytes. The `CreditCard` class is a simple Java Bean that can be easily mapped onto XML.

```
public class CreditCard implements Serializable {
    …
    public CreditCard() {}
    public void setIssuer(String param) …
    public String getIssuer() …
    public void setName(String param) …
    public String getName() …
```

```
        public void setNumber(String param) …
        public String getNumber() …
        public void setExpiry(String param) …
        public String getExpiry() …
}
```

To make a better basis for creating a service we can build a `wrapper` class that removes the extra step of getting a key and only exposes types that can be easily mapped to XML.

```
public class EncryptionServiceWrapper {
    public byte[] encryptCard(String passPhrase, CreditCard card) …
    public CreditCard decryptCard(String passPhrase, byte[]
                                  encryptedCard) …
}
```

Launching the Web Service wizard

To expose this new wrapper class in JDeveloper, we will launch the **Create Java Web Service** wizard by right-clicking on the class.

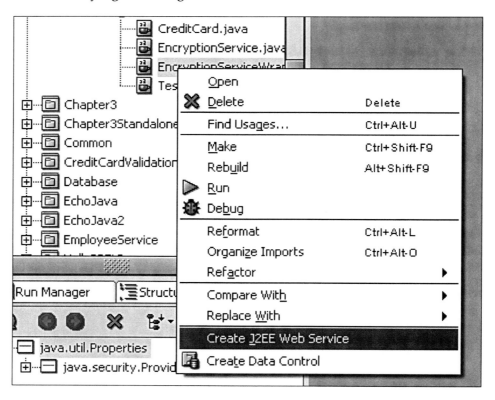

Select deployment platform

We can then select how we want the web service to be implemented in Java. Unless we are deploying to an earlier version of OC4J, we should choose **J2EE 1.4**.

The web service version determines how the Java class is wrapped or annotated to expose the web service.

Select service name

The name of the service is arbitrary. Because we started by generating a service specifically for a given Java class, we cannot change the **Component To Publish**.

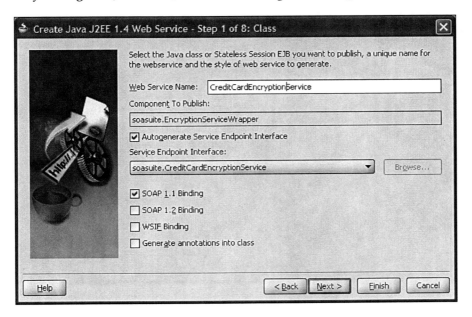

For maximum interoperability it is best to stay with SOAP 1.1 binding. Auto generation of the service endpoint means that the endpoint name and address will be selected by JDeveloper; at runtime the physical address will be modified to reflect the container that the service is hosted on.

Select message format

The message format determines how the service serializes the data for transmission. The formats determine which options are available later in the wizard. The document wrapped style passes a single parameter on the wire that is a holder for the individual parameters.

Wrapped and literal styles

The different encoding styles cause the message to be packaged differently. The wrapped styles cause each message to have a single message part and a root XML element that has all the native parameters underneath. The literal style causes a message to have multiple parts, each part has its own separate root element that corresponds to the native parameters on the implementing class.

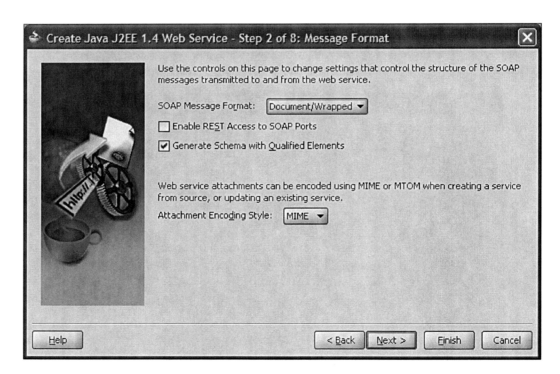

Provide custom serializers

Having selected the message format we will be prompted to provide any custom XML to Java mappings. Generally, we will not require these unless we want to use a pre-existing XML Schema for our parameter types. We may also use this to provide precise control about how a Java class is transformed into XML through the use of a serializer. This is a topic outside the scope of this book.

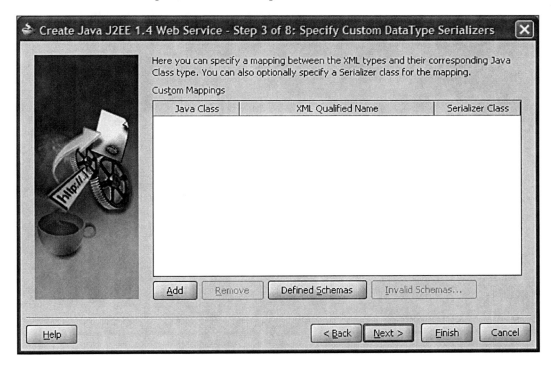

Mapping

If we don't have an existing schema to map onto, the mapping step in the wizard allows us to control the generation of an XML Schema to describe our Java classes. It is here that we specify the namespaces to be used for our service definition and service types.

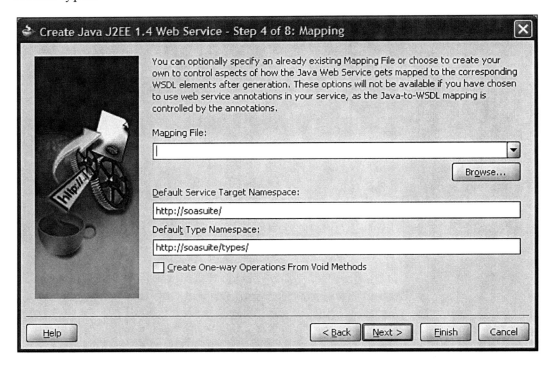

Select methods

In this step, we can verify which methods we wish to include in our service.

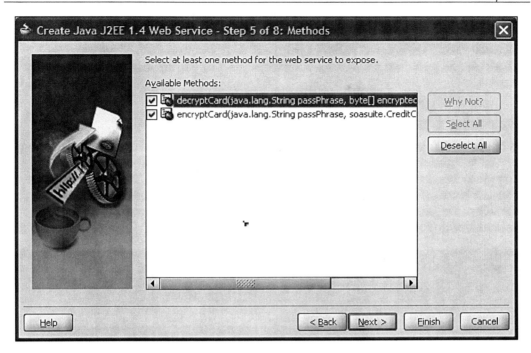

We have the option to remove unwanted methods from the service. If a method is grayed out, choosing **Why Not?** will explain why that method cannot be included in the service.

This is generally a good point to click the **Finish** button to generate the web service. This service may now be deployed to an application server and used within the SOA Suite. Actual deployment steps will depend on the target application server. However, the steps are the same as for deploying any JEE application to an application server.

Creating services from scratch

There are times when the functionality that we require does not already exist and so we need to create it from scratch. The languages of choice for doing this with SOA Suite are Java and PL/SQL. The choice of language will be determined by several factors including:

- Available skills
- Complexity of logic—more computational and conditional centric logic favours Java
- Complexity of data—more data-centric logic favours PL/SQL

Creating a Java service from a WSDL

Previously we have created services from existing functionality. Now let us look at how we can generate the service wrappers to let us implement the functionality we need.

Starting the wizard

We begin with a project into which we import a WSDL document or create one using the WSDL builder in JDeveloper. The WSDL we will use describes a credit card encryption service similar to the one we have previously used. To launch the wizard we select **New...** from the **File** menu of JDeveloper. Within the **New Gallery,** we then select the **Java Web Service from WSDL** item under the **Business Tier Web Services** category.

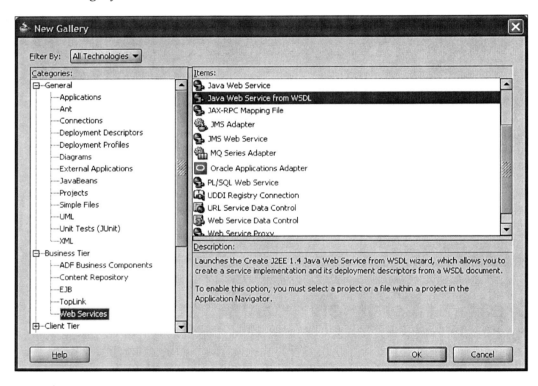

Choosing the WSDL

Within the wizard we first need to choose the appropriate WSDL document from which we want to generate a web service implementation. The **WSDL Document URL** drop down not only shows all the WSDL documents within this JDeveloper application but also allows us to browse for WSDL in the file system or in a UDDI repository.

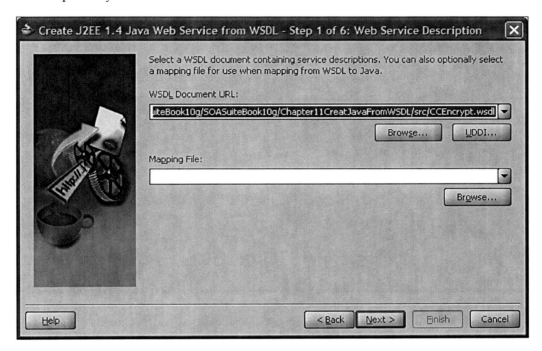

The optional **Mapping File** field allows us to control the names and types of Java classes corresponding to our XML Schema.

Choosing the mapping options

When we come to Step 2—**Default Mapping Options** we have some new choices to make. This screen allows us to describe the name and packages of generated Java classes.

`Soa.bookGenerated` Java classes will be created in the Java package identified by the **Package Name**. Classes generated to describe parameters and return types are created in the Java package identified by **Root Package for Generated Types**.

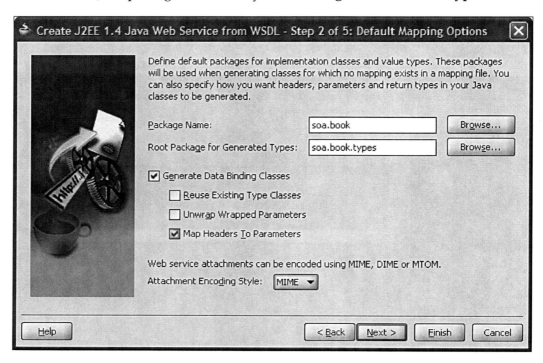

A couple of extra fields provide more control over the mapping. If the WSDL identifies the use of any specific SOAP headers, **Map Headers to Parameters** allows these to be mapped as additional parameters to the Java class, avoiding the need to write message handlers to extract the headers. If the underlying parameter types have already been mapped and exist, checking **Reuse Existing Type Classes** will cause the code generator to not generate any classes for parameter types, however the mapping file should have been used in this case to map existing classes onto the appropriate XML types.

Clicking **Finish** at this point will cause the wizard to generate appropriate Java classes.

The generated Java

The wizard will generate a number of different classes:

- An implementation class—`CreditCardEncryptionServiceImpl`—that we must use to provide the functionality of the service.

- An interface—`CreditCardEncryptionService`—that defines the service interface in Java.

- A number of data structure classes—`CreditCard`, `DecryptCardRequest`, `DecryptCardResponse`, `EncryptCardRequest`, and `EncryptCardResponse`—that represent the parameters into the service and/ or its return value as well as any other data types required.

- A descriptor to map the service WSDL and associated XML Schema onto the generated Java classes—`CreditCardEncryptionServiceService-java-wsdl-mapping.xml`.

The only class that needs to be altered is the implementation class. This is shown as follows:

```
public class CreditCardEncryptionServiceImpl {
    public DecryptCardResponse decryptCard(DecryptCardRequest request)
    {
      return null;
    }

    public EncryptCardResponse encryptCard(EncryptCardRequest request)
    {
      return null;
    }
}
```

Any class initialization must go into the class constructor. Any other functionality should be referenced from the methods generated for that functionality, such as decryptCard being used to provide a mechanism for decrypting an encrypted credit card.

Once the methods have been implemented, the new service can be deployed to an application server and is available for use.

Summary

In this chapter we have explored how we can create business focussed services that conform to the canonical model principles discussed in Chapter 10. Some services can be exposed directly using the web services wizard in JDeveloper. Other services may need to be transformed through the Service Bus before they match the canonical form. Finally, we can map to canonical form using methods in the native language and then expose those methods as a canonical service. Choice of language for creating new services is largely driven by the skills available and the nature of the service — data centric or computational logic centric.

Services can also be specified first and then a Java template generated. Currently JDeveloper only supports generation of Java templates.

12
Building Validation into Services

Once we have divided our solution up into a number of composite components, one of the next questions we typically get is:

Where should I put my validation and how should I implement it?

At first glance this may seem like an obvious question, but once you consider that a service may be made up of other services, it becomes clear that you could potentially end up implementing the same validation in every level.

Apart from the obvious performance implications, you also have the issue of having to implement and maintain the same validation at multiple points within the solution.

When you get down to an individual service, you still have many considerations around where in the service you place the validation and how best to implement it. Particularly if you want the flexibility to be able to change the validation within a service without having to redeploy it.

This chapter gives guidance on how best to address this question. It examines how we can implement validation within a service using XSD validation, Schematron and Business Rules as well as within the service itself. With each of these options it looks at the pros and cons and how they can be combined to provide a flexible validation strategy.

Finally, we look at validation within the context of the overall solution, and provide guidelines around which layer within the architecture we should place our validation.

Using XML Schema validation

A service exposes one or more operations, these operations provide the entry point for the outside world, so it provides the obvious starting point for implementing validation in our service.

The interface for each of these services is defined by its WSDL contract, with the core structure of the data being exchanged being defined by the XML Schemas. So XSD validation provides an excellent way to implement the initial level of validation.

When implementing schema based validation, we have two basic approaches —which are either to implement strongly typed web services or loosely typed services.

Strongly typed services

With strongly typed services, we use XML Schema to very precisely specify the exact structure of each element within our XML instance. For example, if we look at the definition of CreditCard within the oBay canonical model a strongly typed version may be defined as follows:

```
<xsd:complexType name="tCreditCard">
  <xsd:sequence>
    <xsd:element name="cardType"          type="tCardType"/>
    <xsd:element name="cardHolderName"    type="tCardHolderName"/>
    <xsd:element name="cardNumber"        type="tCardNumber" />
    <xsd:element name="expiryMonth"       type="tExpiryMonth"/>
    <xsd:element name="expiryYear"        type="tExpiryYear"/>
    <xsd:element name="securityNo"        type="tSecurityNo" />
  </xsd:sequence>
</xsd:complexType>

<xsd:simpleType name="tCardType">
  <xsd:restriction base="xsd:string">
    <xsd:enumeration value="MasterCard"/>
    <xsd:enumeration value="Visa"/>
  </xsd:restriction>
</xsd:simpleType>

<xsd:simpleType name="tCardHolderName">
  <xsd:restriction base="xsd:string">
    <xsd:maxLength value="32"/>
  </xsd:restriction>
</xsd:simpleType>

<xsd:simpleType name="tCardNumber">
  <xsd:restriction base="xsd:integer">
```

```
      <xsd:pattern value="[0-9]{16}"/>
    </xsd:restriction>
  </xsd:simpleType>

  <xsd:simpleType name="tExpiryMonth">
    <xsd:restriction base="xsd:integer">
      <xsd:minInclusive value="1"/>
      <xsd:maxInclusive value="12"/>
    </xsd:restriction>
  </xsd:simpleType>

  <xsd:simpleType name="tExpiryYear">
    <xsd:restriction base="xsd:integer">
      <xsd:minInclusive value="2008"/>
      <xsd:maxInclusive value="9999"/>
    </xsd:restriction>
  </xsd:simpleType>

  <xsd:simpleType name="tSecurityNo">
    <xsd:restriction base="xsd:integer">
      <xsd:pattern value="[0-9]{3}"/>
    </xsd:restriction>
  </xsd:simpleType>
```

With this approach, we have very precisely defined the following restrictions:

- Valid card types are either MasterCard or Visa
- Credit card number is a 16 digit integer
- The expiry month must be between 1 and 12
- The expiry year must be a four digit integer with a minimum value of 2008
- The security code is a 3 digit integer

The advantage with this approach is that we have a far more explicit definition of the interface, providing a far more robust and tightly controlled entry point for our service. From a client perspective, it provides a far clearer understanding of what does or doesn't constitute a valid data structure.

From an implementation perspective, by placing the majority of the validation in the service contract we have removed the need for the underlying service to build in this validation, simplifying the construction of the actual service.

However, the major disadvantage with this approach is that the tighter the constraints, then the more resistant to change a service becomes.

For example, if oBay decided to accept American Express as payment, then `CardType` would need to be updated to contain an additional enumeration, `CardNumber` would need to be amended to accept 15 digit numbers and `SecurityCode` amended to accept 4 digit numbers.

This would require oBay to release a new version of their XML Schema and a corresponding new version of any service which relies on `CreditCard` in any of its operations.

In addition, every New Year, a new version of the canonical model would be required to update `ExpiryYear` as appropriate.

 You could also argue that it's perfectly valid to have details of an expired credit card, in which case you would not want to put this constraint in the Canonical Data Model.

Loosely typed services

With a loosely typed approach, we use XML Schema to define the overall structure of the XML instance, that is, what elements may appear in the document, whether they are optional or mandatory and how often they may occur, but provided minimal constraints around the content of each element. Using this approach our definition of CreditCard could be as follows:

```
<xsd:complexType name="creditCard">
  <xsd:sequence>
    <xsd:element name="cardType"        type="xsd:string"/>
    <xsd:element name="cardHolderName"  type="xsd:string"/>
    <xsd:element name="cardNumber"      type="xsd:integer"/>
    <xsd:element name="expiryMonth"     type="xsd:integer"/>
    <xsd:element name="expiryYear"      type="xsd:integer"/>
    <xsd:element name="securityNo"      type="xsd:integer"/>
  </xsd:sequence>
</xsd:complexType>
```

This is about as loose a definition as we could provide, though we could have gone one step further and made every element a string.

The major advantage of this approach is that the service is far more conducive to change. Following on from our previous example, if oBay decided to accept American Express as payment, then no changes would be required to the schema or service contract.

However, the key disadvantage with this approach is that we have far less control over the data that comes into our service and thus need to rely on the required validation being implemented elsewhere within our service.

What we want to avoid is coding the majority of this validation into the service itself, as this can over-complicate the implementation of the service, resulting in the same validation being implemented in multiple services (possibly inconsistently) as well as making changed harder to manage, as we would have to update the service code every time the validation rules changed.

Another disadvantage with this approach is that the service contract provides far less guidance to the consumer of the service as to what constitutes valid data, thus additional documentation would be required along with the service to define this.

Combined approach

Rather than use one approach exclusively, the key here is to strike the right balance and use schema validation to provide at least an initial sanity check of the data, that is, the data is of correct type (for example integer, date) and that the size of the data is within reasonable limits.

For example, with the loosely coupled schema definition, all our fields could be of any length. Often this data will at some point be persisted in a database, if a service consumer issued a request with elements containing data larger than the underlying data store then this could cause the service to fail.

These types of validations can easily be overlooked by developers, yet cause problems that are hard to diagnose at run time; by ensuring that we perform some level of sanity checking at the service entry point we can prevent these issues from occurring.

This also prevents services being called with significantly oversized payloads, which could have performance implications for the system if allowed to permeate through the application.

For elements which are far less prone to change, we can define tighter constraints around the content of those elements, to remove as much validation as possible from the underlying service implementation.

However, we would still like to abstract out as much of the validation logic from the underlying service as possible. This not only makes the service simpler to implement, it also makes the service more reusable as we could potentially provide different validation depending on the context in which it is used. Fortunately this is where Schematron comes in.

Using schema validation within BPEL PM

Schema validation of incoming and outgoing XML documents is enabled within BPEL PM, through appropriate configuration of the `validateXML` property; this can take one of the following three values:

- `strict`: Schema validation will be applied to the XML document, if the XML document fails validation then an exception will be thrown.

- `warning`: Schema validation will be applied to the XML document, if the XML document fails validation then BPEL will log this in the audit trail of the appropriate activity (that is, `invoke`, `reply`, `receive`), but **no** exception is thrown.

- `none`: No schema validation is applied.

This property is set at the domain level within BPEL, with a default setting of **none**, that we can then override at the Partner Link level by configuring it appropriately.

[Note in releases prior to 10.1.3.4, this property takes the value of `true` and `false`, which maps to `strict` and `none` respectively.]

Validation of inbound documents

Within a BPEL process, the `receive` activity will validate inbound documents if its corresponding Partner Link is configured (either at the Partner Link or domain level) to validate XML. If the validation results in an exception being thrown, then the `receive` activity will throw the exception.

For a synchronous operation, if the BPEL process doesn't handle the exception then the `receive` activity will return a fault to the client. However, for an asynchronous operation no fault is returned to the client.

Validation of outbound documents

Within a BPEL process, the `invoke` and `reply` activities will validate outbound documents if their corresponding Partner Link is configured to validate XML. As with inbound documents, if the validation results in an exception being thrown, then the corresponding `invoke` or `reply` activities will throw the exception.

Validation between BPEL processes

If we have a BPEL process invoking another BPEL process, there are some subtle nuances we need to be aware of. This is because there are two possible points where the validation could occur.

Validation for synchronous interactions

Consider the following synchronous interaction, shown as follows:

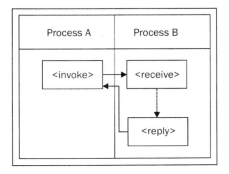

The first point where XML validation could occur is in the invoke activity in process A, the second in the receive activity in process B. If the validation is carried out in the invoke activity, and an exception is raised, then no message will be sent and process B will never be invoked.

However, if the validation is carried out in the `receive` activity in process B, the message will be sent and an instance of process B will be created to process the message.

Assuming the exception isn't handled in process B, then the `receive` activity will return a fault to process A, which will be re-thrown by the invoke activity in process A. This is the same fault that the invoke would have thrown if it carried out the validation.

So functionally it makes no difference, but if we carry out the validation in the receive we have the overhead of sending the message and instantiating a new instance of process B.

Validation for asynchronous interactions

Consider a similar scenario but this time for an asynchronous interaction shown as follows:

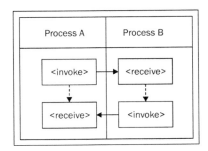

As before, the validation could occur in either the invoke or receive activity, if the invoke activity carries out the validation, the result will be identical to our synchronous example.

If the validation happens in the receive activity, we get a different result. This is because, with asynchronous interactions, the message isn't delivered directly to the process, rather it's placed in the message delivery queue.

The message will then be removed from the queue and delivered to process B; if an error occurs then the receive activity will throw an exception, which if it isn't handled will result in the message being placed back in the queue for recovery at a later point in time.

If this happens then process A will potentially wait forever for a response to come. So in this scenario, we should look to either carry out the validation in the initial invoke, or use a fault handler to catch any validation exceptions raised by the receive activity.

Setting validateXML for a BPEL domain

The BPEL Console is used to configure the validateXML property for a BPEL domain. To do this log in to the console for the required domain and click on the **Configuration** tab, from here click on the **Domain** sub tab.

This will list all the configuration properties for the BPEL domain, if you scroll to the bottom of the list you will see the **validateXML** property, shown in the following screenshot:

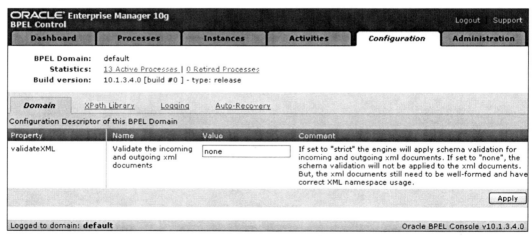

Modify this to the required value and click **Apply**; this will update the property to contain the new value and apply it with immediate effect.

Setting validateXML for a PartnerLink

To specify the validateXML property for a PartnerLink, open the **Partner Link** within the BPEL process and select the **Property** tab shown as follows:

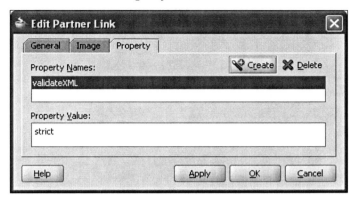

Next click **Create**. This will pop up a window with a drop down containing properties you can set on the Partner Link. Select **validateXML** and then for the **Property Value** specify the required setting.

When finished, save the BPEL process and deploy it to the BPEL Server in order for it to take effect.

Using schema validation within the service bus

Within the Service Bus, schema validation is carried out using a **Validate** action, which is typically invoked during a pipeline stage or route node.

The **Validate** action provides an additional degree of flexibility when compared to BPEL PM, in that rather than validate the entire payload of either an inbound or outbound document, you can choose to validate just a fragment of the XML document which you specify using XPath.

Upon completing validation, you can specify that the **Validate** action records the result of the validation, either `true` or `false` in a variable or that it should throw an exception if the validation fails.

Validation of inbound documents

When processing an inbound document, it's good practice to perform validation as early as practical within the flow as this prevents unnecessary processing of an invalid document.

This typically means creating a validation stage at the first stage within the Request Pipeline of a pipeline pair.

If we look at the operation updateCreditCard which forms part of the UserAccount service, a typical XML instance for this operation would appear as follows:

```
<soap:Envelope xmlns:soap="http://schemas.xmlsoap.org/soap/envelope">
 <soap:Body xmlns:tns="http://xmlns.packtpub.com/obay/bs/UserAccount"
            xmlns:usr="http://schemas.packtpub.com/obay/usr"
            xmlns:cmn="http://schemas.packtpub.com/obay/cmn">
    <tns:updateCreditCard>
      <usr:userId>jsmith</usr:userId>
      <cmn:creditCard>
        <cmn:cardType>MasterCard</cmn:cardType>
        <cmn:cardHolderName>John Smith</cmn:cardHolderName>
        <cmn:cardNumber>4570126723982904</cmn:cardNumber>
        <cmn:expiryMonth>10</cmn:expiryMonth>
        <cmn:expiryYear>2010</cmn:expiryYear>
        <cmn:securityNo>528</cmn:securityNo>
      </cmn:creditCard>
    </tns:updateCreditCard>
  </soap:Body>
</soap:Envelope>
```

If we wanted to add a validation step to check the creditCard details, then we would add a validation stage (for example, Validate Credit Card) at the start of the Request Pipeline.

To add a validation action, click on the validate stage within the Request Pipeline and select **Edit Stage**. This will bring up the **Edit Stage Configuration** window. Click on **Add an Action | Message Processing | Validate**. This will insert the following **Validate** action into our stage.

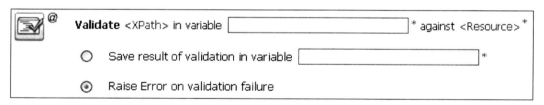

In the **variable** text field, enter the name of the variable which contains the XML fragment we wish to validate, that is, **body** in our example. Next, we need to specify which part of the **body** variable we want to validate. To do this, click the **<XPath>** link to bring up the **XPath Expression Editor** and define the appropriate XPath expression.

In our case we want to validate the **creditCard** fragment from our **body** variable, so our expression is defined as follows:

```
./tns:updateCreditCardProcessRequest/cmn:creditCard
```

Next we need to specify which schema element or type we wish to validate against; click on the **<Resource>** link and select **Schema** from the drop down, this will display the **Select a XML Schema** window, as shown in the following screenshot:

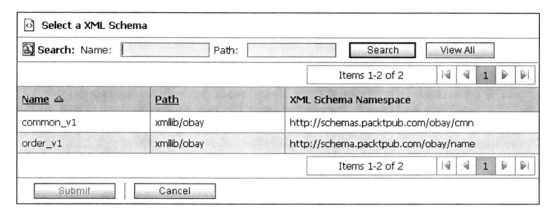

Select the required schema, that is, **common_v1** in our case and this will launch the **Select a Schema definition** window, shown as follows:

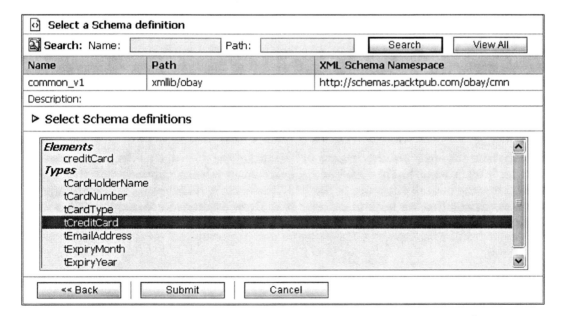

This lists all the types and global elements defined in the XML Schema. From here we select the element or type we wish to validate our XML fragment against. So for our example, select **tCreditCard** and hit **Submit**.

Our completed validate action will look as follows:

At run time, if the validation fails then the validate action will throw an exception. Typically we would define a **Stage Error Handler** for our validation stage to catch the exception and handle it appropriately; we look at how to do this in Chapter 13 — *Error Handling*. If we don't define an error handler, the Service Bus will return the default validation fault to the caller of the service.

Validation of outbound documents

Within the Service Bus we can also use the validate action to check any outbound documents. Typically we would do this just prior to invoking any external service, and we would do this in a similar fashion for inbound documents.

However, strictly speaking, if we have received a valid inbound document and our service has been **correctly** implemented, it shouldn't be generating any invalid XML.

In reality this is not always the case, so in many scenarios it still makes sense to include this level of validation. Though if we follow this approach too strictly we run the risk of over-validation which we will cover in more detail in the following section.

Using Schematron for validation

Schematron provides another means of validating the message payload of a web service. It takes a markedly different approach from schema validation, in that rather than check the overall structure of the XML instance, it enables you to specify one or more assertions that we wish to enforce. If all these assertions are met the document is deemed to be valid.

These assertions are specified using XPath, so it allows us to specify constraints that can't be expressed using XML Schema. For example following on from the example above, we can define the following validations on credit card.

- If the card type is American Express then the card number should be 15 digits in length, otherwise it should be 16 digits.
- If the card type is American Express then the security code should be 4 digits in length, otherwise it should be 3 digits.
- The expiry date, which consists of the `expiryMonth` and `expiryYear` elements, should be in the future.

For each assertion we can also specify meaningful diagnostic messages, which indicate why an assertion hasn't been met (as opposed to schema validation messages which aren't always so enlightening).

The other advantage of using Schematron is that it enables us to modify the assertions for a document without the need to change the schema.

However, rather than consider Schematron as alternative approach to XML Schema validation, we see it very much as complementary. Thus we would use XML Schema to validate the core structure of the XML, but not make those checks too granular. Rather we will place those checks along with ones that can't be expressed in XML Schema in Schematron.

Overview of Schematron

One of the advantages of Schematron is that being based on XSLT makes it extremely easy to learn. Effectively it has several key constructs, and once these are understood you are ready to unleash the full power of the tool.

So before we look at how to use Schematron within SOA Suite, we will give a quick introduction to Schematron itself. Readers who are familiar with Schematron may still want to skim this section, just to understand some of the idiosyncrasies of how Schematron behaves within the Oracle SOA Suite.

If we look at the operation `updateCreditCard` which forms part of the `UserAccount` service, a typical XML instance for this operation would appear as follows:

```
<soap:Envelope xmlns:soap="http://schemas.xmlsoap.org/soap/envelope">
 <soap:Body xmlns:tns="http://xmlns.packtpub.com/obay/bs/UserAccount"
            xmlns:usr="http://schemas.packtpub.com/obay/usr"
            xmlns:cmn="http://schemas.packtpub.com/obay/cmn">
   <tns:updateCreditCard>
     <usr:userId>jsmith</usr:userId>
```

```
      <cmn:creditCard>
        <cmn:cardType>MasterCard</cmn:cardType>
        <cmn:cardHolderName>John Smith</cmn:cardHolderName>
        <cmn:cardNumber>4570126723982904</cmn:cardNumber>
        <cmn:expiryMonth>10</cmn:expiryMonth>
        <cmn:expiryYear>2010</cmn:expiryYear>
        <cmn:securityNo>5285</cmn:securityNo>
      </cmn:creditCard>
    </tns:updateCreditCard>
  </soap:Body>
</soap:Envelope>
```

A Schematron which checks that the credit card type is MasterCard or Visa could be written as follows:

```
<?xml version="1.0" encoding="UTF-8"?>
<schema xmlns="http://www.ascc.net/xml/schematron">
  <ns uri="http://schemas.packtpub.com/obay/cmn" prefix="cmn"/>
  <pattern name="Check Credit Card Type">
    <rule context="cmn:creditCard">
      <assert test="cmn:cardType='MasterCard' or
                    cmn:cardType='Visa'">
        Credit Card must be MasterCard or Visa
      </assert>
    </rule>
  </pattern>
</schema>
```

From this we can see a Schematron is made of four key components: `pattern`, `rule`, `asser`, and `ns` contained within the `schema` element. We'll examine these elements one by one, starting with the inner most element and working out.

Assertions

The `assert` element as its name suggest is used to define the constraints to be enforced within an XML document. In the above Schematron we have defined the following `assert` element.

```
<assert test="cmn:cardType = 'MasterCard' or cmn:cardType = 'Visa'">
    Credit Card must be MasterCard or Visa
</assert>
```

We can see it contains the `test` attribute which specifies an XPath expression, which should return a boolean value. If the test expression evaluates to `true`, then the assertion has been met.

If the test evaluates to `false` then the assertion has failed and the document is invalid. When this happens Schematron will raise an error and the content of the `assert` element (i.e. `Credit Card must be MasterCard or Visa`) is returned as an error message.

Rules

Asserts are defined within a `rule` element. Each rule has a `context` attribute, which contains an XPath expression used to specify the nodes within an XML instance to which the rule should be applied.

In effect it will perform a select on the root node of the service payload, which may result in a node set containing zero, one or more nodes. Each node returned will then be validated against all asserts defined within the rule.

In the case of the `valCreditCard.sch` Schematron, we have defined the following rule:

```
<rule context="cmn:creditCard">
   ...
</rule>
```

We have specified a *relative* context of `cmn:creditCard`, which will match against any occurrence of `creditCard` regardless of where it appears in the XML payload. The advantage of this is that we can use the same Schematron to validate any occurrence of `cmn:creditCard` regardless of which operation it is used in.

In the case of the `updateCreditCard` operation, the rule will return just a single node, `cmn:CreditCard` shown as follows, to which our single assertion will be applied.

```
<cmn:creditCard>
  <cmn:cardType>MasterCard</cmn:cardType>
  <cmn:cardHolderName>John Smith</cmn:cardHolderName>
  <cmn:expiryMonth>10</cmn:expiryMonth>
  <cmn:expiryYear>2010</cmn:expiryYear>
  <cmn:securityNo>5285</cmn:securityNo>
</cmn:creditCard>
```

In the case where we have multiple assertions defined for a rule, if more than one assertion fails for a particular node, then Schematron will return a diagnostic message for each failed assertion.

Patterns

Rules are defined with a `pattern` element. Each `pattern` can hold a collection of one or more associated rules. Pattern contains a single attribute name, which contains free format text used to describe the rules contained within it.

In our `valCreditCard.sch` Schematron, we have defined the following pattern:

```
<pattern name="Check Credit Card Type">
   ...
</pattern>
```

When processing an XML instance, Schematron will apply each pattern against the XML instance in pattern order. When checking against a pattern, Schematron will check the XML instance against each rule contained within the pattern in rule order.

Namespaces

Namespaces are declared using the `ns` element. This has two attributes — `uri` which is used to define the namespace URI and `prefix` which is used to define the namespace prefix.

For example, in our credit card validation Schematron we define the namespace `http://schemas.packtpub.com/obay/cmn` with the following:

```
<ns uri="http://schemas.packtpub.com/obay/cmn" prefix="cmn"/>
```

Schema

The root element of a Schematron document is the `schema` element defined within the namespace `http://www.ascc.net/xml/schematron`. In our example we've made this the default namespace so we don't have to prefix any of the Schematron elements.

```
<?xml version="1.0" encoding="UTF-8"?>
<schema xmlns="http://www.ascc.net/xml/schematron">
   ...
</schema
```

Intermediate validation

So far we have just implemented some basic validation that we could have quite easily have performed using XML Schema. However, to give you a feel for the real capability of Schematron we will also look at some validation requirements that can't be implemented using XSD.

Cross field validation

An area where Schematron excels is cross field validation, for example if we wanted to check that `cardNumber` is 16 digits long for MasterCard and Visa, and 15 digits long for American Express, we could write the following assertion:

```
<rule context="cmn:CreditCard">
  <assert test="((cmn:cardType='MasterCard' or
                  cmn:cardType='Visa') and
                  string-length(cmn:cardNumber) = '16') or
                 (cmn:cardType='American Express' and
                  string-length(cmn:cardNumber) = '15')">
    Invalid Card Number.
  </assert>
</rule>
```

Using XPath predicates in rules

The above approach, though perfectly valid, could become quite verbose, especially once we start to add additional checks for specific card types. For example, in case we want to check the length of `securityCode` based on `cardType`.

Another approach is to use an XPath predicate within the rules context attribute to narrow down the context to a specific card type. For example we can specify a set of assertions for credit cards of type `MasterCard` as follows:

```
<rule context="cmn:creditCard[cmn:cardType='MasterCard']">
  <assert test="string-length(cmn:cardNumber) = '16'">
    Mastercard card number must be 16 digits.
  </assert>
  <assert test="string-length(cmn:securityNo) = '3'">
    Security code for Mastercard must be 3 digits.
  </assert>
</rule>
```

Using this approach we can specify a different rule for each card type, allowing us to maintain assertions for each card type independently from one another as well as simplifying the process of adding new card types.

Using XPath 2.0 functions

In the above assertion we are just testing that `cardNumber` is 16 characters in length, we are not checking that it's an actual integer, rather we are relying on schema validation for this.

There is nothing wrong with this approach, but what if some cards allowed alphanumeric numbers? In this scenario we would need to declare `cardNumber` as a string and then carry out specific validation in Schematron to check the format of the element based on `cardType`.

For this we can use the `matches` function, to test whether the content of the element conforms to a particular regular expression. However, this is an XPath 2.0 function, so in order to use this within Schematron we need to define its namespace. We do this in exactly the same way as we would for any other namespace, that is:

```
<ns uri="http://www.oracle.com/XSL/Transform/java/oracle.tip.
          pc.services.functions.Xpath20" prefix="xp20"/>
```

We can then create an assertion that matches the `cardNumber` as shown:

```
<assert test="xp20:matches(cmn:cardNumber, '[0-9]{16}')">
  Mastercard number must be 16 digits.
</assert>
```

Date validation

Schematron is also an excellent method for validating dates based on the current time, for example we need to check that the expiry date for the credit card is not in the past.

To do this we need to check that the expiry year of the credit card is greater than the current year, or that the expiry year of the credit card equals the current year and the current month is less than or equal to the expiry month of the card.

To do this we could write the following test:

```
cmn:expiryYear > xp20:year-from-dateTime(xp20:current-dateTime()) or
(cmn:expiryYear= xp20:year-from-dateTime(xp20:current-dateTime()) and
cmn:expiryMonth>=xp20:month-from-dateTime(xp20:current-dateTime()) )
```

Element present

Another requirement is to check whether an element is present or not. We can do this with XML Schema by defining an element as being mandatory. However, whether an element is optional or mandatory may well be based on values in other fields.

For example, if we had made `securityNo` optional within our schema definition, but we wanted to make it mandatory for American Express, we could write the following rule:

```
<rule context="cmn:creditCard[cmn:cardType='American Express']">
  <assert test="cmn:securityNo">
    Security No must be specified
  </assert>
</rule>
```

Note, this will only check to see if the element is present in the XML instance. It doesn't actually check if it actually contains a value. The simplest way to check this is to use the string-length function as shown:

```
<rule context="cmn:creditCard[cmn:cardType='American Express']">
  <assert test="cmn:securityNo and string-length(cmn:securityNo)>0">
    Security No must be specified
  </assert>
</rule>
```

Using Schematron within BPEL PM

BPEL PM includes a Schematron validation service which allows you to validate an XML instance against a Schematron. The service is invoked just like any other service via a partner link, and in the event of a validation failure, returns a `ValidationException` fault that contains a list of errors. We can then use a fault handler to catch the fault and handle it appropriately.

Creating a Partner Link for the Validation Service

The WSDL file for the validation service is contained in the `bpm-services.jar` that is installed as part of the SOA Suite. This file can be located in the directory:

```
<SOA_HOME>\bpel\system\services\lib
```

Take a copy of this JAR, and extract the file:

```
oracle\tip\pc\services\validation\validation.wsdl
```

We can then use this WSDL to define a Partner Link in the normal way. The `validationService` defines a single operation `validation`. It takes two parts; `instanceFile` which contains the XML to validate and `ruleFile` which contains the Schematron.

 If you look at the bindings section of the WSDL you will see that it provides this service via java bindings, meaning that the validation service is invoked via java (as opposed to SOAP over HTTP), giving us better performance. This is an area that we will examine in more detail in Chapter 17 — *The importance of Bindings*.

Creating a Schematron file

To create a Schematron within our BPEL project, in the **Applications Navigator** right-click on your BPEL Project and select **New**. This will launch the gallery for creating new project resources, from here select **File** (under the **General category**) and click **OK**.

This will bring up the **Create File** dialogue; give the file an appropriate name (for example `valCreditCard.sch`) and click **OK**. This will create the file in the resources folder of our BPEL project.

Creating the file in the resource folder ensures that JDeveloper will include the file in BPEL Suitcase when we deploy the BPEL process to the server, which will allow the BPEL process to easily access the content of the file at runtime.

Once defined, we can use JDeveloper to edit the file in order to define our Schematron.

Invoking the validate operation

To invoke the validate service, drag an invoke activity onto our BPEL process in the normal way and create an input and output variable.

The input variable takes two parts: `instanceFile` which contains the XML to validate and `ruleFile` which contains the Schematron. The following figure shows the structure of the input it expects.

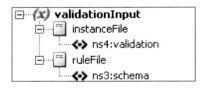

Assigning the instanceFile

The `instanceFile` contains a single element; `validation` defined as an `xsd:anyType`; which we need to populate with the XML to be validated.

Note, the `validation` operation expects the `validation` element to contain a single element; any more than this will cause it to return an error.

So in our example, if we use a standard copy operation such as the following:

```
<copy>
   <from variable="inputVariable" part="payload"
         query="/client:updateCreditCard"/>
```

```
    <to variable="schematronInput" part="instanceFile"
        query=/ns4:validation/>
</copy>
```

To map the content of updateCreditCard to validation, we will end up with a validation element that looks like the following:

```
<validation xmlns="http://xmlns.oracle.com/pcbpel/validationservice">
    <usr:userId>jsmith</usr:userId>
    <cmn:creditCard>
        <cmn:cardType>MasterCard</cmn:cardType>
        <cmn:cardHolderName>John Smith</cmn:cardHolderName>
        <cmn:cardNumber>4570126723982904</cmn:cardNumber>
        <cmn:expiryMonth>10</cmn:expiryMonth>
        <cmn:expiryYear>2010</cmn:expiryYear>
        <cmn:securityNo>285</cmn:securityNo>
    </cmn:creditCard>
</validation>
```

Here, we can see the validation element contains the two elements: userId and creditCard, which if we submitted to the validation service would cause it to throw an error as it expects only a single element.

One way to fix this is to add a remove operation to our assign activity, to delete the userId element. To do this, within the **Assign** activity click on **Create** and select **Remove Operation** as shown in the screenshot:

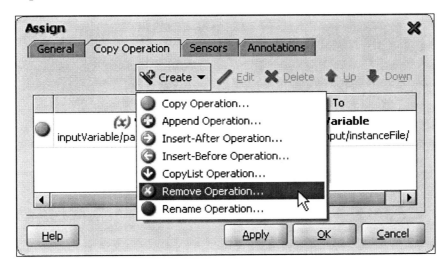

This will present us with the **Create Remove Operation** window, as shown in the following screenshot:

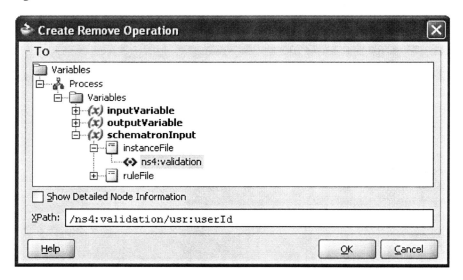

Here we just need to specify the node that we wish to delete, so in our example we just expand the **schematronInput** tree and select **ns4:validation**.

Since this is defined as `xsd:anyType` we will need to manually enter the XPath expression to remove the required node, which in our example is **/ns4:validation/ usr:userId**.

Assigning the ruleFile

The `ruleFile` contains a single element; `schema` defined as an `xsd:anyType`, which needs to contain the Schematron we wish to validate our XML against.

To copy the content of our Schematron file (for example, `valCreditCard.sch`) into `schema` we can use the `ora:doc` XPath function, found under the category **BPEL XPath Extension Functions** in the **Expression Builder**.

This function reads in the content of the specified file, parses it and returns it as an XML node, so for our purposes we have the following `copy` command:

```
<copy>
  <from expression="ora:doc('valCreditCard.sch')"/>
  <to variable="schematronInput" part="ruleFile"/>
</copy>
```

Sharing a Schematron between processes

As we have already observed, our `valCreditCard` Schematron can be used to validate a `creditCard` element in any BPEL Process in which it is used.

Rather than create a copy of the same Schematron file in each BPEL project which uses it, a better approach is to have a single copy of the Schematron that is referenced by all processes.

As with XML Schemas, BPEL PM also allows you to deploy any other XML document directly to the server, by placing it under the same directory structure, namely:

```
<SOA_HOME>\bpel\system\xmllib
```

The XML document will then be made available at the following URL:

```
http://server:port/orabpel/xmllib/<document name>
```

We can still use the `ora:doc` XPath function as before to read in the content of the file, but rather than specify a relative file name we now need to specify its URL.

For example, if we placed `valCreditCard.sch` in the following directory:

```
<SOA_HOME>\bpel\system\xmllib\obay\sch
```

We would modify the above call to `ora:doc` to the following:

```
ora:doc('http://host:port/orabpel/xmllib/obay/sch/valCreditCard.sch')
```

This has a number of distinct advantages. Firstly, you can ensure all your processes use the same version of a particular Schematron. Secondly, if we need to modify our validation rules we just need to update a single Schematron and redeploy it to the server. In addition any BPEL process which references that Schematron will automatically pick up the modified version, without us having to redeploy it.

Using Schematron with the service bus

The service bus does not support Schematron validation. However, it does provide a Java Callout Action that allows you to invoke a Java method within a message flow.

One approach would be to implement a lightweight Java class which wrappers the Schematron classes and exposes a single method (similar to the Schematron validation service in BPEL) which can then be invoked using a Java Action in the service bus.

Putting validation in the underlying service

So far we have looked at using XML Schema and Schematron to put validation either in the service contract or mediator layer in order to provide initial validation of a service invocation, before we actually invoke the underlying service. This provides a number of benefits, including:

- Simplifies the development of validation within the actual service as it can now rely on the fact that it is receiving relatively sensible data.

- Allows us to implement a more generic service, since business specific validation can be provided at a higher level within the service. This makes the service more reusable, as it can be used in multiple scenarios each with different validation requirements.

- Makes change easier to manage, as changes to business rules which impact the overall validation of the service can happen at either the schema or Schematron level and thus may require no changes to the actual underlying service

- By placing the validation in a centralised place, which can be reused across multiple services, it enables us to implement the same validation across multiple services in a consistent fashion. This also makes change simpler to manage as we only have to make the changes once as opposed to everywhere the validation is required.

However, at some point, we will still be required to put some level of validation in the underlying service itself. For example, take our `updateCreditCard` operation, despite all our checks we can't be completely sure that the credit card itself is actually a valid card and that the card name, security number, and so on correspond to the given card number. To validate this, we will still need to call out to an external validation service.

In addition, we still need to validate that the userId provided as part of the operation is a valid user within our system.

Using Business Rules for validation

One option for implementing validation checks within your service is to separate them out as a Business Rule. This allows us to implement the validation just once and then share it across multiple services. This shares a number of advantages with the approaches already discussed, including:

- Simplifies development of rules, as we only need to implement it once

- Rules are implemented consistently across multiple services

- Easier to maintain as rules only need to be modified once should a change be required

When implementing a service using BPEL, the use of rules for validation is a pretty natural fit. But natively rules is implemented in Java, so comes with a Java API making it relatively straightforward to call from any services implemented in Java.

In addition, you can also expose a rule set as a web service, either in the standard way you would expose a Java code as a web service, or just by wrapping the rule in a decision service embedded within a Synchronous BPEL process.

Coding in validation

While providing an extra option for validation, using Business Rules will not be appropriate in every case. In these scenarios the only remaining option is to implement the validation in code.

However, even when we take this approach, we can still follow the same pattern that we used for Business Rules, namely to separate out the validation from the core service so that it can be used in multiple services and also consider the option of providing a means to maintain the validation rules without the need to modify actual code.

Returning validation failures in synchronous services

When putting the validation in the underlying service, apart from carrying out the validation we also need a mechanism for returning any validation failures to the client, ideally with some meaningful information about why the error occurred.

For synchronous services the mechanism for achieving this is to return a SOAP Fault to the service caller. A SOAP Fault contains four pieces of information, namely:

- `faultcode`: This provides a high-level indication as to the cause of the fault. SOAP 1.1 defines the following fault codes: `VersionMismatch`, `MustUnderstand`, `Client`, or `Server`. As the fault is as a result of an error in the message payload which the client needs to fix, we should return a fault code of type `Client`, unless we are returning a custom fault code.

- `faultstring`: This should contain a human-readable description of why the fault occurred, that is, the reason for the validation failure.

- `faultactor`: This provides details of where in the message path the fault occurred. If the failure occurred somewhere other than the final destination of the SOAP message then this must be present to indicate where. For our purpose, we can leave this blank.

- `detail`: This is an optional element, which can be used to provide further detail about why the fault occurred. We only need to provide this if the `faultstring` does not provide sufficient information for the client to handle the error.

Defining faults

Unless returning a basic fault, that is, using a predefined fault code and no structured content within the `soap:detail`, it is good practice to define the fault as part of the WSDL contract defining your service.

Faults are defined by adding the appropriate `fault` elements to the `operation` declarations. A fault has two attributes: `name` which corresponds to the fault code returned in the soap fault and `message` which will contain additional information about the fault and is returned within the `soap:detail` element.

For example to define a fault for the `updateCreditCard` operation we would just add the following `fault` element to our definition, shown as follows:

```
<operation name="updateCreditCard">
  <input message="tns:updateCreditCard "/>
  <output message="tns:updateCreditCardResponse "/>
  <fault   name="tns:invalidCreditCard"
  message="tns:invalidCreditCardFault "/>
</operation>
```

There is nothing to stop a service returning a fault which is undeclared in its service contract. However, by declaring the fault, the service consumer has the opportunity to handle the fault in an appropriate manner. By knowing the structure of the fault detail is able to process it in a more meaningful way.

Custom fault codes

Often it is desirable to define a custom fault, particularly for services that may return a number of faults, as this can simplify fault handling for the service consumer (because they can implement targeted fault-handling mechanisms for each type of fault).

SOAP 1.1 allows custom fault codes to be implemented through the use of the dot notation, for example we could define a fault code of `client.invalidCreditCard` in the SOAP namespace (`http://schemas.xmlsoap.org/soap/envelope/`). However, this can result in namespace collision and interoperability issues so is not WS-I Basic Profile compliant, and should be avoided.

Instead custom fault codes should be defined within their own namespace, for example we have defined our `invalidCreditCard` fault code to be in the same namespace as the actual `userManagement` service.

> While defining custom faults within their own namespace is WS-I Basic Profile compliant, WS-I Basic Profile still encourages that you use the standard SOAP 1.1 fault codes and use the detail element to provide any extra information.

Validation failures in asynchronous services

If an asynchronous service needs to return a fault to a client, it can't do this in the reply message in the same way that a synchronous service can. This is because an asynchronous service consists of two one-way operations, the first containing the original request, the second a callback from the service containing the result.

To return a fault we need to do this within the callback. We have two basic options to choose from, the first is to return the success or otherwise with the content of the standard callback and allow the client to inspect the content to determine whether the service was successfully invoked or not.

The other is to define additional operations on the callback port specifically for the purpose of returning an error message. The latter of these is the preferred approach as it allows the client to implement separate handlers for callbacks indicating errors (in much the same way we can implement separate fault handlers for each type of fault returned with synchronous services).

In many ways it's helpful to think of the operation name as being the equivalent of the fault code, and the message payload of the operation can be used to hold the equivalent of the remainder of the fault information (for example, fault string and detail).

For example, one way to define an asynchronous version of our `updateCreditCard` operation is as follows:

```
<portType name="userManagement">
  <operation name="updateCreditCard">
    <input message="usr:updateCreditCard "/>
```

```
    </operation>
  </portType>

  <portType name="userManagementCallback">
    <operation name="updateCreditCardCallback">
      <input message=" usr:updateCreditCardCallback "/>
    </operation>

    <operation name="invalidCreditCard">
      <input message="usr:invalidCreditCard"/>
    </operation>
  </portType>
```

The final callback operation (highlighted in the code), is the equivalent of the fault defined within our synchronous service.

Layered validation considerations

Within a single composite application we have a certain amount of control over what validation to put in the schema, Schematron, and the underlying services. This allows us to design and implement these in a coordinated fashion so that they can work in synergy with one another.

However, once we start assembling services from other composite applications, then the lines of demarcation and thus which service is responsible for which validation becomes less clear.

There are a number of potential strategies which can be adopted, but each has its own strength and weaknesses. We examine some of these in the following sections, but in reality there is not always a simple answer and it really comes down to good design and being aware of the issues.

Dangers of over validation

Probably the "safest" approach is to make each service fully responsible for its own validation, and thus perform whatever validation is required regardless of what validation is performed by any other service in the chain.

However, this could have potential performance implications. Apart from the obvious overhead of performing the same work several times, it could introduce potential points of contention within the system.

If we take the `updateCreditCard` operation, at some point our application will need to fully validate the card. To do this, it will need to call out to an external web service. If we follow the approach of performing this validation in every service involved in the operation, and the request has to go through n layers of services, then that would require n callouts to the external service with the implied latency of making n callouts. Not to mention that the card company might wonder why this card is being validated so many times!

Another issue with this approach is that the validation may be implemented several times, not always identically, resulting in inconsistent validation that is hard to change. This can be addressed by using shared XML Schema, Schematron, and Business Rules validation.

Dangers of under validation

An alternate approach is to push the responsibility of validation down to the lowest service in the chain on the basis that if an error occurs, then it will catch the error which will be propagated up the chain and returned to the original consumer of the service.

Again on the surface this approach seems fine. However, the main issue here is if we have to undo any work as a result of the error, which we could have avoided if we had caught it earlier. For example, if have a service A which is a composite composed of service B and service C, the call to service B may succeed and only the call to C fail, in which case we may need to undo any work carried out by service B.

Negative coupling of validation

Another issue that arises with service composition is that a high level component which calls other components effectively *inherits* the validation of the lower level components.

The strategy we recommend here is that we put the minimal amount of validation in the lower-level component and put the more restrictive constraints in the higher level components.

Assuming the service is only designed for internal use, that is via other components within our control, this approach works well. We can mandate that any additional validation that is required is applied in a higher level component.

For those components that we need to expose directly to external consumers, we can still follow this approach, by implementing a wrapper component with the required validation and then exposing this externally.

This approach allows us to develop more generic lower-level components, which are easier to reuse while at the same time minimizing over and under validation.

Summary

In this chapter, we've looked at how we can implement validation within an individual service through a combination of XSD validation, Schematron, and Business Rules.

Ideally we should use XSD validation to check the overall sanity of the data, but in order to provide a greater level of flexibility abstract out the business specific validation into a separate component such as Schematron. This provides greater flexibility to change the validation for a component without the need to redeploy a new version of it.

In situations where Schematron can't provide the required validation, we've looked at how we can use Business Rules to build this into the underlying service implementation, again giving us the flexibility to change the validation without having to redeploy the service.

Finally, we've looked at some of the issues and potential strategies for validation when combing multiple services; while there are no simple solutions, by at least having an appreciation of the issues we are able to take these into account in the design of our overall solution.

13
Error Handling

Handling errors or faults is an important consideration for SOA based applications, especially if you consider that a solution is likely to be a loose assembly of independent components each with varying levels of resilience, throughput, and availability.

How faults are handled depends on a number of factors, whether it's a business or system fault, was the service, where the fault originated, called synchronously or asynchronously, and whether the interaction between the client and the component detecting the fault is synchronous or asynchronous.

A business fault is loosely defined as one we know about in advance, in that it is defined as part of the service contract and so represents a legitimate state within the business process. How we handle a fault of this type is largely driven by business requirements, and so it makes sense to handle these within the context of the process.

A system fault, conversely, is one that is unexpected in nature, and could occur to any component in the solution. Such faults are often caused by infrastructure problems, such as a network outage or a service being unavailable. Often these are temporary and can be handled by retrying the service at a later time.

The interaction between the client and the component detecting the fault also influences how we handle it. If asynchronous the component has time to resolve the problem; for example, if the fault occurred due to a service being unavailable, it can retry it later.

With synchronous interactions, we only have a small window in which to resolve the fault before the client times out waiting for our component and raises its own fault. With this style of interaction, often all we can do is catch the fault, undo any partially completed activities so that we leave the system in a consistent state, and then return a fault to the client.

In this chapter we examine to how to handle faults within our composite applications. We first examine the catch and compensate activities that BPEL provides and how we can use them to handle business faults. Next we look at how to leverage the BPEL PM Fault Management Framework to simplify the handling of system faults within BPEL.

In the final section of this chapter, we look at the mechanisms the service bus provides for handling faults and how we can use these in our overall fault management strategy.

Business faults

A business fault is one that is defined in the WSDL of the service; how we define the fault depends on whether a service is synchronous or asynchronous.

Defining faults in synchronous services

Synchronous services signal faults by returning a fault element in place of the defined output message for the service. These faults are defined in the WSDL of the service, and are denoted by the `<fault>` element.

For example, the oBay application implements a dummy `CreditCard` service, which includes the operation `verifyCreditCard`; the definition of the operation is as follows:

```
<portType name="CardServices">
    <operation name="verifyCreditCard">
        <input     message="tns:verifyCreditCard" />
        <output    message="tns:verifyCreditCardResponse"/>
        <fault     name="invalidCreditCard"
            message="tns:invalidCreditCardFault"/>
    </operation>
</portType>
```

As well as defining the standard input and output messages for the operation, it lists a fault message (highlighted above) that could be returned in place of the defined output operation. An operation can define zero, one, or many faults for an individual operation; they are similar in construct to an output message, except that they must also be named so that the client can distinguish which fault has been returned.

 When a `soap:Fault` is generated, the `faultcode` will contain the fault name (for example `tns:invalidCreditCard` in the above example) and the `detail` element will contain the content of the fault message.

Defining faults in asynchronous services

Asynchronous services don't explicitly support the concept of faults; this is because the result of an asynchronous service is returned in a separate callback operation. So to signal a fault, the service will need to define additional callbacks, typically one extra callback per fault. If we take our credit card example and rewrite it as an asynchronous service, we get the corresponding WSDL:

```
<portType name="CardServices"
  <operation name="verifyCreditCard">
    <input message="tns:verifyCreditCard"/>
  </operation>
</portType>
<portType name="CardServicesCallback"
  <operation name="creditCardVerified">
    <input message="tns:creditCardVerified" />
  </operation>
  <operation name="invalidCreditCard">
    <input message="tns:invalidCreditCard" />
  </operation>
</portType>
```

Here we can see that we've defined a second callback operation (highlighted above). This corresponds to the fault we defined in the synchronous operation. If we examine this, we can see we've used the fault name as the operation name in the callback, and while we have two different messages, in reality they are identical — we have just used different names as we want to stick to our naming conventions.

It is still possible for the invocation of an asynchronous service to return a fault. This can occur when the system is unable to successfully deliver the invocation message to the asynchronous service, for example the network connection is down. This type of fault we would treat as a system fault as opposed to a business fault.

Handling business faults in BPEL

Within a BPEL process, any call to a PartnerLink could result in a fault being raised. Other activities within a process can also result in a fault being thrown (for example due to a selection failure within an `assign` activity), and in addition the process itself may need to signal a fault.

When a fault occurs in a BPEL process, the process must first catch the fault; otherwise the process will terminate with a state of `closed.faulted`. Once caught the next step is to decide whether the fault can be handled locally within the process or whether it needs to be returned to the client.

If the interaction between the client and the process is synchronous, it provides limited opportunity to correct the cause of the fault and retry the activity. For example if the fault occurred due to a service not being available, we can retry the service in the hope that its outage was very temporary, but if we wait for the service to come back up then the client of our BPEL process is likely to time out and raise its own fault.

So with synchronous interactions, all we can really do is catch the fault, undo any partially completed activities so that we leave the system in a consistent state, and then return a fault to the client.

The client itself may be a BPEL process, or another SOA component, again if the interaction between this component and its client is also synchronous, it will typically need to return its own fault, and so on up the chain until the interaction between a client and a component is asynchronous in nature.

With asynchronous interactions, we have a lot more flexibility to handle the fault within the context of the process, as the client is unlikely to timeout (though we still need to allow for the fact that the client may only wait so long).

If the fault is temporary in nature, such as a service not being available, we can wait for the issue to be resolved and retry the activity later. However, this type of fault should be handled using the Fault Management Framework (which we will cover later in this chapter). This allows us to focus on handling business faults within our BPEL process, which keeps our process simpler and easier to maintain.

Handling business faults is just a natural extension to the process, in that we need to model the process to cater for these types of scenarios. For example if a fault occurred due to invalid data, then in a synchronous interaction we would just return details of the fault to the client, while in an asynchronous interaction we could create a Human Workflow Task for someone to capture the correct data in order that the process can resume.

Catching faults

The first step in handling a fault is to catch it. Within BPEL we do this using a `<catch>` branch, which can either be attached to a scope or the process. With a catch branch, we specify the name of the fault to be caught and the series of activities to be carried out in that event.

Once the catch branch has completed, processing will continue with the next activity following the scope in which the fault was caught, assuming of course another fault hasn't been thrown.

We can define as many catch branches as we want for a scope, and, in addition, we can also attach a `<catchAll>` branch which will catch any fault not caught by any of the specific `<catch>` activities.

When a fault is raised, the BPEL engine will first check the current scope to determine a suitable catch or catch all branch. If the fault is not caught, the BPEL engine will then check the containing scope for an appropriate fault handler, and so on up to process level.

If the fault is not caught at this level, then the process will terminate with a status of `closed.faulted`. If the interaction between the client and the process is synchronous, then the fault will be automatically returned to the client. However, if the interaction is asynchronous then the fault will **not** be returned, with the potential result being that the client may hang waiting for a response that is never sent.

Adding a catch branch

To demonstrate this we will look at the `UserRegistration` process which needs to carry out a number of checks; for example that the requested `userId` isn't already in use, that the supplied credit card is valid. Should one of these checks fail, we need to catch the fault and then return a reply to the client to indicate that an error has occurred.

To achieve this we will place each validation step in its own scope, and define a fault handler for each one. To add a catch branch to a scope, click on the **Add Catch Branch** icon for the scope; this will add an empty catch branch to the scope as shown in the following figure:

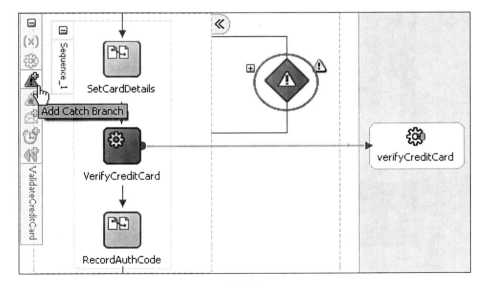

The next step is to specify the type of fault that you want to catch; to do this double-click on the catch branch icon (circled in the previous screenshot). This will bring up the **Catch** dialogue as shown in the following figure:

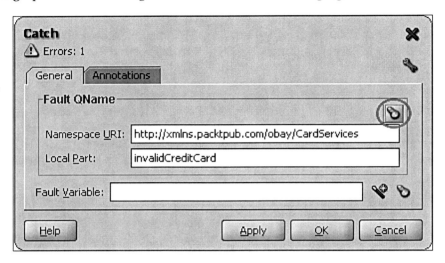

Click on the flashlight for the **Fault QName** (circled in the previous screenshot) and this will launch the **Fault Chooser** dialogue. From here you can browse to the fault that we want to catch; in our case this is the **invalidCreditCard** fault defined in the WSDL file of the **CreditCardServices** Partner Link.

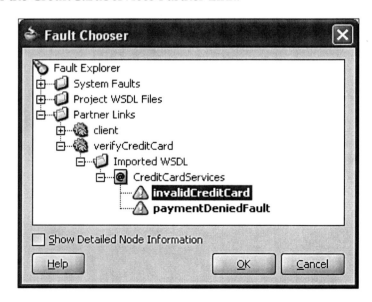

There is also the option to specify a fault variable to hold details of the fault returned; this should be of type `Message` and match the message type defined for the fault, that is `client:invalidCreditCardFault` in the case of the fault `invalidCreditCard` (as defined in the WSDL file for this service).

Once we have caught the fault, we need to specify the activities to perform in order to handle the fault. In our case we need to undo any activities completed in previous scopes, using the compensate activity before we return the fault `invalidUserDetails` to the caller of this process.

However, the current scope is not the correct context for triggering the required compensation (we will see why in a moment), so our fault handler needs to capture the reason for the fault and throw a new fault that can be handled at the appropriate place within our process.

Throwing faults

To do this expand the catch branch for the **Fault Handler** by clicking on the **+** symbol, and drag a **Throw** activity into it.

To specify the fault we wish to throw, double-click the **Throw** activity to bring up the dialogue to configure it, as shown in the following screenshot:

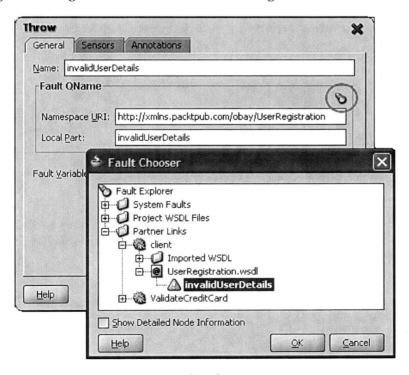

Next click the flashlight to bring up the **Fault Chooser**. This time we want to browse to the fault we wish to throw which is the `invalidUserDetails` fault, which is defined in the WSDL file for the **UserRegistration** process.

We also want to record the reason for the invalid user details, so we need to define a fault variable to hold this. The simplest way to do this is by clicking on the magic wand icon to create a variable of the right type, though you should specify that the variable is local to the scope as opposed to global.

Finally, we've added a simple assign activity before our throw activity to populate our fault variable, so our final catch branch looks as follows:

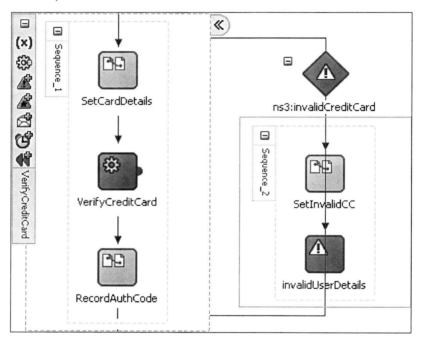

Compensation

As part of the user registration process we need to check that the requested userId is not already in use. We do this by attempting to insert a record into the `obay_user` table (where `userId` is the primary key).

If this succeeds we know the `userId` is unique and at the same time prevents anyone else from acquiring it (on the off chance that two requests with the same userId are submitted at the same time).

We do this before verifying the credit card, the result being that if the credit card fails verification we end up with a user record for the specified userId in the `obay_user` table. This will cause the next request to fail when the user resubmits their request with corrected credit card details.

 An alternative approach would be to verify the credit card first before validating the userId; however, with this approach if the user chooses multiple userIds that are already taken, their credit card would be validated several times which could cause issues with the card company.

To prevent resubmission of user registrations from failing, we need to undo the creation of the user record; one way of achieving this is to use the compensation model provided by BPEL.

This allows us to break a BPEL process up into logical components using scopes. For each scope we can define a compensation handler that will contain a sequence of one or more activities to reverse the effects of the activities contained within that scope.

In our case we need to define a compensate handler on the `CreateUser` scope, which deletes the user record created by the scope.

Defining compensation

To define the compensation activities for a scope, click on the **Add Compensation Handler** icon for the scope, this will add an empty compensation branch on the scope as shown in the following figure:

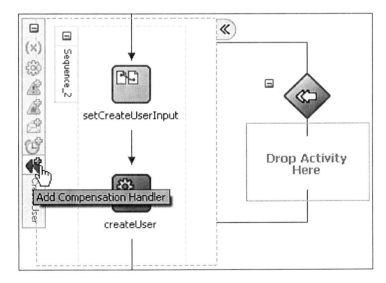

Once you've created your compensation handler, simply add the activities that need to be carried out to undo the effect of the scope; in our case we just need to call the `deleteUser` operation on the `UserManagement` service.

Triggering a compensation handler

Compensation handlers aren't triggered automatically, rather they need to be explicitly invoked using the **Compensate** activity, which can only be invoked from within a fault handler or another compensation handler.

When the compensate activity is executed, it will only invoke the compensation handlers for those scopes **directly** contained within the scope for which the fault handler is defined. Or if invoked in a fault handler at the process level (as in our example), it will only execute the compensation handlers for the top level scopes.

The compensation handlers will only be invoked for those scopes which have completed successfully, and will be invoked in reverse order to that which they were completed. That is the compensation handler for the most recently completed scope will be invoked first, and then the next most recent and so on.

If a scope whose compensation handler has been invoked contains scopes for which compensation needs to be performed, then it will need to call the compensate activity within its own compensation handler.

 If a scope doesn't have an explicit compensation handler defined for it, then it will have a default compensation handler which just invokes the compensate activity.

Adding a compensate activity

For our purposes we need to trigger the compensate activity at the process level, so to do this we have defined a fault handler on the process to catch the `invalidUserDetails` fault thrown by our previous fault handler.

Once done, we will add a **Compensate** activity as the first activity within our fault handler. To configure it, double-click the **Compensate** activity to bring up the dialogue as shown:

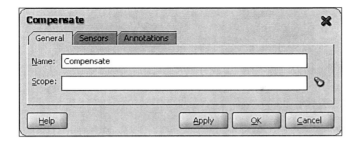

Here we have the option of specifying a **Scope** name to restrict it to invoking the compensation handler for that scope. For our purposes we want to invoke the compensation handler for all top level scopes so have left it blank.

Returning faults

If at run time the verifyCreditCard operation returns a fault of type invalidCreditCard then this will be caught by the catch branch we defined on the VerifyCreditCard scope.

This fault handler will throw an invalidUserDetails fault, which will get caught by the catch branch defined against our process. This will execute the compensate activity triggering the compensation handler on the CreateUser scope, which will delete the previously inserted user record.

The final step is to return an invalidUserDetails fault to the caller of the BPEL process. To return a fault within BPEL we use the **Reply** activity. The difference is to configure it to return a fault as opposed to a standard output message, as shown in the following screenshot:

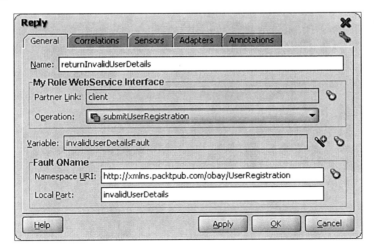

Here we have configured the **Partner Link** and **Operation** as you would for a standard reply.

However, for the **Variable** we need to specify a variable that contains the content of the fault to be returned. In our case this is the content of the fault caught by our process level fault handler (and populated by the fault handler for the ValidateCreditCard scope).

Finally we need to specify that an invalidUserDetails fault should be returned. Specify this by clicking on the flashlight in the **Fault QName** panel to launch the now familiar **Fault Chooser**. After returning the fault, the process will complete.

If a fault had been triggered at the step of creating the user record (for example because the userId was already in use), then an invalidUserDetails fault would have been thrown in the fault handler for this scope. The process would follow the same flow as outlined above, apart from the fact that the compensation handler for the CreateUser scope would not have been triggered as the scope never completed.

Asynchronous considerations

As we pointed out earlier, asynchronous services don't explicitly support the concept of faults, so it's worth examining how we would manage the above scenario if all the messaging interactions were asynchronous.

As we covered earlier, an asynchronous version of the CreditCard service would require two callbacks, creditCardVerified and invalidCreditCard, which would be the equivalent of our fault in the synchronous example.

Within our VerifyCreditCard after our invoke activity, instead of having a receive activity to receive the callback we would need a pick activity with two onMessage branches, one for each callback. The branch for invalidCreditCard would be the equivalent of our synchronous fault handler above, and would contain the same activities as its synchronous equivalent.

We would still have the fault handler defined for our process, which would catch the fault thrown by our onMessage branch for invalidCreditCard.

The activities of this fault handler would be similar to the fault handler in our synchronous version. We would still call the compensate activity, but rather than use the reply activity to return a fault, we would now use the invoke activity to invoke the appropriate callback to signal invalid user details.

Using the fault management framework

The Oracle SOA Suite provides a sophisticated framework for handling invocation faults within BPEL PM. Without the framework, when a BPEL process invokes a service, if an error occurs the fault is returned to the BPEL process to handle.

This is fine for a business fault as we need to handle it in a way appropriate to the business process as covered above.

But for system faults, such as network problems resulting in a service becoming temporarily unavailable, implementing the handling of this at the process level can be protracted, often requiring the same fragments of BPEL to be implemented in every process.

For managing these types of faults, BPEL PM provides a fault handling framework which allows us to define policies for handling faults which occur when a BPEL process executes an invoke activity.

When a fault occurs the framework intercepts the fault before it is returned to the BPEL process. It then attempts to identify an appropriate fault policy to handle the fault. If it finds one the policy is executed and, assuming the fault is resolved, the BPEL process continues as if nothing happened.

A policy consists of two basic components, the faults that you wish to catch and, once caught, the actions you wish to take, such as retry the service or perform manual recovery actions from the BPEL Console.

Defining a fault policy

Re-examine the `UserRegistration` process at the point that it invokes the credit card service to verify the user's card details. Apart from the business faults that could be returned, it could also return a system fault such as the following:

```
<soap:Body xmlns:soap="http://schemas.xmlsoap.org/soap/envelope"
           xmlns:tns="http://schema.packtpub.com/obay/flt">
  <soap:Fault>
    <faultcode>tns:TransportFault</faultcode>
    <faultstring>Transport Run Time Error</faultstring>
    <detail>
      <tns:fault>
        <tns:code>380002</tns:code>
        <tns:summary>Connection Error</tns:summary>
        <tns:detail>
          ...
```

```
        </tns:detail>
      </tns:fault>
    </detail>
  </soap:Fault>
</soap:Body>
```

Indicating that it's unable to call the service because of a transport problem, the code of 380002 is displayed indicating that this is probably due to a temporary problem. For this kind of scenario, we can define a fault policy to catch this error and re-try the service.

The outline of the fault policy for our credit card service is shown as follows:

```xml
<?xml version="1.0" encoding="UTF-8"?>
<faultPolicy version="2.0.1" id="ValidateCreditCardPolicy"
            xmlns:env="http://schemas.xmlsoap.org/soap/envelope/"
            xmlns="http://schemas.oracle.com/bpel/faultpolicy">
  <Conditions>
    ...
  </Conditions>
  <Actions>
    ...
  </Actions>
</faultPolicy>
```

From this we can see a fault policy consist of the top level element faultPolicy, with the attribute id, which is used to uniquely identify our policy (as we can define multiple policies per BPEL domain).

The policy itself is divided into two sections — the Conditions section, which defines the faults we wish to handle, and the Actions section, which defines the actions to take in order to recover from the fault.

Each fault policy should be defined in a separate XML file, which should be placed in the directory:

```
<SOA_HOME>\bpel\domains\<domain_name>\config\fault-policies
```

Here, <domain_name> corresponds to the domain to which the policy applies. The file can have any name, but for the purpose of clarity it is recommended naming it after the fault policy ID, so ValidateCreditCardPolicy.xml in our scenario.

Defining fault policy conditions

The first section of a fault policy defines the conditions that we wish to handle and contains a list of one or more faultName elements that we want our policy to handle. For the above example, we could define the following:

```
<Conditions>
  <faultName xmlns:tns="http://schema.packtpub.com/obay/faults"
             name="tns:TransportFault">
    <condition>
      <test>$fault.payload/tns:fault/tns:code="380002"</test>
      <action ref="ora-retry"/>
    </condition>
    <condition>
      <action ref="ora-human-intervention"/>
    </condition>
  </faultName>
  <faultName>
    <condition>
      <action ref="ora-human-intervention"/>
    </condition>
  </faultName>
  ...
</Conditions>
```

Specifying the <faultName>

A faultName element is used to define a specific fault which we wish to handle; it contains a single attribute name, which specifies the fault code (i.e. tns:TransportFault in the previous example) of the fault to handle.

Note, a faultcode is defined as a QName type, which has a format of:

```
prefix:faultName
```

Here, prefix maps to a namespace. So within the faultName element we need to define the namespace to which the prefix is mapped, otherwise we won't get a match.

We can also specify a faultName element without a name attribute, which will match all faults. This allows us to define a generic catch-all policy for any fault not handled by a more specific policy.

Specifying the <condition>

The faultName element defines one or more conditions; each condition consists of an optional test element and an action reference.

The test element allows us to specify an XPath expression which is evaluated against the content of the fault; if the XPath expression evaluates to true, the condition is considered a match and the action referenced within the action element will be executed.

Otherwise the fault management framework will look to evaluate the next condition, and so on until it finds a match. A condition without a test element will always return a match.

In the above policy, we have defined the following test for our first condition:

```
<test>$fault.payload/tns:fault/tns:code="380002"</test>
```

Where the variable `$fault.payload` maps to the root element within the `payload` part of our SOAP Fault, so the above test is the equivalent of:

```
/soap:Fault/detail/tns:fault/tns:code="380002"
```

Which for the fault in our example will evaluate to `true`, so the Fault Management Framework would execute the action `ora-retry`; if `tns:code` contained some other value, then it would move onto the next condition. As this doesn't include a test element it will result in a match and execute the `ora-human-intervention` action.

 The `message` element for some faults, including the extension faults defined by BPEL PM, contains multiple parts, for example `code`, `summary`, and `detail`. To evaluate the content of any of these parts, just append the part name to `$fault.`, so to check the content of the `code` part you would specify `$fault.code`.

Defining fault policy actions

The second part of our fault policy defines the actions referenced in the `Conditions` section; this consists of an `Actions` element, which contains one or more `Action` elements.

Each `Action` element contains an `id` attribute, which is the value referenced by the action `ref` attribute within the conditions. For the conditions defined in the above policy, we have defined two actions: `ora-retry` and `ora-human-intervention` as shown here:

```
<Actions>
  <Action id="ora-retry">
    <retry>
      <retryCount>5</retryCount>
      <retryInterval>15</retryInterval>
      <exponentialBackoff/>
      <retryFailureAction ref="ora-human-intervention"/>
    </retry>
  </Action>
  <Action id="ora-human-intervention">
    <humanIntervention/>
  </Action>
</Actions>
```

The content of the action element is used to specify and configure the actual action to be executed by the fault management framework, which can be one of `retry`, `humanIntervention`, `rethrow`, `abort`, `replayScope`, or `javaAction`.

Retry action

The retry action instructs the fault management framework to retry a failed service invocation until it is successful or it reaches a specified limit. In the above example we have specified that we will retry the service five times; if after this the invoke is still failing we have specified that we want to invoke the `ora-human-intervention` action.

If we didn't specify this, the fault management framework would just re-throw the fault to the BPEL process for it to handle.

The retry action takes a number of parameters that allows us to configure how it behaves, these are defined as follows:

- `retryCount`: Specifies the maximum number of retries before this action completes with a failure status.

- `retryInterval`: Specifies the period in seconds between retries.

- `exponentialBackoff`: An optional element which takes no parameters. When specified, if a retry fails, the interval between this retry and the next retry is double that of the previous interval. In the above example the first retry would occur after 15 seconds, the second after 30 seconds, the third after 60 seconds, and so on.

- `retrySuccessAction`: An optional element with a single attribute `ref`. This references another action to be taken upon successful retry of a service. This should only be used to reference a Java action (see below), which we can use to generate an alert.

- `retryFailureAction`: An optional element with a single attribute `ref`, that allows you to define the action to be carried out should all retries fail.

For scenarios where the interaction between a BPEL process and its client are synchronous, we should only use small retry periods. This is because we are suspending the BPEL process between retries; thus if the retry period is too long then the client which invoked the BPEL process could timeout while waiting for a response.

Human intervention action

For errors which are more permanent, the `humanIntervention` action gives us the ability to suspend a process; once suspended we can log into the BPEL console to manually handle the fault.

From within the console we can perform a number of actions. These include manually retrying the service, with the option of modifying the input payload in case this is causing the error, or in the event that the service can't be called, we can get the process to skip the invoke activity and manually create the output that should have been returned by the service. We look at how we can do this as well as other possible options in the next section.

Because we are pausing the BPEL process, we should only use this action if the interaction between the BPEL process and its client is asynchronous otherwise the client will timeout while waiting for the problem to be resolved.

Re-throw action

For errors that we don't want handled by the fault management framework, we can use the `rethrowFault` action to re-throw the fault to our BPEL Process.

This is often useful when we have defined a generic fault handler to catch all faults, but want to exclude certain faults. For example, if we look at the fault policy defined above, the final handler within our conditions section is defined as follows:

```
<faultName>
  <condition>
    <action ref="ora-human-intervention"/>
  </condition>
</faultName>
```

This will catch all faults that have not yet been handled. This is exactly what we want for any unknown system faults, however, we want business faults to be explicitly handled by our BPEL process.

The re-throw action allows us to do just this; we can define a fault handler that catches our business faults, such as the following:

```
<faultName xmlns:tns="http://xmlns.packtpub.com/obay/CardServices"
           name="invalidCreditCard">
  <condition>
    <action ref="ora-rethrow-fault"/>
  </condition>
</faultName>
```

This will then invoke the following action:

```
<Action id="ora-rethrow-fault">
  <rethrowFault/>
</Action>
```

This will re-throw the fault to our BPEL process.

Abort action

This action causes the BPEL process to terminate. It's the equivalent of executing a `terminate` activity directly within the BPEL process. Note, in both cases no response is returned to the client of the BPEL Process.

An `abort` action takes no parameters and is defined as follows:

```
<Action id="ora-terminate">
  <abort/>
</Action>
```

Replay scope action

This action causes the fault management framework to return a replay fault to the BPEL process. This fault will be automatically caught by the scope in which the fault is thrown and trigger the BPEL engine to re-execute the scope from the beginning.

A `replay scope` action takes no parameters and is defined as follows:

```
<Action id="ora-replay-scope">
  <replayScope/>
</Action>
```

Java action

This enables us to call out to a custom Java class as part of the process of handling the fault. The class must implement the interface `IFaultRecoveryJavaClass`, which defines two methods:

```
public void handleRetrySuccess(IFaultRecoveryContext ctx );
public String handleBPELFault( IFaultRecoveryContext ctx );
```

The first method `handleRetrySuccess` is called after a successful retry of an invocation, otherwise `handleBPELFault` is called.

The class is not intended to handle a fault, but more for generating alerts, and so on. For example, you could use invocation of the method `handleBPELFault` to generate a notification that there is a problem with a particular endpoint, and likewise use the invocation of the method `handleRetrySuccess` to generate a notification that the problem with the endpoint has now been resolved.

The method `handleBPELFault` also returns a string value, which can be mapped to the next action to be invoked by the framework, for example, if we defined the following javaAction:

```
<Action id="ora-java">
  <javaAction className="mypackage.myClass"
      defaultAction=" ora-human-intervention ">
    <returnValue value="RETRY" ref="ora-retry"/>
    <returnValue value="MANUAL" ref="ora-human-intervention"/>
  </javaAction>
</Action>
```

The `javaAction` element takes two attributes: `className` which specifies the Java class to be invoked and `defaultAction` which specifies the default action to be executed upon completion of the Java action.

Within the `javaAction` element we can specify zero, one or more `returnValue` elements, each of which maps a value returned by `handleBPELFault` to a corresponding follow-up action to be executed by the fault management framework.

In the previous example, we have specified that for a return value of `RETRY` the framework should execute the `ora-retry` action, and that if a value of `MANUAL` is returned, then it should execute the `ora-human-intervention` action.

If no mapping is found for the return value, then the `defaultAction` specified as part of the `javaAction` is executed. This gives us the flexibility to calculate how we wish to handle a particular fault at run time.

Binding fault policies

To put a fault policy into operation, we need to specify the invoke activities within a BPEL process that the fault policy is to be applied; this is known as binding.

We can bind fault policies to Partner Links, Port Type or Processes, and we can define these either for a specific process or an entire domain.

Binding fault polices at the process level

Bindings are configured for an individual process by including a `faultPolicyBindings` section in its `bpel.xml` file. This is defined after the `partnerLinkBindings` section, as shown:

```
<?xml version = '1.0' encoding = 'UTF-8'?>
<BPELSuitcase>
  <BPELProcess id="UserRegistration" src="UserRegistration.bpel">
    <partnerLinkBindings>
      ...
      <partnerLinkBinding name="CreditCardServices">
        <property name="wsdlLocation">CardServices.wsdl</property>
      </partnerLinkBinding>
    </partnerLinkBindings>
```

```
    <faultPolicyBindings>
      <process faultPolicy="UserRegPolicy"/>
      <partnerLink faultPolicy="ValidateCreditCardPolicy
            xmlns:ccd="http://xmlns.packtpub.com/obay/CardServices">
        <name>CreditCardService</name>
        <portType>ccd:CardServices</portType>
      </partnerLink>
    </faultPolicyBindings>
  </BPELProcess>
</BPELSuitcase>
```

Defining bindings on the process

The `process` element is an **optional** element, which allows us to specify the default fault policy for a BPEL process; it contains a single attribute `faultPolicy`, which contains the `id` of the fault policy to be used for the process.

In the previous example we have specified that the `UserRegistration` process should use `UserRegPolicy` as its default fault policy.

Defining bindings on the PartnerLink

After the process binding, we can specify one or more `partnerLink` elements; each of which allows us to bind a fault policy to a specific Partner Link or Port Type. It contains a single attribute `faultPolicy`, which contains the `id` of the fault policy to be used for this binding.

Within the `partnerLink` elements, we specify zero or more `name` elements and zero or more `portType` elements.

The `name` element should contain the name of a PartnerLink within the process that we wish to bind the fault policy to, while the `portType` element should contain the name of the service port type as defined in the WSDL file that we wish to bind the fault policy to.

At first glance it may appear that there is little difference between binding the policy to either the partner link name or port type; however, it is quite possible to use the same port type within multiple partner links, each with their own name.

Binding fault policies at the domain level

In addition to specifying our fault policy bindings at the process level, we can also define this at the domain level; we do this by modifying the `fault-bindings.xml` file for the domain as appropriate. This file can be found at:

```
<SOA_HOME>\bpel\domains\<domain_name>\config\fault-bindings.xml
```

Here, `<domain_name>` corresponds to the domain to which the binding applies.

The structure of this file is the same as the `faultPolicyBindings` section of the `bpel.xml` file (and defined in the schema `fault-policy-binding.xsd`).

When defining bindings for Partner Links at the domain level, it's less error prone to define them for the port type, as opposed to the partner link name. It's unlikely that developers will always name partner links consistently; therefore as long as the same WSDL definition is being used to access a particular service, then the port type will always be the same.

Binding resolution

At run time when a fault occurs, the fault management framework will attempt to find a condition with a corresponding action that matches the fault.

It does this by first attempting to locate an appropriate fault policy binding, by looking for a binding in the following order:

- Partner Link name binding in `bpel.xml`
- Port type binding in `bpel.xml`
- Process binding in `bpel.xml`
- Partner Link name binding for the domain
- Port type binding for the domain
- Process binding for the domain

Once it finds a binding, it will check the fault policy to find a matching condition, and then execute its corresponding action. If no matching condition is found, it will then move to the next binding level; it will continue this process until either a matching condition is found or all binding levels have been checked.

Human intervention in BPEL Console

To manage processes suspended pending human intervention, we need to log into the BPEL Console. Once logged on, click on the **Activities** tab. This by default will list all activities with a state of pending (that is, awaiting human intervention) as shown in the following screenshot:

Activities 1 - 2					
	Activity Label	Instance	Process	Due	Fault Name
☐	⇒⚙ verifyCreditCard	370003	UserRegistration (v. 1.0)	no date	invalidCreditCard
☐	⇒⚙ verifyCreditCard	370001	UserRegistration (v. 1.0)	no date	invalidCreditCard

If you click on the activity label of a suspended process (for example, **verifyCreditCard** in the previous screenshot), then the Console will bring up the recovery screen for that activity, as shown:

From here you can carry out any of the standard recovery actions available in the fault management framework, such as retrying the service, re-throwing the exception, aborting the process, or replaying the scope. Plus it provides the ability to skip the failed invoke by selecting the continue activity.

In addition, we can get the value of any process variable, as in the screenshot, where we've fetched the variable verifyCreditCardInput that contains the message submitted to the failed invoke activity. From here we can also update the content of this or any other process variable.

This gives us a number of options for managing the fault, including changing the input variable and retrying the service or setting the output variable from a service and skipping the invoke activity.

Change the input variable contents and retry

A common cause for failure could be due to the input for the service being invalid; in the above example we may have provided an invalid security number for the credit card. One way to correct this is to modify our input and retry the service.

To do this, select the variable to update from the **Available Variables** drop down, that is, `verifyCreditCardInput` in the previous example and click **Get**. This will return the current content of the variable.

Next we can update `securityNo` to contain the correct value and click **Set** to update the content of the variable within the BPEL process.

Finally from the **Actions available** drop down select **Retry** and then click **Recover**; this will cause the BPEL process to retry the failed invoke activity with the updated variable and, if successful, to then continue with the remainder of the process.

Set the output variable and continue

Another scenario is that for whatever reason we are unable to call the service. For example in the above scenario the `verifyCreditCard` service is not available.

One way around this is to fallback to manual processing and for a service rep to phone the credit card company to verify the card and get an authorisation code. We can then manually update the appropriate variables within our process and continue processing.

To do this select the variable we want to update from the **Available Variables** drop down, that is, `verifyCreditCardOutput` in the previous example and click **Get**. This will return the current content of the variable, which in our case will be empty as it has yet to be initialized.

Next we need to enter the XML fragment that it should have contained if the service had been successfully invoked. A simple way to do this is click **Skeleton Value**; the console will then generate an empty XML skeleton of the variable into which we can enter the values.

Once we have specified the content of the variable, click **Set** and this will update the content of the variable within the BPEL process.

Finally from the **Actions available** drop down select **Continue** and then click **Recover**. This will cause the BPEL process to skip the failed invoke activity and continue with the remainder of the process.

 This is only useful for synchronous or one-way invocations. This is because if we skip the invoke activity for an asynchronous two-way invocation, then when the process reaches the corresponding receive activity it will end up waiting forever.

Handling faults within the service bus

Before we look at how to handle faults inside a proxy service, it's worth taking a step back to revisit our SOA architecture and the purpose of the Virtual Service layer.

Essentially this layer provides a proxy service based on our canonical model, which is responsible for routing requests to the appropriate application service. In the process of which it will validate and transform the input message into the one expected by the application service and vice versa for the response.

Within our proxy service an error can occur at the validate stage (as discussed in the previous chapter) in which case the proxy service needs to generate and return an appropriate fault to the client.

In addition when we call out to an external service, either to enrich the input message as part of the transformation or at the route stage, a fault could occur. This could either be a business or a system fault.

A business fault, by our definition, is just another **valid** response that can be returned by our application service, so the role of the proxy service is to transform that fault from an application specific one, to one defined in the WSDL of the proxy service which it can then return to its client.

In the case of a system fault, one option for the proxy service is to return the fault without modification directly to the client, and let it work out how to handle it.

However, it makes sense to define a standard set of system faults within our architecture that we map all other system faults to. This will simplify the implementation of standardized error handling for such faults across our applications.

With system faults that are temporary in nature, it may be tempting to build in the functionality to retry them; however, as we've already established, we only have a small window in which to resolves the fault before the client times out.

So we need to follow a strategy that avoids multiple layers in our composite application retrying temporary errors, because the role of the virtual service layer is to provide a standardized representation of the underlying service, including faults. As a guideline we will not attempt to retry transient faults within this layer.

 One scenario where it makes sense to retry a business service, is where it has multiple endpoints. In this scenario if a call to one endpoint fails, the service bus can be configured to retry an alternate endpoint for the same business service.

Handling faults in synchronous proxy services

The basic strategy for handling faults within the service bus is essentially the same regardless of whether it is a business or system fault. That is to catch the fault, undo any partially completed activities so that we leave the system in a consistent state and map the underlying fault to a "standard" fault, which is then returned to the client.

If we examine the `CreditCard` service used by the above BPEL process, this is actually a proxy service implemented on the service bus. OBay accepts MasterCard and Visa, and in our scenario each of these card providers supplies their own service for card verification and payment processing.

The role of the `CreditCard` proxy is to provide a standardized service, independent of card type. It will then route requests to the appropriate service, based on the card being used.

As part of this process, the proxy service will transform the request from the oBay canonical form into the specific format required by the card provider and vice versa for the response.

If during execution of the proxy service an error occurs, the role of the proxy service is to intercept the fault and then map it to a specific type of fault, either a business fault defined by the proxy service or a standard system fault.

Raising an error

When an error occurs, the service bus performs a number of steps. First it will populate the `$fault` variable with details of the error. Next if the error was caused by the external service returning a fault, it will update the `$body` variable to hold the actual fault returned.

For example if the `verifyMasterCard` operation returned the following fault:

```
<env:Body xmlns:env="http://schemas.xmlsoap.org/soap/envelope/">
  <env:Fault xmlns:mcd="http://xmlns.packtpub.com/MasterCard">
    <faultcode>mcd:invalidMasterCard</faultcode>
    <faultstring>business exception</faultstring>
    <faultactor>cx-fault-actor</faultactor>
    <detail>
     <invalidCard xmlns="http://xmlns.packtpub.com/MasterCard ">
       <code>DECLINED</code>
       <desc>MasterCard Declined</desc>
```

```
      </declined>
    </detail>
  </env:Fault>
</env:Body>
```

This would be intercepted by the service bus, which would then populate $fault with the following:

```
<con:fault  xmlns:con="http://www.bea.com/wli/sb/context">
  <con:errorCode>BEA-380001</con:errorCode>
  <con:reason>Internal Server Error</con:reason>
  <con:location>
    <con:node>RouteToVerifyMasterCard</con:node>
    <con:path>response-pipeline</con:path>
  </con:location>
</con:fault>
```

Where errorCode and its corresponding reason provide an indication of the type of error that occurred, common error codes include:

- BEA-380001: Indicates an internal server error, including the return of a fault by a SOAP service.
- BEA-380002: Indicates a connection error, such as the SOAP service not being reachable or available.
- BEA-382500: Indicates that a service callout returned a SOAP Fault.

We can also see from the content of the location element that the error occurred in the response pipeline of RouteToVerifyMasterCard node. This information can be useful if we are implementing a more generic error handler at either the pipeline or service level.

In addition to populating the $fault variable the $body variable will now contain the actual SOAP Fault returned by the external service.

Finally the service bus will raise an error, which if not handled by the proxy service will result in the service bus returning its own fault to the client of the proxy service.

Defining an error handler

The first step in handling an error is to catch it. Within a proxy service we do this using an error handler, which can be defined at the route, stage, pipeline, or service level.

When the service bus raises an error, it will first look to invoke the error handler on the route node or stage in which the error occurred.

If one isn't defined or the error handler does not handle the error, then the service bus will invoke the error handler for the corresponding pipeline. Again if the error isn't handled at the pipeline level, it will invoke the service level error handler and if not handled at this level then the service bus will return a `soapenv:Server` fault, with the `detail` element containing the content of `$fault`.

A fault is only considered **handled** if the error handler invokes either a reply or resume action. The reply action will immediately send the content of `$body` as a response to the client of the proxy service and completes the processing of the proxy, while a resume action will cause the proxy service to continue, with processing resuming on the next node following the node on which the error handler is defined.

For faults returned by external services it makes sense to define our error handler as close to the error as possible, that is on the route node, as we can handle the error in the context in that it occurred, simplifying the logic of our error handler.

For more generic errors, such as a connection error (for example, `BEA-380002`), we can define a higher level error handler at either the pipeline or service level.

In the case of our `CreditCard` service, this means defining an error handler on the route nodes for each endpoint, to handle errors specific to each service callout, and defining a generic error handler on the service itself.

Adding a route error handler

To define an error handler on a route node, click on it, and select the option **Add Route Error Handler** as shown in the following screenshot:

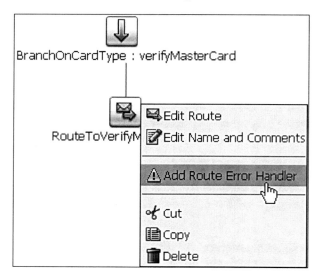

This will open the **Edit ErrorHandler; Route Node** window, where we can configure the error handler. An error handler consists of one or more stages, first we need to add a stage and name it accordingly (for example, **HandleVerfifyMasterCardFault**) as in the following example:

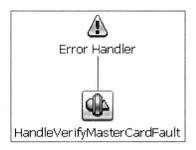

The first step within our error handler is to check whether we have received a SOAP Fault or something more generic. To do this we just need to add an If... Then... action, which checks if the value of $fault/ctx:errorCode is either BEA-382500 or BEA-380001.

 While the service bus reserves the error BEA-382500 for SOAP Faults, we find that when we return a custom SOAP Fault, that the service bus raises an error of type BEA-380001. So we check for both error codes to be safe.

Checking the type of SOAP Faults

Next we need to check the SOAP Fault returned (which will be in $body) so that we can handle it appropriately.

If we examine the WSDL for our verifyMasterCard operation, we can see that it could potentially return one of two faults, mcd:declined and mcd:invalid, each of which needs to be mapped to a fault returned by our proxy service.

At first glance this all looks pretty straightforward. We just need to define an **If...Then...** action, with a branch to test for each type of fault returned and generate the appropriate fault to return.

For example, to test for a fault of type mcd:declined, we could define a branch with a condition such as the following:

```
$body/soap-env:Fault/faultcode = 'mcd:declined'
```

However, if we look at faultcode more closely, we can see its type is QName, with a format of prefix:faultName (for example, mcd:declined), where prefix is mapped to a namespace in the soap:Fault element (for example, http://xmlns.packtpub.com/MasterCard).

The issue here is that there is no guarantee that the same prefix will always be used, which could cause our condition to be incorrectly evaluated.

Getting the qualified fault name

To ensure that our test condition is correctly evaluated we need to fully resolve the QName. We can do this using XQuery function resolve-QName. This takes two parameters. The first contains the QName that we wish to resolve (that is faultcode), the second contains an element in which the namespace prefix is defined (that is soap:Fault). This gives us a function call that looks like the following:

```
fn:resolve-QName($body/soap:Fault/faultcode, $body/soap:Fault)
```

As we will need to test this value multiple times, rather than embed this within our if condition, we can use an **Assign** action to assign it to a variable (for example, $faultcode).

Our modified condition to test for a fault of type mcd:declined, would now look like the following:

```
$faultcode = '{http://xmlns.packtpub.com/MasterCard}declined'
```

We can now define an If... Then... action, with one branch for each fault we want to test for, plus an else branch to cover any unexpected faults.

Creating a SOAP Fault

Once we know the fault returned by the external service, we can generate the appropriate fault to be returned by the proxy service and assign this to the $body variable.

The simplest way to do this is create an Assign action, and for the **XQuery Text**, directly specify the actual SOAP Fault to be returned, as shown in the following screenshot:

```
▷ XQuery Text | XQuery Resources | XSLT Resources | Dynamic XQuery

<soap:Body xmlns:soap="http://schemas.xmlsoap.org/soap/envelope/"
        xmlns:tns="http://xmlns.packtpub.com/obay/ivs/CreditCard">
 <soap:Fault>
   <faultcode>tns:invalidCreditCard</faultcode>
   <faultstring>Invalid Credit Card</faultstring>
   <detail>
     <fault xmlns="http://schemas.packtpub.com/obay/flt">
       <code>DECLINED</code>
       <summary>Credit Card Declined</summary>
       <detail>{fn:concat($body//mcd:code, ': ', $body//mcd:desc)}</detail>
     </fault>
   </detail>
 </soap:Fault>
</soap:Body>
```

Handling unexpected faults

In the case of unexpected faults, we have two choices, one is to return the fault as is and let the client figure out how to handle it, the other is to return a generic fault indicating that an unexpected error occurred. Typically we would recommend the latter approach as this will simplify error handling for the client.

It is often prudent to record details of the fault that occurred. For example if it's occurring frequently we may wish to add a specific branch to our error handler to manage a fault of this type, especially if it allows our client to make a more informed choice on how to handle the error.

One way of achieving this is to use the **Report** action; this takes two parameters; the first is the message we want to report, the second is zero, one or more name value pairs which we can use to search for specific reports.

In the case of error handler, we have configured it to capture details of the actual fault message, with a single key of the format `BusinessService=$outbound/@name` (which will evaluate to `BusinessService=VerifyMasterCard`) as shown in the following screenshot:

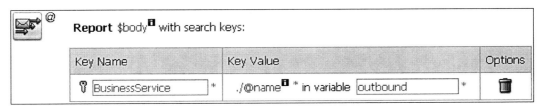

At run time this will cause a record containing the specified information as well as additional metadata to be written to the Service Bus Reporting Data Stream. The metadata includes information such as the error code, inbound service name, URI and operation and the outbound service, URI and operation.

By default the service bus is configured to write this data to a reporting data store which can then be queried from the service bus console. To view the report data click on the **Operations** tab and then click on **Message Reports** (under **Reporting**).

This will bring up the **Summary of Message Reports**, where you can search for report entries against a number of criteria, including data range, inbound service name, error code and the report key (defined in the **Report** action). From here you can click on a report entry to view its metadata and the actual message.

 The Reporting Stream can be configured to write data to a number of targets including JMS Queues, database, file, and so on.

Returning a SOAP Fault

Once we have populated our $body variable with the appropriate SOAP Fault, the final step is for our proxy service to return it.

We do this by using a **Reply** action. The key here is to configure it to **Reply with Failure**, as shown in the following screenshot. This will cause the service bus to generate an **HTTP 500** status, indicating a fault.

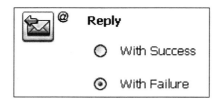

Once the reply has been sent the processing of the request is completed and no further processing will be done.

This completes the definition of our error handler for our **RouteToVerifyMasterCard** node, which looks as follows:

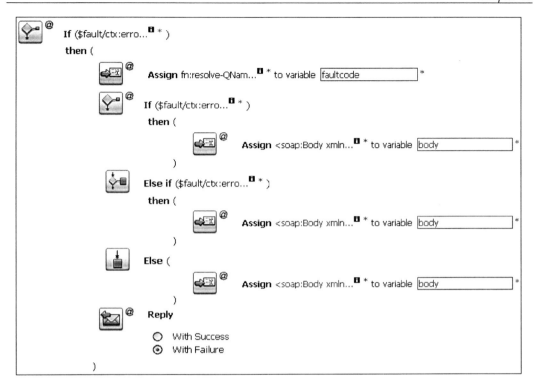

If an error other than a SOAP Fault occurs, then this handler will still be invoked, but because we don't handle it (that is, execute a Reply or Resume activity). Then the service bus will look to invoke an Error Handler on a higher level stage.

Adding a Service Error Handler

For handling errors other than those caused by SOAP Faults, we typically want to define a generic error handler at the service level. To do this click the **Proxy Service** icon and select **Add Service Error Handler** as shown in the following screenshot:

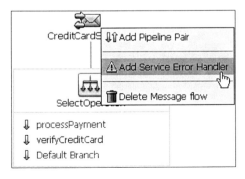

In here we need to create a stage in which to define our error handling logic as we did for our route node error handler.

For errors which have been raised for a reason other than a SOAP Fault being returned by the external client, we just need to check the error code in `$fault` so that we can map it to an appropriate system fault.

When generating a system fault, rather than try to map a specific service bus error to a corresponding SOAP Fault, we need to think about how the client may handle the fault. Typically this will be driven by whether it is a permanent or transient fault.

Handling permanent faults

Permanent faults are ones where by the same submission will continue to cause an error. This could be due to a number of reasons, including invalid security credentials, erroneous data contained within the message payload, or an error within the actual service itself (that is, the request is valid, but for whatever reason the service is unable to process it).

For each type of error, a corresponding error code is defined by the service bus which can be accessed in the `$fault` variable at run time. These error codes are categorized into the following subsystems: transport, message flow, action, security, and UDDI.

Within our generic service level error handler, we typically want to use an `If...Then...` action to check which error category the error code falls into and then map it to a corresponding SOAP Fault. This follows a similar approach to the one we used for mapping business services faults to corresponding faults defined by the proxy service.

Once we have populated our `$body` variable with the appropriate SOAP Fault, we would then use a `Reply` action as before to return it to the client.

This ensures that any client of the proxy service will only have to deal with the business faults defined in the WSDL of the service and a handful of pre-defined system faults that any of the proxy services could return.

 If we look at a BPEL process, this approach makes it very simple to write a fault policy for managing a small, well-defined set of system faults and within the BPEL process define fault handlers for the known business faults.

Generating alerts

When a permanent fault occurs it may indicate that we have an underlying problem in the system. So in addition to returning a SOAP Fault to the client, we may wish to notify someone of the problem.

One way to do this would be through the report action we looked at earlier, but in some cases we may have an issue that requires more immediate attention. For example we have an attempted security violation or there is an error in the actual logic of a recently deployed proxy service.

For these situations we can use the **Alert** action to publish an alert to an appropriate destination, which could be a JMS Queue, Email, SNMP Trap, or Reporting Data Stream.

To add an alert, click **Add an Action | Reporting | Alert**; this will insert an **Alert** action into our error handler, like the one shown as follows:

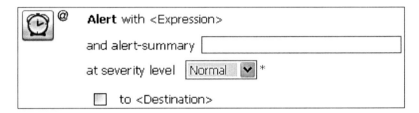

To specify the content of the alert, click on **<Expression>**. This will launch the XQuery Expression Editor, where we can define the alert body as required. We can also specify an optional **alert-summary**, which is presented according to the destination. For example it will form the subject line for an email notification. If this is left blank, then it defaults to **ALSB Alert**.

The severity level can take a value of **Normal**, **Warning**, **Minor**, **Major**, **Critical**, or **Fatal**. These don't have specific meanings, so you can attach your definitions to each of these values; though when we configure alerting for the proxy service (see below) we can opt to filter out alerts based on their severity level.

To specify the recipient of the alert click on **<Destination>**. This will launch the **Select Alert Destination** window, where we can search for and select any previously defined destination. If we don't specify a destination then the alert will be sent to the console.

Destinations are created and configured in the service bus console; this gives us the flexibility to change the actual recipient of the alert at a later point in time, just by re-configuring the destination appropriately.

Enabling alerts

For pipeline alerts to be generated, you must first enable them, otherwise Alert actions will just be skipped during the execution of the proxy service. Alerts need to be enabled in two places, first at the server level and then at the proxy service level.

To enable them globally, click on the **Operations** tab with the service bus console and then select **Global Settings**. This will display the **Global Setting** window. From here ensure the option **Enable Pipeline Alerting** is checked.

Once enabled globally, we can then specify settings for a proxy service. Select the proxy service and then click on the **Operational Settings** tab as shown in the following screenshot:

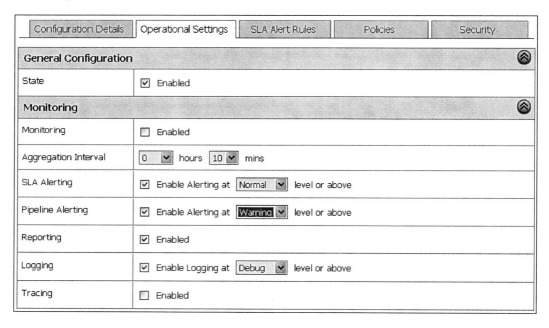

Select the check box for **Pipeline Alerting** and then, from the **Enabling Alerting at** drop down, select the level of alerting required. This will suppress the generation of any alerts with a lower severity. So in this example we have enabled alerting at **Warning** level or above, so any alert actions in the proxy service with a severity level of **Normal** will be skipped.

Handling transient faults

Transient faults, typically manifest themselves as non-responsive URI's (that is no response is being received for a particular service endpoint), which the service bus indicates with the error code `BEA-380002`.

In this scenario, we have already established that for a synchronous proxy service there is limited scope to take any corrective action. However, for services which provide multiple endpoints, one option is to retry an alternate endpoint.

Retrying non-responsive business service

A business service allows you to configure multiple endpoints for a service, which it can load balance requests across (using a variety of algorithms). This can be useful when a particular endpoint becomes non-responsive, as we can configure the business service to automatically retry an alternative endpoint.

Edit a Business Service (obay/BusinessService/VerifyMasterCard)	
Transport Configuration	
Protocol*	http
Load Balancing Algorithm	round-robin
Endpoint URI*	Format: http://host:port/someService http:// [Add] **EXISTING URIS** **OPTIONS** http://host1:80/orabpel/obay/VerifyMasterCard/1.0 ⇧ ⇩ ✎ 🗑 http://host2:80/orabpel/obay/VerifyMasterCard/1.0 ⇧ ⇩ ✎ 🗑
Retry Count	1
Retry Iteration Interval	30
Retry Application Errors	⊙ Yes ○ No

When we have multiple URIs specified for an endpoint, if the initial call to an endpoint fails, the business service will immediately attempt to invoke an alternate URI. It will continue to do this until either successful, the **Retry Count** is reached or all online URIs have been tried.

If at this point the retry count has not been reached, the business service will wait for the duration specified by the **Retry Iteration Interval** before iterating over the endpoints again.

Finally you need to ensure that we set **Retry Application Errors** to **No**, otherwise any SOAP fault returned by the business service will be treated as a failure and will prompt the service bus to retry.

In this example, where we have defined two URIs, if the first call fails then the service bus will immediately call the second URI. If this fails then it will have reached the retry limit and the underlying error will be returned to the proxy service. If the retry count was two, then it would wait 30 seconds before attempting one final retry.

Handling faults in one-way proxy services

The service bus also allows you to define one-way proxy services, where the client issues a request to the service bus and then continues processing without ever receiving a response. This is often referred to as fire and forget.

The approach for handling errors for one-way proxy services is quite different from that of synchronous services. For transient errors, it makes absolute sense to retry the Business Service until we are successful as no one is going to timeout waiting for a response.

For permanent errors, we can't return a fault to the client and let them resolve it. Rather we need to alert a third party so that they can take some corrective action to resolve the error, and then re-run the request.

One way to do this is to publish an alert notification to a JMS Queue. We could do this directly or go via the alerting mechanism described above. The content of the alert will typically need to contain details of the actual error so that we know what corrective action to perform, the proxy service invoked and its payload, so that we can re-invoke the proxy with the original payload once the issue has been resolved.

Once we've published the alert, we also need to implement something on the other end of the JMS Queue to process it. One approach would be to implement this as a BPEL process, containing a human workflow task to correct the error. Once corrected then the BPEL process could re-invoke the proxy service.

Summary

Over the course of this chapter we've taken a detailed look at some of the key considerations we need to take into account when handling errors within a SOA based application.

This includes whether the interaction between the components involved is synchronous or asynchronous, whether the error is a business or system error and is it permanent or transient in nature. In addition, we've examined how the error and the handling of it is likely to impact other components at different layers within our composite.

With this is mind, we have outlined an overall approach for handling errors within our composite apps, and how to implement this in BPEL PM and the Service Bus.

14
Message Interaction Patterns

In every business process, messages are exchanged between participants. So far we have only looked at simple interactions, that is a single request followed by a reply, whether synchronous or asynchronous.

Asynchronous messaging adds additional complexities around the routing and correlation of replies. In this chapter, we will look at how BPEL PM uses WS-Addressing to manage this and in situations where this can't be used, examine how we can use correlation sets in BPEL to achieve the same result.

As part of this we look at some common, but more complex, messaging patterns and requirements; such as:

- How we can handle multiple exchanges of messages, either synchronous or asynchronous between two participants.
- How BPEL can be used to aggregate messages from multiple sources.
- And though not strictly a message interaction pattern, examine one technique for process scheduling.

Finally, as we explore these patterns, we take the opportunity to cover some of BPEL's more advanced features, including FlowN, Pick, and Dynamic Partner Links.

Message routing

A key requirement in any message exchange is to ensure that messages are routed to the appropriate service endpoint. Initial web service implementations were built using SOAP over HTTP, primarily because HTTP is well understood and is able to leverage the existing Internet infrastructure.

However, one of the limitations of HTTP is that it is stateless in nature, and thus provides no support for conversations requiring the exchange of multiple messages. With synchronous interactions this is not an issue, because the response message for a particular request can be returned in the HTTP response.

However, with asynchronous interactions this is a more serious limitation. To understand why, look at the diagram below. The diagram shows a simple asynchronous interaction between two processes, A and B. In this case the interaction is started by process A initiating process B, which does some work before sending a response back to process A.

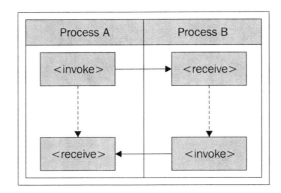

This all looks pretty straightforward, until you consider how it actually works. The first thing to note is that this consists of two operations, one for the initial invocation, the other for the response. Each operation (or message) is sent as separate HTTP POST (with the HTTP response being empty).

When we invoke an operation on a BPEL process, the BPEL engine will either invoke a new process to handle it, as with the initial request, or route it through to the appropriate instance of an already running process.

This is where the complexity comes in. While this example shows Process A invoking Process B, it could potentially be invoked from multiple clients, for example another process or an external client, so how does Process B know the service endpoint it needs to invoke for the call back?

Secondly, assuming we have multiple instances of Process A and B running at the same time; once we have routed the message to the correct service endpoint, how does the BPEL engine know which instance of the Process A to route the response from Process B to?

WS-Addressing

To solve these issues, the BPEL engine makes use of WS-Addressing, which provides a standardized way of including all the addressing specific information as SOAP headers within a SOAP message.

To demonstrate how WS-Addressing achieves this, let us look at the WS-Addressing headers BPEL PM inserts into our request and response messages in the previous example.

Request message with WS-Addressing

The initial request sent by BPEL PM with WS-Addressing headers inserted looks something like the following:

```
<env:Envelope xmlns:env="http://www.w3.org/2003/05/soap-envelope"
  xmlns:wsa="http://schemas.xmlsoap.org/ws/2003/03/addressing"
  xmlns:ptns="http://xmlns.oracle.com/ProcessA">

<env:Header>
  <wsa:ReplyTo>
    <wsa:Address>http://hostname:80/orabpel/default/ProcessA/1.0/
                 ProcessB/ProcessBRequester</wsa:Address>
    <PortType>ptns:ProcessBCallback</PortType>
    <ServiceName>ptns:ProcessBCallbackService</ServiceName>
  </wsa:ReplyTo>
  <wsa:MessageID>uuid://hostname/ProcessA/aaaaaaaa</wsa:MessageID>
</env:Header>
<env:Body>
  ...
</env:Body>
</env:Envelope>
```

From this we can see that we have two additional elements present in the SOAP header. The first element, `wsa:ReplyTo` contains the `wsa:Address` element which specifies the endpoint that Process B should send its asynchronous response to. Secondly, it contains the property `wsa:MessageId` which uniquely identifies the conversation, which as we will see in a moment is used to correlate the response message to the original requestor.

Response message with WS-Addressing

When sending our response message, the response will be sent to the address specified in the `wsa:ReplyTo` endpoint reference. In addition, if we look at the message below, we can see that it contains the property `<wsa:RelatesTo>` which contains the message ID specified in the original message.

It's this value that enables the endpoint to correlate the response back to the original request. In our case this enables the BPEL engine to route the response from Process B back to the instance of Process A which sent the original request.

```
<env:Envelope xmlns:env="http://www.w3.org/2003/05/soap-envelope"
```

```
     xmlns:wsa=http://schemas.xmlsoap.org/ws/2003/03/addressing>

<env:Header>
  <wsa:RelatesTo> uuid://hostname/ProcessA/aaaaaaaa</wsa:RelatesTo>
</env:Header>
<env:Body>
  ...
</env:Body>
</env:Envelope>
```

Additional message exchanges

In the above example, it's quite feasible for Process A and Process B to send multiple messages to each other; any further exchange of messages between the two process instances will just contain the same `<wsa:RelatesTo>` property within the SOAP header.

For example, after receiving a response from Process B, Process A sends a second request to process B. Instead of re-sending the `wsa:ReplyTo` element and a new `wsa:MessageId`, it will just include the `<wsa:RelatesTo>` element containing the original message ID.

This provides sufficient information for BPEL PM to route the request through to the correct instance of Process B; if Process B then needs to send a second response to Process A it will just use the address specified in the `wsa:ReplyTo` element contained in the first request message and embed the `<wsa:RelatesTo>` property as before.

Using BPEL correlation sets

For situations where WS-Addressing isn't appropriate or available, BPEL provides the concept of correlation sets. Essentially correlation sets allow you to use one or more fields present in the body of all correlated messages (for example, `orderId`) to act as a pseudo-conversation ID (equivalent to the `<wsa:MessageID>` and `<wsa:RelatesTo>` properties in WS-Addressing).

A correlation set consists of one more properties; these properties are then mapped using property aliases to the corresponding field in each of the messages that are being exchanged. The combined value of these properties at run time should result in a unique value (as least unique across all instances of the same process), that allows the BPEL engine to route the message to the appropriate instance of a process.

Using correlation sets for multiple process interactions

A common requirement is for a client to make multiple invocations against the same instance of a process. The first is pretty much the same as a standard synchronous or asynchronous request, but all subsequent requests are subtly different as we now need to route the request through to the appropriate instance of an already running process rather than initiate a new instance.

Take the UserRegistration process; this is a long running process which needs to handle multiple synchronous requests during its lifecycle. The first operation submitUserRegistration is called by the client to initiate the process, which validates all the provided user information and returns a confirmation of success or otherwise.

The only information that is not validated at this stage is the email address; for this the process sends an email to the provided address containing a unique token which the user can use to confirm their address.

Once they have received the email they can launch their browser and submit the token. The web client will then invoke the confirmEmailAddress operation. It's at this point we need to use correlation sets to route this request to the appropriate instance of the UserRegistration process.

Defining a correlation set property

The first step is to choose a unique field that could act as a property. One such approach would be to use the userId specified by the user. However, for our purposes we want to use a value that the user will only have access to once they have received their confirmation email, so will use the token contained in the email.

To create a property, within the **Structure** view for the BPEL process, right-click on the **Properties** folder and select **Create Property...** as shown in the following screenshot:

This will launch the **Create CorrelationSet Property** window. Give the property a meaningful name, such as **EmailToken** and then click the flashlight to launch the **Type Chooser** and select the appropriate schema type (for example, xsd:string) as shown in the following screenshot:

Defining correlation set

Once we've defined our Correlation Set Property(s), the next step is to define the Correlation Set itself.

Correlation Sets can be defined either at the process level or for a particular scope. In most cases the process level will suffice, but if you need to have multiple correlated conversations within the same process instance, for example, iterations through a `while` loop, then define the Correlation Set at scope level.

Within the BPEL **Structure** view expand the **Correlation Sets** folder, and then the **Process** folder, and right-click on the **Correlation Sets** folder and from the menu select **Create Correlation Set...** as shown in the following screenshot:

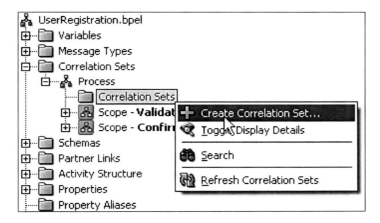

This will launch the **Create Correlation Set** window displayed in the following screenshot. Give the correlation set a meaningful name, such as **EmailTokenCS** in our case, and then select the **+** symbol to add one or more properties to the correlation set. This will bring up the **Property Chooser** where you can select any previously defined properties.

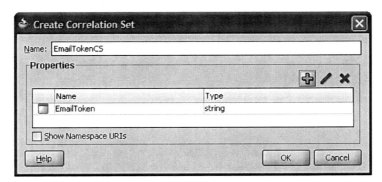

Using correlation sets

Next we need to specify which messages we wish to route with our correlation set. For our purposes we want to use the Correlation Set to route the inbound message for the operation `confirmEmailAddress` to the appropriate process instance.

To configure this, double-click the receive activity for this operation to open the **Receive** activity window and select the **Correlations** tab as shown:

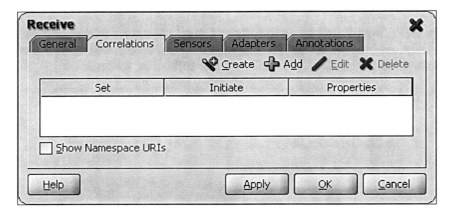

Next select the **+** symbol; this will launch the **Correlation Set Chooser** as shown in the following screenshot:

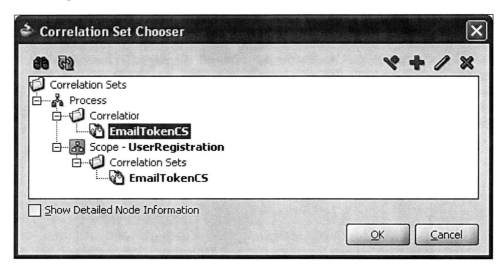

From here we can select the **EmailTokenCS** we defined previously. Click **OK** and this will return us to the **Correlations** tab, showing the newly added correlation.

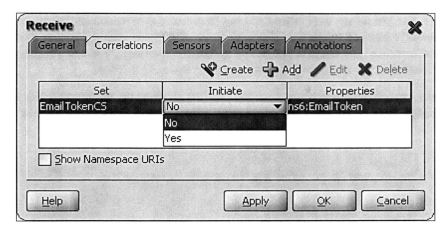

We can see here that we have to specify one additional property **Initiate**. This is used to specify which message should be used to initiate the correlation set.

Initializing the correlation set

As you would expect, the value of the property(s) contained in the first message exchanged in any sequence of correlated messages must be used to initiate the value of each property contained within the correlation set.

However, rather than implicitly initialize the correlation set based on the first message exchange, BPEL expects you to explicitly define which message activity should be the first in the sequence by setting the **Initiate** property to **Yes**.

 If we try to initialize an already initialized correlation set, or try to use a correlation set that isn't initialized, then a run-time exception will be thrown by the BPEL engine. Likewise, once initialized, the value of these properties must be identical in all subsequent messages sent as part of the sequence of correlated messages, or again the BPEL engine will throw an exception.

When initializing a correlation set, any outbound message can be used to achieve this. However, there are practical restrictions on which inbound messages can be used to initiate a correlation set, since the process must first **receive** the inbound message before it can use it to initialize a correlation set.

Essentially, if an inbound message is used to create a new instance of a process, or is routed through to the process by another mechanism (for example, a different correlation set) then it can be used for the purpose of initiating our correlation set.

In our case, we are using the correlation set to route the inbound message for the confirmEmailAddress operation through to an already running process instance, so we need to initialize the correlation set in an earlier message. We can do this within the invoke activity for the sub-processs validateEmailAddress.

We define a correlation set for an Invoke activity as we would for any message based activity, that is, we open its properties window and select the **Correlations** tab as shown in the following screenshot:

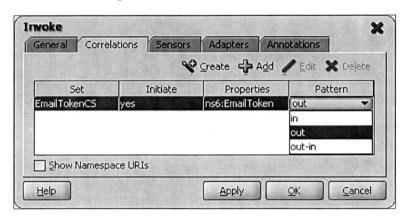

However, you may notice that when creating a correlation for an Invoke activity, we are required to set the additional attribute **Pattern**. This is because, unlike any other message activity, Invoke can consist of two messages, the initial outbound request, and an optional corresponding inbound response. The pattern attribute is used to specify to which message the Correlation Set should be applied; that is, **out** for the outbound request, **in** for the inbound response and **out-in** for both.

Since validateEmailAddress is a one-way operation, we need to set the **Pattern** attribute to **out**.

Note that if you choose to initiate the correlation with an **out-in** pattern, then the outbound request is used to initiate the Correlation Set.

Defining property aliases

Once the messages to be exchanged as part of our Correlation Set have been defined, the final step is to map the properties used by the Correlation Set, to the corresponding fields in each of the messages exchanged.

To do this, we need to create a property alias for every **Message Type** exchanged that is, i.e. validateEmailAddress and confirmEmailAddress in our User Registration example.

To create an alias, within the **Structure** view for the BPEL process, right-click on the **Property Aliases** folder and select **Create Property**, this will launch the **Create Property Alias** window, as shown:

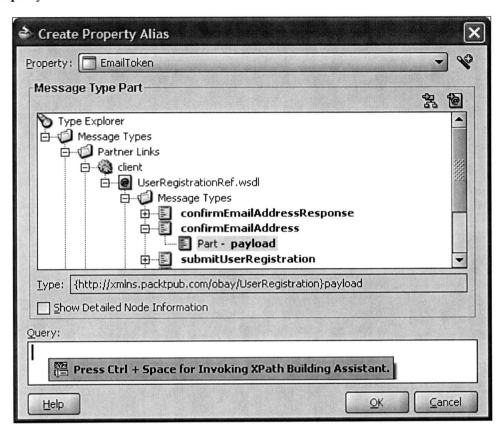

In the **Property** drop down, select the property that you wish to define the alias for and then using the **Type Explorer** navigate through the **Message Types, Partner Links** down to the relevant **Message Type** and **Part** that you want to map the property to.

This will activate the **Query** field, where we specify the XPath for the field containing the property in the specified message type. Rather than type it all by hand, press *Ctrl + Space* to use the **XPath Building Assistant**.

Once we have defined an alias for each of the messages exchanged within our correlation set, we can view them within the **Structure** view of the BPEL process as shown in the following screenshot:

This completes the definition of our Correlation Set.

 A BPEL process can define multiple Correlation Sets, and messages exchanged within a BPEL process can be exchanged in zero, one, or more correlation sets. When a message is involved in multiple Correlation Sets, it can be the same or different fields that are mapped to a corresponding property. You will of course require a separate property alias for each correlation set.

Message aggregation

A typical messaging requirement is to aggregate multiple related messages for processing within a single BPEL process instance. Messages are aggregated using a common correlation Id, in much the same way as we covered above.

The other challenge is to determine when we have all the messages that belong to the aggregation. Typically, most use cases fall into two broad patterns:

- **Fixed Duration**: In this scenario we don't know how many messages we expect to receive, so will process all those received within a specified period of time.

- **Wait For All**: In this scenario we know how many messages we expect to receive; once they have been received we can then process them as an aggregated message. It's usual to combine this with a timeout in case some messages aren't received so that the process doesn't wait forever.

An example of the first pattern is the oBay auction process. Here, during the period for which the auction is in progress, we need to route zero or more bids from various sources to the appropriate instance of the auction. Then once the auction has finished, select the highest bid as the winner. The outline of the process is shown on the next page.

From this, we can see that the process supports two asynchronous operations, each with a corresponding callback, namely:

- `initateAuction`: This operation is used to instantiate the auction process. Once started, the auction will run for a preset period until completing and then invoke the callback `returnAuctionResult`, to return the result of the auction to the client which initiated the auction.

- `submitBid`: This operation is used to submit a bid to the auction. The operation is responsible for checking each bid to see if we have a new highest bid, and if so updates the current bid price appropriately, before returning the result of the bid to the client. The process then loops back round to process the next bid.

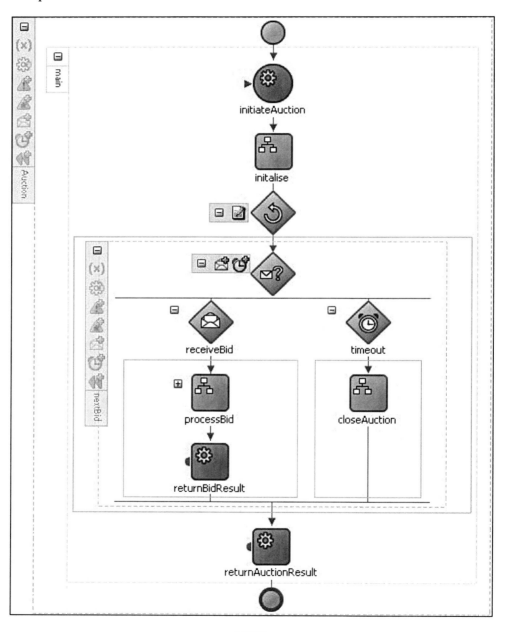

Message routing

The first task for the aggregator is to route bids through to the appropriate instance of the auction process. As with our earlier `UserRegistration` example, we can use a correlation set to route messages to the appropriate instance. In this example, we will create a correlation set based on the element `auctionId`, which is included in the message payload for `initateAuction` and `submitBid`.

At first glance this looks pretty straightforward, as we can use correlation sets for aggregation in much the same way as we have already covered. However, this scenario presents us with an additional complexity, which is that a single instance of a BPEL process may receive multiple messages of the same type at approximately the same time.

To manage this we need to implement a queuing mechanism, so that we can process each bid in turn before moving onto the next. This is achieved by implementing the interaction between the client submitting the bid and the auction process as asynchronous.

With asynchronous operations, BPEL saves received messages to the BPEL delivery queue. The delivery service then handles the processing of these messages, either instantiating a new process or correlating the message to a `waiting`, `receive`, or `onMessage` activity in an already running process instance.

If a process is not ready to receive a message, then the message will remain in the queue until the process is ready.

This introduces a number of complexities over our previous correlation example. This is because a BPEL process can only support **one inbound Partner Link** (for example, client), for which the BPEL engine generates a corresponding concrete WSDL which defines all operations that can be invoked against that BPEL process (as well as any corresponding callbacks).

When BPEL generates the WSDL it includes the appropriate WS-Addressing header definitions for each of the operations. However, only operations which are used to instantiate a process, that is, `initiateAuction` in the case of the auction process, include WS-Addressing headers to hold the reply to address and message ID.

Correlating the callback

The first complexity this causes is that whenever a client submits a request to the auction process via the `submitBid` operation, it doesn't include a message ID, so we can't use WS-Addressing to correlate the response of the auction process back to the client.

At first, the obvious answer might appear to be just to use the `auctionId` to correlate the result of the bid back to the client. However, while the `auctionId` allows us to uniquely identify a single instance of an auction, it doesn't allow us to uniquely identify a bidder. This at first may seem strange, but recall we may have several clients calling the auction process at the same time, and thus all waiting for a response. We need to ensure that each response is returned to the appropriate instance.

Thus the calling client will need to pass a unique key in the `submitBid` request message (for example, `bidId`) that the auction process can include in the response. Assuming we are using BPEL to implement the client, we then need to implement a correlation set based on this property in the calling process, so that the BPEL engine can route the response to the appropriate instance of the client process.

Specifying the reply to address

The second complexity is that whenever a client submits a request to the auction process via the `submitBid` operation, it doesn't include a `replyToAddress` within the SOAP header.

As a result the BPEL engine doesn't know which address to send the reply to; or rather it will attempt to send the reply to the process which initiated the auction. It was this request which contained the `wsa:ReplyTo` header specifying the callback endpoint for the client Partner Link.

This highlights the other issue, namely our auction process supports two callbacks, one to return the auction result and the other to return the bid result. Yet the `replyToAddress` on the Partner Link is being fixed with the initial invocation of the process, forcing both callbacks to be routed to the same endpoint, which is not what we want.

Creating a proxy process

At this point, you may be thinking that this all may be too complex. However, the solution is rather straightforward and that is to use a proxy process, which supports the same operations as the auction process.

With this approach the client invokes either the `initateAuction` or `submitBid` operation on the proxy, which then forwards the request to the auction process. The auction process then returns the result to the proxy, which then returns it to the original client.

This not only solves the problem of having a fixed reply to address, but has the additional benefit of shielding the client from having to use Correlation Sets, as it can use WS-Addressing to communicate with the proxy.

Using the pick activity

Our proxy process needs to support both operations, `initateAuction` and `submitBid`, that is, either operation can be used to **initiate** an instance of the proxy process. To achieve this, we will use the `<pick>` activity at the start of our process, in place of a `<receive>` activity.

A pick activity is similar to a receive activity; the difference being that with a pick activity you can specify the process waits for **one** of a set of events, events can either be the receipt of a message or an alarm event (which we look at later in this chapter).

Each message is specified in a separate `<onMessage>` branch, each branch containing one or more activities to be executed on receipt of the corresponding message. To use a pick activity, drag a `<pick>` activity from the **Process Activities** list of the **Component Pallet** on to your process.

As the pick activity is used to receive the initial message which starts the process, we need to set the `createInstance` attribute on the activity. To do this, double-click the pick activity to open the **Pick** activity window as shown below, and select the **Create Instance** checkbox.

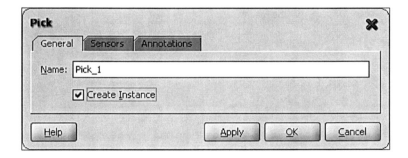

Next, within the process diagram, click on the + symbol to expand the `<pick>` activity. By default it will have two branches illustrated as follows:

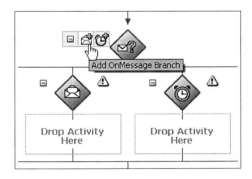

The first branch contains an `<onMessage>` component, with a corresponding area where you can drop a sequence of one or more activities that will be executed if the corresponding message is received.

The second branch contains an `<onAlarm>` sub-activity, with a corresponding area for activities. It doesn't make sense to have this as part of the initial activity in a process, so right-click on the `onAlarm` sub-activity and select **delete** to remove it

We require two `OnMessage` branches, one for each operation that the process supports. For this, click on the **Add OnMessage Branch** icon (highlighted in the previous diagram) to add another `<onMessage>` branch.

The next step is to configure the `onMessage` branch. Double-click on the first branch to open the **OnMessage Branch** activity window as shown in the following screenshot:

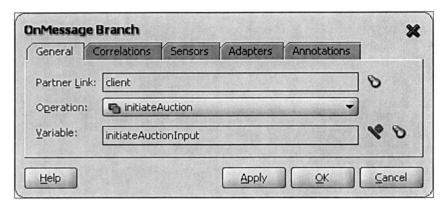

As we can see an **OnMessage Branch** is configured in a similar fashion to a **Receive** activity. For the purpose of our proxy, we will configure the first `onMessage` branch to support the `initateAuction` operation (as shown in the previous screenshot) and the second `onMessage` branch to support the `submitBid` operation.

Each branch will just contain an invoke and receive activity to call the corresponding operation provided by the auction process, and a final invoke activity to return the result of the operation to the caller of the process.

Defining the correlation sets

For our proxy process we need to define a Correlation Set for the `submitBid` operation, to ensure that replies from the `Auction` process are routed through to the correct instance of the `AuctionProxy` process.

As mentioned earlier, this requires us to include a unique `bidId` within the `submitBid` message. To generate this we can use the XPath function **generateGUID**, which is available under the category **BPEL XPath Extension Function** within the expression builder.

Note, we don't need to define a correlation set for the `initateAuction` operation, as the corresponding operation on the auction process is still using WS-Addressing.

Completing the aggregation

All that remains is to add in the logic that enables the process to determine when the aggregation is complete. For a scenario where we know how many messages we expect, every time we receive a message we just need to check whether there are any outstanding messages and proceed accordingly.

However, for scenarios where we are waiting for a fixed duration, as is the case with our auction process, it's slightly trickier. The challenge is that for the period over which the auction is running, the process will spend most of its time in a **paused state**, waiting for the receive activity to return details of the next bid.

So the only opportunity we have within the logic of our process to check whether the duration has expired is after the receipt of a bid, which may arrive long after the auction has completed or not at all (since the auction has theoretically finished).

Ideally what we want to do is place a timeout on the `Receive` activity, so that it either receives the next bid or times out on completion of the auction, whichever occurs first.

Fortunately, this can be easily accomplished by replacing the `Receive` activity for the `submitBid` operation with a `Pick` activity. The `Pick` would contain two branches: an `onMessage` branch configured in an identical fashion to the `Receive` activity and an `onAlarm` branch configured to trigger once the finish time for the auction has been reached.

To configure the onAlarm branch, double-click on it to open the **OnAlarm Branch** activity window as shown in the following screenshot:

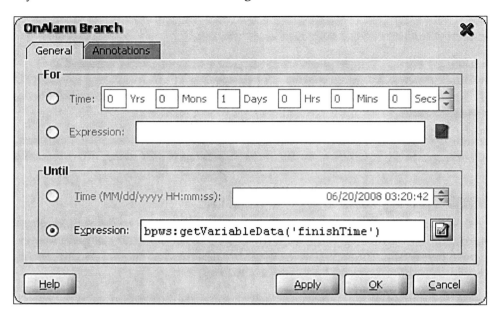

We can see that an onAlarm branch is configured in a similar fashion to a Wait activity in that we can specify the Pick waits **For** a specified duration of time or **Until** a specified deadline. In either case you specify a fixed value or specify an XPath expression to calculate the value at run time.

For our purposes we have pre-calculated the finish time for the auction based on its start time and duration, and have configured the Pick activity to wait until this time.

When triggered, the process will execute the activities contained in the **OnAlarm** branch and will then move onto the activity following the Pick. In the case of our auction process, the branch contains just a single activity which sets the flag auctionComplete to true, causing the process to exit the while loop containing the Pick activity. Upon exiting the loop, the process calculates and returns the auction result before completing.

Scheduling services

A common requirement is to schedule a process or service to run at regular intervals. For example, the oBay `accountBilling` process is required to be run once every night. One approach would be to use a scheduling tool; there are a number of tools available for this, including:

- **Quartz:** This is an open-source, Java-based scheduler. The advantage of Quartz is that it is already used internally by the BPEL engine for scheduling, so is available to use as part of the SOA Suite platform. However, this approach requires knowledge of the API as well as Java.
- **Oracle Database Job Scheduler**: Provided as part of the Oracle Database, such as Quartz. It is available regardless of which platform you are running the SOA Suite on (assuming you are using Oracle as the backend database). However, it requires knowledge of PL/SQL.

While these are all perfectly valid approaches, they all require knowledge of components outside the SOA suite; an alternate approach is to use BPEL to implement the scheduler.

One approach is to implement a BPEL process which continuously loops, with the sole purpose of launching other scheduled BPEL processes. However, as the process never dies, this will result in an ever increasing audit trail, causing the objects persisted in the database as well as the in-memory size of the process to grow over time, which eventually will have a negative impact on the performance of the engine.

A better approach is to have an XML file that specifies a series of one or more services (or jobs) to be scheduled. We can then use the file adapter to read this file and trigger a scheduling process which can invoke each of the scheduled jobs. Once all jobs have been triggered then the scheduling process can be allowed to complete.

The trick with this approach is to re-cycle the scheduling file; that is, in the process of reading the file, the file adapter will move it to an `archive` directory. To ensure the scheduling process is re-run every day, we need to move the file back into the directory being polled by the adapter. We can do this using the scheduling process.

Defining the schedule file

For our oBay example, we are simply going to create a scheduling process that is run once at the start of the day; the schedule file will then contain details of each job to be run, and at what time during the day. The schema for our scheduling file is as follows:

```
<?xml version="1.0" encoding="utf-8"?>
<xsd:schema xmlns:xsd="http://www.w3.org/2001/XMLSchema"
```

```
                        xmlns="http://xmlns.packtpub.com/obay/xsd/sch"
                        targetNamespace="http://xmlns.packtpub.com/obay/xsd/sch"
                        elementFormDefault="qualified" >
    <xsd:element name="schedule"              type="tSchedule"/>
    <xsd:element name="job"                   type="tJob"/>

    <xsd:complexType name="tSchedule">
        <xsd:sequence>
            <xsd:element name="startTime" type="xsd:time"/>
            <xsd:element ref="job" minOccurs="1"
                                maxOccurs="unbounded"/>
        </xsd:sequence>
    </xsd:complexType>

    <xsd:complexType name="tJob">
        <xsd:sequence>
            <xsd:element name="endpoint"  type="xsd:string" />
            <xsd:element name="startTime" type="xsd:time"/>
            <xsd:element name="jobDetail" type="xsd:anyType"/>
        </xsd:sequence>
    </xsd:complexType>

</xsd:schema>
```

The bulk of the schedule file is made up by the Job element; with each schedule file containing one or more jobs. The job elements contains three elements:

- endpoint: Defines the endpoint of the service to invoke.

- startTime: Defines the time that the service should be invoked.

- jobDetail: Defined as xsd:anyType; is used to hold details specific to the service being invoked.

For the purpose of our accountBilling process our schedule file looks as follows:

```
<?xml version="1.0" encoding="UTF-8" ?>
<schedule xmlns="http://xmlns.packtpub.com/obay/xsd/sch">
  <startTime>0:2:55.125</startTime>
  <job>
    <endpoint>
      http://localhost:80/orabpel/obay/accountBilling/1.0/
    </endpoint>
    <startTime>T02:00:00</startTime>
    <jobDetail>
    </jobDetail>
  </job>
</schedule>
```

Using FlowN

To ensure that our schedule process supports the concurrent execution of jobs, we need to process them in parallel. If the number of branches/jobs was fixed at design time, we could use the `<flow>` activity to achieve this.

For our scenario, the number of branches will be determined by the number of jobs defined in our scheduling file. For cases such as these we can use the `<flowN>` activity; this will create N branches, where N is calculated at run time.

Each branch performs the same activities and has access to the same global data, but is assigned an index number from 1 to N to allow it to look up the data specific to that branch.

To use a `FlowN` activity, drag a `<flowN>` activity from the **Process Activities** list of the **Component Pallet** on to your process. Double-click on it to open the **FlowN** activity window as shown in the following figure:

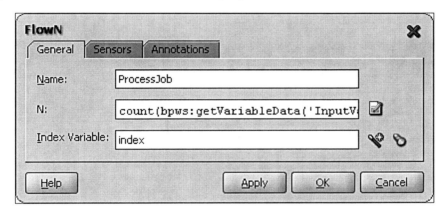

In addition to the activity **Name**, it takes two parameters. The first parameter is **N** which contains an XPath expression used at run time to calculate the number of parallel branches required. This typically uses the `count` function to count the number of nodes in a variable. In our case, we need to calculate the number of `job` elements, so our expression is defined as follows:

```
count(bpws:getVariableData('InputVariable','schedule',
                          '/sch:schedule/sch:job'))
```

The second parameter, **Index Variable**, is used to specify the variable into which the index value will be placed at run time. While we have defined this as a global variable, each branch will be given its own local copy of the variable containing its assigned index number.

Accessing branch specific data in FlowN

The first step within the **flowN** branch is to get a local copy of the data that is to be processed by that specific branch, that is, the **Job** in our case.

Before we do this we need to ensure that we are working with local variables, otherwise each branch in the **flowN** will update the same process variables. The simplest way to achieve this is to drop a scope (which we've named **ProcessJob**) as the activity within the **flowN** branch, and to then define any branch specific variables at the scope level and perform all branch specific activities within the scope.

In this case, we have created a single variable `JobInputVariable` of type `Job`, which we need to populate with the job element to be processed by the **flowN** branch. To do this, we need to create an XPath expression that contains a **predicate** to select the required job based on its position with the node set, in effect doing the equivalent of an array lookup in a language such as Java.

The simplest way to achieve this is to create a standard copy operation, as shown in the following screenshot:

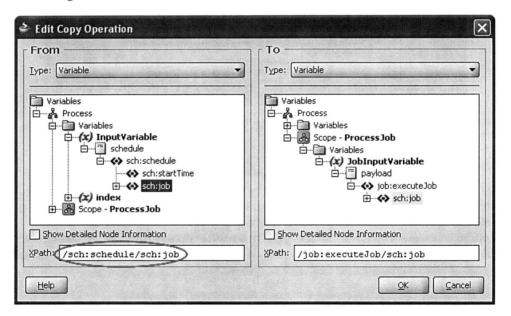

Next we need to modify the **From XPath** expression (circled in the previous screenshot) so that we only select the required job based on the value of the index. To do this, modify the XPath to add a position based predicate based on the index, to obtain an expression that looks something like the following:

```
/sch:schedule/sch:job[bpws:getVariableData('index')]
```

The next step within our branch is to use a `Wait` activity to pause the branch until the `startTime` for the specified job.

Dynamic Partner Links

The final step within our branch is to call the service as defined by the endpoint in the `Job` element. Up to now we've only dealt in BPEL with static Partner Links, where the endpoint of a service is defined as design time.

However, BPEL also provides support for dynamic Partner Links, where we can override the endpoint specified at design time, with a value specified at run time.

Define common interface

While we can override the endpoint for a partner link, all other attributes of our service definition remain fixed. So to use this approach we must define a common interface that all of our **Job** services will implement. For our purpose we've defined the following abstract WSDL:

```xml
<?xml version="1.0" encoding="UTF-8"?>
<definitions name="Job">
  <types>
    <schema>
      <import namespace="http://xmlns.packtpub.com/obay/xsd/sch"
              schemaLocation="../schedule.xsd"/>

      <element name="executeJob" type="client:tExecuteJob"/>

      <complexType name="tExecuteJob">
        <sequence>
          <element ref="sch:Job"/>
        </sequence>
      </complexType>
    </schema>
  </types>

  <message name="executeJob">
    <part name="payload" element="tns:executeJob"/>
```

```
    </message>

    <portType name="Job">
      <operation name="executeJob">
        <input message="tns:executeJob"/>
      </operation>
    </portType>

    <plnk:partnerLinkType name="Job_PL">
      <plnk:role name="Job_Role">
        <plnk:portType name="tns:Job"/>
      </plnk:role>
    </plnk:partnerLinkType>

  </definitions>
```

Examining this, we can see that we've defined a simple one-way operation (executeJob) that our scheduling process will invoke to initiate our job. For simplicity, we have defined the content of the input message to be that of the job element that we used in our scheduling file.

Define Job Partner Link

Before we can define a Job Partner Link within our Schedule process, we need a WSDL file complete with bindings. The simplest way to do this is to deploy a default process that implements our abstract WSDL. To do this, create a BPEL process (such as JobService) based on our predefined WSDL contract (as described in Chapter 10). The process just needs to contain a simple Receive activity as it should never be called.

Note that for any other service that we wish to invoke as a job, we will need to create a process based on our abstract WSDL, and then once created implement the process as required to carry out the job.

Once we've deployed our default JobService process we can create a Partner Link and invoke it within our scheduler process just as would any other service.

Create endpoint reference

To dynamically invoke the appropriate endpoint at run time we need to update the endpoint reference before invoking the service. To do this, we need to create variable of type EndPointReference (as defined by WS-Addressing) **containing just the** <Address> **element** and populate this with the endpoint of the Job service that we want to invoke.

This is important, because if we create an `EndpointReference` containing any of the other optional elements, then if we try to invoke the Partner Link, the BPEL engine will throw a fault.

 To create a variable of type `EndpointReference`, you will need to import the WS-Addressing schema (located at `http://<host>:<port>/orabpel/xmllib/ws-addressing.xsd`).

To populate the address element, use a transformation activity rather than an assign activity, as shown in the following screenshot:

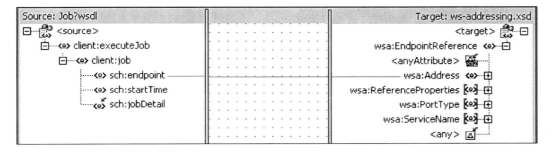

If we use an `assign` too directly to populate the `<Address>` element, then BPEL by default would create an initialized `<EndpointReference>` element containing all the other optional elements (each with an empty value).

Update Endpoint

Finally, we use another copy rule to dynamically set the partner link. The key difference here is that the **target** of the copy rule is the **JobService PartnerLink**, as shown in the following screenshot:

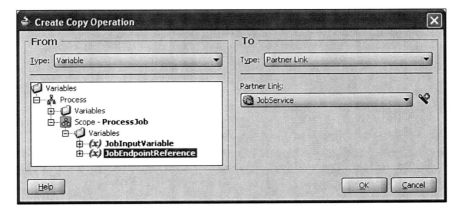

Now when we invoke the **JobService** via the Partner Link it will dynamically route the request to the updated endpoint.

Re-cycling the scheduling file

As we've already covered, the scheduling process is triggered by the file adapter reading in the `schedule.xml` file. As part of this activity, the file adapter will move it to an `archive` directory, to ensure that the file is processed just once.

However, in our case we actually want the file adapter to process the scheduling file on a daily basis. To do this we need to move the file back into the directory being polled by the adapter.

For the purpose of this we have defined the following two directories:

```
<SOA_HOME>/scheduler/config
<SOA_HOME>/scheduler/execute
```

When creating our scheduling process, we have configured the file adapter to poll the `execute` directory on a regular basis (for example, every five minutes), and archive processed files to the `config` directory.

When the `schedule.xml` file is placed into the `execute` directory for the first time, this will trigger file adapter to pick up the file and launch the scheduler process, and at the same time move the schedule file into the `config` directory.

Within the scheduler process, we then invoke the file adapter to move the `schedule.xml` file from the `config` directory back to the `execute` directory (see Chapter 3 — *Service Enabling Existing Systems* for details on how to do this). However, rather than invoke the `moveFile` operation immediately, we have placed a `wait` activity in front of it that waits until the `startTime` defined at the head of the schedule file, as shown:

```
<?xml version="1.0" encoding="UTF-8" ?>
<schedule xmlns="http://xmlns.packtpub.com/obay/xsd/sch">
    <startTime>0:2:55.125</startTime>
    <job>
       ...
    </job>
</schedule>
```

This has a couple of advantages, the first is we use the `schedule.xml` file to control when the scheduling process is run, as opposed to configuring the file adapter to poll the `execute` directory once every 24 hours and then deploy the process at the right time to start the clock counting.

The other advantage is that most of the time the `schedule.xml` file resides in the `config` directory. Thus, while the file is in this directory we can go in and modify the schedule to add new jobs or update and delete existing jobs, which will then be picked up the next time the scheduler is executed.

Summary

In this chapter, we have looked at the more advanced messaging constructs supported by the Oracle BPEL PM. We have also seen how we can use this to support some of the more complex but relatively common message interaction patterns used in a typical SOA deployment.

We have also used this as an opportunity to introduce some of the more advanced BPEL activities and features such as the Pick and FlowN activity as well as Dynamic Partner Links.

We have not covered every possible pattern. Yet, hopefully you should now have a good understanding of how BPEL PM utilizes WS-Addressing and Correlation Sets to support message interactions that go beyond a single synchronous or asynchronous request and reply. You should now be able to apply this understanding to support your particular requirements.

15
Workflow Patterns

So far we've used workflow for simple task approval in conjunction with the worklist application. However, human workflows are often more complex, often involving multiple participants as well as requiring the task list to be integrated into the user's existing user interface rather than accessed through a standalone worklist application.

In this chapter, we look at these common requirements. First, we examine how to manage workflows involving complex chains of approval, including parallel approvers and the different options that are available. Next, we look at the Workflow Service API and how we can use that to completely transform the look and feel of the workflow service.

Managing multiple participants in a workflow

The process for validating items which have been flagged as suspicious is a classic workflow scenario that may potentially involve multiple participants.

The first step in the workflow requires an oBay administrator to check whether the item is suspect. Assuming the case is straightforward they can either approve or reject the item and complete the workflow.

This is pretty straightforward; however, for grey areas the oBay administrator needs to defer making a decision. In this scenario we have a second step in which the item is submitted to a panel who can vote on whether to approve or reject the item.

There are two approaches to model this workflow, one is to model each step as a separate Human Task, the other is to model it as a single Human Task containing multiple assignments and routing policies. Each approach has its own advantages and disadvantages, so we will look at each in turn to understand the differences.

Using multiple assignment and routing policies

For our `checkSuspectItem` process, we are first going to take the approach of combining the two workflow steps into a single Human Task. The first step in the workflow is the familiar single approval step, where we assign the task to the `oBayAdministrator` group.

The task takes a single un-editable parameter of type `suspectItem`, which contains the details of the item in question as well as why it has been flagged as suspect. The definition of this is shown as follows:

```
<xsd:element name="suspectItem"          type="act:tSuspectItem"/>

<xsd:complexType name="tSuspectItem">
  <xsd:sequence>
    <xsd:element name="item"          type="act:ItemType"/>
    <xsd:element name="reasonCode"    type="xsd:string" />
    <xsd:element name="reasonDesc"    type="xsd:string"/>
  </xsd:sequence>
</xsd:complexType>
```

Determining the outcome by a group vote

For the second step in the workflow we are going to define a participant type of **Group Vote**; this participant type allows us to allocate the same task to multiple participants in parallel. The task definition form for a group vote is shown in the following figure:

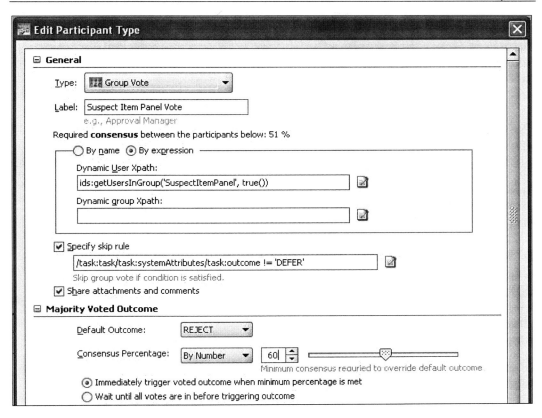

Assigning participants

The first requirement is to allocate this task to all users in the voting panel. To enable this, we've defined the group `SuspectItemPanel` within our user repository. We don't want to allocate the task to the group, as this would only allow one user from the group to acquire and process the task. Rather we want to allocate it to all members of the group. To do that we can use the Identity Service XPath function `ids:getUsersInGroup`, as illustrated here:

```
ids:getUsersInGroup ('SuspectItemPanel', false())
```

Note the second parameter is a Boolean which, if set to `true`, will only return **direct** members of the group. Setting it to `false` causes it to return all members of the group.

Doing this will effectively create and assign a separate sub-task to every member of the group.

Skipping the second step

There is an issue with this approach so far, in that the second step will always be executed regardless of what happens in the first step. To prevent this we've specified the following skip rule:

```
/task:task/task:systemAttributes/task:outcome != 'DEFER'
```

The skip rule lets you specify an XPath expression which evaluates to a boolean value. If it evaluates to `true` then the corresponding participant will be skipped in the task.

In our case we are testing the outcome taken by the oBay administrator in the previous step. If they didn't defer it, that is they chose to either accept or reject the item, then this step is skipped.

Sharing attachments and comments

When panel members are considering their decision they may want to confer with one another. By default anyone assigned a task will be able to see comments and attachments made by participants in previous steps of the task (that is, the oBay administrator), however, they won't be able to see comments made by other panel members.

To enable the sharing of attachments and comments between panel members we've selected the **Share comments and attachments** checkbox.

Deciding on the outcome

The final part of the group vote is to specify what the outcome is in the event that not all members are in agreement. There are two parts to this; the first is to specify what the default outcome is if there isn't agreement, in our case we want to REJECT the item.

The second part is to specify what constitutes agreement, this can either be unanimous, that is, everyone must agree, or default outcome is selected. Alternatively, you can specify that only a majority need to be in agreement and what the size of that majority should be.

The size of the majority can be a fixed amount (60% as in our case), or can be based on an XPath expression which could calculate this value dynamically at run time.

The final option you have is to specify whether all votes should be counted or if once we have sufficient votes on which to make a decision the outcome should be triggered. In this scenario, any outstanding sub-tasks will be withdrawn.

In our case the panel consists of three members, so as soon as two have approved the task, the required consensus will have been achieved and the third member will have their task withdrawn.

Using multiple Human Tasks

The other approach to this workflow is to model each step as a separate Human Task in its own right, each with a single assignment and routing policy.

With this approach you get a lot more control over how you want to handle each step, because most of the run-time behavior of the human task is defined at the task level, allowing you to specify different parameters, expiration policies, notification settings, and task forms for each step in the workflow. In addition, on completion of every step, control is returned to the BPEL process, allowing you to carry out some additional processing before executing the next step in the workflow.

One of the draw backs of this approach is that you need to specify a lot more information (roughly n times as much, where n is the number of tasks that you have), and often you may be replicating the same information across multiple task definitions as well as having to specify the handling of outcomes for multiple tasks within your BPEL process.

This not only requires more work upfront, but results in a larger and more complicated BPEL process that is not so intuitive to understand and often harder to maintain.

Linking individual Human Tasks

The other potential issue is that the second task doesn't include the comments, task history, and attachments from the previous task. In our case this is important as we want members of the panel to see any comments made by the oBay administrator before they deferred the task.

BPEL allows us to link tasks within the same BPEL process together; to do this double click on the task in the BPEL process that you wish to link to a preceding task. This will open the **BPEL Human Task** configuration window; from here select the **Advanced** tab and you will be presented with a variety of options.

If you select the checkbox **Include task history from**, then you will be presented with a drop down listing all the preceding Human Tasks defined in the BPEL process as illustrated in the following figure:

By selecting one of these, your task is automatically linked to that task and will inherit its task history, comments, and attachments.

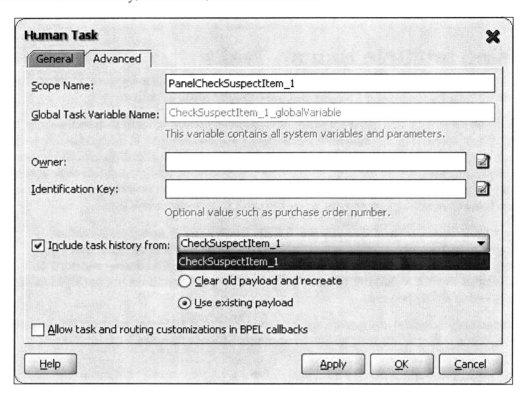

The final choice is whether you wish to use the payload from the previous task or create a new payload. This is decided by selecting the appropriate option.

Using the workflow API

If we look at the Order Fulfillment process, which is used to complete the sale for items won at auction, it is a prime candidate for Human Workflow as it will need to proceed through the following steps in order to complete the sale:

- Buyer specifies shipping details (for example address and method of postage)
- Seller confirms shipping cost
- Buyer notifies the seller that a payment for the item has been made
- Seller confirms receipt of payment

- Seller notifies the buyer that the item has been shipped
- Buyer confirms receipt of item

You may recall from Chapter 9 (*oBay Introduction*) that we've decided to build a custom user interface (UI) for oBay's customers. As part of the UI we need to enable users to perform each task required to complete the Order Fulfillment process.

One way to achieve this would be to use the Worklist Portlets and embed them directly within the oBay UI. However, oBay want to make the user experience a lot more seamless, so that users are not even aware that they are interacting with any kind of workflow system.

The Workflow Service provides a set of API's just for this kind of scenario. These are exposed as a set of Web Services with support for SOAP and Java WSIF bindings, as well as an equivalent set of Java API's.

Indeed the Worklist application uses the same API's. However, rather than invoke these API's directly from our oBay UI, we are going to build our own Task Based Business Service which acts as a façade around these underlying services. This will give us the architecture depicted in the following diagram:

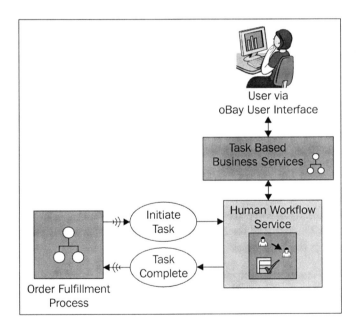

As we will be using BPEL to implement our Task Based Business Services it makes sense to us the Java WSIF Web Service API (in the same way that any BPEL process containing a Human Task does).

If you compare this to our architecture outlined in Chapter 9, you will notice that we've decided not to wrap a virtual service layer around the workflow service; there are two key reasons for this.

First, if you look at the service description for the workflow services they already provide a very well-defined abstract definition of the service. Hence if you were to re-design the interface they probably wouldn't look a lot different.

Second, whenever we include a Human Workflow task within our process, JDeveloper automatically generates a lot of code which directly uses these services. Thus if we wanted to put a virtual layer over these services we would need to ensure that all our Human Workflow tasks also went via this layer, which is not a trivial activity.

So the reality is adding in a virtual services layer would gain us very little, but would take a lot of effort and we would lose a lot of the advantages provided by the development environment.

Defining the order fulfillment Human Task

For our `OrderFulfillment` process, we are taking the approach of combining all six workflow steps into a single Human Task (the `OrderFulfillment.task`). Now this isn't a perfect fit for some of the reasons we've already touched on, so we will look at how we address each of these issues as we encounter them.

Within our task definition we've defined two possible **Outcomes** for the task either COMPLETED or ABORTED (where for some reason the sale fails to proceed). In addition, in the BPEL Human Task configuration window we have configured the **Task Title** to be set to the item title, and set the **Initiator** to be the seller of the item.

Specifying task parameters

A key design consideration is to decide on what parameter(s) we are going to pass to the task, taking in to account that we need to pass in the superset of parameters required by each step in the workflow.

For our task we will have a single parameter of type `order` which contains all the data required for our task; the definition for this is shown as follows:

```
<xsd:element name="order"     type="act:tOrder"/>

<xsd:complexType name="tOrder">
  <xsd:sequence>
    <xsd:element name="orderId"        type="xsd:string"/>
```

```
      <xsd:element name="itemId"        type="act:tItemId"/>
      <xsd:element name="orderDesc"     type="xsd:string" />
      <xsd:element name="sellerId"      type="act:tUserId"/>
      <xsd:element name="buyerId"       type="act:tUserId"/>
      <xsd:element name="orderDetails"  type="act:tOrderDetails" />
      <xsd:element name="shipTo"        type="act:tShipTo" />
    </xsd:sequence>
  </xsd:complexType>

  <xsd:complexType name="tOrderDetails">
    <xsd:sequence>
      <xsd:element name="orderDate"     type="xsd:date"/>
      <xsd:element name="status"        type="xsd:string"/>
      <xsd:element name="quantity"      type="xsd:int"/>
      <xsd:element name="itemPrice"     type="xsd:decimal" />
      <xsd:element name="subTotal"      type="xsd:decimal" />
      <xsd:element name="shippingPrice" type="xsd:decimal" />
      <xsd:element name="total"         type="xsd:decimal" />
    </xsd:sequence>
  </xsd:complexType>

  <xsd:complexType name="tShipTo">
    <xsd:sequence>
      <xsd:element name="shippingName"           type="xsd:string"/>
      <xsd:element name="shippingAddress"        type="act:tAddress"/>
      <xsd:element name="additionalInstructions" type="xsd:string"/>
    </xsd:sequence>
  </xsd:complexType>
```

Before we go any further, it's worth spending a moment to highlight some of the key components of this:

- **Order Id:** Potentially we could have multiple orders per auction (for example, if oBay were to support a Dutch auction format at some point in the future), so every order will need its own unique identifier.

  As we have made the decision to have a single Human Task, we have a one-to-one mapping between an order and an OrderFulfillment human task. We will use the task number as our order number.

- **Ship To**: This contains the details provided of where the item is to be sent to as well as the preferred delivery method. This needs to be specified by the buyer in the first step of the workflow.

- **Shipping Price**: Once the buyer has specified the shipping details, the seller can confirm the cost of shipping. This needs to be added to the `subTotal` to calculate the `total` amount payable.
- **Status**: This field is updated after every step to track where we are in the order fulfillment process.

The most obvious problem from our requirement is that at each step in the process, we will need to update different fields in the `order` parameter, and that some of these fields are calculated.

If we were using the default simple task forms generated by JDeveloper for the worklist application then this poses a problem because you can only specify at the parameter level whether it is read only or editable and this will be the same at every step in the task.

One work around is to customize the generated form, which is definitely possible if not entirely straightforward. However, in our scenario, as we are developing our own custom built user interface rather than the worklist application, this issue is easily solved.

Specifying the routing policy

For the `OrderFulfillment` task, we have specified six **Assignment and Routing Policies,** one for each step of the workflow. Each one is of type **SingleApprover** and is assigned dynamically to either the seller or buyer as appropriate, as illustrated in the following screenshot:

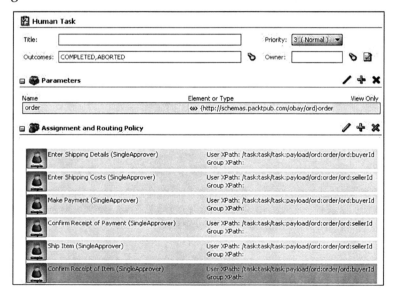

Notification settings

The only other potential issue for us is that we need to share generic notification settings for each step in the workflow; for our purpose this is fine as we just want to send a generic notification to our seller or buyer every time a task is assigned to them to notify them that they now need to perform an action in order to complete the sale.

However, if we wanted to send more specific notifications, then we can do that from the BPEL process itself using the notification service. By default the BPEL process will only receive a callback from the Workflow Service upon completion of the task.

However, if you open up the BPEL Human Task configuration window and select the **Advanced** tab, you will see a checkbox with the option **Allow task and routing customizations in BPEL callbacks**.

If you select this, your BPEL process will be modified to also receive callbacks when either a task is assigned, updated, or completed as well as when a sub-task is updated.

It does this by replacing the `Receive` activity which receives the completed task callback with a `Pick` activity embedded within a `While` activity that essentially loops until the task is completed, as illustrated:

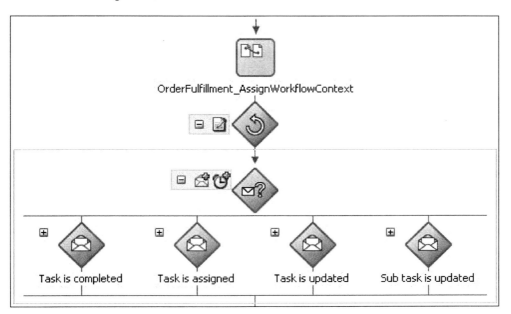

As you can see the `Pick` activity contains an `onMessage` branch for each potential callback; you then just add any additional processing that is required to the appropriate `onMessage` branch.

In our case we might add a switch to the **Task is assigned** branch to check where we are in the workflow and then based on that generate the appropriate notification.

Querying task instances

Now that we have defined out **Order Fulfillment** task, the next step is to implement our task based Business Services that will act upon it. If we look at the type of interactions that the user will have with our Order Fulfillment task, they split into two categories. The first being query-based tasks and the second being tasks which change the state of the workflow task. We will look at the query based tasks first.

By analyzing our requirements we can see that we need to support the following query-based operations:

- `getSoldItems`: Returns a list of all items sold by the specified seller, and provides details of those items which have an outstanding task assigned to the seller.

- `getPurchasedItems`: Similar to the previous operation but returns a list of all items bought by the specified buyer.

- `getOrderDetails`: Returns detailed information about a specific order.

It's worth noting that the first two operations are not just returning the current task list for either the buyer or seller, but rather a complete list of all applicable items, regardless of whether the task is currently allocated to the buyer or seller.

We are going to implement each of these operations as a separate BPEL process. To do so we will make use of the **Task Query Service** provided by the Workflow Service; this provides a number of methods for querying tasks based on a variety of search criteria including status, keywords, attribute values, and so on.

Defining a Partner Link for the Task Query Service

The WSDL for the Task Query Service is defined in the file `TaskQueryService.wsdl` which can be found in the directory:

```
<SOA_HOME>\bpel\system\services\schema
```

The WSDL itself imports a number of other WSDL's and schemas, some of which in turn import additional schemas, all of which can be located in the same directory. In total we need to include the following files in our BPEL project:

- `TaskQuery.xsd`
- `TaskQueryService.wsdl`
- `TaskQueryService.xsd`
- `TaskQueryServiceInterface.wsdl`
- `UserMetadata.xsd`
- `WorkflowCommon.xsd`
- `WorkflowTask.xsd`

We could import these files one by one into our BPEL processes; however, that would be quite tedious. A quicker approach is to copy them directly into our BPEL project.

 An alternative approach would be to deploy these files to the BPEL Server so they can be referenced via a URL as described in Chapter 10.

The following screenshot shows the file structure of a BPEL project within JDeveloper.

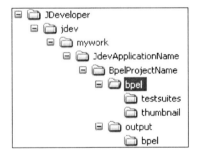

If you copy all of the above files into the highlighted `bpel` sub-directory, JDeveloper will automatically include them in your project. However, before we can use these files to create a PartnerLink we need to make a couple of minor modifications.

Modifying TaskQueryServiceInterface.wsdl

The `<types>` section of the `TaskQueryServiceInterface.wsdl` file contains four `import` statements, the last of which (at the time of writing) contains an error. If we look at the following fragment of XML from this file, we can see that the import statement includes the attribute `location`.

```
<import namespace="http://xmlns.oracle.com/bpel/.../taskQueryService"
        location="TaskQueryService.xsd"/>
```

We need to rename this attribute to `schemaLocation` as shown here:

```
<import namespace="http://xmlns.oracle.com/bpel/.../taskQueryService"
        schemaLocation="TaskQueryService.xsd"/>
```

Modifying TaskQueryService.wsdl

The other modification we need to make is to update the `location` attribute of the `soap` address for the Task Query Service defined in `TaskQueryService.wsdl`.

```
<service name="TaskQueryService">
  <port name="TaskQueryServicePort"
        binding="tns:TaskQueryServiceSOAPBinding">
    <soap:address location="http://localhost:8888/integration/Task
                            QueryService"/>
  </port>
</service>
```

We need to modify `location` to point to the actual endpoint of the Task Query Service, so set the value of location to:

```
http://<hostname>:<port>/integration/services/TaskQueryService/
                                              TaskQueryService
```

Here `hostname` represents the name of the machine on which the SOA Suite is running and `port` represents the port number.

 It's not just a case of modifying the `hostname` and `port`; we also need to modify the remainder of the URL.

Creating the Task Query Service PartnerLink

Once we have copied these files into our project directory and modified them as described above, we are ready to create a partner link.

From this point on, we follow the standard approach for creating a PartnerLink; namely drag a PartnerLink from the **Services** section in the **Component Palette** onto your BPEL process. Click on the icon to **Browse WSDL Files From Local File System** and browse to and select our modified `TaskQueryService.wsdl`.

When prompted to make a local copy of the WSDL file and create a WSDL file that defines PartnerLink types select **Yes** in both cases.

User authentication

As with the Worklist application, the task query service will only return details of tasks for which you have access, such as the task is assigned to you or you are the task owner or initiator (see Chapter 6 for details).

For authentication purposes, the `authenticate` operation is provided, this takes an element of type `credential` which consists of the following parameters:

- `login`: User ID as defined to the underlying Identity Service.
- `password`: Corresponding password for the specified user.
- `identityContext`: The identity service enables you to configure multiple identity repositories, each containing it's own set of users. Each repository is identified by its realm name.

    The `identityContext` should be set to the name of the realm in which the user is defined. Note: jazn.com is the default realm installed out of the box.

- `onBehalfOfUser`: An optional element, which allows a user with administrative privileges to create a workflow context on behalf of another user by specifying their user id here.

Upon successful authentication, a `workflowContext` is returned which is then used in any subsequent calls to the workflow service.

> If you are calling a single workflow service, you can provide the authentication details as part of that service invocation, instead of a separate call to the authentication service. This removes the overhead of having to make two calls to the query service.

Create credential element

When creating the `credential` element, we need to ensure that it doesn't include an empty `onBehalfOfUser` element. The service will try to create a workflow context for this `empty` user, which of course will fail and return an error.

This is an easy error to make, because the first time we use an assign statement to populate any sub-element of credential, for example doing a copy to populate the `login` element, BPEL PM, by default, will create an initialized `credential` element containing all its sub-elements including `onBehalfOfUser` (each with an empty value).

A simple way round this is to assign a fragment of xml, such as the following:

```xml
<credential xmlns="http://xmlns.oracle.com/bpel/workflow/common">
  <login/>
  <password/>
  <identityContext>jazn.com</identityContext>
</credential>
```

Directly to `credential`, this acts as a template into which we can copy the required values for `login` and `password`. We do this using a copy operation within an assign statement, the key difference being that we specify an **XML Fragment** as the **From Type** as shown in the following screenshot:

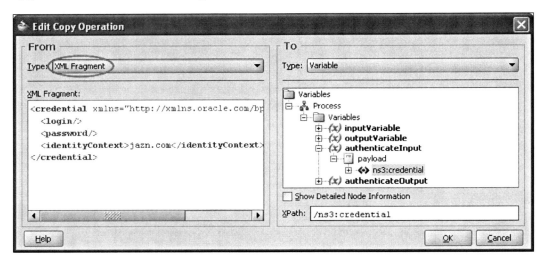

Note, we have specified the default namespace in the `credential` element so that all elements are created in the appropriate namespace.

Querying tasks

The `queryTask` operation returns a list of tasks for a user, which you can filter based on criteria similar to that provided by the Worklist application. The following diagram shows the structure of the input it expects.

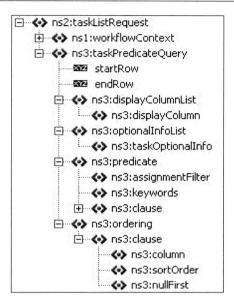

We can see the `taskListRequest` consists of two elements: the `workflowContext`, which should contain the value returned by our authentication request and other is the `taskPredicateQuery`, which defines the actual query that we wish to make.

The `taskPredicateQuery` consists of the following core elements:

- `displayColumnList`: Allows us to specify which attributes of the task (for example, title, created by, created date, etc) we want to be included in the result set.

- `optionalInfoList`: Allows us to specify any additional information we want returned with each task, such as comments, task history, etc.

- `predicate`: Used to specify the filter conditions for which tasks we want returned.

- `ordering`: Allows us to specify one or more columns on which we want to sort the result set.

The two attributes `startRow` and `endRow` are used to control whether the entire result set is returned by the query or just a subset. To return the entire result set, set both attributes to zero. To only return a subset of the result set then set the attributes appropriately. For example to return the first ten tasks in the result set, you would set the `startRow` equal to 1 and the `endRow` equal to 10.

Specifying the Display Column List

The `displayColumnList` element list contained within the `taskPredicateQuery` allows us to define which task attributes (or columns) we want returned by our query.

Simply include in here one `displayColumn` entry per task attributes we want returned, valid values include `TaskNumber`, `Title`, `Priority`, `Creator`, `CreatedDate` and `State`.

 For a full list of `task attributes` see the list of **WorklistColumns** defined in the **Constant Field Values** section of the **Workflow Services Java API Reference** that comes with the Oracle BPEL Process Manager documentation.

These tend to match the column names in the WFTASK table in the BPEL PM Database schema.

If we look at the WSDL definition for the `getSoldItems` operation we can see that it returns the values `orderNo`, `itemId`, `orderDesc`, `buyerId`, `itemPrice`, `totalPrice`, `saleDate`, `orderStatus`, `lastUpdateDate`, and `nextAction`.

At first glance only a couple of these match to actual task attributes; when we created the task we set the task `title` to hold `orderDesc` and the task attribute `updatedDate` maps to `lastUpdateDate`.

In addition, we have decided to use `taskNumber` for the `orderNo` as this makes it a lot simpler to tie the two together.

However, the remaining fields are all held in the task payload which we can't access through the `queryTask` operation. One solution would be to call the `getTaskDetails` operation for every row returned, but this would hardly be efficient. Fortunately we have an alternative approach and that is to use Flex Fields.

Flex fields

Flex fields are a set of generic attributes attached to a task which can be populated with information from the task payload. This information can be displayed in the task listing as well as used for querying (and defining workflow rules in the worklist application).

Populating Flex Fields

The simplest way to initialize the Flex fields is in the BPEL process which creates the task. If you click on the plus sign next to a Human Task activity, this will expand the task showing you the individual BPEL activities that are used to invoke it, as illustrated in the following figure:

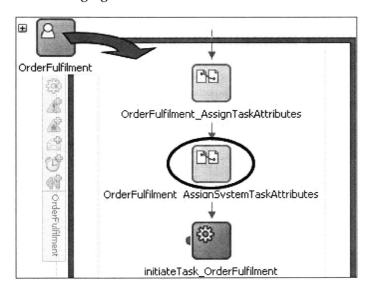

You will see that this starts with a number of assign activities, the second one of which (circled) is used to set the system attributes. To set the Flex fields simply open the assign activity, and add an extra copy statement for each Flex field required.

For our purposes we will set the following Flex fields in our Order Fulfillment task.

Flex field	Attribute
textAttribute1	itemId
textAttribute2	buyerId
numberAttribute1	salePrice
numberAttribute2	totalPrice
dateAttribute1	saleDate
textAttribute3	orderStatus
textAttribute4	nextAction

You will need to update the **local variable** `initiateTaskInput` which will be defined in the scope with the same name as the Human Task (`OrderFulfillment` in our case). The Flex fields are located in the `systemMessageAttributes` element of the `task` element as illustrated in the following screenshot:

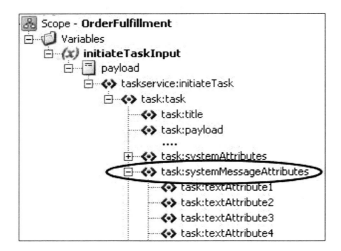

Accessing Flex fields

Once we have populated the Flex fields we can access them in our query just like any other task attribute. This will give us a `displayColumnList` that looks as follows:

```
<displayColumnList
    xmlns="http://xmlns.oracle.com/bpel/workflow/taskQuery">
  <displayColumn>TaskNumber</displayColumn>
  <displayColumn>Title</displayColumn>
  <displayColumn>UpdatedDate</displayColumn>
  <displayColumn>TextAttribute1</displayColumn>
  <displayColumn>TextAttribute2</displayColumn>
  <displayColumn>NumberAttribute1</displayColumn>
  <displayColumn>NumberAttribute2</displayColumn>
  <displayColumn>DateAttribute1</displayColumn>
  <displayColumn>TextAttribute3</displayColumn>
  <displayColumn>TextAttribute4</displayColumn>
</displayColumnList>
```

Specifying the query predicate

The next step is to specify the query predicate so that it only returns those tasks that we are interested in. We will first look at the query we need to construct to return all sold items for a particular seller.

The following diagram shows the structure of the query predicate. The `assignmentFilter` allows us to specify a filter based on who the task is **currently** assigned to. Valid values are `All`, `My`, `Group`, `My+Group`, `Reportees`, `Creator`, `Owner`, `Previous`, or `Admin`.

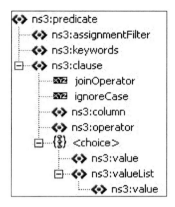

For our purpose we need to list all tasks related to items sold by the specified seller; so we will need to include those items which have tasks currently assigned to the buyer.

You may recall that when we defined our workflow we assigned the initiator (or creator) of the task to be the seller, so we can use `Creator` as the `assignmentFilter`.

So far our query will return all tasks created by the specified user, which could potentially include tasks created in other workflows, so we need to add an additional filter to further restrict our query.

One approach would be to use the `keywords` filter. This is an optional search string, which, if specified, will only return tasks where the string is contained in the task title, task identification key, or one of the task text Flex fields. However, this probably won't result in the most efficient query, so we should use an alternative if available.

For this we need to use the `clause` element (shown in the figure above). This allows us to specify one of more clauses against any of the task attributes.

One such attribute is the `TaskDefinitionName`, which contains the name that we assigned to our task when we defined it in JDeveloper (that is, `OrderFulfillment`). Adding a clause to filter on this would give us the following predicate:

```
<predicate xmlns="http://xmlns.oracle.com/bpel/workflow/taskQuery">
  <assignmentFilter>Creator</assignmentFilter>
  <clause joinOperator="AND">
    <column>TaskDefinitionName</column>
```

```
        <operator>EQ</operator>
        <value>OrderFulfillment</value>
      </clause>
    </predicate>
```

Using Flex fields in the query predicate

Specifying the query predicate for the buyer isn't quite so simple as we want to list all tasks related to items bought by the specified buyer, so we will need to include those items which have tasks currently assigned to various sellers.

Unlike the seller's query, we can't use the `Creator` value as our assignment filter, and we can't use `My` either as this only return tasks currently assigned to us. Hence, the only option we have is to use `All` as our assignment filter. However, this will return all tasks currently in the system, so we need to find a way of restricting the list to just those tasks required by the buyer.

As you may recall we have already defined the Flex field `textAttribute1` to hold the `buyerId`, so we just need to add an extra clause to our predicate to test for this condition. This will give us a predicate that looks as follows:

```
<predicate xmlns="http://xmlns.oracle.com/bpel/workflow/taskQuery">
  <assignmentFilter>All</assignmentFilter>
  <clause joinOperator="AND">
    <column>TextAttribute1</column>
    <operator>EQ</operator>
    <value>$buyerId</value>
  </clause>
  <clause joinOperator="AND">
    <column>TaskDefinitionName</column>
    <operator>EQ</operator>
    <value>OrderFulfillment</value>
  </clause>
</predicate>
```

where `$buyerId` needs to be substituted with the actual `userId` of the buyer.

Ordering the data

The `ordering` element list contained within the `taskPredicateQuery` allows us to define which task attributes we want to order our result set by. For our purpose we want to order by sale date, which is held in `dateAttribute1`; this gives us an `ordering` element which looks as follows:

```
<ordering xmlns="xmlns.oracle.com/bpel/workflow/taskQuery">
    <clause>
        <column>DateAttribute1</column>
        <sortOrder>ASCENDING</sortOrder>
    </clause>
</ordering>
```

 The simplest way to create the `taskPredicateQuery` is to create an **XML Fragment** which can act as a template for the query and assign this with a single `copy` statement. Then just add any additional copy statements for those values which need to be specified at run time in order to modify the template generated value appropriately.

Getting task details

The final query based operation we need to implement is `getOrderDetails`, which returns the order details for the specified `orderNo`. The Task Query Service provides two similar operations `getTaskDetailsByNumber` and `getTaskDetailsById`.

As the `orderNo` corresponds to the `taskNumber`, it makes sense to call the `getTaskDetailsByNumber` operation. This just takes the standard `workflowContext` and the `taskNumber` as its input.

The only slight area of complexity is extracting the order from the task payload. This is because `payload` is defined as `xsd:any`, which means it can contain any value. Because of this the XPath mapping tool can't determine the structure of the payload and thus can't visually map the **From** part of the operation.

Thus you have to create the XPath manually. The simplest way to do this is to create a mapping from the task to your target variable using the visual editor and then modify the XPath manually as shown in the following screenshot:

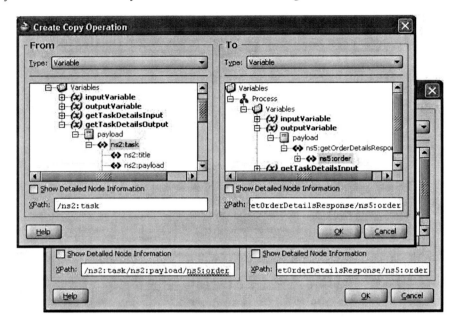

Updating a task instance

Our second category of Task Based Business Service is the one that allows the buyer or seller to perform actions against the workflow task. For the purpose of this section we will look at the implementation of the setShippingDetails operation, though the other operations submitInvoice, notifyPaymentMade, confirmPaymentReceived, notifyItemShipped, and confirmItemReceived all follow the same basic pattern.

setShippingDetails is used to complete the first step in the workflow, namely update the task payload to contain the shipping name and address of the buyer as well as provide any additional shipping instructions. Finally it needs to set the outcome of the current step to COMPLETED so that the task moves on to the next step in the workflow. The following diagram shows the input fields for this operation.

From this we can see it contains the buyer's `credentials`, required to authenticate with the Workflow Services, the `orderNo` which we will use to locate the appropriate order fulfillment task, and the actual `shipTo` details which we will use to update the task.

To implement this operation we are going to make use of the Task Service provided by the Workflow Service; this provides a number of operations which act on a task.

Defining a PartnerLink for the Task Service

The WSDL for the Task Service is defined in the file `TaskServiceWSIF.wsdl` which can be found in the directory:

    <SOA_HOME>\bpel\system\services\schema

The WSDL itself imports a number of other WSDLs and schemas, some of which in turn import additional schemas, all of which can be located in the same directory. In total we need to include the following files in our BPEL project:

- `RoutingSlip.xsd`
- `TaskService.xsd`
- `TaskServiceInterface.wsdl`
- `TaskServiceWSIF.wsdl`
- `WorkflowCommon.xsd`
- `WorkflowTask.xsd`

To include these files within our project, we can copy them into the `bpel` sub-directory in the same way we described earlier for the Task Query Service and create a corresponding PartnerLink.

An alternative approach is to add a **Human Task** activity to our BPEL process. In doing so, JDeveloper will automatically add all the required resources to our project. This is because BPEL makes use of the same Task Service to create a workflow task in the first place. We can then remove the actual Human Task activity from our process.

Using the updateTask operation

Most of the tasks provided by this service are granular in nature and only update a specific part of a task. Thus they only require the `taskId` and the corresponding part of the task being updated as input.

However, our operation needs to update multiple parts of a task, that is, the order held in the task payload, the corresponding Flex fields and the task outcome. For this we will use the `updateTask` operation. The following diagram shows its expected input:

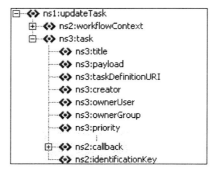

From this we can see that it expects the standard `workflowContext` as well as the **complete** updated `task` element.

The simplest way to achieve this is to use the Task Query Service to get an up-to-date copy of our `task`. We do this in exactly the same way we did for our `getOrderDetails` operation, but then modifying it as appropriate and calling the `updateTask` operation to make the changes.

Updating the task payload

The only area of complexity is updating the `order` directly within the task payload. This is for the same reason we mentioned earlier when implementing the `getOrderDetails` operation; as the payload is defined as `xsd:any`, we can't use the XPath mapping tool to visually map the updates.

The simplest way to work around this is to first extract the `order` from the task payload into a local variable (which we do in exactly the same way that we did for our `getOrderDetails` operation).

Once we've done this we can update the `shipTo` element of the `order` to hold the shipping details as well as update its status to **Awaiting Shipping Costs** to reflect the next step in the workflow.

Once we have updated the `order`, we must insert it into the task payload; this is essentially the reverse of the copy operation we used to extract it.

Updating the task Flex fields

Once we have updated the task payload we then need to update the corresponding
Flex fields so that they remain synchronized with the order. We do this using an
`assign` activity in a similar way that we used to set the Flex fields when creating
the task in our `OrderFulfillment` process.

Updating the task outcome

Finally, we need to set the task outcome for the current step (this is effectively the
same as specifying a task action through the worklist application). In our case we
have defined two potential outcomes: COMPLETED or ABORTED.

For `setShippingDetails` (as with all of our operations), we want to set the task
outcome to COMPLETED. Note that this won't actually complete the task, rather it
completes the current assignment, and in our case since all our routing policies are
single approver, it will complete the current step in the workflow and move the task
on to the next step. Only once the final step is completed will the task complete and
control be returned to the `OrderFulfillment` BPEL process.

To set the task outcome, we only need to set the `outcome` element (located
in the task `systemAttributes` element) to COMPLETED. However, it isn't
quite that straightforward; if you look at the actual task data returned by the
`getTaskDetailsByNumber` operation, the `outcome` element isn't present.

Thus, if we use a standard copy operation to try to assign a value to this element we
will get an XPath exception.

Instead what we need to do is create the `outcome` element and its associated value
and append it to the `systemAttributes` element. To do this within the assign
activity, use an **Append Operation** as shown in the following diagram:

The simplest way to create the `outcome` element is to use an **XML Fragment** and append it to the `systemAttributes` element as shown in the following screenshot:

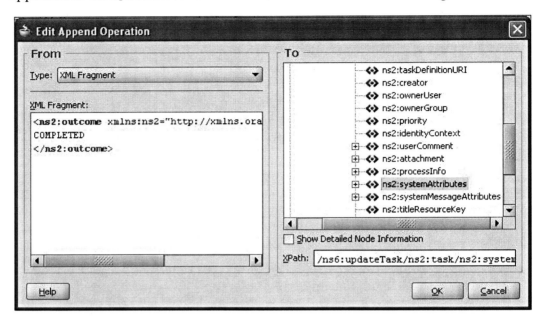

Once we've done this we will have a completed task, so that all that remains to do is call `updateTask` to complete the operation.

Summary

Human workflow is a key requirement for many projects. Quite often these are a lot more demanding than just a simple approval. In this chapter, we've looked at some of the more complex, yet common use cases and shown how these can be addressed in a relatively straightforward fashion by the Workflow Service.

In addition, we've demonstrated how we can use the Workflow API to completely abstract out the underlying Workflow Service and present a completely different appearance to the consumer of the service.

While we have not covered every detail of the Workflow Service, you should now have a good appreciation of some of its more advanced features, the versatility this gives you and more importantly how you can apply them to solve some of the more common workflow requirements.

16
Using Business Rules to Implement Services

We have looked at how we can use the rules engine to define business rules, which can then be invoked as decision points within a BPEL process. The examples we have used so far have been pretty trivial; however, the rules engine uses the Rete Algorithm, which was developed by researchers into Artificial Intelligence in the 1970s.

Rete has some unique qualities when compared to more *procedural-based* languages such as PL/SQL, C, C++, or Java, making it ideal for evaluating a large number of interdependent rules and facts.

This not only makes it simpler to implement highly complex rules than would typically be the case with more procedural based languages, but also makes it suitable for implementing particular categories of first class business services.

In this chapter, we look in more detail at how the rule engine works. Once armed with this knowledge, we write a set of rules to implement the auction algorithm, responsible for determining the winning bid according to the rules set out in Chapter 9—*oBay Introduction*.

How the rule engine works

So far we have only dealt with very simple rules that deal with a single fact. Before we look at a more complicated ruleset that deals with multiple facts it's worth taking some time to gain a better understanding of the inner workings of the rules engine.

The first thing to take into account is that when we invoke a ruleset, we do it through a rules session managed by the decision service. When using the decision service, it first asserts the facts passed in by the BPEL process. Next, it executes the ruleset against those facts, before finally retrieving the result from the rule sessions.

Asserting facts

The first step is for the decision service to assert all the facts passed by the BPEL process into the working memory of the rules sessions, ready for evaluation by the rules engine.

When defining the decision service, it's important to check the box **Check here to assert all descendants from the top level element**. Otherwise, only the top level XML element will be asserted as a fact.

Once the facts have been asserted into working memory, the next step is to execute the ruleset.

Executing the ruleset

Recall that a ruleset consists of one or more rules, and that each rule consists of two parts: a rule condition, which is composed of a series of one or more tests, and an action-block or list of actions to be carried out when the rule condition evaluates to `true` for a particular fact or combination of facts.

It's important to understand that the execution of the rule condition and its corresponding action block are carried out at two very distinct phases within the execution of the ruleset.

Rule activation

During the first phase, the rules engine will test the rule condition of **all** rules to determine which facts or combination of facts the rule conditions evaluate to `true`. A group of facts that together cause a given rule condition to evaluate to `true`, is known as a *fact set row*, with a *fact set* being a collection of all *fact set rows* that evaluate to `true` for a given rule.

In many ways it's similar to the concept of executing the rule condition as a query over the facts in working memory, with every row returned by the query equivalent to a fact set row, and the entire result set being equivalent to the fact set.

For each fact set row, the rules engine will activate the rule. This involves adding each fact set row with a reference to the corresponding rule to the agenda of rules which need to be fired. At this point, the action block of any rule has **not** been executed.

When rule activations are placed on the rule agenda, they are ordered based on the priority of the rule, with those rules with a higher priority placed at the top of the agenda.

When there are multiple activations with the same priority, the most recently added activation is the next rule to fire. However, it's quite common for multiple activations to be added to the ruleset at the same time; the ordering of these activations is not specified.

Rule firing

Once all rule conditions have been evaluated, then the rule engine will start to process the agenda. It will take the rule activation at the top of the agenda and execute the action block for the fact set row and the corresponding rule.

During executing of the action block, the rule may assert new facts, assert updated facts, or retract exiting facts from the working memory. As the rule engine does this, it may cause existing activations to be removed from the agenda, or may add new activations to the agenda.

When an activation is added to the agenda, it will be inserted into the agenda based on the priority of the rule. If there are already previous activations on the agenda with the same priority, the new activation will be inserted in front of these activations. This means that the set of new activations will be processed before any of the older activations with the same priority, but after any activation with a higher priority.

> If a rule asserts a fact that is mentioned in its rule condition, and the rule condition is still `true`, then a new activation for the same fact set row will be added back to the agenda. So the rule will be fired again. This can result in a rule continually firing itself and thus the ruleset never completing.

Once the rule engine has completed the execution of the action block for an activation, it will take the next activation from the agenda and process that. Once all activations on the agenda have been processed then the rule engine has completed execution of the ruleset.

Retrieve result

Once the ruleset has completed, the decision service will query the working memory of the rule session for the result, specifically the facts that we configured the decision service to watch, which the decision service will then return to the BPEL process.

Note, for each fact that we have configured the decision service to watch, we should ensure that just a single fact of that type will reside within the working memory of the decision service upon completion of executing the ruleset. If zero or multiple facts exist, then the decision service will return an exception to the BPEL process.

Session management

Before executing a ruleset, the decision service must first obtain a rule session. Creating a rule session involves creating a `RuleSession` object and loading the required repository, which has significant overhead. Instead of creating a new `RuleSession` to handle each request, the decision service maintains a pool of shared objects that it uses to service requests.

When we invoke a decision service within a BPEL process, the decision service will allocate `RuleSession` object from this pool to handle the request.

In most scenarios, we will choose to assert the facts, execute a ruleset and retrieve the result within a single operation. At the end of this, the final step is to reset the session, so that it can be returned to the pool of `RuleSession` objects and reused to handle future requests. This pattern of invocation is known as a stateless request, as the state of the session is not maintained between operations.

However, the decision service also supports a stateful invocation pattern, which enables you to split these steps across multiple operations when more flexibility is required.

For example, you can assert some facts within the first invocation, execute the ruleset and retrieve the results (without resetting the session). Based on the result, you may then take one of multiple paths within your BPEL process. At which point you may re-invoke the decision service, asserting some additional facts, re-execute the ruleset, retrieve an updated result, and then reset the rule session.

However, stateful sessions should be used with care as the state of the rule session is **not** persisted as part of the dehydration of a BPEL process, so won't survive a server shutdown.

Debugging a ruleset

Because the order in which rules and facts are evaluated are not specified for rules with equal priority, when you don't get the result you are expecting it can potentially be quite hard to debug. In these situations it can be extremely useful to see what facts are being asserted, the activations that are being generated and the rules as they are being fired.

The decision service can be configured to log these events, by specifying the following properties:

- `watchFacts`: Logs information about each fact as it is asserted, retracted, or modified within the working memory of a ruleset. As each fact is asserted, it is given a numeric identifier prefixed with `f-`, which uniquely identifies that fact within the rule session.

- `watchActivations`: Logs information about each rule activation as it's placed on the agenda, including details of the facts in the row fact set for the activation.

- `watchRules`: Logs information about each rule as it fires, detailing the rule fired as well as the facts in the row fact set causing the rule to fire.

These properties must configured by adding them to the `decisonservices.xml` file shown as follows:

```
<?xml version = '1.0' encoding = 'UTF-8'?>
<decisionServices xmlns="http://xmlns.oracle.com/bpel/rules">
  <ruleEngineProvider name="obay.ob1" provider="Oracle">
    <repository type="File">
      <file>repositoryresource:obay.obr</file>
    </repository>
    <properties>
      <property name="watchRules">true</property>
      <property name="watchActivations">true</property>
      <property name="watchFacts">true</property>
    </properties>
  </ruleEngineProvider>
  ...
</decisionServices>
```

This file isn't available within JDeveloper as part of the BPEL project. Hence it needs to be manually opened and modified using JDeveloper or a text editor. The file can be found in the following directory

```
<Project Dir>\decisionservices\AuctionService\war\WEB-INF\classes
```

Here, `<Project Dir>` is the home directory of the BPEL project using the decision service. Once you have set these properties you still have to configure the BPEL domain to log these events, by setting the logger `default.collaxa.cube.services` to `debug`.

Using DM.println to add additional logging

Even with the above logging information, it can be useful to produce more fine grain logging within your ruleset. You can do this using the DM.println function within your ruleset.

This function can be used either within your own functions or called as part of the action block for a rule. Again to enable these statements to be written to the BPEL *domain* log, you need to set the logger default.collaxa.cube.services to debug.

Using business rules to implement an auction

A good candidate for a service to implement as a ruleset is the oBay auction service. You may recall that we looked at the oBay auction process in Chapter 14 ; what we didn't cover in this chapter is the actual implementation of how we calculate the winning bid.

In this scenario our facts consist of the item up for auction and a list of bids which have been submitted against the item. So we need to implement a set of rules to be applied against these bids in order to determine the winning bid.

Defining our XML Facts

The first step in implementing our ruleset is to define our XML Facts; we can create these using the auction.xsd that we defined as part of our canonical model for oBay, shown as follows:

```xml
<?xml version="1.0" encoding="windows-1252"?>
<xsd:schema xmlns:xsd="http://www.w3.org/2001/XMLSchema"
            xmlns="http://schema.packtpub.com/obay/auc"
            targetNamespace="http://schema.packtpub.com/obay/auc"
            elementFormDefault="qualified" >

    <xsd:element name="auctionItem"              type="tAuctionItem"/>
    <xsd:element name="bids"                     type="tBids"/>
    <xsd:element name="bid"                      type="tBid"/>

    <xsd:complexType name="tAuctionItem">
      <xsd:sequence>
        <xsd:element name="auctionType"     type="xsd:string"/>
        <xsd:element name="startTime"       type="xsd:dateTime" />
        <xsd:element name="endTime"         type="xsd:dateTime" />
        <xsd:element name="startingPrice"   type="xsd:double" />
```

```
        <xsd:element name="reservePrice"  type="xsd:double"/>
        <xsd:element name="winningPrice"  type="xsd:double"/>
        <xsd:element name="winningBid"  minOccurs="0" type="tBid"/>
        <xsd:element name="bidHistory"    type="tBids"/>
      </xsd:sequence>
    </xsd:complexType>

    <xsd:complexType name="tBids">
      <xsd:sequence>
        <xsd:element name="bid" type="tBid" minOccurs="0"
                                       maxOccurs="unbounded" />
      </xsd:sequence>
    </xsd:complexType>

    <xsd:complexType name="tBid">
      <xsd:sequence>
        <xsd:element name="bidId"      type="xsd:string" />
        <xsd:element name="bidderId"    type="xsd:string" />
        <xsd:element name="bidtime"    type="xsd:dateTime"/>
        <xsd:element name="maxAmount"  type="xsd:double"/>
        <xsd:element name="bidAmount"  type="xsd:double"/>
        <xsd:element name="status"      type="xsd:string"/>
      </xsd:sequence>
    </xsd:complexType>

  </xsd:schema>
```

Examining this we can see that this maps nicely to facts that we have already identified. We have the element auctionItem which maps to our auction fact.

This has a start and end time during which bids can be received, a starting price and a reserve price (which defaults to the starting price if not specified). It also contains an optional winning bid element, which holds details of the current winning bid for the auction (if there is one) as well the bid history element, which contains details of all failed bids.

When we first create an auction, we won't have received any bids. So initially our auctionItem will not contain a winning bid and the bid history will be empty, as in the following example:

```
<auctionItem>
  <auctionType>STD</auctionType>
  <startTime>2008-09-01T15:45:48 </startTime>
  <endTime>2008-09-08T15:45:48</endTime>
  <startingPrice>1.00</startingPrice>
```

```
    <reservePrice>5.00</reservePrice>
    <winningPrice>0.00</winningPrice>
    <bidHistory/>
  </auctionItem>
```

Against this we need to apply one or more bids; this is contained within the fact bids, which contains one or more bid elements of type tBid.

 As part of the auction process, as each bid is submitted to the BPEL process, it will assign a unique ID to the bid (within the context of the auction), set the bidtime to the current time and set the status of the bid to NEW, before submitting it to the Auction ruleset.

So, for example, if we submitted the following set of bids against the above item:

```
<bids>
  <bid>
    <bidId>1</bidId>
    <bidderId>jcooper</bidderId>
    <bidtime>2008-09-06T12:27:14</bidtime>
    <maxAmount>12.00</maxAmount>
    <bidAmount>0.00</bidAmount>
    <status>NEW</status>
  </bid>
  <bid>
    <bidId>2</bidId>
    <bidderId>istone</bidderId>
    <bidtime>2008-09-07T10:15:33</bidtime>
    <maxAmount>10.00</maxAmount>
    <bidAmount>0.00</bidAmount>
    <status>NEW</status>
  </bid>
</bids>
```

we would want the rule engine to return as an updated auctionItem fact that looked like the following.

```
<auctionItem>
  <auctionType>STD</auctionType>
  <startTime>2008-09-01T15:45:48 </startTime>
  <endTime>2008-09-08T15:45:48</endTime>
  <startingPrice>1.00</startingPrice>
  <reservePrice>5.00</reservePrice>
  <winningPrice>10.50</winningPrice>
  <winningbid>
```

```
      <bidId>1</bidId>
      <bidderId>jcooper</bidderId>
      <bidtime>2008-09-06T12:27:14</bidtime>
      <maxAmount>12.00</maxAmount>
      <bidAmount>10.50</bidAmount>
      <status>WINNING</status>
    </winningbid>
    <bidHistory>
      <bid>
        <bidId>2</bidId>
        <bidderId>istone</bidderId>
        <bidtime>2008-09-07T10:15:33</bidtime>
        <maxAmount>10.00</maxAmount>
        <bidAmount>10.00</bidAmount>
        <status>OUTBID</status>
      </bid>
    </bidHistory>
  </auctionItem>
```

Defining the decision service

Once we have created our dictionary containing our XML facts, we can create an empty ruleset (called **Auction** in our example). At this point we can already create a decision service to invoke the ruleset.

For the Auction Decision Service we need to pass in two facts: AuctionItem and Bids and return the single fact AuctionItem as shown in the following screenshot:

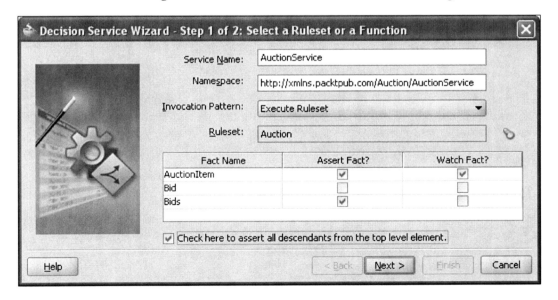

At this point we can actually save and run the ruleset from our Auction Process. Assuming everything works as expected, it will return a result containing details of the actual auction item that we passed in. All that remains now is for us to write the rules to evaluate our list of bids.

Using a global variable to reference the result set

When we configure a decision service, we specify one or more facts that we want the decision service to watch (that is, `AuctionItem` in the previous example); these are often referred to as the **result set**.

Many of our rules within the ruleset will require us to update the result set. For example, every time we evaluate a bid, we will need to update the `AuctionItem` fact accordingly, either to record a bid as the new winning bid or add it to the bid history as a failed bid.

When a rule is fired, the action block is only able to operate on those facts contained within its local scope, which are those facts contained in the fact set row for that activation. Or put more simply, the rule can only execute actions against those facts which triggered the rule.

This means that for any rule which needs to operate on the result set, we would need to include the appropriate test within the rule condition in order to pull that fact into the fact set row for the activation. So, in the case of our Auction ruleset, we would need to add the following statement to every rule which needed to operate on the `AuctionItem` fact:

```
AuctionItem is a AuctionItem
```

This just adds an extra level of complexity to all our rules, particularly if you have multiple facts contained within the result set. It's considered better practice to define a global variable which references the result set, which we can access within the action block of any rule and within any function we define.

Defining a global variable

To create a global variable, from within the **Definitions** tab, select the **Variables** folder. This will bring up the **Variables Summary**, which lists all the variables currently defined to our ruleset. Click **Create** to bring up the **Variable** editor page as shown in the screenshot.

Here we have defined a variable of type **AuctionItem** and given it a corresponding name and alias. For the purpose of clarity, we tend to prefix all variables with **var** to indicate that it's a global variable.

If we check the box **Final** the variable is fixed, that is, it becomes a constant, which can then be used within the test part of a rule. However, as we want to be able to update the variable we have left this unchecked.

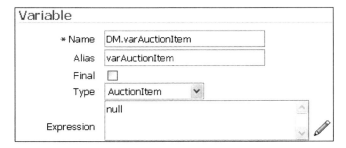

Finally, we can define an expression to initialize the variable. With XML facts you would often call a function to create the fact and initialize the variable. In our case, we want to initialize it to reference the `AuctionItem` fact passed in by the decision service.

Since variables are created and initialized prior to asserting any facts, we will need to define a rule to do this once `AuctionItem` has been asserted. So here we are just setting our variable to **null**.

Defining a rule to initialize a global variable

As you can see from the following diagram, the rule to initialize our global variable is pretty straightforward.

The key point worth noting is that we have specified a priority of **100** (the default is 0) for the rule. This is to ensure that this rule is fired before any of the other rules which reference this variable.

Writing our auction rules

The next step is to write the rules to determine the winning bid. We could write a very simple rule to find the highest bid by writing a rule condition statement such as the following:

```
winningBid is a TBid
There is no case where otherBid is a TBid and
    otherBid.maxAmount > winningBid.maxAmount
```

This will match the bid which has no other bids with a greater bid amount. However, if we examine the bidding rules of an auction, we can see that the highest bid doesn't always win.

The reason being that once a successful bid has been placed, the next bid has to be equal to the winning amount plus a full bid increment; otherwise it's not a valid bid. In addition if two maximum bids are equal, then the bid that was placed first is deemed the winning bid.

Evaluating facts in date order

In other words we need to evaluate our bids in date order, the earliest first, and then the next, and so on. Once a bid has been processed, its status will be set to WINNING, OUTBID, or INVALID as appropriate.

So we need to write a rule to select a bid with a status of NEW which has an earlier bidtime than any other bid with a status of NEW. This can then be evaluated against our auction rules to determine its success or otherwise.

The first part of the rule condition is straight forward; we just need to implement a pattern such as:

```
nextBid is a TBid and
    nextBid.status == "NEW"
```

This will of course match all bids with a status of NEW.

Checking for non-existent fact

So we need to define a second pattern that checks to see if no other bids exist (with a status of NEW) with an earlier bid time; in other words we have to check for the non-existence of a fact.

We do this by defining a pattern of type There is no case which will fire once if there are no matches, that is, no earlier bids. So our extended rule condition is implemented as follows:

```
nextBid is a TBid and
    nextBid.status == "NEW"
There is no case where anotherBid is a TBid and
    anotherBid.status == "NEW" &&
    anotherBid.bidtime.before(nextBid.bidtime)
```

This condition works as follows; the first test will select all the bids with a status of NEW. For each bid selected it will execute the second test where it will select all other bids with a status of new and an earlier bid time; if no bids are selected then this test will evaluate to true and the rule will be activated and placed on the agenda.

When the activation is placed on the agenda, only the fact referenced by nextBid is included in the fact row set, because for the rule condition to be true, anotherBid won't actually reference any other bid.

Using Calendar functionality

You may have noted that the property bidtime, which is defined within our schema as xsd:datetime maps to a java.util.Calendar. When comparing properties of type Calendar within a rule, we can't use the standard operators (such as >, >=, <= and <) to do this.

Rather we need to use the appropriate methods (for example before, after) provided by the Calendar class. Now we could write our own functions that wrap these methods calls, or alternatively as we have done above invoke them directly within our rules.

In order to do this, we first need to import the java.util.Calendar class as a Java fact within our dictionary. Once we have done this, the rule editor won't expose the methods. Rather we need to specify that our test is an **Advanced Test** and manually enter the code.

Updating the bid status

Once we have located the next bid, we need to set its status to NEXT and re-assert it; we do this with the following statements in our action block.

```
Assign nextBid.status = "NEXT"
Assert nextBid
```

An interesting side effect is that as soon as we assert our modified bid, the rule engine will re-apply the test condition and potentially find another bid with a status of **"NEW"**, that is, the next bid to be processed after this one.

On finding this bid, it will place a new activation on the agenda for this rule referencing this new bid. To prevent this rule from firing before any of the rules which process bids with a status of **"NEXT"**, we have set the priority of this rule to **0**.

So the complete rule to get the next bid is defined as follows:

Rule

* Name	GetNextBid
Description	
Priority	0

If

New Pattern Delete

☐ 🖉 **nextBid** is a **TBid** and
   nextBid.status == "NEW"

☐ 🖉 There is no case where **anotherBid** is a **TBid** and
   anotherBid.status == "NEW" && anotherBid.bidtime.before(nextBid.bidtime)

Then

New Action Delete

☐ 🖉 Assign nextBid.status = "NEXT"

☐ 🖉 Assert nextBid

Using inference

Once we have identified the next bid, we could then, within the same rule, include the logic to determine the success or otherwise of the bid. However, when processing a bid, we have to deal with the following three potential scenarios:

1. The next bid is higher than the current winning bid.

2. The current winning bid is higher than or equal to the next bid.

3. This is our first bid and thus by default it is our winning bid.

Before evaluating a bid we also need to check that it's valid; specifically we must check:

- The max bid amount is greater than or equal to the starting price of the item.
- The max bid amount is greater than the current winning price plus one bidding increment.

If we encompassed all these checks within a single rule, we would end up with a very complex rule.

For example, to write a single rule for the first scenario, we would need to write a rule condition to identify the next bid, validate it and finally check if it is higher than the current winning bid, so would end up with a rule condition such as this:

```
nextBid is a TBid and
    nextBid.status == "NEW"

There is no case where anotherBid is a TBid and
    anotherBid.status == "NEW" &&
    anotherBid.bidtime.before(nextBid.bidtime)

auctionItem is a TAuctionItem and
    nextBid.maxAmount >= auctionItem.startingPrice

winningBid is a TBid and
    winningBid.status == "WINNING" &&
    nextBid.maxAmount >= winningBid.bidAmount +
                    getBidIncrement (winningBid.bidAmount)
    nextBid.maxAmount >  winningBid.maxAmount
```

We would then need to re-implement most of this logic for the other two scenarios.

Better practice is to use inference, that is, if A implies B, and B implies C, then we can infer from this that A implies C. In other words, we don't have to write this all within a single rule; the rule engine will automatically infer this for us.

In our scenario this means writing a rule to get the next bid (as covered above). Next, writing two rules to validate any bid with a status of next, these rules will **retract** any invalid bids and update their status to reflect this. Finally we need to write three rules, one for each of the scenarios identified above to process each valid bid.

The only thing we need to take into account is that the validation rules must have a higher priority than the rules which process the next bid. Hence, that they retract any invalid bids before they can be processed.

Processing the next valid bid

Using inference we can now write our rules to process the next bid on the basis that we already know which bid is next and that the bid is valid. Using this approach, the rule condition for the first scenario where the next bid is higher than the current winning bid, would be specified as:

```
nextBid is a TBid and
    nextBid.status == "NEXT"

winningBid is a TBid and
    winningBid.status == "WINNING" &&
    winningBid.maxAmount < nextBid.maxAmount
```

This, as we can see, is considerably simpler than the previous example.

If this evaluates to `true` for our next bid, then we have a new winning bid and need to take the appropriate actions to update the affected facts as well as the result set.

The first action we need to take is to calculate the actual winning amount by adding one bidding increment to the maximum amount of the losing bid. So the first statement in our rules action block is as follows:

```
Assign nextBid.bidAmount = winningBid.maxAmount +
                    getBidIncrement (winningBid.maxAmount)
```

Where `DM.getBidIncrement` is a function that calculates the next bid increment, based on the size of the current winning amount.

Next, we need to update its status to `WINNING` and re-assert the bid in order that it will be re-evaluated as a winning bid by our ruleset.

In addition, we need to update the status of our previous winning bid to `OUTBID` and retract, if from the rule space, as we no longer need to evaluate it.

Using functions to manipulate XML Facts

As part of the process of evaluating a new winning bid, we also need to update our result set. This includes creating a new XML element of type `TBid` to hold the details of the losing bid and insert this into the `bidHistory` element as well as updating the `winningBid` element with details of our new winning bid.

To create new instances of XML elements we need to use the corresponding JAXB `ObjectFactory` class that the rule author generated when we imported the auction schema.

Rather than performing this manipulation of the XML structure directly within the action block of our rules, it's considered best practice to implement this as a function, which can then be called from our rule. This helps keep our rules simpler and more intuitive to understand.

So for the above purpose we need to define two functions `assertWinningBid` and `retractLosingBid`.

Asserting a winning bid

To record details of a new winning bid in the result set, we have defined the function `DM.assertWinningBid`, which takes a single parameter `bid` of type `TBid`, used to pass in a reference to the winning bid. The code for this function is as follows:

```
// Update Status of Winning Bid
bid.setStatus("WINNING");
assert(bid);

// Update result set with details of Winning Bid
varAuctionItem.setWinningPrice(bid.getBidAmount());

com.packtpub.schema.obay.auction.TBid winningBid =
varAuctionItem.getWinningBid();

// Create Winning Bid if one doesn't exist
if (winningBid == null)
{
    com.packtpub.schema.obay.auc.ObjectFactory of =
        new com.packtpub.schema.obay.auc.ObjectFactory();

    winningBid = of.createTBid();

    varAuctionItem.setWinningBid(winningBid);
}

winningBid.setBidAmount(bid.getBidAmount());
winningBid.setBidderId(bid.getBidderId());
winningBid.setBidId(bid.getBidId());
winningBid.setBidtime(bid.getBidtime());
winningBid.setMaxAmount(bid.getMaxAmount());
winningBid.setStatus(bid.getStatus());
```

Looking at this, we can see it breaks into two parts. The first part updates the status of the winning bid to 'WINNING', and asserts the bid. Now, we didn't need to include this functionality within the function, we could have achieved the same result within the rule itself be defining the following actions:

```
Assign nextBid.status = "WINNING"
Assert nextBid
```

We need to process a winning bid in multiple rules; including this in the function both simplifies our rules and ensures that we handle winning bids in a consistent way. Either approach is valid; it just comes down to personal preference.

However, to indicate to callers of the function that we are asserting the winning bid in the function, we have prefixed the name of the function with `'assert'`.

The second part of the function is used to update the result set with details of the winning bid. The first line updates the element `winningPrice` to contain the bid amount of the winning bid.

The next set of code is more interesting. First it calls the method `getWinningbid()` on the result set to get a reference to the winning bid element. This may return null, as the `AuctionItem` may not currently have a winning bid (that is, if this is the first winning bid).

To create any new XML elements we need an appropriate `ObjectFactory`, so we create a new instance of one with the following line of code:

```
com.packtpub.schema.obay.auc.ObjectFactory of =
    new com.packtpub.schema.obay.auc.ObjectFactory();
```

Next we use the `ObjectFactory` to create a new element of type `TBid` as follows:

```
winningBid = of.createTBid();
```

Finally we update the winning bid element in `AuctionItem` to point to this newly created element as follows:

```
varAuctionItem.setWinningBid(winningBid);
```

Once we've done this we update the details of the `winningBid` element with those of the `bid` element.

The final thing to note is that we are not asserting `varAuctionItem` or any of the elements we have added to it. Hence, none of these changes will be visible to our ruleset, which is exactly what we want. This is because we are using the result set as a place to build up the result of executing our ruleset and thus don't want it included in the evaluation.

Retracting a losing bid

To record details of a losing bid in the result set, we have followed a similar approach and defined the function DM.retractLosingBid, which takes a single parameter bid of type TBid. The code for the function is as follows:

```
// Update Status of Losing Bid
bid.setStatus("OUTBID");
bid.setBidAmount(bid.getMaxAmount());
retract(bid);

// Record Details of Bid in Result Set
com.packtpub.schema.obay.auc.TBid losingBid = DM.cloneTBid(bid);

java.util.List bidHistory = varAuctionItem.getBidHistory().getBid();

if (bidHistory.isEmpty()) {
    bidHistory.add(losingBid);
}
else {
    bidHistory.add(0,losingBid);
}
```

Looking at this, we can see that, as with the previous function, it breaks into two parts. The first part updates the status of the losing bid and then retracts it. The second part of the function is used to record details of losing bid within the bidHistory element of our result set.

The first line of this part calls the function DM.cloneTBid to create a new element of type TBid and initialize it with the values of the losing bid using a approach similar to the one previously used to create a new winning bid element.

Once we've done that, we then add it to the bidHistory element. The bid history itself is a collection of bid elements. JAXB implements this as a java.util.List, the method getBid returns a reference to this list.

The final part of the function inserts the losing bid at the start of this list, so that the bid history contains the most recently processed bid at the start of the list.

Rules to process a new winning bid

With our functions defined, we can finish the implementation of the rule for a new winning bid, which is shown in the following screenshot:

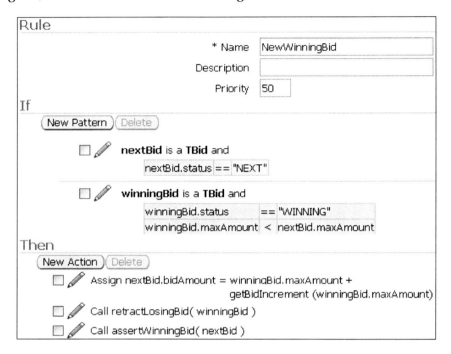

Due to the use of inference to simplify the rule condition and the use of functions to manipulate the result set, the final rule is very straightforward.

The only thing we need to take into account is the priority of the rule, which we have set to **50**. This is to ensure that the validation rules for a bid have a higher priority so that they are fired first.

Validating the next bid

For the above rule to be complete we need to define the rules which validate the next bid before we process it; the two conditions that we need to check are:

- The max bid amount is greater than or equal to the starting price of the item.
- The max bid amount is greater than the current winning price plus one bidding increment.

To validate that max bid amount is greater than or equal to the auction starting price, we have defined the following rule:

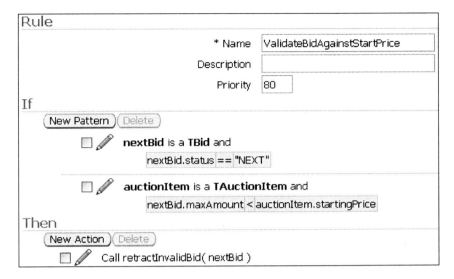

The function `retractInvalidBid` is almost identical to the function `retractLosingBid`, the only difference being that it sets the status of the bid to `'INVALID'`.

We have also defined a similar rule, `validateBidAgainstWinningPrice` to validate that the max bid amount is greater than the current winning amount plus one bidding increment.

Each of these rules has a priority of **80**, which is higher than the rules for processing the next bid. This ensures that any invalid bids are retracted before they can be processed.

Rule to process a losing bid

The rules to handle the other potential outcomes for the next bid, namely where it's our first bid, and thus by default a winning bid or a losing bid, are straightforward, apart for one exception. The rule for the scenario where the next bid is a losing bid is shown here:

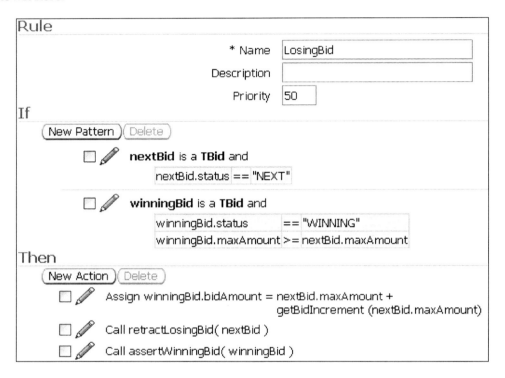

If we look at the first action that sets the bid amount of the winning bid equal to the maximum amount of the losing bid plus the next bid increment, there is a possibility that this could cause the bid amount to exceed the maximum amount specified.

For example if the maximum bid was $10, with the current winning amount being $5, then it would be valid for the next bid to be $10. This bid would fail but the new winning amount according to the above would be $10.50.

Capping the winning bid amount

To prevent this from happening we need to write another rule to test if the winning amount of the bid is greater than its maximum amount and if it is then set the winning amount equal to the maximum amount. The rule for this is shown in the following screenshot:

```
Rule
                              * Name    CapWinningBid
                            Description
                             Priority    90
If
   ( New Pattern )( Delete )
       ☐ ✎   winningBid is a TBid and
                    winningBid.status      == "WINNING"
                    winningBid.bidAmount   >  winningBid.maxAmount
Then
   ( New Action )( Delete )
       ☐ ✎   Assign winningBid.bidAmount = winningBid.maxAmount
       ☐ ✎   Call assertWinningBid( winningBid )
```

The rule itself is straightforward. But as this rule is being used to correct an inconsistent state we have given it a priority of **90** so that it is fired even before the validation rules.

Complete ruleset

In total we have eight rules within our Auction ruleset; these are listed below in order of priority.

Rule	Priority
InitialiseVarAuctionItem	100
CapWinningBid	90
ValidateBidAgainstStartPrice	80
ValidateBidAgainstWinningPrice	80
FirstBid	50
NewWinningBid	50
LosingBid	50
GetNextBid	0

The first rule is just used to initialize the global variable, which references the result set. The next rule, CapWinningBid, ensures that we don't breach the maximum amount for a bid. The next two rules: ValidateBidAgainstStartPrice and ValidateBidAgainstWinningPrice are just simple validation rules.

The majority of the work is done in the next three rules: `FirstBid`, `NewWinningBid` and `LosingBid`, each of which deals with one of the three possible outcomes each time we have to process a new bid. The final rule, `GetNextBid`, is used to ensure that we process each bid in date order.

Performance considerations

In the example we've been working on the basis that every time we receive a new bid we add that to our list of bids received and then submit the auction and the entire list of bids to the ruleset for evaluation.

The obvious issue with this technique is that we are re-evaluating all bids that we have received from scratch every time we receive a new bid.

One possible solution would be to have a stateful rule session. With this approach we would first submit the auction item to the decision service, but no bids. Then, as we receive a bid, we could assert that against the ruleset and get the updated result back from the decision service.

The issue with this (as we discussed at the start of this chapter) is when the BPEL process dehydrates, which in the case of our auction process will happen each time we wait for the next bid, the rule session is not persisted. Consequently, whenever the server is restarted we will lose the rules session of any auction in progress, which is clearly not desirable.

Managing state within the BPEL process

One alternative is to use the BPEL process to hold the state of the rule session. With this technique we need to ensure that all relevant facts contained within the rule session are returned within the facts that the decision service is watching.

Next time we invoke the decision service, we can re-submit these facts (along with any new facts to be evaluated) and re-assert them back into a new rule session.

In the case of our Auction ruleset, the relevant facts that need to be maintained between invocations are `auctionItem` and `winningBid` which is contained within `auctionItem`.

With this approach, each time we receive a new bid we just need to assert the auctionItem element as returned by the previous invocation of the ruleset and the new bid (within the bids element). As a result, each time we submit a new bid, rather than re-evaluate all bids to determine the winning bid, we just need to evaluate the new bid against the winning bid, which is clearly more efficient.

To support this, we do not have to make any modifications to our ruleset, because we have implemented it in such a way that it supports either asserting all bids in one go or submitting them incrementally.

The only remaining drawback with this approach is that the ruleset will still assert all bid objects contained within the bidHistory element of auctionItem into working memory. While this won't change the outcome, it still means all these bids will be evaluated in the process of firing the rules, though none of them will cause an activation to happen.

Where we have only a relatively small number of facts this doesn't really cause a problem, but if the number of facts is in the high hundreds or order of 1000s, then this may make a noticeable difference.

Using functions to control the assertion of facts

The reason that all facts are asserted into the working memory of the rule session is that we checked the box **Check here to assert all descendants from the top level element**.

This causes the function assertXPath to be called for each fact passed in by the decision service, which causes all the descendants of the fact elements to be asserted at run time.

An alternative is to leave this unchecked and write a function for each fact passed in that asserts just the desired facts. So in our case we would write a function to assert the winningBid element in auctionItem and all the bid elements contained in bids.

Summary

The Business Rules Engine is built on a powerful inference engine, which it inherits from its roots in the Rete Algorithm. We spent the first part of this chapter explaining how the rule engine evaluates facts against rules. The operation of the Rete algorithm can be a challenge to completely understand, so re-reading this section may be beneficial.

However, once you have an appreciation for how the rule engine works and can start "thinking in Rete", you have a powerful tool not just for implementing complex business rules but also a certain type of service.

We demonstrated this by developing a complete ruleset to determine the winning bid for an auction. Looking at the final list of rules, we can see that we needed relatively few to achieve the end result, and that none of these were particularly complex.

As is the case when implementing a more typical decision services, we have the added advantage that we can easily modify the rules that implement a service without having to modify the overall application, giving us an even greater degree of flexibility.

The Importance of Bindings

17

When we talk about web services, most people assume that we are going to bind (that is, connect) to the service using SOAP over HTTP. Indeed, this is often the case; however, Oracle SOA Suite supports binding to web services over multiple protocols. This chapter looks at the different bindings supported and the various advantages they have, including better support for transactions and improved performance.

The web services stack

To understand how bindings affect our applications, we need to put them into the context of the web services stack. For the purposes of this discussion, we focus only on the exposure of services within the web services stack, ignoring composition of services through BPEL and the service bus.

Logical view of web services stack

A logical view of the web services stack is shown in the following diagram and identifies three key components:

1. A service description layer that provides a consistent view of how services are described. In particular, it must describe what interfaces are supported by the service, what messages are used by those services, and finally how those services are mapped onto physical formats and transport facilities. This role is fulfilled by WSDL, the Web Services Description Language which is covered in more detail in the next section.

2. A message format for transmission of service requests and service responses. This is normally described by SOAP, the Simple Object Access Protocol. However, as the diagram shows, other message formats are possible.

3. A physical transport mechanism for delivery of messages. This may be covered by a SOAP profile, such as SOAP over HTTP (the most commonly used mechanism) or SOAP over FTP. However, it is also possible to have other transports being used with non-SOAP message formats.

The join between the service description layer and the message layer is known as the binding of the service, and specifies how the actual communication protocols are used by the service. This binding provides a wrapper to a physical service implementation, which may be in Java, C#, or some higher level implementation mechanism such as BPEL or a service bus.

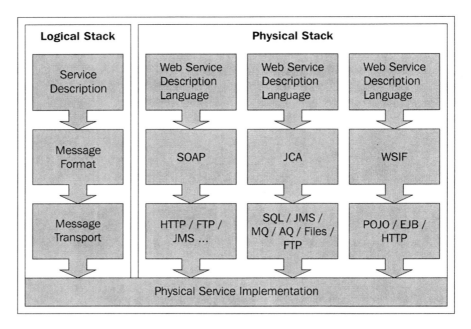

Physical view of web services stack

When we look at physical implementations of the web services stack, we notice that virtually all implementations use WSDL to describe the service. This provides a high degree of inter-operability at the tool layer in particular, as tools only need to understand WSDL to make use of a service.

The most common description of message formats is done by using SOAP. SOAP allows messages to be described using XML, either with an XML Schema definition or through SOAP specific XML descriptions. When SOAP and XML is not being used, the message formats are generally mapped onto very specific native formats, such as Java objects or SQL types.

SOAP is very flexible about how messages are physically transported. A SOAP message may be transported across HTTP or some other protocol, such as JMS or FTP. In contrast, other bindings tend to be limited to a single transport, such as a Java binding that would use Java types to describe messages, but then only offer the option of directly calling **Plain Old Java Objects** (POJOs).

Understanding Web Service Description Language (WSDL)

We will now look at how the Web Service Description Language (WSDL) describes services, before exploring why we have a need for all these different binding layers. WSDL describes the interfaces supported by a service. It also describes the data they expect to receive and send, and the operations within those interfaces.

How to read WSDL

In Chapter 10, we looked at how to build a WSDL document. It is easy to get confused by all the parts of a WSDL file. Hence, in this section we will look at what they are and how they fit together. The example below shows a sample WSDL file with key elements highlighted. We will look at the basic structure of a WSDL file by examining each element in turn.

```xml
<?xml version="1.0" encoding="UTF-8" ?>
<definitions targetNamespace="urn:ChangeCurrencyInterface"
    xmlns="http://schemas.xmlsoap.org/wsdl/"
    xmlns:tns="urn:ChangeCurrencyInterface"
    … >
  <types
    <xsd:schema elementFormDefault="qualified">
      <xsd:import schemaLocation="OBayCanonical.xsd"
                    namespace="http://www.obay.example"/>
    </xsd:schema>
  </types>
  <message name="ChangeCurrencyRequestMessage">
    <part name="in" element="ccs:ChangeCurrencyRequest"/>
  </message>
  <message name="ChangeCurrencyResponseMessage">
    <part name="return" element="ccs:ChangeCurrencyResponse"/>
  </message>
  <portType name="ChangeCurrencyPortType">
    <operation name="ConvertCurrency">
      <input message="tns:ChangeCurrencyRequestMessage"/>
      <output message="tns:ChangeCurrencyResponseMessage"/>
```

```
            </operation>
        </portType>
        <binding name="ChangeCurrencyServiceSoapHttp"
                 type="tns:ChangeCurrencyPortType">
        <soap:binding style="document"
                    transport="http://schemas.xmlsoap.org/soap/http"/>
        <operation name="ConvertCurrency">
          <soap:operation
soapAction="urn:ChangeCurrencyInterface/ChangeCurrencyService.wsdl/
ConvertCurrency"/>
            <input>
              <soap:body use="literal"/>
            </input>
            <output>
              <soap:body use="literal"/>
            </output>
          </operation>
        </binding>
        <service name="ChangeCurrencyService">
        <port name="ChangeCurrencyPort"
            binding="tns:ChangeCurrencyServiceSoapHttp">
            <soap:address location="http://www.example.com"/>
        </port>
    </service>
</definitions>
```

<definitions>

A WSDL document is an XML document, and it has a root element called
<definitions>. The definitions element provides a wrapper for a set of definitions.
The set of definitions may be named through an optional name attribute. The
definitions in the document are:

- Types: Used to define content of messages
- Messages: Used to define parameters of operations
- Port Types: Used to define collections of logical operations
- Bindings: Used to define concrete protocols and data formats
- Ports: Used to define concrete endpoints for bindings
- Services: Used to group sets of related ports

The following diagram shows how these definitions relate to each other.

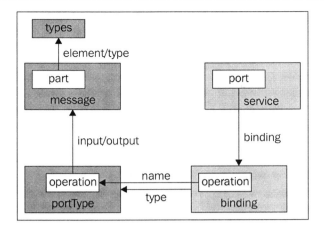

WSDL concepts in a 3GL

It is useful to map WSDL concepts onto a third generation language, such as Java to clarify what they mean.

portType is like a Java interface; it contains operations that are like Java methods.

messages are like the input parameters or return value of a Java method.

binding and service are like a Java class in that they identify a concrete mapping of an interface onto a physical implementation.

\<types>

A WSDL document may include a \<types> element, which is used to define data types that will be used later. These types are normally described using XML Schema, and may also be brought in from an external XSD file. This is good practice as they may well be reusable in several services. The types element will almost always include an XML Schema document shown as follows:

```
<types>
   <xsd:schema elementFormDefault="qualified">
      <xsd:import namespace="http://www.obay.example"
                  schemaLocation="../OBAYSchema/OBayCanonical.xsd"
      />
   </xsd:schema>
</types>
```

<message>

The types defined are used to create messages defined by one or more `<message>` elements. Messages are the units of data transfer between service provider and service requestor. Messages are identified by their `name` attribute. The messages themselves may consist of several parts, identified by the `<part>` element. Each part is either a type (common in RPC style web services) or an element (seen in doc style web services). Hence parts depend upon the types. These types could include primitive types such as `string` or `int`.

RPC and Document Style Web Services

RPC and Document Style refers to the way in which the web service encodes the messages. RPC style expects there to be an element indicating the operation and the data is encoded according to SOAP encoding rules, for example, allowing for cyclic graphs to be passed. Document style expects to pass the messages as XML documents that conform to an XML Schema. Generally doc style are viewed as preferable because of the ability to transform the documents en-route using XSLT transforms. See Chapter 10 for a more detailed discussion of different web service styles.

Parts are identified by their `name` attribute and will have either an `element` attribute to indicate the root element of the part or a `type` attribute to indicate the type of the part.

```
<message name="ChangeCurrencyRequestMessage">
  <part name="in" element="ccs:ChangeCurrencyRequest"/>
</message>
<message name="ChangeCurrencyResponseMessage">
  <part name="return" element="ccs:ChangeCurrencyResponse"/>
</message>
```

A message may have more than one part.

<portType>

The messages are grouped together into exchanges using the `<portType>` element. A `portType` defines an interface or abstract service. The `portType` is identified by its `name` attribute. Within the definitions element, a `portType` must have a unique name. Associated with the `portType` are one or more `<operation>` elements. Operations are identified by their `name` attribute. Each operation through the use of an `<input>` and/or an `<output>` element specifies a message and its direction. A normal request/reply operation would have an input message followed by an output message. There is also a `<fault>` element to allow for exceptions to be thrown by an operation.

```
<portType name="ChangeCurrencyPortType">
   <operation name="ConvertCurrency">
      <input message="ChangeCurrencyRequestMessage"/>
      <output message="ChangeCurrencyResponseMessage"/>
   </operation>
</portType>
```

<binding>

Everything we have discussed so far is abstract, and has no concrete implementation. As we move to the right-hand side of the diagram we move from the abstract to the concrete.

The <binding> element provides a concrete implementation of the abstract portType identified by the bindings type attribute, specifying for example the use of SOAP over HTTP. Bindings are identified by the name attribute. For each operation in the portType there may be a corresponding <operation> tag in the binding that will describe the mapping of the message onto the physical transport mechanism. Operations are identified by their name attribute.

Note that the binding details themselves are in a different namespace. This is because the WSDL specification is extensible to allow for many different kinds of bindings, not just SOAP over HTTP.

```
<binding name="ChangeCurrencyServiceSoapHttp"
         type="tns:ChangeCurrencyPortType">
   <soap:binding style="document"
                 transport="http://schemas.xmlsoap.org/soap/http"/>
   <operation name="ConvertCurrency">
      <soap:operation
soapAction="urn:ChangeCurrencyInterface/ChangeCurrencyService.wsdl/
ConvertCurrency"/>
      <input>
         <soap:body use="literal"/>
      </input>
      <output>
         <soap:body use="literal"/>
      </output>
   </operation>
</binding>
```

\<service\>

Finally, the concrete service itself is identified by the `<service>` element. A service groups together a related set of functionality into a logical service implementation. The service is identified by its `name` attribute. The service is associated with one or more `<port>` elements. Each port has a name attribute to identify it and in turn it identifies the binding supported by this port through the `<binding>` attribute. Because the bindings in turn refer to the `portTypes`, we have a link between the ports exposed by a service and the abstract ports defined earlier in the WSDL. When using SOAP bindings the port also includes an `<address>` element, which provides the physical endpoint for the port.

```
<service name="ChangeCurrencyService">
    <port name="ChangeCurrencyPort"
          binding="tns:ChangeCurrencyServiceSoapHttp">
        <soap:address location="http://www.example.com"/>
    </port>
</service>
```

It is worth noting that a service may have multiple ports that use different bindings but refer back to the same `portType`. This allows the service to have multiple ways of requesting its service. For example, one binding may be through SOAP over HTTP and another may be through a direct mapping onto an Enterprise Java Bean. We will explore this latter possibility later in the chapter.

The case for different bindings

The binding describes how the abstract XML interface and data type is mapped onto the physical data format and transport. The ability of WSDL to describe different bindings other than SOAP begs the question of why. There are at least three answers to this. Let us look at them in detail.

Connectivity

It is useful to be able to connect to a resource without the need for that resource to provide a SOAP interface. For example, when connecting to a database, it may be easier to have a binding that maps onto SQL data types and a database specific transport layer than it is to create a wrapper service for every service required. This increases the range of services that may be used without the need for separate wrappers.

Transactionality

Although there are efforts under way to provide a mechanism for transactional support using SOAP, there is currently no effective way of supporting traditional transactional services. Using a native binding such as JDBC or JCA allows a service to be accessed as part of a database transaction. For example, a BPEL flow may remove a message from MQ series using MQ native protocols, transform it, and apply it to a database using native database protocols. In this case the steps could all occur as part of the same XA transaction.

Performance

SOAP messaging provides great inter-operability but has never won any records for performance when compared to native protocols. Where performance is important, using native bindings rather than SOAP can be critical.

JCA bindings

Java Connector Architecture, JCA, is a standard way in Java to access a wide range of resources. A JCA resource adapter may provide an interface to many different types of resource including databases, packaged applications, and mainframes. Java Enterprise Edition (JEE) containers, such as WebLogic and WebSphere, provide JCA frameworks that allow registered adapters to be made available to hosted components as though they were native container resources. JCA adapters may also participate in transactions.

JCA bindings are probably the most commonly used non-SOAP binding in the SOA Suite. This is because they are used extensively by the adapter wizards to provide access to a wide range of native resources. Generally, the JCA bindings are generated by the wizards with no need for further work by the developer.

JCA bindings actually differ a lot in the way in which they map the WSDL message onto a physical format. But where they are common is in their use of Java Connector Architecture (JCA) adapters to provide the physical wrapper to the service. Across all JCA adapters/bindings the wizard will offer the opportunity to identify a JNDI location for the JCA resource. Either develop your own consistent notation for this or pay attention to the location generated by the wizard.

Most JCA adapters describe both a JNDI lookup for the JCA resource and also embed a description of the JCA resource used to generate the adapter. For example, a database adapter WSDL binding will have a lookup to a JCA database adapter at a specific JNDI location but it will also have a description of the database connection used by the wizard to interrogate the database to build the WSDL.

At run time, the JCA binding will first attempt to find a resource by looking up the JNDI location, for example /eis/DB/MyDB. If this name does not exist, or in other words if there is no resource adapter bound to this JNDI location, then the binding will use the connection properties used by the wizard that have been embedded in the WSDL.

When deploying to any system other than your embedded SOA Suite instance in JDeveloper, it is good practice to ensure that the JNDI location referenced does indeed have a resource of the correct type. It is also good practise to make sure that this is a pooled resource so that resource usage can be monitored and controlled by the application server infrastructure. Configuring of JCA resources is container specific and you will need to consult your container's documentation to find out how to bind adapters to particular JNDI locations.

Java bindings

In Chapter 11, we looked at how to create a Java web service that used SOAP protocols. In this section, we will explore how we can directly access that same Java without the need for using SOAP. This will improve performance as we do not have to send the message over HTTP but instead can invoke the Java directly.

Creating a Java binding

Using the example in Chapter 11, let's create a web service with Java bindings. We begin by right-clicking on the service wrapper class and selecting **Create J2EE Web Service**. This launches the **Create Java Web Service** wizard.

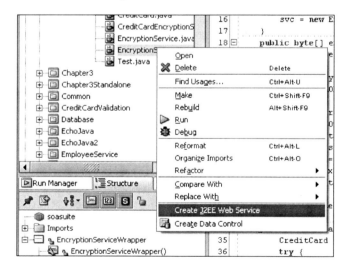

We must select the **J2EE 1.4 (JAX-RPC) Web Service** option, as this is the only option that currently supports Java binding.

We can then select the web service name and choose the bindings that we want to provide, in this case just the WSIF binding which provides a WSDL wrapping around our service. Selecting **Autogenerate Service Endpoint Interface** causes JDeveloper to automatically create a Java interface extending `java.rmi Remote` which is needed when creating a web service wrapper. If we are not generating any other bindings, we need to select **Next** to advance to the next configuration screen. We do not need to provide any additional configuration for the **Specify Custom Data Type Serializers** screen, and so can skip it by selecting **Next**. Similarly we can skip the **Mapping** screen. These two screens can be used to customize how data is transformed to/from XML, and how the mapping works between the WSDL interface and the Java interface.

By choosing a **Java binding (WSIF)** we are avoiding the overhead of SOAP and HTTP, but limiting ourselves to invoking a local service.

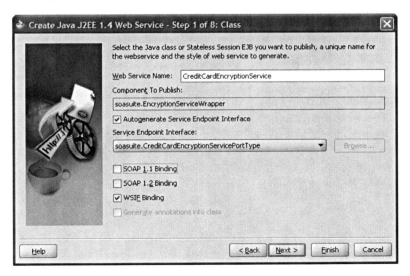

We now have the opportunity to select the methods to be exposed as part of the service. This allows us to limit the functionality of the Java that we are exposing through the web service.

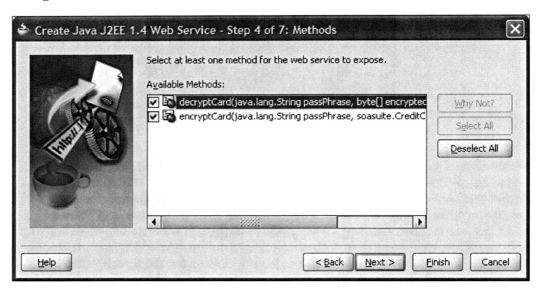

Having selected the methods we desire, and having clicked **Finish**, the required WSDL description of the service and any necessary wrapper classes, such as the Java interface corresponding to the WSDL Port Type, will be generated.

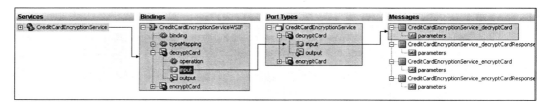

Note that before using the service, it is necessary to copy the Java classes so that they can be found by the appropriate SOA Suite component. For example, by copying the classes onto the SOA Suite server in the $ORACLE_HOME/bpel/system/classes directory, they can be found at run time by the BPEL Process Manager. Classes placed here are available to all BPEL processes.

Service bus bindings

The Oracle Service Bus is very flexible in its use of bindings. When creating a Business Service or a Proxy it is possible to specify the bindings to be used on the **Transport Configuration** screen. The choice of transports available is different depending on whether we are configuring a Business Service or a Proxy.

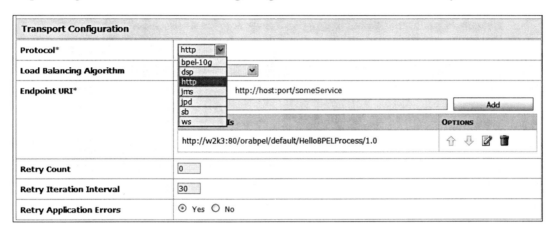

When configuring a Business Service transport described by WSDL we have the following protocol options available.

- **http**: For normal HTTP or HTTPS connections, this can be used for SOAP over HTTP services.

- **jms**: For message-based interfaces.

- **ws**: For endpoints that support **Web Services Reliable Messages (WSRM)** protocol, a reliable message delivery protocol for web services.

- **sb**: An optimized protocol for communicating with another Oracle Service Bus domain.

- **bpel-10g**: An optimized protocol that communicates with Oracle BPEL processes.

- **dsp**: A protocol optimized for communication with **Oracle Data Service Integrator (ODSI)**, formerly known as AquaLogic Data Services Platform, a mechanism for performing a federated data query across multiple data sources.

- **jpd**: A protocol optimized for communicating with **WebLogic Integration (WLI)**, an earlier integration product from BEA and now supported by Oracle.

The different transports allow for better performance or more reliable messaging than simple SOAP over HTTP. The transports available when defining a Proxy Service described by WSDL include **http, jms, ws,** and **sb** as already described. The other three mentioned, **bpel-10g, dsp,** and **jpd** are not supported for inbound traffic to the service bus. There is, however, another transport supported by Proxy services, which is **local**.

- **local**: A protocol that restricts the Proxy service to be called only by other proxy services.

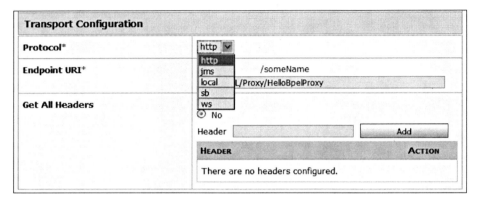

The local transport is highly optimized for using internally by the service bus. In addition to being highly performing, is also very reliable, having exactly once invocation semantics. Exactly once invocation semantics means that when called there will be a single invocation of the proxy with no retries.

Summary

Bindings allow us to control the way in which SOA Suite components interact with services. Different bindings provide different benefits, such as transactionality or better performance.

Generally when considering bindings, we do not have to worry too much about the low level details. The key questions we need to ask are:

- Does this service already exist? In this case, we use the existing service without concerning ourselves about the bindings it uses.
- Can this service be created by use of an adapter wizard? In this case, we use the appropriate adapter wizard to generate the required service without concerning ourselves about the bindings other than to make a note to create the appropriate JCA resource at the correct JNDI location.

- Does this service require very high throughput? In this case, we may want to consider using an adapter or Java binding to improve performance, even if a SOAP binding already exists.

- Does this service require true transactionality? In this case, we want to use a JCA binding so that the SOA Suite can combine multiple interactions into a single database or XA transaction, giving us tight transactionality. Note that when doing this, we are relying on the underlying implementation of the bindings to provide transactionality rather than on any higher level constructs. Hence, we have more tightly coupled our services together.

Most of our binding choices will be dictated by the nature of the service required, and only occasionally will the latter two questions enter into our considerations.

18
Packaging and Deployment

In this section, we will look at how to package a set of SOA Suite components for deployment in different environments. We will also look at some of the deployment topologies that may be used at run time to provide scalability. We will focus principally on the BPEL Process Manager as this has some of the more complex requirements for mapping of services.

The need for packaging

When developing software, we generally use a local development environment to create our SOA artefacts. In some cases this may be entirely on the developers' machine, at other times the developer will have access to a shared development server. In either case there will usually be the need to move the artefacts from the development environment into a test environment and eventually into a production environment.

Problems with moving between environments

Within our SOA artefacts we will have references to other artefacts such as service endpoint locations and rule repository locations. In addition the configuration for some components, particularly adapter services will probably be different between environments, for example, database locations and file locations may be different between different locations. We need to have a means of modifying these various environment dependant properties.

Types of interface

Within the development environment we will build many of the artefacts in a thick client design tool such as JDeveloper or Workshop and then deploy directly into the development run-time environment. As we move into test and/or production we do not want our operators to have JDeveloper or other design time environments, we would prefer that they had a set of command line tools and/or web interfaces to deploy components. Often they will be unable to use JDeveloper to deploy because of firewall restrictions.

Web interfaces

Web interfaces are handy for rapid deployment of components into a new environment, and they generally make it easy to configure any changes that are required. Web interfaces, however, are not easy to automate and so are not ideal for deployment that must be repeated across multiple stages, such as test, pre-production, and production environments.

Command line interfaces

Command line interfaces are often a little harder to work with, but have the huge advantage that they are easy to script, making it possible to have a repeatable deployment process. This is important enough for the move from test to production, but becomes even more important when we consider that we may wish to set up a data recovery environment or other multiple environments.

In a well-managed environment the use of deployment scripts is essential to ensuring a consistent way of deploying SOA Suite artefacts across different environments.

SOA Suite packaging

Unfortunately the current release of SOA Suite is not consistent in the way in which it packages the different components. Each SOA Suite component such as BPEL or service bus has a different way of packaging its artefacts for deployment. In this section, we will examine each component to see how it is packaged and how best to manage deployment across multiple environments.

Oracle Service Bus

An Oracle Service Bus project may be deployed from the Workshop IDE or imported from the service bus console by selecting the **System Administration** tab and then selecting the **Import Resources** link. In a similar fashion it is possible to export resources from the service bus console by selecting the **Export Resources** link.

When exporting a project or group of projects from the service bus by clicking on the **Export** button, the project is exported in a JAR file package called `sbconfig.jar` by default that may be saved from the browser.

The JAR file generated may be deployed to another service bus domain by importing it, and then editing the project settings to have the correct configuration.

Unlike BPEL there is no concept of versioning in the service bus and so once deployed it is generally easier to maintain the existing deployment rather than replace it completely; however complete projects may be replaced if necessary. Chapter 10 talks about how versioning may be applied in the service bus.

Individual service endpoint locations can be edited directly from within the service bus console. Potentially, every business service may need modifying for the correct environment.

It is also possible to use the **WebLogic Scripting Tool (WLST)** to migrate projects between environments.

Oracle BPEL Process Manager

The deployment unit of a BPEL process is the BPEL suitcase. The BPEL suitcase may be deployed to a BPEL Process Manager using the web interface accessed from the **Processes** tab of the BPEL console. A BPEL suitcase is generated when a BPEL process is compiled, either in JDeveloper or using an `Ant` task generated by JDeveloper. The location of the BPEL suitcase is displayed in the message log during BPEL compilation; it is usually generated in the `$PROJECT_HOME/output` directory. When deploying from JDeveloper into BPEL Process Manager the BPEL suitcase is used to transfer all the information required by the process. The same is true whether deploying the suitcase manually through the web interface or through an `ant` task.

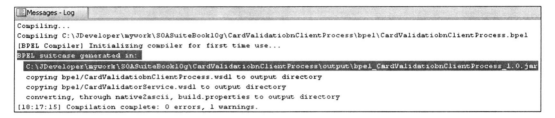

Deploying a BPEL process using the BPEL Console

Clicking the **Deploy New Process** link on the **Processes** tab of the BPEL Console provides access to the **Deploy New BPEL Process** screen. Here we can browse for the BPEL suitcase and then deploy it.

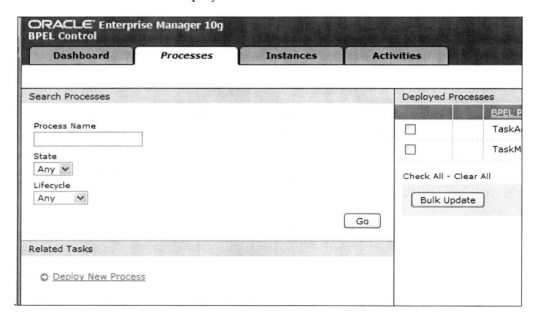

Note that some browsers may not properly close the BPEL suitcase after uploading it to the BPEL Process Manager. If this occurs then it will not be possible to regenerate the suitcase with the same version number. To work around this either close and reopen the browser or regenerate to a new version number

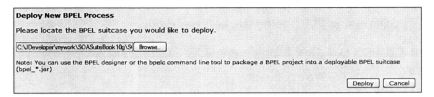

After deploying the process we receive a confirmation screen confirming that the process was successfully deployed.

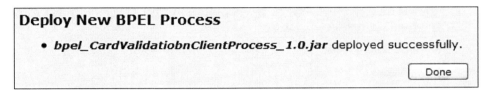

Deploying a BPEL process using 'ant'

JDeveloper automatically generates an ant script that may be used to deploy BPEL processes from the command line or from within JDeveloper. The script is called **build.xml** and is found in the **Resources** section of the JDeveloper project and is located in the top level project folder. This contains all the ant targets required to build and deploy BPEL processes from the command line. Associated with it is a properties file called **build.properties** that contains property definitions referenced by the **build.xml** file.

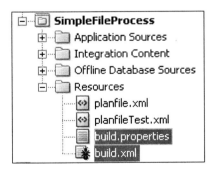

The following `ant` tasks relating to build and deployment are available:

- `deploy_test` will compile and deploy the BPEL process and run any test cases associated with the BPEL process.
- `deploy` will compile and deploy the BPEL process.
- `test` will deploy BPEL test cases and run them.

These three top level tasks are supplemented by a number of lower level tasks. For example:

- `pre-build` allows additional tasks to be associated with the deploy step; these execute before the process-deploy step. This may be used to check source code out of a source code repository.
- `process-deploy` validates, builds, and deploys the BPEL process and any associated human workflow or rules. It does this by using a number of tasks, all of which are self-explanatory:
  - `validateTask`
  - `compile`
  - `deployProcess`
  - `deployTaskForm`
  - `deployDecisionServices`
- `post-build` allows additional tasks to be associated with deploy step; these execute after the process-deploy step.

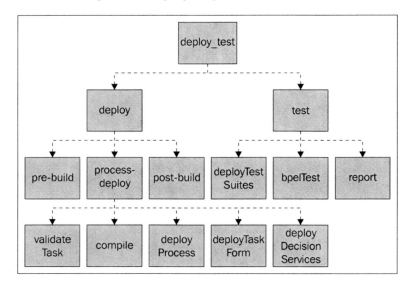

The `ant` script uses some key properties that may be configured through the `build.properties` file. Properties that may require changing include:

- `http.hostname` and `http.port` should point to the hostname and port number of the BPEL Process Manager server that you wish to deploy to.

- `domain` which refers to the BPEL domain.

- `rev` which refers to the BPEL process version number.

- `admin.user` and `admin.password` which are the credentials used when connecting to the BPEL server.

The `ant` scripts can be used from the command line, providing a way to automate the process of deployment and so ensuring a consistent way of deploying processes to servers. In the following sections, we will look at how the configuration of the BPEL process can be modified for different deployment environments.

Enabling web service endpoint and WSDL location alteration

When deploying between environments we typically want to modify the endpoint details to reflect the new environment which will have different hostnames for its services. This can be done by adding a `location` property to the partner links in `bpel.xml`, as shown in the example below, which changes a partner link to point to a service located on a web services manager gateway.

```
<BPELSuitcase>
  <BPELProcess id="SimpleFileProcess" src="SimpleFileProcess.bpel">
    <partnerLinkBindings>

      ...
      <partnerLinkBinding name="CardValidatorService">
        <property name="wsdlLocation">
          CardValidatorService.wsdl
        </property>
        <property name="location">
                http://w2k3/gateway/services/SID0003001
        </property>
      </partnerLinkBinding>
    </partnerLinkBindings>
    ...
  </BPELProcess>
</BPELSuitcase><partnerLinkBinding name="CardValidatorService">
```

It is not currently possible to modify the location via the BPEL Console.

By specifying the `partnerlink` property, `wsdlRuntimeLocation`, it is possible to point to a different WSDL at runtime. Care must be taken with this property. However, as often the BPEL designer will generate a wrapper around published WSDL to provide partner role information, and hence the generated WSDL would need modifying to point to the run-time WSDL.

In summary, endpoint location changes can be handled by the `location` property in the partner link in the `bpel.xml`. WSDL location changes may be handled in a similar way with the `wsdlRuntimeLocation` property if the WSDL already has partner roles. If the WSDL does not have partner roles then the `import` statement in the generated WSDL will need to be modified to point to the correct WSDL location.

Enabling adapter configuration

In addition to web service endpoints changing in different environments, we often want to modify the configuration of adapters. Many adapters make use of JEE resources, and so the JEE container just needs to be correctly configured with the resource names. For example, the database adapter uses a JNDI lookup to find its data source. Similarly the JMS adapter uses a JNDI lookup to find its queues. Some adapters however, such as the file adapter, do not have a JNDI lookup.

The file and FTP adapters provide the concept of a logical location for the directory in which they search for input for example. Creating a logical location in the file adapter wizard causes a logical location element with the name of the logical location to be added to the activation agent element in the `bpel.xml` file as shown:

```
<BPELSuitcase>
  <BPELProcess id="SimpleFileProcess" src="SimpleFileProcess.bpel">
    <partnerLinkBindings>
      <partnerLinkBinding name="ReadNewCustomerFileService">
        <property name="wsdlLocation">
          ReadNewCustomerFileService.wsdl
        </property>
      </partnerLinkBinding>
      ...
    </partnerLinkBindings>
    <activationAgents>
      <activationAgent
        className="oracle.tip.adapter.fw.agent.jca.JCAActivationAgent"
            partnerLink="ReadNewCustomerFileService">
        <property name="NewCustomerFileDirectory"
                type="LogicalDirectory">c:\FileTransfer\Inbound
        </property>
        <property name="portType">Read_ptt</property>
```

```
        </activationAgent>
      </activationAgents>
    </BPELProcess>
  </BPELSuitcase>
```

This location must be specified before deployment but may then be edited at run time by selecting the process in the BPEL Console from the dashboard or the **Processes** tab and then selecting the **Descriptor** tab for the process. The logical name may be updated to point to the correct file location on the BPEL Process Manager server and the process updated by clicking **Update Descriptor**.

XML Schema locations

XML Schemas are often referenced through relative links from a WSDL file. In which case updating the WSDL location will make the XML Schema files available. However, sometimes the XML Schema files are stored separately with their own URLs. In this case the URLs will usually be embedded in the WSDL file referencing them and each reference will need to be updated before redeploying the process to the correct environment.

XSL imports

Any XSL files that reference external schema will also need to be updated before deployment.

BPEL deployment framework

Modifying the `bpel.xml` file or altering descriptors through the console provide a degree of customisation for different environments, but it is all done using a single property at a time and requires a lot of work for each environment, especially when it is considered that individual WSDL files may also need to be updated. In earlier versions of SOA Suite it was possible to use `ant` scripts to automate a lot of this substitution, but it was a resource intensive process to set up. There is a better way in SOA Suite 10.1.3.4 and later versions—the deployment framework.

The deployment framework combines the BPEL suitcase with a deployment plan that updates multiple files in the BPEL suitcase with the correct values for the deployment environment. Different deployment plans can be created and maintained for each deployment plan.

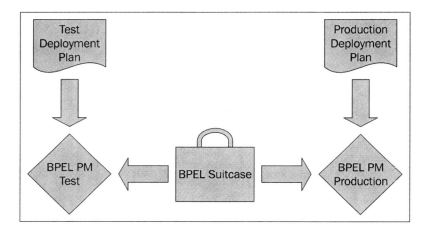

It is possible to generate a template BPEL deployment plan from a BPEL suitcase which can be customized and used with the base BPEL suitcase at deployment time to update the various URLs and properties.

The steps to customize the BPEL suitcase for each environment are as follows:

- Create a deployment template from the BPEL project or suitcase that will be used as the basis for the deployment plans.
- Create a deployment plan based on the template for each target environment.
- Attach the appropriate deployment plan to the BPEL suitcase or project prior to deploying in the target environment.
- Deploy the BPEL process into the target environment.

Creating a deployment plan template

To create a deployment template we need to add the following commands to the `build.xml` ant file that is built by JDeveloper and found in the **Resources** folder of our BPEL project.

```
<target name="generate_plan_from_project">
  <generateplan planfile="${process.dir}/planfile.xml"
              verbose="true"
              overwrite="true"
              descfile="${process.dir}/bpel/bpel.xml"/>
</target>
<target name="generate_plan_from_suitcase">
  <generateplan planfile="${process.dir}/planfile.xml"
              verbose="true"
              overwrite="true"
suitcase="${process.dir}/output/bpel_${BPELSuitcase.
BPELProcess(id)}_${rev}.jar"/>
</target>
```

This creates two new ant targets: `generate_plan_from_project` and `generate_plan_from_suitcase`. These both create a template deployment plan, either directly from the project files, or from a generated suitcase. A BPEL suitcase is only generated when a BPEL project is deployed or when the project is "made", so if using the option to generate from a suitcase it is necessary to ensure that the suitcase has previously been created. If the suitcase generated is a revision other than 1.0 then it is necessary to set the revision property in the `build.properties` file that is found in the **Resources** folder of the BPEL project in JDeveloper.

```
# Change below if deploying with process revision other than 1.0
rev = 1.1
```

The `generateplan` command in `ant` uses four attributes:

* `suitecase` or `descfile` is the source information for the deployment plan
* `planfile` is the location of the planfile template to be generated
* `overwrite` will replace any existing planfile of the same name
* `verbose` turns up the level of reporting

A sample deployment plan template is shown as follows. Note the use of two elements:

- `<replace>` is used to replace the value of a property within a specific part of the `bpel.xml`
- `<searchReplace>` is used to `<search>` for a string in WSDL and XSD files and `<replace>` it with another string

```xml
<?xml version="1.0" encoding="UTF-8"?>
<BPELDeploymentPlan xmlns="http://schemas.oracle.com/bpel/deployplan">
    <BPELProcess id="SimpleFileProcess">
        <configurations/>
        <partnerLinkBindings>
            <partnerLinkBinding name="ReadNewCustomerFileService">
                <property name="wsdlLocation">
                    <replace>ReadNewCustomerFileService.wsdl</replace>
                </property>
            </partnerLinkBinding>
            <partnerLinkBinding name="WriteNewCustomerDBService">
                <property name="retryInterval">
                    <replace>60</replace>
                </property>
                <property name="wsdlLocation">
                    <replace>WriteNewCustomerDBService.wsdl</replace>
                </property>
            </partnerLinkBinding>
            <partnerLinkBinding name="CardValidatorService">
                <property name="wsdlLocation">
                    <replace>CardValidatorService.wsdl</replace>
                </property>
                <property name="location">
<replace>http://w2k3/chapter18/CardValidatorServiceSoapHttpPort
                                                    </replace>
                </property>
            </partnerLinkBinding>
        </partnerLinkBindings>
    </BPELProcess>
    <wsdlAndSchema
name="CardValidatorService.wsdl|DBAdapterOutboundHeader.
wsdl|fileAdapterInboundHeader.wsdl|NewCustomerFile.
xsd|ReadNewCustomerFileService.wsdl|WriteNewCustomerDBService.
wsdl|WriteNewCustomerDBService_table.xsd">
        <searchReplace>
            <search/>
            <replace/>
        </searchReplace>
    </wsdlAndSchema>
</BPELDeploymentPlan>
```

Creating a deployment plan

Having created a template, we can use this to create deployment plans for each specific environment. We do this by creating a copy of the deployment plan by selecting **Save As** from the file menu in JDeveloper and then editing the <search> and <searchReplace> tags to match our target environment.

We will search and replace all instances of our local development machine hostname—w2k3, with the name of our test server—testserver, across WSDL, and XSD files. To do this we modify the search and replace elements shown as follows:

```
<wsdlAndSchema name="*">
  <searchReplace>
    <search>w2k3</search>
    <replace>testserver</replace>
  </searchReplace>
</wsdlAndSchema>
```

This will cause the BPEL Process Manager to search all WSDL and schema files "*" in the suitcase at deployment time and replace the string w2k3 with the string testserver. Note that it is possible to have multiple <searchReplace> elements.

Attaching a deployment plan to a BPEL suitcase

Having created and saved a deployment plan specific for one or more environments we will want to deploy our process into an environment. Before doing this we must first attach the specific deployment plan to the BPEL suitcase. We do this using the following ant command.

```
<target name="attach_plan">
  <attachplan planfile="${planfile}" verbose="true"
              overwrite="true"
suitcase="${process.dir}/output/bpel_${BPELSuitcase.
BPELProcess(id)}_${rev}.jar"/>
</target>
```

This will create a file bpeldeployplan.xml in the BPEL suitcase. This is the deployment plan that will be used at deployment time by the BPEL Process Manager. Note that the name of the deployment plan to use is encoded as an Ant property planfile that must be set in the build.xml. Once attached the deployment plan will be executed when the BPEL suitcase is deployed. The planfile property can be set from the ant command line, allowing a different plan to be attached in each environment.

Modifying ant to use deployment plan

In addition to adding the two tasks above to the `build.xml` file, it is possible to add the attachment of the plan file as part of the regular deploy process. This is done by modifying the dependencies of the `process-deploy` task by adding the `attach_plan` dependency after the compile dependency.

```
<target name="process-deploy"
    depends="validateTask, compile, attach_plan, deployProcess,
            deployTaskForm, deployDecisionServices" />
```

When building and deploying with `ant`, the deployment plan will be attached to the suitcase before the suitcase is deployed to the target environment. This allows us to provide a different deployment plan for each environment. After attaching the named plan to the suitcase, the suitcase can be deployed from the command line.

Note that use of command line properties allows us to script the whole deployment process, making it easy to reproduce in different environments.

A different deployment plan file may be specified by having a separate `build.properties` file for each environment, which is needed anyway because the `build.properties` will specify the target machine name, port number, and administrator credentials. The deployment file may also be specified by setting the `ant` property `planfile` on the command line.

Oracle Web Services Manager (OWSM)

OWSM provides a command line interface to export components and properties from an OWSM configuration and then import them into a different configuration. The components to be exported are selected through the use of an export instructions file called `LMTInstructions.xml`. This file specifies which components and also which, if any, custom steps are to be exported. The `export` command uses this file to create a representation of the OWSM configuration in an export directory which can then be moved to the target environment. The components to be imported into an environment are specified in an import instructions file. This import instructions file, also called `LMTInstructions.xml`, is then used by the `import` command to import the components and their associated policies into the target environment.

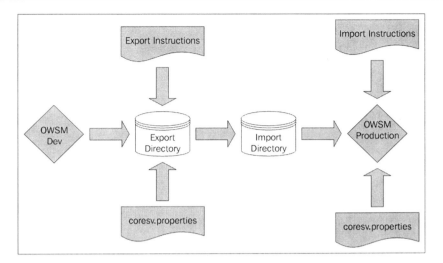

The export and import directories are specified in the coresv.properties file
found in the $SOA_HOME/owsm/bin directory. The following properties are used:

- db.export.dir specifies the export directory
- db.import.dir specifies the import directory

The export file, LMTInstructions.xml, lists the components to be exported.
If a component is a gateway then individual services must also be specified.

```xml
<?xml version="1.0"?>
<lmt-instructions>
  <transferable-objects>
    <component id="C0003001">
      <service id="SID0003001">
      </service>
    </component>
    <component id="C0003003">
    </component>
  </transferable-objects>
</lmt-instructions>
```

In the example above, a gateway component (C0003001) is exported together
with a single service (SID0003001) associated with that gateway. An agent
component (C0003003) is also exported. Objects are exported by running the
exportTransferableObjects command from the $SOA_HOME/owsm/bin directory.

```
owsm\bin>wsmadmin exportTransferableObjects
Buildfile: C:\oracle\SOA10.1.3\owsm\bin\..\scripts\exportDBData.xml
```

```
validate.DBPassword:
    [input] Database Password:

exportTransferableObjects:
    [java] Directory c:\FileTransfer\OWSM\18Nov2008-09-10-39AM has
been created
 successfully. Please check export logs in this directory

BUILD SUCCESSFUL
Total time: 5 minutes 7 seconds
```

This will create a sub-directory named with the current time in the export
directory. This directory will consist of a number of sub-directories. To import the
configuration into another OWSM environment it is necessary to copy the complete
directory sub-tree to the target environment.

An import instructions file is created to select which components to import. Note
that not all components must be imported.

```xml
<?xml version="1.0"?>
<lmt-instructions>
  <transferable-objects>
    <component id="C0003001"
      import-name="ImportedGateway"
      url="http://w2k3:80/gateway"
      monitor-rmi-host="localhost"
      monitor-rmi-port="3118"
      monitor-soap="http://localhost:80/coreman/services/
                              CoremanMeasurementClient"
      monitor-type="rmi"
      create-new="true"
      type="Gateway"
      mapped-to-component-id="">
      <service id="SID0003001"
        import-name="ImportedService"
        version="1.0"/>
    </component>
    <component id="C0003002"
      import-name="ImportedServerAgent"
      url=""
      monitor-rmi-host="localhost"
      monitor-rmi-port="3118"
      monitor-soap="http://localhost:80/coreman/services/
                              CoremanMeasurementClient"
      monitor-type="rmi"
```

```
        create-new="true"
        type="ServerAgent"
        mapped-to-component-id="">
    </component>
  </transferable-objects>
</lmt-instructions>
```

The `import` instructions have a number of properties which allow the import to be customized to the new environment.

Important component properties are listed below:

- `id` is the component ID in the source system and hence in the export directory
- `import-name` is the name of the component when imported into the new environment
- `url` is the endpoint associated with a gateway
- `monitor-*` properties are the location of the monitor and should match the target topology
- `type` is the type of component — Gateway, Server-Agent, or Client-Agent
- `create-new` indicates if this should be a new component (`true`) or if it should replace an existing component (`false`)
- `mapped-to-component-id` is a component ID to be replaced in the target environment if create-new is `false`

An initial deployment will usually have create-new set to `true`. Subsequent deployments will usually have create-new set to `false` so that updates are applied rather than new components created.

Service component properties are very similar to the component properties in that they specify a service ID and import-name. The service component also has useful properties, as outlined below, to enable the service definition to be customized for the target environment.

- `wsdl` is the location of the WSDL for this service in the target environment.
- `url` is the endpoint of the service in the target environment.

It is also possible to override step properties within a pipeline to customize those for the target environment by using the pipeline-property element and specifying the step and property to be modified.

Objects are imported by running the `importTransferableObjects` command from the `$SOA_HOME/owsm/bin` directory.

```
owsm\bin>wsmadmin importTransferableObjects
Buildfile: C:\oracle\SOA10.1.3\owsm\bin\..\scripts\importDBData.xml

validate.DBPassword:
    [input] Database Password:

BUILD SUCCESSFUL
Total time: 8 seconds
```

This will read the sub-directory identified in the `coresv.properties` file and apply any substitutions specified in the `LMTInstructions.xml` file. This provides us with the same policies as existed in the source system.

Oracle rules

Rules will generally not change between environments and can be deployed as a complete repository.

Business activity monitoring

BAM provides a command line tool called `iCommand` to assist in exporting and importing BAM components such as data object definitions and reports as well as data objects themselves. It is possible to select subsets of components, making it easy to move just the updated components from a development to a test and/or production environment.

Commands

`ICommand` allows a number of different operations through the `cmd` parameter which can take the following values:

- `export`: Exports the selected components and/or values
- `import`: Imports the selected components and/or values
- `delete`: Deletes the selected components
- `rename`: Renames components
- `clear`: Clears data from a given object

There are other commands related to Enterprise Link, an ETL component used by BAM.

Selecting items

Items are identified using a file like syntax such as /Samples/Employees. There are a number of parameters that may be used to select items in different ways:

- name: Selects items explicitly by name, for example,
  name=/Samples/Employees.
- match: Selects items by using a DOS style pattern, for example,
  match=/Samples/*.
- regex: Selects items by using a regular expression, for example,
  regex="/Samples/[A-Za-z]* Sales".
- all: Selects all components.

The queries above may be combined with the following parameters to further restrict the items selected:

- type: Restricts the items exported by type such as type=Folder or type=DataObject.
- dependencies: Includes dependent objects in the selection.
- contents: Includes (value 1 or unspecified) or excludes (value 0) the contents of a data object, for example, contents=0.
- layout: Includes (value 1 or unspecified) or excludes (value 0) the data object type definition for example layout=0.

Using iCommand

When migrating items between environments we will generally not want to move the actual contents of the data. We would like to move only the layouts. For example, to export the layouts but not the contents for all the Sales data objects we issue the following command:

```
C:\BAM\bin>icommand cmd=export regex="[a-zA-Z]* Sales"
file=SalesDataObjects.xml contents=0
Oracle BAM Command Utility
10g Release 3 (10.1.3.3.0) [Build 3 5 6008 0, ADC Version 1004.0]
Copyright (c) 2002, 2008 Oracle.
All rights reserved.
Exporting Data Object "/Samples/Film Sales"...
Data Object "/Samples/Film Sales" exported successfully (0 rows).
Exporting Data Object "/Samples/Media Sales"...
Data Object "/Samples/Media Sales" exported successfully (0 rows).
Exporting Data Object "/Samples/Product Sales"...
Data Object "/Samples/Product Sales" exported successfully (0 rows).
3 items exported successfully.
Items were exported to 1 files.
```

This generates a file that can be used to import the definitions into another BAM instance. The generated file `SalesDataObjects.xml` is in the format shown as follows:

```
<?xml version="1.0" encoding="utf-8"?>
<OracleBAMExport Version="1004.0" Build="3.5.6008.0">
  <DataObject Version="14" Name="Film Sales" ID="_Film_Sales" Path="/
Samples" External="0">
    <Layout>
      <Column Name="Region" ID="_Region" Type="string" MaxSize="100"
            Nullable="1" Public="1" />
      ...
      <Indexes />
    </Layout>
  </DataObject>
  <DataObject Version="14" Name="Media Sales" ID="_Media_Sales"
Path="/Samples" External="0">
  ...
  </DataObject>
</OracleBAMExport>
```

Note that it is possible to edit the contents of the exported data files and this can provide a means to batch load reference data from another system into BAM.

To import from a file `employees.xml` we issue the command:

```
C:\BAM\bin> icommand cmd=import file=Employees.xml
Oracle BAM Command Utility
10g Release 3 (10.1.3.3.0) [Build 3 5 6008 0, ADC Version 1004.0]
Copyright (c) 2002, 2008 Oracle.
All rights reserved.
Data Object "/Samples/Employees" already exists, ID ignored.
Data Object "/Samples/Employees" already exists, "Layout" section
ignored.
Importing contents of Data Object "/Samples/Employees"...
Data Object "/Samples/Employees" imported successfully (3 rows).
1 items imported.
```

The `import` command will always import the full contents of the file into the target BAM instance.

Deployment architectures

During development, generally all SOA Suite components will be deployed on a single server, sometimes using a database on the same machine, sometimes on a separate machine. When moving into a production environment there will often be a requirement to run multiple instances of SOA Suite. In this section, we will consider some of the consequences of this requirement and other configurations.

Running multiple instances of SOA Suite gives us two advantages: resilience and scalability. Resilience means that the loss of a single instance of SOA Suite will not impact the running of the system. Scalability means that as additional instances are added the capacity of the system will increase. Generally, SOA Suite scales almost linearly with additional instances. The bottleneck for scalability usually becomes the database used as a dehydration store in BPEL.

The database used by the SOA Suite can be scaled by using Oracle Real Application Clusters which provides multiple instances of a single database to provide scalability as well as resilience.

SOA Suite deployment architectures

The smallest deployments will usually have the SOA suite on one server and connect to the database on a separate server. This configuration is simple to install and there are no particular requirements to consider when deploying SOA Suite components.

A variation on the simple deployment adds a front-end web server machine for additional security when providing or consuming services outside the corporate firewall. This machine will usually sit in a DMZ with a firewall on either side of it.

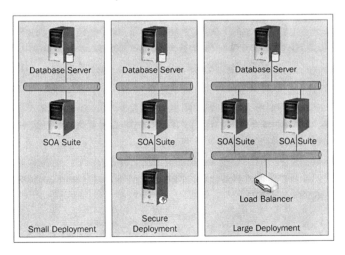

Larger deployments will usually consist of multiple instances of SOA Suite installed on multiple machines. In this case an external load balancer will usually be required to load balance incoming requests across the multiple instances.

In the current release it is likely that Oracle Service Bus will be deployed on a different application server instance to the rest of the SOA Suite. These instances may be on the same or separate machines.

Using an external web server or load balancer

When using an external web server or load balancer then the hostname that receives requests is not the same as the hostname that will process the request. For example clients will need the address of the web server or load balancer, not the SOA Suite address. Hence when the SOA Suite advertises services externally then it must use the web server or load balancer hostname, not the hostname of the SOA Suite instance providing the information. Furthermore, when multiple instances of SOA Suite are involved, it is necessary to provide additional information to enable the multiple instances to operate as a single cluster.

Apart from the BPEL Process Manager the components of the SOA Suite generally need little additional configuration to operate with multiple instances. However, there are few extra tasks to perform around the BPEL Process Manager.

BPEL Process Manager specifics

Within the BPEL Process Manager we configure this external address and other cluster settings in the `collaxa-config.xml` file found in the `$SOA_SUITE_HOME/bpel/system/config` directory. These settings can also be modified from the **Configuration** tab of the BPEL admin console at `http://hostname:port/BPELAdmin`.

* `soapServerUrl` is the endpoint published in the WSDL files and should point to the name of the front-end web server or load balancer.
* `soapCallbackUrl` is the address used when providing a callback address through WS-Addressing.
* `enableCluster` is the property that tells a BPEL instance that it is part of a cluster of instances executing processes in the same domain and using the same dehydration store.
* `clusterName` is the arbitary name of the cluster. All nodes in the same cluster should have the same cluster name as well as the same multi-cast or `jgroup` specification.

```xml
<property id="soapServerUrl">
  <name>BPEL soap server URL</name>
  <value>http://w2k3:80</value>

  <comment>
    <![CDATA[
      This URL is published as part of the SOAP address of a process
      in the WSDL file.<p/>
      The hostname and port for this URL should be customized to
      match the hostname of your system and the port of your HTTP
      gateway.
    ]]>
  </comment>
</property>

<property id="soapCallbackUrl">
  <name>BPEL soap callback URL</name>
  <value>http://w2k3:80</value>

  <comment>
    <![CDATA[
      This URL is sent by the server as part of the asynchronous
      callback address to the invoker. <p/>
      The hostname and port for this URL should be customized to
      match the hostname of your system and the port of your HTTP
      gateway.
    ]]>
  </comment>
</property>

<property id="enableCluster">
  <name>Cluster enable flag</name>
  <value>true</value>

  <comment>
    <![CDATA[
      Specify the value to true if you want to enable clustering. By
      default the clustering service is disabled.
    ]]>
  </comment>
</property>


<property id="clusterName">
  <name>Cluster Id</name>
  <value>w2k3:80</value>

  <comment>
    <![CDATA[
```

```
        clusterName specifies the name of the bpel cluster.<p/>
        The cluster is defined by the clusterName, multi-cast address
        and multi-cast port.Changing any one of those parameter puts
        the bpel server instance in a different cluster.
        Value for clusterName property needs to be the same for all
        bpel nodes in a cluster in order for them to find each
        other.<p/>
        In addition to having distinct cluster names for each cluster,
        you should use a different multicast address or port for each
        cluster.<p/>
        You can change the multicast address or port in the
        bpel/system/config/jgroups-protocol.xml
    ]]>
    </comment>
</property>
```

Configuration and implications of running multiple instances impact the BPEL Process Manager more than other SOA Suite components because this is the component that deals with long running processes that exist beyond the life of a single interaction. It is important that the configuration of the process manager is set up correctly to enable processes to be executed on any node in the instance, allowing for a single process instance to execute on different nodes at different times.

For multiple SOA Suite instance in a single subnet, it is possible to use network multi-cast to find other instances. If there are nodes on other subnets then it is necessary to configure the explicit hostnames on every node. In either case the configuration resides in the `jgroups-protocol.xml` file found in the `$SOA_SUITE_HOME/bpel/system/config` directory.

Note that these configuration settings must be applied to each individual BPEL Process Manager instance.

Web services manager

Although OWSM will run across multiple instances of SOA Suite, some components must be disabled. Only one machine can run the OWSM monitor and only one machine can run the OWSM console, although there may be multiple policy managers and gateways.

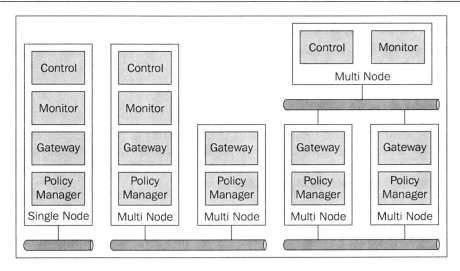

Console and monitor

After installing SOA Suite on multiple nodes it is necessary to first set up the node that will run the console. We do this by configuring OWSM for the load balancer or front-end web server by setting the following properties in the `$SOA_HOME/owsm/config/ccore/ui-config-installer.properties` file:

- `ui.pm.server.httpHost` specifies the name of the load balancer or front-end front-end web server
- `ui.pm.server.httpPort` specifies the port of the load balancer or front-end web server

We then redeploy the console by using the command:

```
wsmadmin deploy console
```

If necessary we can undeploy the policy manager by the following command:

```
wsmadmin undeploy policymanager
```

We then un-deploy the OWSM console and monitor from all nodes that do not require it. This is done by issuing the following commands on all nodes that will not be hosting the monitor or console:

```
wsmadmin undeploy monitor
```

```
wsmadmin undeploy control
```

Gateways and agents are deployed as outlined in Chapter 20.

Oracle Service Bus

The Oracle Service Bus will take advantage of an underlying WebLogic cluster to provide a clustered environment.

Business activity monitoring

BAM deployment is different to the rest of the SOA Suite deployment because in 10.1.3 and earlier releases it is a Windows application and can only be deployed on a Windows platform. In release 11g this will change as BAM has been ported to run as a Java application within an application server.

BAM is made of several components:

- Active Data Cache: Holds the data in memory and updates aggregates in response to new data arriving.
- Event Engine: Monitors information in active data cache for certain conditions and performs associated actions defined in rules.
- Report Server: Provides reports to end users.
- Report Cache: Maintains shared views in memory for better performance.

In addition it uses Microsoft Internet Information Server (IIS) as a web-server platform and requires a database to act as a repository.

Only a single instance of Active Data Cache may be active at any one time; however, the other components may all be replicated to improve scalability and availability. High availability of the Active Data Cache may be achieved by using a cold failover configuration.

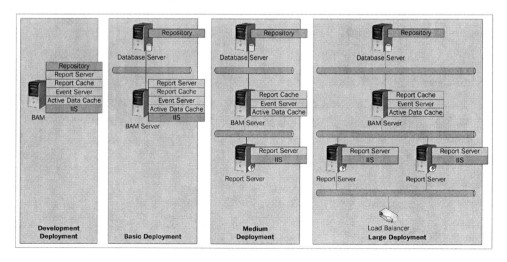

Moving the report server to a separate machine allows BAM to scale to support a larger client population. Multiple report servers may be run to allow even larger user populations.

Local hostnames

Generally when running clustered environments it is a good idea to have the front-end hostname in the `hosts` file of each machine. However, instead of pointing to the IP address of the load balancer or the web front end, it could point to the loopback address (`127.0.0.1`) on the host in question to ensure that, where possible, communication occurs on the same host, reducing latency and network traffic. This approach works well when components are co-hosted in the same container because generally they will all be available at the same time. There are problems with using the loopback address if it is possible for some components on a box to be available and others to be down. If a component is down on the local box then instances on other machines will be ignored, losing the benefit of a high availability architecture.

Summary

The SOA Suite provides facilities for moving configurations between different environments using either web-based tools or command-line tools. Generally, the use of command-line tools allows deployment to be more repeatable through scripting. Some properties must be modified during the move from one environment to another and there are some facilities in the SOA Suite to make this easier.

When deploying installations of more than one instance, either for throughput or resilience, care must be taken with the deployment, particularly with the use of hostnames.

19
Testing Composite Applications

In this chapter, we will focus on the tools in JDeveloper and the SOA Suite that assist you in testing the components of your SOA application. The basic principles of testing are the same in SOA as in other software development approaches. You start testing the lowest level components and gradually build up to a complete system test before moving into user acceptance testing. You may also be required to undertake some form of performance testing.

We will begin our discussion by looking at the manual testing of individual components and services in the SOA Suite. We will then investigate the importance of repeatable testing before moving on to discuss automated testing and the testing framework available in the Oracle SOA Suite. Finally, we will discuss how a system may be performance tested.

Tests can be run in either of the two fashions. They can be run manually, by a dedicated testing team, or they can be automated. Manual testing tends to be run only when the software is deemed almost ready for release due to the cost of people to run the tests. Automated tests are to be preferred as they potentially allow the test suites to be run on all the intermediate builds of software, providing management with a heartbeat of the robustness of the release under development. We will look at support for both models of testing within the SOA Suite.

SOA Suite testing model

The SOA Suite has two distinct methods of testing SOA artefacts. They may be tested in a one-off fashion through a test service client or they may be tested in a repeatable fashion through the SOA Suite test framework. In either case it is necessary, at the very least, to generate appropriate input data to the artefact being tested.

The illustration shows a simple composite service that is invoked by a client and in turn invokes two services before completing. The details of the composite service are not relevant at this point, and the composite could consist of a service bus pipeline, a BPEL process, or both. Note that the nature of the composite defines several interfaces; the composite exposes a client interface and in turn makes use of interfaces exposed by the two services. We will use this simple example to explore how to perform different levels of test.

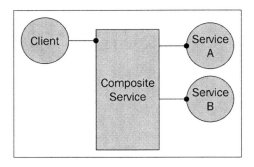

One-off testing

Within a development environment it is very useful to run a quick test of a process or interaction to ensure that it behaves as expected. These one-off tests can be run from the BPEL Console and the Service Bus console as explained in the following section.

Testing BPEL processes

All deployed, BPEL processes have a test client created for them. This is accessed by clicking on the process in the BPEL dashboard or processes list and selecting the **Initiate** tab. The test service client in the BPEL Process Manager is very good when you want to quickly test that the process you have deployed is behaving as expected. It allows you to specify the input parameters through the web interface, including a choice of HTML or XML input formats. The example below from the BPEL Process Manager console shows how the HTML format makes it very easy to focus on just the input fields required rather than having to be concerned with the exact XML format required by the composite.

Posting the XML message will cause the BPEL process to be invoked and any results will then be available through the console. Verification of the accuracy of the results must be done manually by the developer. Later in this chapter, we will examine how the testing of results may also be automated.

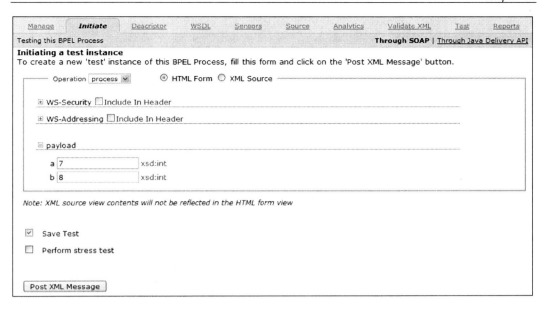

If you have a very complicated interface you may not want to have to enter the parameter values every time you test the process. Clicking the **Save Test** checkbox will save the parameters for the next time the test client is entered. Note, however, that these parameters are only saved for the current version, and are lost if the process is redeployed with the same version. However, these parameters can be saved as the default input to a process as follows.

Enter the desired parameters in the **HTML Form**. Switch to the **XML Source** view by selecting the radio button, you will now see a SOAP message constructed to contain the input to the process. Copy the XML to the clipboard.

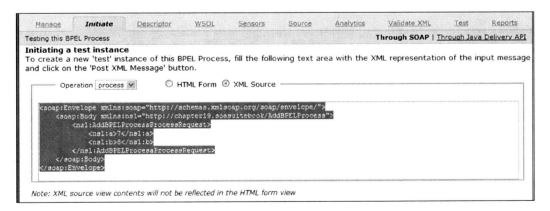

Now within JDeveloper click on the **Deployment Descriptor Properties ...** icon at the top of the visual BPEL editor.

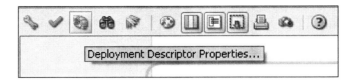

This brings up the **Deployment Descriptor Properties** dialog where we can select the **configurations** tab and click the **Create** button to create a new configuration property. The **defaultInput** property allows us to define the default input to the BPEL process. Whatever input we provide here will be used to create an initial default test message in the BPEL console client tester. This will be deployed to the BPEL Process Manager with the process.

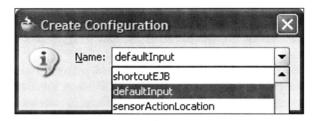

The XML from the BPEL Console test client can then be pasted into the property value area. When the process is deployed this will form the default message used by the test client. This is very useful to allow a developer to quickly do a sanity check on their process and ensure that it works for at least one use case, but it still requires the developer to manually enter any parameters other than the single default set.

The easiest way to get the default input is to deploy the process and then use the HTML form to create the correct input. The process can then be updated to include the **defaultInput** property and redeployed with the same version number. Changes to the input format will require changes to the XML input. Unless the change is very extensive it will generally be easier to edit the XML directly rather than repeat the steps of deploying the process, generating a sample input and then pasting that input back into JDeveloper.

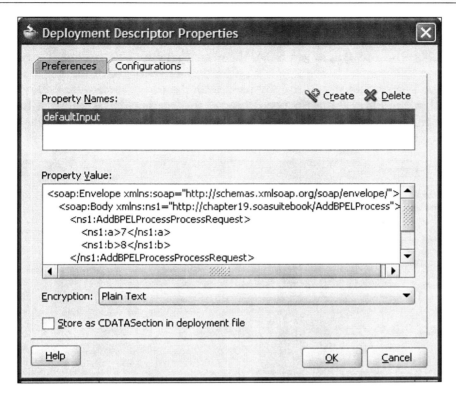

Use of the test client

The test client should not be part of the formal testing strategy. It should be used by developers to get immediate feedback on the correctness of their composite, not as part of a formal validation process.

Testing the service bus

The service bus also provides a simple client testing interface. In BPEL the only option is to test the entire process, but in the service bus we can test either the business service (the back end service) or the proxy service (the service bus interface). After navigating to the folder containing the proxy or business service the tester is invoked by clicking on the bug icon.

Name △	Resource Type	Actions	Options
MultiplyService	Proxy Service		

This brings up the test client. For a SOAP service, the test client allows the specification of the message parameters in the SOAP body through the payload text box as well as the addition of any SOAP headers that may be required. There are two options that control how the call is submitted and what additional information is collected. The direct call is normally used with the proxy service and allows additional information about the processing of the message to be collected through the use of the trace option. This can be invaluable in tracing problems in the service bus pipelines or routing services.

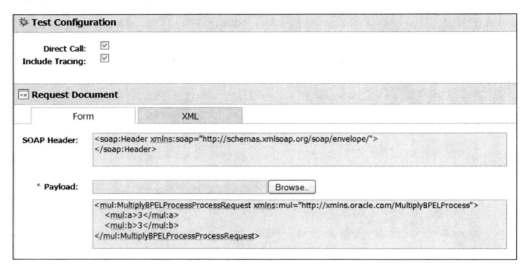

The output from the test client can be checked manually for accuracy.

Automated testing

Up to this point the testing we have investigated is manual based requiring human intervention. For more extensive testing we require an automated test framework which is just what is included in the BPEL Process Manager.

The BPEL test framework

The BPEL Process Manager includes a test framework that supports the following:

- Aggregation of multiple tests called "test cases" into a "test suite"
- Generation of initial messages
- Validation of input into, and output from, services and composites
- Simulation of service interactions

- Reporting of test results
- Reporting of BPEL code coverage

The BPEL test framework may be thought of as similar to the Java unit test framework JUnit.

BPEL test suites

Individual test cases are grouped into a test suite at the level of an individual JDeveloper project. Note that in the current release this is only supported for a single process. Multiple processes would require multiple test suites. Multiple test cases in a single test suite can be executed with a single request, automating much of the testing.

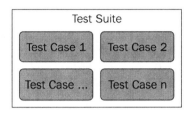

Individual test cases will be used to test different conditions. Each individual test case will result in a single instance of the BPEL process being created. So a test suite with 100 test cases could have 100 BPEL process instances created as a result of a single user request.

To create a new test suite in JDeveloper just right-click on the **Test Suites** folder in a BPEL project and select **Create Test Suite...**.

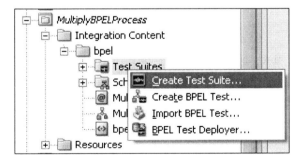

Name the test suite and then you are ready to create your first test case. The easiest way to create a test case is to download it from the BPEL console. This requires the following steps:

- Run a test case with the desired parameters as described in the section *Testing BPEL processes*
- Select the **Test** tab for the desired instance
- Save the target of the link **Save as unit test (.xml)**

The unit test that is saved describes the input parameters to the process as well as any interactions with partner links. When saving the file it is a good idea to give the test case a descriptive name that will distinguish it from other test cases. The unit test is imported into the JDeveloper project by right-clicking on the **Test Suites** folder and selecting **Import BPEL Test...**.

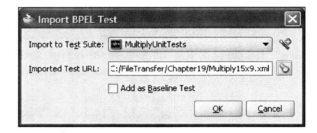

Note that we can also create a new test case from scratch by selecting the **Create BPEL Test...** option. This gives us an empty BPEL test case to which we need to add an input message. The content of the input message can be obtained in the same way as we obtained the default input message for our process.

Data validation

The testing framework allows validation to be applied to the inputs and outputs of either the process as a whole, or individual services. Validation is performed through an assertion. An assertion is a statement about the expected behavior of the process at this point. For example, an assertion may identify that the value of the output of a process should be a particular value. When the test case is run the actual value of the output will be compared to the expected value and if they do not match the test case will fail.

We can add assertions to a test case to ensure that we get the expected result. We do this by opening the imported test case in JDeveloper. Each test case provides a design view similar to the BPEL process design view. Within the design view of the test case, assertions are added by right-clicking on it and selecting **Asserts**. This brings up the **BPEL Test Settings** dialog. Note that assertions may be added to any activity in the BPEL process but usually they are added to check the output of the process and the input and/or output of service calls made by the process.

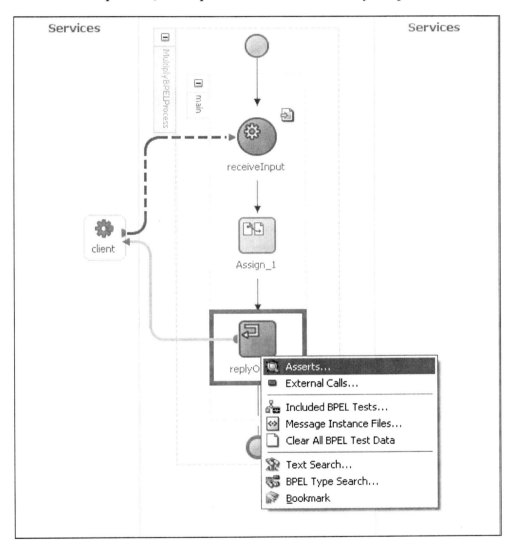

Within the **BPEL Test Settings** dialog we can choose to make a number of different types of assertion. These are:

- **Value Assert**: This allows us to test the value of a BPEL variable, usually the input or output variable of an activity.

- **Activity Executed Assert**: This lets us verify the number of times an activity is executed within our BPEL process; this is usually used within loops to ensure that we execute the loop the expected number of times.

- **XML Assert**: This allows us to compare the XML of a variable directly with an XML fragment. Note that we can make multiple assertions about the same activity.

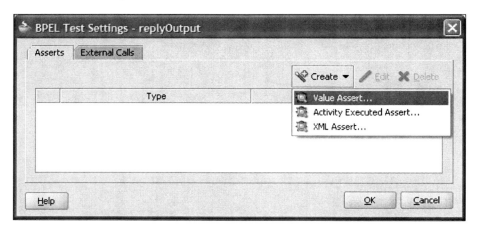

In addition to the **Asserts** tab, there is also an **External Calls** tab that allows the execution of custom validation code written in Java. We will focus just on the creation of value asserts.

Creating a value assert leads us to the **Create Value Assert** dialog box. We can use the flashlight icon to select a variable and construct an xpath expression to the value we wish to test. Comparisons can either be numeric or string values. If we choose a string value, then it is possible to specify a regular expression as the expected value. This is useful if we know the general format of the expected response but not the specific values.

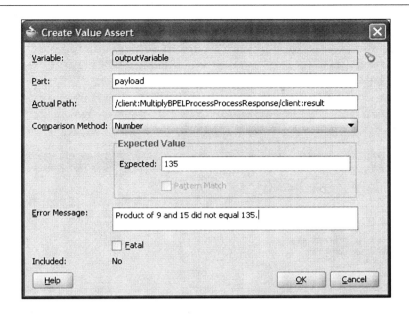

If the assertion fails, the **Error Message** field is displayed in the BPEL test console. This can be used to give information about why the test failed. The **Fatal** checkbox is used to indicate what the process should do if the assertion fails. When the **Fatal** checkbox is checked then the process will terminate if the assertion fails; if it is not checked then the process will continue to execute.

 Note that in releases used in writing this book, setting the **Fatal** checkbox could cause unstable behavior in the process manager and should not be used. Assertion failures will be flagged when the test case is run only if they are not fatal. Until there is better support for **Fatal** in BPEL, it is best to ensure that it is not selected.

Deploying the test suite

The test suites and their included test cases are all deployed to the BPEL run time by right-clicking on the **Test Suites** folder and selecting **BPEL Test Deployer**. This brings up the **BPEL Test Deployer** dialog box. This dialog enables us to select the actual test suites to be deployed to BPEL server instances. After selecting the tests to be deployed then click the **Deploy** button to deploy them to the selected servers. The status of deploying the test suites will appear in the **Status** window of the dialog box.

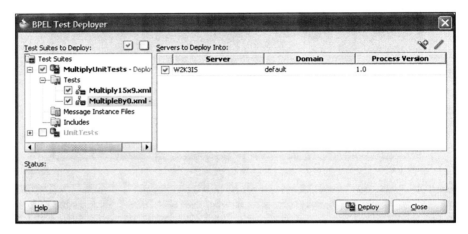

Running the test suites

The deployed test suites will appear in the SOA Console in the process **Test** tab. The interface allows all or a subset of tests to be selected and then executed by clicking the **Execute Tests** button. The **maximum concurrent instances** field allows for concurrent execution of tests.

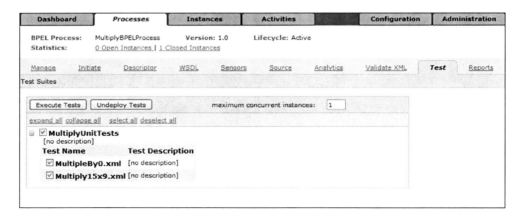

The results of the tests are displayed in the **BPEL Test Report** screen that appears after clicking on the **Execute Tests** button.

BPEL Test Report

Test Parameters

Process ID:	MultiplyBPELProcess (v. 1.0)
Start date:	06 October 2008 22:00:06
Completion Date:	06 October 2008 22:00:10
Test Suites:	MultiplyUnitTests
Workers:	1

Summary Report

Total	Initiated	Completed	Successful	Success Rate	Process Coverage
4	4	4	3	75%	100%

Detail Report

☐ Display Failures Only

✓ **FractionalInputs (MultiplyUnitTests)**	View Instance Flow
✓ **MultipleBigNumbers (MultiplyUnitTests)**	View Instance Flow
✓ **MultipleBy0 (MultiplyUnitTests)**	View Instance Flow
✗ **Multiply15x9 (MultiplyUnitTests)** Less	View Instance Flow

Message	Expected	Actual
Product of 9 and 15 did not equal 135!	134	135

The test report displays the summary and count of tests executed, and also gives error messages of any failed assertions. The test report also provides an analysis of code coverage in the test suite. Code coverage is the percentage of BPEL activities executed in the process. BPEL processes may have paths that are not executed in all cases. This may be due to `switch` or `pick` activities that explicitly provide alternate paths, or it may be due to compensation and exception handlers that will not always be invoked. The process coverage is a useful measure to verify that your test suite is at least exercising all the activities in the process under test. If you are not covering all the activities then consider adding additional test cases to cover all paths.

Note that although it is desirable in the total test suite to have 100% coverage of the BPEL code, this is a necessary but not sufficient condition to ensure that the BPEL has been fully exercised.

Partner link handling in test cases

Getting a BPEL process to cover all possible code paths often requires us to get specific behaviors from sub-processes or other partner links. This can be difficult to create using the test client in the BPEL console. We need more control over the behavior of partner links. The BPEL test capability is quite sophisticated in how it handles partner links. Partner links may be handled in one of three ways:

- Direct call to the partner link
- Emulated call to the partner link
- Invoke a test case for the partner link (only for BPEL processes)

If no reference is made to the `invoke` or `receive` activity then it is directly executed. Alternatively the partner link interaction may be emulated, with pre-defined values being returned. This is what happens when we download a test case from the BPEL Console, all the partner link calls are emulated. The final option allows us to test a network of BPEL processes.

To modify the handling of a partner link in JDeveloper, open the test case, right-click the activity we wish to control, and select **Emulate Invoke Message** to bring up the **BPEL Test Settings** dialog with the **Emulate** tab being in focus.

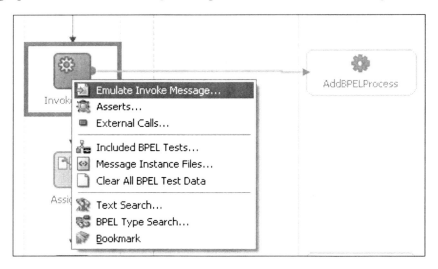

In the dialog we have the three options for interacting with the partner link displayed as radio buttons. We select the correct radio button for the type of interaction we require. To emulate an interaction we are allowed to specify either the inbound message or the fault generated by the partner link. In either case we can select the details of the message or fault manually or we may load it from a message file deployed with the test suite. Message files are a handy way to reuse messages across several test cases; specifying them in message files makes it easier to update the messages if the schema they are based on alters.

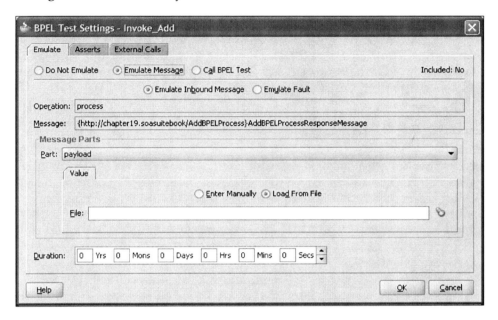

A note on message flow nomenclature

Messages flowing into the process under test are identified as inbound messages. Messages flowing out of the process under test are identified as outbound messages. When dealing with a synchronous invoke this can be misleading as the inbound message is the response from the partner link. Always thinking of oneself as sitting inside the process under test makes it easier to understand what is meant by the message flow directions. Outbound messages do not need to be emulated because they are generated by the process under test; only inbound messages may need emulation.

Note that in addition to specifying the message or fault payload it is also possible to specify a duration, making the emulation more realistic and giving the possibility of performing additional types of testing relating to timing of responses, for example simulating long delays to enable time-outs to be tested. In addition to using messages generated by the BPEL test console, it is also possible to take the input request generated by the test client in the BPEL Console and paste that into this window. Often the HTML format is easier to enter data into, and then the view can be switched to an XML view in the test client and copied and pasted into this dialog.

Simulation of process to process interactions

When emulating a partner link interaction we can invoke another BPEL process and have it executed under the control of a given test script. This allows us to test the interactions between running BPEL processes.

Baseline scripts

When importing a test case it is possible to import it as a baseline script by checking the **Add as Baseline Test** checkbox. Baseline scripts can be thought of as template scripts that can be overridden in specific test cases. Baseline scripts can be included in other test cases, but are not executed on their own. To execute an imported baseline script we would create a new test case and then include the baseline script by right-clicking the **Include BPEL Tests** menu option. Within the **Included BPEL Tests** dialog that appears, we can add a single baseline test. This baseline test forms the basis of our new test case. It is possible to override the behavior of the baseline test case just by specifying alternative emulations or test cases to execute. Note that if the baseline interaction is emulated or invokes another test case then it is not possible to cancel this emulation or test case, it can only be overridden with another emulation or test case.

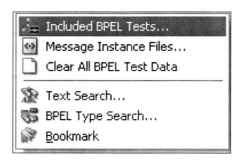

A common use for a baseline script would be to have a number of emulated interactions. Individual test scripts could then override a single interaction, perhaps changing the response values or altering the emulation into a fault to exercise different paths through the BPEL process. Typically each test script would have a different assertion on the message returned to the caller of the process.

Regression testing

One of the hallmarks of an ongoing successful software system is regression testing. Regression testing is the process of creating a series of tests for a software system and then repeating those tests every time a new release of the software is produced. As defects are discovered in the field and fixed, test cases are produced and these test cases are then added to the set of regression tests. This process helps to ensure that, once fixed, the same defect does not reappear in future releases of the software. In this fashion the number of tests to which a software system is subject to increases over time. Note that regression tests should be performed at all levels of testing from unit testing up to system testing.

Use of test suites

Test suites should always be used to collect related tests on a BPEL process. They can then be used to run multiple tests with minimal user intervention and so provide a useful regression testing environment.

System testing

Although the BPEL Console refers to **Unit Tests**, it is possible to test large portions of the system through the BPEL test framework. By creating a process that exercises all external interfaces to the system a large amount of system testing can be performed through the testing framework.

In the example below the client injects a number of messages into the system, but then either no emulations, or minimal emulations are performed to allow for the entire system to be exercised. This is because when no emulation is specified then the actual partner link will be invoked. This effectively tests both the individual services, which may themselves be composites, and the composite assembly itself. This type of testing only delivers high level success or fail information around individual use cases. Because many of the services will themselves be complex assemblies it is not possible in this type of testing to drill down into the exact reason why an individual test case may fail. However, this type of testing does provide a high level of confidence that the whole system interacts correctly because there is a minimum of emulation.

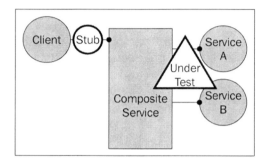

This type of configuration may also be used to test individual composites in the context of the actual services that they will use.

Composite testing

The problem with the system test is that it may fail for many reasons and often those reasons will be unclear. Composite-level testing allows us to isolate the individual composites and test them against their specifications. To do this, we inject requests from the client and stub out the services used by the composite so that we have complete control over all interactions between the composite and the services it interfaces with.

This type of testing is good for identifying defects in the composite, but must be treated with care as individual services may behave differently from the stubbed-out (emulated) versions of those services.

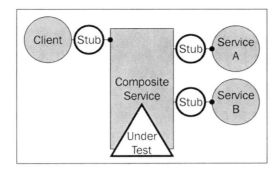

Component testing

The framework was designed for testing BPEL processes but may also be used to provide a test harness for individual services as shown in the following figure. In this case, a pass through assembly is provided that allows injection of messages into the service. The BPEL process and the service are then configured with suitable assertions to ensure the service is behaving as expected.

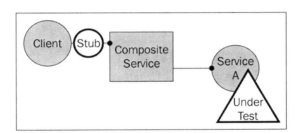

Unit testing

Unfortunately, the SOA Suite doesn't provide any specific low-level unit testing of individual components with the exception of XSL, although it may be emulated to an extent as described in the previous section. JDeveloper may also be used to run JUnit test cases which can interact with low level services. However, this is done outside the scope of the SOA Suite.

JDeveloper does have an XSL test tool that may be used to validate XSL transformations before deploying them as part of a service bus or BPEL deployment.

Performance testing

Although the SOA Suite provides as part of the test client the facility to run multiple queries concurrently against an interface, this should not be substituted for proper performance testing. The test client multiple thread interface has the following limitations:

- **Single message input**: All inputs to the service have the same input message. Depending on how the service is written this may improve performance, for example, because after the first request all the data pulled from the database is available in memory rather than having to be fetched from disc.

- **Limited scalability**: The clients and servers are all part of the same system and run on a single machine. This is not a realistic scenario and precludes testing how well the system scales.

- **Doesn't use test framework**: The test framework provides detailed feedback on multiple types of test and this is missing from the simple client interface.

The test client interface is good for quick basic performance testing, but any real world performance testing should use a more complete testing framework provided by Oracle Enterprise Manager testing tools or third parties such as Mercury Interactive.

User interface testing

The SOA Suite is focused on services rather than user interfaces and so any user interface interaction with the services must be driven from another test tool. Similar to performance testing this is something for which other products should be used. Although there is a certain amount that can tested by performing a system test as described earlier, this does not fully test all the ways in which a Web or thick client application may interact with the services exposed. There is no substitute for a proper end-user interface testing tool to be used alongside the SOA Suite testing framework.

Summary

In this chapter, we have examined testing in SOA Suite, starting with simple one-off tests and then moving on to examine the BPEL test framework that provides a repeatable testing framework for BPEL processes and any services called from a BPEL process.

The SOA Suite testing framework can be used to provide a rigorous environment to support regression tests. In order to get the best out of this framework it is necessary to invest effort in building test cases alongside the composites themselves. The following checklist may be useful:

1. Always develop test cases alongside the composites.
2. Always develop test cases for standalone services by creating appropriate composites as test harnesses.
3. Add new test cases for defects discovered in the field that were not caught by existing test cases.
4. Emulate services to allow test cases to focus on composites.
5. Directly call services (don't emulate) to allow test cases to interact with real endpoints.

It is best to build tests when the components themselves are being built; this allows us to validate our components incrementally and immediately.

Test early, test often!

20
Defining Security and Management Policies

In this chapter we will investigate how service-oriented computing makes security more complicated before exploring how to secure our service infrastructure and monitor it.

Security and management challenges in the SOA environment

Moving to service-oriented architecture brings with it a number of benefits that we have explored throughout this book, such as improved re-use, strong encapsulation of business services, ability to rapidly construct new composite services, and applications. However, there is one area in which SOA makes life much harder, and that is in the area of security and management. By security we mean the process of ensuring that individuals and applications can only access the information and invoke the processing which is allowed to them. By management we mean the task of ensuring that a system is capable of delivering the required services when requested.

Evolution of security and management

The challenges that SOA brings to the security and monitoring space are made clearer when we look at the evolution of computing. The original computer systems provided a single centralized system with a single access mechanism via a terminal. These mainframe systems provided their own security and required external parties (users) to authenticate, at which point they were restricted in their access by the internal security protocols of the system. In a similar fashion monitoring was a case of monitoring the status of individual components within the central system. This made it very easy to provide strong centralized control of who could access resources, while also retaining a strong ability to monitor individual users, as well as the health of the system.

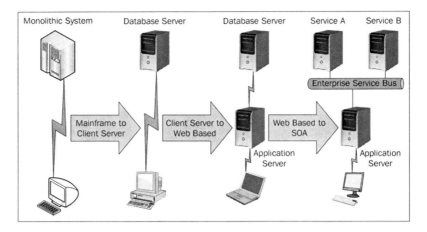

The move to client server systems complicated things because now the actual processing was spread across two machines, the server, generally a database server, and a client, generally a personal computer. The central server was now required to provide external access at a more granular level, potentially protecting individual tables in the database rather than the broader brush application level that was required in the previous generation of centralized systems. This now introduced the problem of coordinating identity across two tiers; the client application would generally authenticate the end user against the server, providing a pass through level of security. Hence the security model was more complex due to more demanding access control requirements, but the authentication model was not greatly different.

However, the move to client server greatly increased the complexity of monitoring the solution. Moving processing off the central system and on to the client meant that it was now necessary to monitor the health of components in the client, and that client was more complex than the terminals used in the previous generation. A particular problem in this environment was the unexpected interactions different applications in the client could have with each other.

The problems of monitoring and managing the distributed client applications led to a pressure to move the processing back into the data centre, which led to a third generation of solution architectures based around web/application servers and web browsers.

This led to further complication of the security infrastructure as now the applications had to maintain links from many different clients and ensure that they enforced appropriate access controls on each individual client. It did however simplify the management environment by bringing the application back into the managed data centre environment. However, the end-to-end environment was now more complex to manage due to there being multiple tiers rather than a single tier, and problems in one tier would impact the entire service offered by an application.

The move to service-oriented architectures can be thought of as a natural progression from the web deployment model, but with the additional complication that now applications are composed from services provided by many individual service providers, potentially on different machines, and in some circumstances the service may be provided outside the company by another company. In the next section, we will examine the management and security challenges that SOA brings.

Added complications of SOA environment

The SOA environment makes it harder to enforce a consistent security policy. It also has a number of moving parts that must be managed. Let us consider each of these challenges in turn.

Security impacts of SOA

Consider a service that is invoked. In order to decide whether to service the request it must determine if the requestor is allowed to access this service. Access may be controlled or restricted based on the invoking code and also based on the originator of the request. Consider a composite application in which user A makes a request of application X which satisfies the request by making a request to service Y which in turn calls service Z.

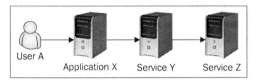

Application X has no more a difficult job in accepting the request in this environment than in a web application. It can require the user to authenticate, potentially via some form of secure certificate or bio-metric based authentication. The challenges come when X starts to invoke services. Service Y must decide if it will honor the request. It has three basic ways to do this:

- Accept requests: Effectively apply no security
- Accept requests from application X: Effectively require the client application or service to be identified and authenticated
- Accept requests from user A: Effectively require some way of propagating the identity of user A through application X into the service

Service Z has the same set of options but instead of application A being the client in this case it is service Y. This potential chaining of services and potential requirements for propagation of identity make it harder to effectively secure the environment. Later on we will look at tools in the SOA suite that can simplify this.

Management and monitoring impacts of SOA

In the same way that we have a more complicated set of security demands in the SOA environment we also have a more complicated set of monitoring requirements. Consider the diagram below which shows how a composite application makes use of services to satisfy users' demands.

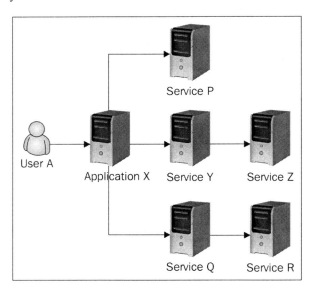

In this case, application X makes use of five services either directly or indirectly to satisfy user requests. We need to monitor the individual services to get any idea as to why an application may be unavailable to an end user. However, this is not sufficient as the some of the services may be required for execution and others may be optional.

For example, consider a shopping site. The catalogue and order entry services must be available to provide a service to the end user, but the fulfillment and payment services need not be available, as they can do their work without the user being online at the time. In this case if the fulfillment service is unavailable then the application can still work but it may have reduced functionality, such as being unable to provide an immediate delivery date.

Another aspect of service monitoring that must be considered is the throughput on individual services. This is important because individual services may be used by multiple applications and so it is possible that an application that previously gave excellent end-user response times may degrade its performance because one of the services it depends on is under heavy load from other applications. Monitoring will allow this risk to be identified early on and corrective action taken.

Securing services

Having looked at the additional complications that SOA brings to the security infrastructure let us examine how SOA Suite enables us to secure our services. We will look at securing services based on what application is calling them as well as securing services based on the end user for whom the request is being made. We will also look at the best places to apply security to our services.

Security outside the SOA Suite

There are several things we can do to secure our services without using the facilities available in the SOA Suite. The following are some of the ways in which we may provide security by configuration of the network and server environment in which our services execute.

Network security

An integral part of a SOA solution will usually be firewalls that restrict access to different networks within the enterprise. A common model is to have a front side network that receives requests from external clients and a back side network that can receive requests from other services but cannot be accessed directly by external clients. Machines that need to be accessed externally will have access to both the front side and back side networks and will act as application bridges between the two, there being no network level connection between them.

Preventing message interception

We can improve security by encrypting all messages between services by using SSL (Secure Socket Layer). This requires the web servers hosting our services to be configured with certificates and only to accept requests across SSL connections. Basically this means disabling HTTP access and only allowing HTTPS access to our servers. This has a performance overhead as all messages must be encrypted before leaving the client machine and decrypted on arriving at the server machine. The server-side encryption may be reduced by use of hardware accelerators, either embedded in the network card or in the network.

If all the machines are on the same physical switch then messages between services are effectively secure because they can only be seen by the client and server machines. This allows us to configure our servers to accept HTTP requests from machines on the same switch but only accept HTTPS requests from machines not on the same switch.

Restricting access to services

We may restrict access to machines based on the IP address of the caller. This is a quick and easy way to provide a layer of protection to our services. Configuring our HTTP servers to only accept requests from well-known clients works well for internal networks but doesn't work for external services. It also leaves us with the problem of reconfiguring our list of acceptable clients when a new client service is added.

Declarative security versus explicit security

A central tenet of service-oriented architecture is to abstract functionality into services that hide implementation details. When we come to security and monitoring these are really facets of a service and can also be provided in a service-oriented fashion. These two key concepts are worth exploring because they are central to making best use of SOA Suite security and monitoring.

Security as a facet

We generally define our services in terms of the functionality (service) that they provide. These services also have attributes that may not be explicitly mentioned in their service data model but are nevertheless an important part of the service. These attributes include availability, response time, and security. Security is an attribute of a service that can be applied without altering the core functionality of the service. For example a service may require that it is only invoked across SSL connections or that it may only be invoked by an authorized user.

Security as a service

Security is itself a service that controls the following:

- Access control: Who may make requests of a service
- Authorization: Who is requesting the service
- Integrity: Can the data be read or altered to or from the service

We can think of security as a service that is applied as a facet to other services. This is the model that is applied within the SOA Suite and particularly the Web Services Manager.

Web Services Manager model

The Web Services Manager allows security to be applied to services and operators to monitor services, without a need to modify the service. The model for this is shown in the figure below:

Access to services (access control) is always through a gateway or agent component supplied by Web Services Manager. The endpoint of the service is exposed as the gateway or agent endpoint.

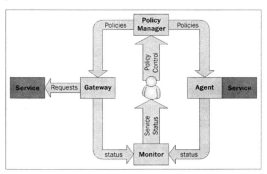

Rules for who can access the service (authorization) and the access they are allowed (access control) are determined by the policies provided by the policy manager component of Web Services Manager. These policies are pushed to individual agents and gateways.

Policies may also specify specific logging requirements or encryption requirements (message integrity) for the data.

Policies are determined by an administrator using the Web Services Manager console and enforced using policy enforcement points. Policy enforcement points are provided by Web Services Manager gateways and agents.

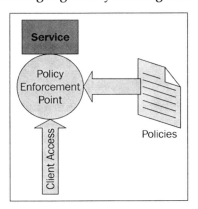

Operators may monitor the performance of services against pre-defined service level agreements by using the web service monitor component. The monitor is informed of service performance by the agent and gateway components.

Policies

A policy consists of a series of steps such as:

- Validate certificate of requestor
- Decrypt message
- Log portion of message

These steps can be thought of as a policy pipeline. Each request for a service must pass through the policy pipeline associated with that service. By defining a policy we can have a consistent way of protecting a number of different services. For example, we may have the following distinct policies:

- Policy for externally accessible services
- Policy for services making financial transactions
- Policy for non-critical services

The first policy may specify a need for encryption of data as well as authentication of clients. The second policy may require strong authentication of clients and special logging steps. The third policy may just perform some simple logging. An internally accessible payments gateway may make use of the second policy, while the same gateway configured for external access may be configured with the first and second policies.

Policies are applied to individual service endpoints.

Agents and gateways

From the preceding discussion it is clear that gateways and agents are the key **Policy Enforcement Points** (PEPs) where the security facet is added to a service. Let's explore how these components differ.

Both gateways and agents are responsible for enforcing policy. The difference is in their physical location. Agents are physically co-located in the same container as the service they are protecting. This has the benefit that agents do not require an additional network hop or inter-process communication to deliver messages to the service. Because of this the physical and logical layout of the agent is essentially the same as shown in the diagram. There is one agent per container which is hosting services.

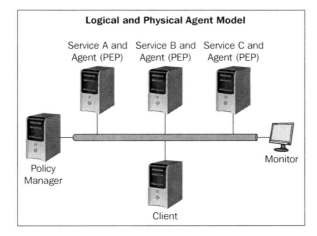

The gateway on the other hand is a centralized policy enforcement point. The service endpoint exposed is that of the gateway, not of the machine on which the service resides. All requests potentially incur an additional network hop as they must go through the machine on which the gateway resides. Although physically the gateway is just another machine on the network, logically it sits in front of the services for which it enforces policies.

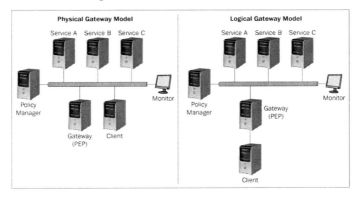

Note that in a production deployment it is possible to have multiple gateways deployed so that a single gateway does not become a single point of failure in the service infrastructure.

Distinctive benefits of gateways and agents

Gateways and agents both achieve the same result of securing and monitoring services, but the different approaches they have provide different benefits. Both gateways and agents can be used together, with some endpoints protected by agents and others protected by gateways.

Benefits of gateways

Following are the benefits of gateways:

- Can protect services running on platforms for which no agent is available, for example a service implemented in Perl
- Does not require modification of service endpoints
- Less intrusive in endpoint platform
- Support message routing
- Support failover

Drawbacks of gateways

Following are the drawbacks of gateways:

- Clients must explicitly target gateway
- Services must be configured to only accept requests from gateways to avoid bypassing of gateway
- Service endpoints must be explicitly registered with gateway

Note that the service bus can also act in the role of a web services gateway, although the 10.3 release does not support the OWSM policies.

Benefits of agents

Following are the benefits of agents:

- Provide true end-to-end security
- Cannot be bypassed by targeting the service directly
- Do not require changes to clients' stored service endpoint
- Potentially faster due to less latency

Drawbacks of agents

Following are the drawbacks of agents:

- Intrusive into services to be monitored/secured
- Cannot convert between transport protocols

Service bus model

The service bus model to securing and monitoring services is similar to the OWSM gateway model in that the service bus sits between the client and the service and can apply policies and monitor performance of services. In the service bus model the policy management server and the policy enforcement point are both parts of the service bus.

Creating gateways and agents

Before we can start creating and applying policies in the Web Services Manager we need to create at least one gateway or agent.

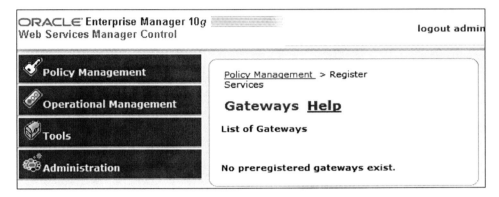

To create gateways or agents we must first log on to the Web Services Manager console at `http://hostname:port/ccore`. We can then select the **Policy Management** tab and then the **Manage Policies** tab.

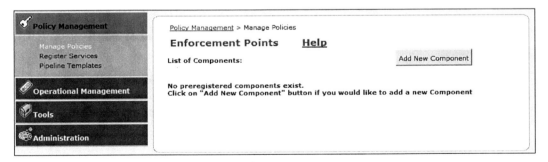

We create gateways and/or agents by clicking the **Add New Component** button. This will bring up an **Add New Component** dialog that will allow selection of the type of component to be registered with the Web Services Manager.

Creating a gateway

When creating a new gateway using the **Add New Component** dialog, we are required to set the **Component Type** to be gateway. The **Component Name** is an arbitrary name to identify the component to operators. The **Component URL** is the endpoint location where the gateway will be deployed. This is usually `http://hostname:port/gateway` where the hostname and port are the host and port number of the application server on which the gateway is to be deployed.

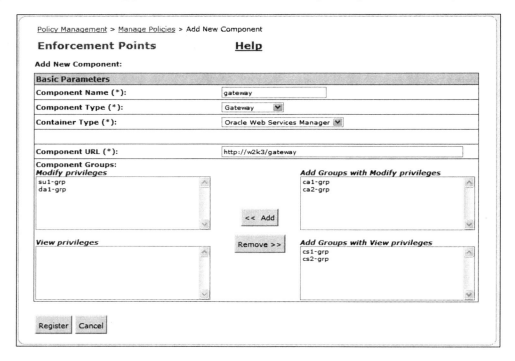

The **Component Groups** fields are used to control who may manage the gateway settings.

The gateway is registered with the Web Services Manager by clicking the **Register** button. This will register the component and create a unique component identifier, which is returned in the confirmation of a successful component registration.

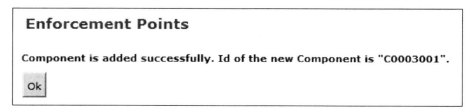

At this point the gateway has been registered with the Web Services Manager but has not been deployed into a container. To do this we need to go to the installation of the SOA Suite and deploy the gateway into a JEE container. We begin by configuring the gateway properties installer file `gateway-config-installer.properties` located in the `owsm/config/gateway` directory.

```
gateway.component.id=C0003001

gateway.repository.url=jdbc:oracle:thin:@//localhost:1521/XE
gateway.repository.driver=oracle.jdbc.driver.OracleDriver
gateway.repository.userid=ORAWSM
gateway.repository.password=????BfaMEtLZAxtnPhGUCTmBfP0=

...
```

In this file we need to set the `gateway.component.id` to be the component ID returned when we registered the gateway in the Web Service Manager Console. If we want to support input protocols other than HTTP SOAP and HTTP XML then they need to be configured in this file as well. After setting the correct component ID we can then deploy the gateway by opening a command prompt in the `owsm/bin` directory and executing the following command:

```
wsmadmin deploy gateway
```

During execution, we will be prompted for the administrator password of the application server into which we are deploying.

```
Buildfile: C:\oracle\SOA10.1.3\owsm\bin\..\scripts\install.xml

validate.oc4jAdminPassword:
    [input] OC4J Administrator Password:
```

Successful deployment will be indicated by a success message.

```
install.buildApps.clean.gateway:
    [delete] Deleting: C:\oracle\SOA10.1.3\owsm\ears\gateway.ear
    [delete] Deleting: C:\oracle\SOA10.1.3\owsm\wars\gateway.war

BUILD SUCCESSFUL
Total time: 1 minute 43 seconds
```

Note that the application server may need restarting in order for the new configuration to take effect.

Having successfully registered a gateway, we now need to tell it about the services available.

Registering gateway services

We register services by clicking on the **Register Services** link of the **Policy Management** menu on the left of the screen. This provides us with a list of gateways. For a given gateway we may drill down into the services for that gateway by clicking on the **Services** link which takes us to a listing of the services currently available on that gateway.

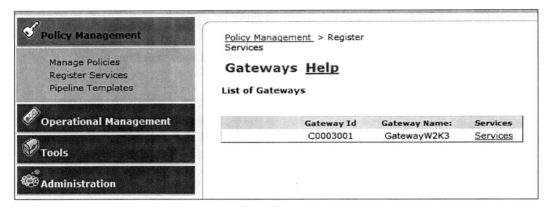

There are two ways to register a service with the gateway. We may **Import Services** by locating them in a service registry or WSIL repository. In this case we need to provide details of the service directory and select the appropriate service within that directory. Alternatively, we may **Add New Service** which allows us to reference a WSDL directly.

Selecting **Add New Service** prompts us to provide a **Service Name** for use by operators and clients of the service. Services may be accessed at the URL `http://host:port/gateway/ServiceName`. We must also provide a **Service Version** identifier that serves to distinguish different services with the same service name. If multiple services with the same name are registered, the last one registered is accessible via the service name.

We must also provide a service WSDL URL which will tell the gateway about the interface to be supported and the endpoint of the web service. Note that the transport exposed by the gateway need not be the same as the transport provided by the service. It is possible to support a variety of different transports for the service to be invoked, including HTTP, HTTPS, JMS, and IBM MQ series.

 There is some overlap in the functionality of the service bus and the Web Services Manager. For example, both are capable of applying security policies as well as performing protocol and format conversions. The Web Services Manager is best used for consistently applying security policies throughout an organization. It is better to use the service bus for abstracting service interfaces and performing protocol and data format conversion. The Web Services Manager should be thought of as the component to provide consistent security policy management in a SOA infrastructure, leaving the service bus to deal with the management of service abstractions.

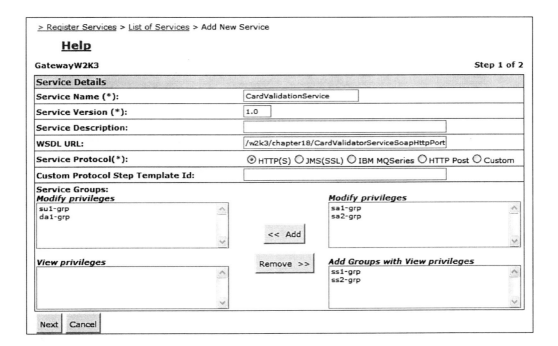

Note that we are configuring the target service transport, not the transport that will receive requests in Web Services Manager. Web Services Manager can be configured to received requests across HTTP, JMS, or MQ series and all registered services will be accessible across all protocols from which OWSM is configured to receive requests.

Clicking **Next** takes us to a second service configuration screen which allows us to configure additional service properties, such as what to do when the service is unavailable.

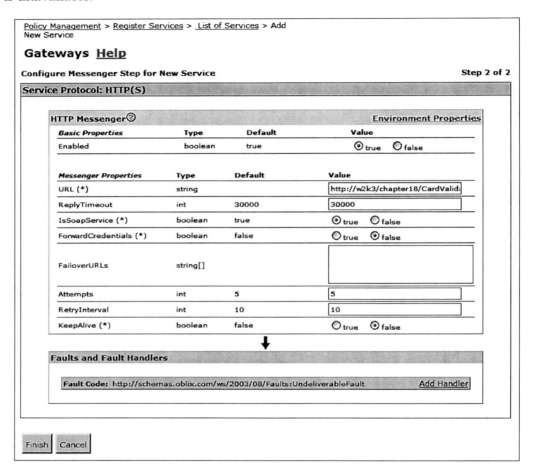

Clicking **Finish** registers the service with the gateway and returns a unique service ID. This service ID may be used to invoke the service from a client.

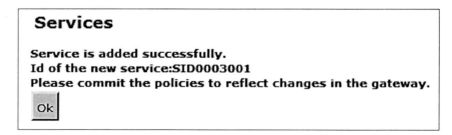

When we register a service with the gateway then we expect all client access to go through the gateway or the policies we register against the service will not be applied. The following table shows how a client may access the service. Services may be accessed using either their service ID or their registered name.

Protocol	Endpoint Address

SOAP over HTTP	`http://GatewayHostname:GatewayPort/gateway/services/ServiceID`
	or
	`http://GatewayHostname:GatewayPort/gateway/services/ServiceName`

XML over HTTP	`http://GatewayHostname:GatewayPort/gateway/xml/ServiceID`
	or
	`http://GatewayHostname:GatewayPort/gateway/xml/ServiceName`

SOAP over JMS or XML over JMS	JMS User Property 'serviceID' set to 'ServiceID' or JMS User Property 'serviceID' set to 'ServiceName'

After registering our service we need to commit the change to have it take effect. This is done by clicking the **commit** link on the list of services associated with the gateway.

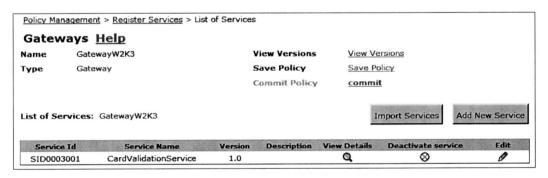

After committing these changes we get a confirmation that the service has been successfully registered.

The list of services registered with a gateway may always be displayed from within the Web Services Manager control by clicking on the **Services** link of the gateway.

Creating an agent

Agents may be installed into Java containers to apply policy directly at the client or service level. There are two kinds of agents in Web Services Manager. Client agents intercept service requests before they leave a client while server agents intercept service requests before they are delivered into a service.

Client and server agents are installed in a similar fashion to the gateway by selecting **Add Component** from the **Policy Management** tab and then choosing the type of component to be deployed: a **Server Agent** or a **Client Agent**.

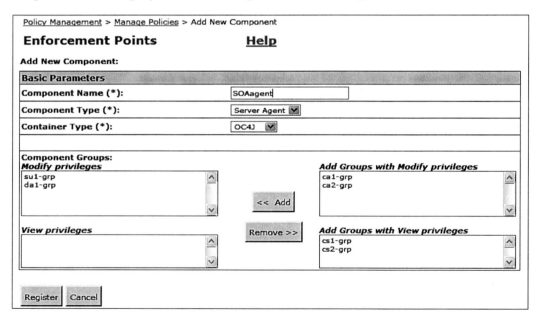

In addition to a name for the agent, the type of container into which the agent is deployed, must also be specified. This type relates more to the web services stack than anything else, hence the listing of **OC4J**, **Axis**, and **Others**. Clicking **Register** causes the agent to be registered and a new component ID returned. This component ID will be used later to configure the deployed agent. The agent is deployed in a slightly different fashion to the gateway. Similar to the gateway, it also has an install configuration file, but this is located in the `owsm/bin` directory and requires different information. The following table summarizes the location and name of the installer configuration files for agents and gateways:

Component	Directory	Filename
Gateway	`Owsm/config/gateway`	`gateway-config-installer.properties`
Client Agent	`Owsm/bin`	`agent.properties`
Server Agent	`Owsm/bin`	`agent.properties`

It is important to ensure that the `agent.componentType`, `agent.containerType` and `agent.containerVersion` properties are correctly set in the relevant installer properties file before running the deployer.

```
#
# agent.componentType can be one of the following
# serveragent - manages webservice providers
# clientagent - manages webservice clients.
# OC4JServerInterceptor - Used an an interceptor for webservice
providers on OC4J
# OC4JClientInterceptor - Used an an interceptor for webservice
providers on OC4J
#
#NOTE - INTERCEPTORS ONLY WORK ON OC4J 10.1.3 +
agent.componentType=OC4JServerInterceptor

#
# agent.containerType can be AXIS, WEBLOGIC, WEBSPHERE, TIBCO-BW or
OC4J
#
# Specifying the container version for OC4J 10.1.3 is a must
#
# The only allowed container type for Interceptor agent is OC4J and
version should be 10.1.3 or higher
#
agent.containerType=OC4J
agent.containerVersion=10.1.3
...

agent.component.id=C0003002
...
```

After verifying that the properties are set correctly then we deploy the agent with the following command:

```
wsmadmin installAgent
```

It is worth noting that `wsmadmin` commands are case sensitive. During deployment we will be prompted for the application server administrator password. Successful deployment is marked by a **BUILD SUCCESSFUL** response. Now that the agent is deployed then it is possible to enable it for specific applications within the JEE container.

Enabling agent services

Monitoring and policy enforcement of agent protected services must be done by going in to the management console for the application server and enabling the agent for services in that application. This will make it possible to apply policies to all or a subset of services in the application.

To enable the agent for a web service in OC4J, log on to the **Application Server Control** and select the container where the agent and the services to be monitored are deployed. Select the **Applications** tab to display a list of deployed applications and select the application containing the services to be monitored. Select the **Web Services** tab to find and drill down into the web service to be monitored. The configuration for the Web Services Agent is available on the **Administration** tab.

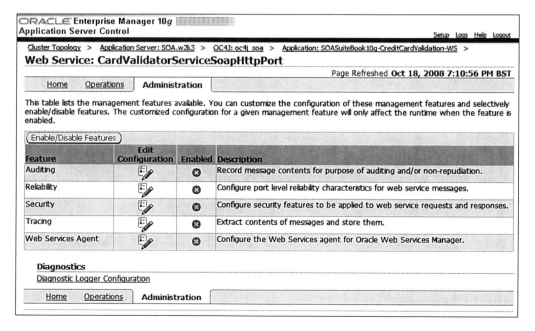

Clicking on the **Edit Configuration** icon for the **Web Services Agent** tab provides access to **Edit Web Services Agent Configuration** dialog. This needs to be configured with the name of the directory associated with the agent, which is the same name as the component ID. This directory is normally located under the home of the SOA Suite install at `owsm/config/interceptors/ComponentID`.

Once this configuration is done then the application server may need restarting and then the service may be managed by the Web Services Manager.

Defining policies

Policies are defined using the Web Services Manager console. A policy can be thought of as a pipeline of steps to be performed on an inbound request and outbound response. Note that OWSM also has pre-request and post-response policy pipelines but these do nothing and will be removed from the product. The request pipeline is the steps executed after the gateway or agent receives the request but before it forwards it on to the service. Similarly the response pipeline is the steps executed by the gateway or agent before forwarding it on to the requestor.

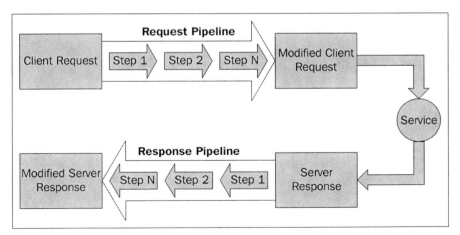

Policies may be used to partially or fully encrypt payloads, provide logging information, transform data, authenticate users, authorize access, or any number of other functions. The table below shows the list of functions supported out of the box by the Web Services Manager. Note that it is also possible to create custom steps written in Java and register them with OWSM. All steps are available by default in the gateway, but a few steps are unavailable in the server or client agents. If a step is available in an agent then it is marked as `true` otherwise it is marked as `false`. The steps associated with a component are accessed by clicking on the **Steps** link in the component list. In addition to the steps listed below it is also possible to register new steps with a component through this link.

Step name	Step description	Server agent	Client agent
Active Directory Authenticate	Authenticate credentials with Active Directory	TRUE	TRUE
Active Directory Authorize	Authorizes request by retrieving roles from Active Directory and checking against roles allowed by service	TRUE	TRUE
Decrypt and Verify Signature	XML Decryption And Signature Verification	TRUE	TRUE
Extract Credentials	Extract Credentials	TRUE	TRUE
File Authenticate	Authenticate username and password against a local .htpasswd file. This step depends on Extract Credentials Step	TRUE	TRUE
File Authorize	Authorize remote user against a local roles file. This step depends on Extract Credentials Step	TRUE	TRUE
Handle Generic Fault	Example generic fault handler step	FALSE	FALSE
Insert Oracle Access Manager Token	Insert Oracle Access Manager Token	FALSE	FALSE
Insert WS BASIC Credentials Step Insert WS BASIC Credentials Step	Insert WS BASIC Credentials	TRUE	TRUE
Ldap Authenticate	Peforms the authentication with a LDAP Server	TRUE	TRUE
Ldap Authorize	Authorizes request by retrieving role from LDAP and checking against roles allowed by service	TRUE	TRUE
Log	Log the request/response message	TRUE	TRUE

Step name	Step description	Server agent	Client agent
Oracle Access Manager Authenticate Authorize	Authenticate and Authorize URLs access with Oracle Access Manager Access Server	TRUE	TRUE
SAML — Insert WSS 1.0 sender-vouches token	Step to Insert SAML token as per WSS 1.0 token profile with Sender-Vouches confirmation method	FALSE	TRUE
SAML — Verify WSS 1.0 Token	Verify SAML tokens as per WSS SAML token profile 1.0	TRUE	FALSE
Sign message	XML Signature	TRUE	TRUE
Sign Message And Encrypt	XML Signature and Encryption	TRUE	TRUE
Siteminder Authentication	SiteMinder Authentication	TRUE	TRUE
Siteminder Authorize	SiteMinder Authorization to be used after SiteMinder Authentication Step	TRUE	TRUE
Verify Certificate	Verify a certificate against a local keystore	TRUE	TRUE
Verify Signature	XML Signature Verification	TRUE	TRUE
XML Decrypt	XML Decryption	TRUE	TRUE
XML Encrypt	XML Encryption	TRUE	TRUE
XML Transform	Transform message using XSL	TRUE	TRUE

It is worth noting that certain steps rely on information being made available by earlier steps. For example the various *Authenticate* steps generally require there to be an extract credentials step beforehand to make the credentials, for example username and password, available. Similarly the *Authorize* steps generally require the corresponding *Authenticate* step to have been performed previously.

Creating a new policy template to perform basic authentication

The easiest way to manage policies is to have a policy template that defines common policy steps to be applied to multiple components. A policy template is a reusable set of policy steps. Templates can be copied into a policy to reduce the amount of work in setting up individual policies. As an example we will create a pipeline template that performs basic authentication with the username and password passed in the HTTP header and the user credentials and roles stored in files. This could then be reused to provide authentication for multiple service policies.

Creating the template

To define a new policy template we go to the **Policy Management** tab in Web Services Manager and select the **Pipeline Templates** link. This allows us to view the current pipeline templates by type of component, gateway, or agent, and pipeline type, request or response. Clicking **Add New Pipeline Template** allows us to define new pipeline templates.

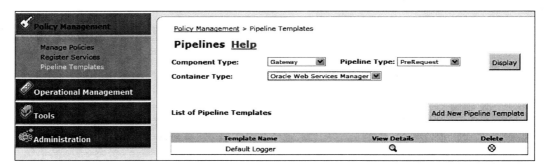

We need to create the pipeline template for a specific pipeline and component type, so these must be correctly selected from the **New Pipeline Template** dialog. We must also provide a name for the template. We can then click the **Next** button.

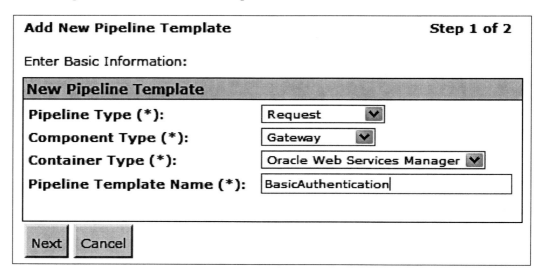

We can now configure the individual pipeline steps in our template. Note that pipeline steps in a template can be fully, partially, or not configured at all. Steps such as **Extract Credentials** may be fully specified if the credentials are located in a well-known location that will be common to all services.

Extracting Credentials

We add a step to our pipeline by clicking the **Add Step Below** link. This prompts us to select a step template such as **Extract Credentials**.

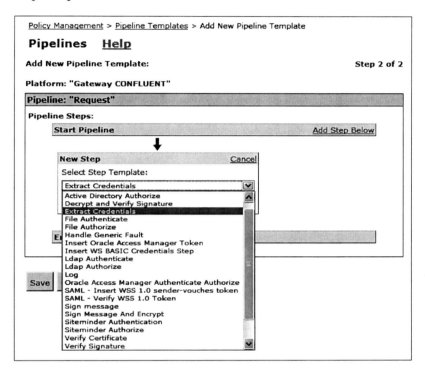

Selecting the template step and clicking **OK** will add an **Extract Credentials** step with default configuration.

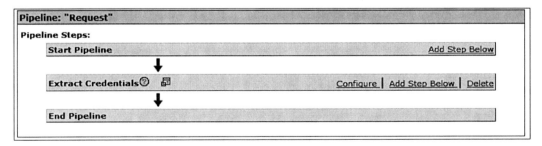

If we expected the configuration to be different for every usage of this template we could leave the step unconfigured. However, in this case we will click **Configure** to ensure that the settings are correct for most uses of the template.

It is the steps in a pipeline template that are copied into a pipeline, not a reference to the pipeline template. Once copied the steps are independent of the template and have no further connection with it. A pipeline is unaffected by any changes made to a pipeline template used in building the pipeline. Similarly changes to the copied steps do not affect the original pipeline template. Web Services Manager does not provide a mechanism for changes in a pipeline template to update the pipelines previously built using that template.

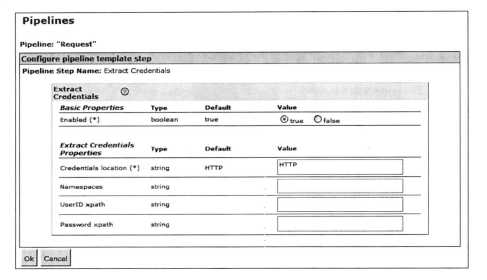

The **Credentials location** field is used to tell OWSM where the credentials are to be found. The options are as follows:

- HTTP: Indicates that the username and password are to be found in the HTTP header which is using HTTP Basic authentication.

- JMS: Indicates that the username is to be found in the JMS header properties.

- WS-BASIC: Indicates the use of WS-I Basic Security profile with the UsernameToken element containing the credentials—note that currently only plaintext passwords are supported.

- XPath Expression: Unlike the previous options this is not a string literal value but an actual XPath expression to the element containing the user credentials.

The first three options require no further configuration. However, if an XPath expression such as soap:Header/soap:Envelope/wsse:Security/ wsse:UsernameToken/ is specified for the **Credentials location** then the remaining fields must be completed.

The **Namespaces** field tells OWSM which namespaces are being used by the XPath expressions in the other three fields. Namespaces take the form of `prefix=namespace` with commas separating multiple namespaces such as `soap=http://schemas.xmlsoap.org/soap/envelope, wsse=http://www.docs.oasis-open.org/wss/2004/01/oasis-200401-wss-wssecurity-utility-1.0.xsd`.

The **UserID xpath** field is appended to the **Credentials location** XPath to give the location of the userID. In a similar fashion the **Password xpath** field is used to derive the location of the password. Note that only `cleartext` passwords are supported for XPath expressions.

> **Securing user credentials**
>
> Although only `cleartext` credentials are supported by the pipeline steps directly, the password could be passed encrypted and then decrypted using the XML decrypt pipeline step or a custom decrypt step before the message passes through the authorization step.

Authenticating a user

We now need to add a step to authenticate the user or in other words verify the identity of a user. OWSM will authenticate using the credentials obtained in the previous step. We must now tell OWSM how to find the stored user credentials against which it must validate the provided user credentials. There are several means of authenticating a user, including the use of standard LDAP servers, and Active Directory. To authenticate against a file we will add a **File Authenticate** step, but the other authenticate steps are used in a similar fashion.

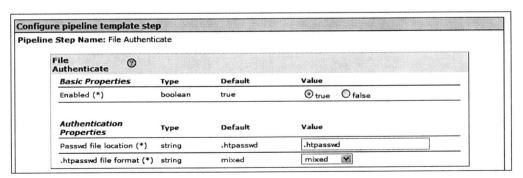

This step requires us to configure a **Password file location** and identify the **.htpasswd** file format. The file location may be either an absolute location or a location relative to $ORACLE_HOME//j2ee/home. The format of the **.htpasswd** file is multiple lines of the form `username:password`.

The actual format of the password portion of the file depends on file format property and may take one of four possible formats:

- md5: Message Digest 5 encoded using the OWSM MD5 algorithm which is not compatible with other implementations such as `user2:{MD5}` `bLdfZSqbUnmOts8iAQV8cw==`.

- sha1: Secure Hash Algorithm encoded.

- plaintext: Unencoded format such as `user2:password2`.

- Mixed: A combination of the above formats. Note that the encoding is identified in the password field, allowing the mixed format to work.

If the decision is taken to use MD5 hash format then the passwords in the `.htpasswd` file must be encrypted using the OWSM admin tool. The user must already have an entry in the `.htpasswd` file and a hashed password may be added by the following command.

```
wsmadmin md5encode <htpasswd file> <username>
```

Authorizing a user

Having authenticated a user we now wish to decide if they are authorized to access the service being protected by this pipeline. To achieve this we use the Authorize step against an appropriate resource such as an LDAP server or in our case a file. Authentication consists of listing a number of roles authorized to access the service and then having OWSM match those roles to the roles associated with the authenticated user. If there is at least one match then the user is authorized. We begin by adding a **File Authorize** step to our pipeline and configuring it.

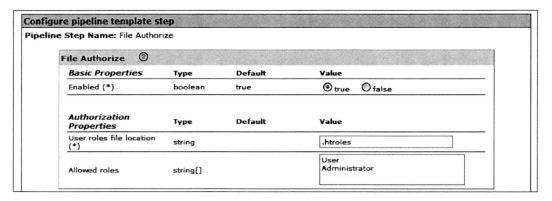

The first item to configure is the **User roles file location**. This tells OWSM where to find the file that lists the roles associated with a user. This may be referenced by a location relative to $ORACLE_HOME/j2ee/home or it may be an absolute path. This file is formatted as XML and has the following structure:

```
<UserRoles>
  <user username="user1" roles="User"/>
  <user username="user2" roles="Admin"/>
  <user username="user3" roles="Viewer"/>
</UserRoles>
```

The root element must be UserRoles and this in turn has one or more user elements. Each user element has a username attribute that identifies a user who will have been previously authenticated. It also has a roles attribute that consists of a comma separated list of roles associated with the user.

In addition to the location of the roles file, the file authorize step also has an **Allowed roles** item that consists of a new line separated list of roles that are allowed to execute the target service. Note that it would be common to not configure this item in a pipeline template as, although the roles file location is probably the same for all services and hence worth configuring in the template, the actual list of roles allowed will probably vary by service and hence is best left to be configured after the template has been applied to a concrete service.

After saving our changes we have now completed the steps in our template.

Saving the pipeline template

We save the pipeline template by clicking the **Save** button.

Note that it is not possible to edit the pipeline template. If changes are required it must be deleted and recreated. The Extract, Authenticate, Authorize pipeline template is a natural sequence. The following diagram shows how both before and after the extract step all users may invoke a service; after the authorize step only users with valid credentials are able to do so; and after the authenticate step only users with the correct roles may invoke the service.

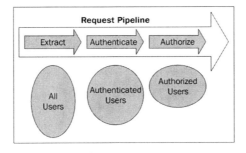

This sequence is represented in OWSM with the following pipeline.

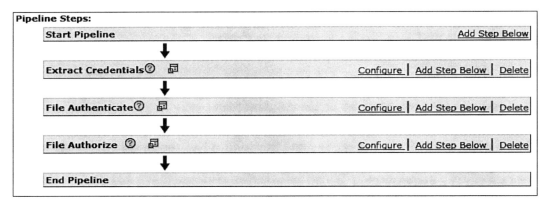

Creating a new policy

Having created our template we now wish to create a new policy, from it that may be applied to a particular service. To create a new policy we first select a component. Policies are defined in the context of a component and are edited by selecting the **Policies** link from the component list.

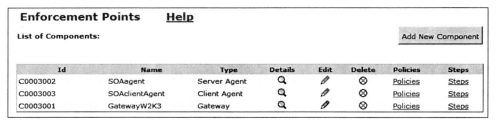

Each component maintains a list of policies and list of URL mapping rules that relate the policy to one or more service endpoints.

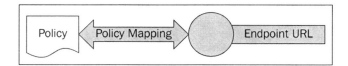

In the case of gateways the names of these policies and their relationship to service endpoints are fixed and provide a separate policy for each registered service, and a fixed URL mapping to the service endpoints.

Creating an agent policy

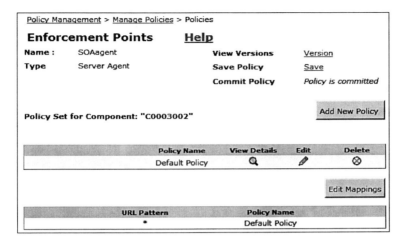

If we choose policies for a client or server agent then we have the option to edit the default policy or create a new policy. The contents of the default policy may be altered but the policy itself cannot be deleted. For agents we maintain a list of policies separate from the endpoints to which those policies apply. We will create a new policy by clicking on the **Add New Policy** button. This brings up a new policy with empty pipelines.

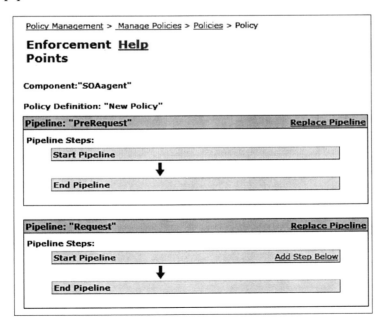

We could add individual steps to the policy in the same way that we created a pipeline template. However, it is now much easier to apply the pipeline template, which we do by clicking on the **Replace Pipeline** link. This takes us to a screen that allows us to select a pipeline template from a list of known templates for this type of agent. Selecting the appropriate template and clicking **Select** allows us to see the individual steps in the template. To make use of the template we click the **Replace** button which causes the pipeline steps to be copied from the template into the new policy.

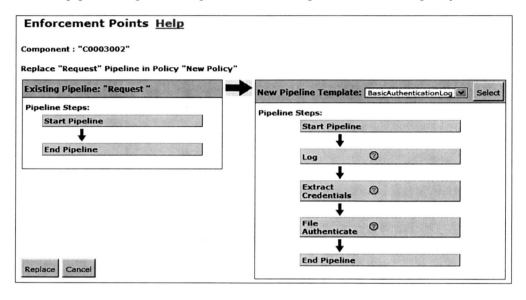

This takes us back to the new policy screen, but now the pipeline will be populated by the steps from the template and if necessary we may configure the individual steps or add additional steps. When we have added the steps we require to both the request and response pipelines and configured them appropriately, then we can click on the **Next** button to take us to the final screen in the new policy creation process.

We must now name our policy and then click **Save** to save it.

Once we have saved the policy we must now decide which endpoints it should apply to. We do this by clicking on the **Edit Mappings** button on the policies screen for our component. This takes us to a mapping editor.

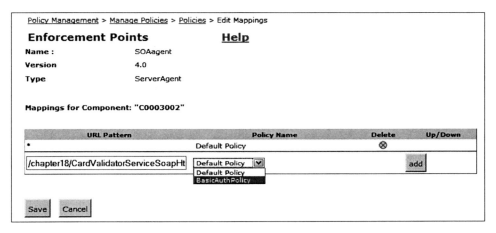

Here we can enter a URL pattern or exact URL that will match against the service or services which we wish to apply the template to. Having entered the mapping details we then click the **Add** button to add the mapping to the list. If there are other mappings we wish to set up then we can add them in a similar fashion. When we have finished adding mappings then click **Save**. This will save our changes to the policy.

After receiving a confirmation screen that our changes have been accepted then we need to activate those changes by clicking **Commit** on the policy management screen.

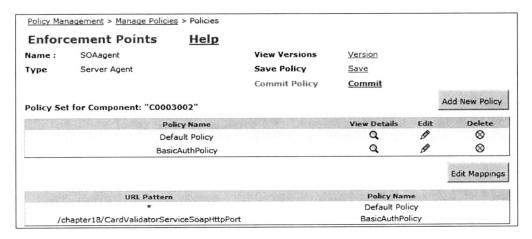

Committing policy changes

Policy changes can be saved up before being applied to the policy enforcement points. This allows multiple related policy changes to be made across components and for them then to all be activated at the same time. Remember that policy changes do not take affect until the commit button is pressed, pushing them out to the policy enforcement points.

Creating a gateway policy

Creating a gateway policy is similar to creating an agent policy except that the application of policies is not as flexible. With gateways, the list of registered services is used by OWSM to derive a list of policies, each named after the service endpoint, and each mapping to a list of the endpoints for the service. For gateways the policy of the service is applied to the endpoints for that policy and only the policy itself can be edited.

Selecting **Edit** for the service we wish to edit a policy to, takes us to the policy pipeline editor, which is edited in the same fashion as the agent policy pipeline that we examined in the previous section. It is worth noting that when the policy is saved it is possible to rename the policy and this will cause the policy mappings for this service to be updated to the new policy name.

Applying a policy through Service Bus Console

Unfortunately in the current release of SOA Suite the Service Bus and the Web Services Manager cannot share policies. In this section we will briefly mention ways in which the service bus may apply security policies to requests. Service Bus distinguishes between accounts that make requests through the service bus, known as service bus accounts, and accounts that make requests of business services, known as service accounts. This distinction is illustrated in the diagram shown:

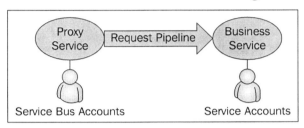

Service accounts

Within OSB business services may have service accounts associated with them. A service account is an account used to provide credentials to a business service. The service account is only used with the outbound message to a business service.

We can create a service account within a project by navigating to the project screen and then selecting **Service Account** from within the **Security** section of the **Resources** list box.

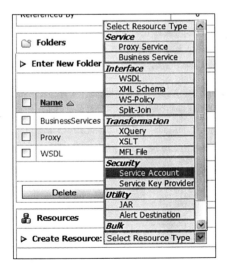

This brings up the **Create a New Service Account** dialog.

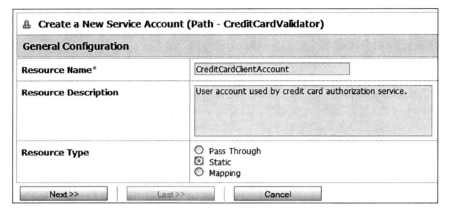

We are required to provide a **Resource Name** to identify the account and allow us to use it later. We must also specify the type of account required (**Resource Type**). There are three different kinds of service account:

- **Pass Through** expects the proxy service to provide credentials and this account will just copy those credentials from the $inbound message to $outbound message. This is useful if the client of the service actually provides credentials in the same security domain.

- **Static** provides a fixed user provided set of credentials. This is useful if the service provider expects to authenticate requests but the same account is to be used by all users, such as a corporate account with a postcode lookup service.

- **Mapping** requires credentials to be provided by the $inbound request and then will map these credentials onto the credentials required by the business service. This is useful if the client of the service and the business service are in different security domains.

We will use the **Static** mapping in this example to authenticate against a service expecting HTTP basic authentication.

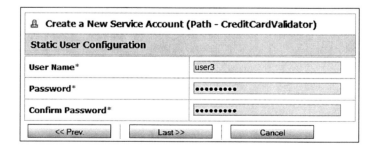

After providing the user credentials and clicking **Last>>** we get a final chance to review and modify settings before saving the new service account.

Using a service account

Having created our service account we can now configure the HTTP transport of the business service to use this account. We begin by selecting the business service and then editing the **HTTP Transport Configuration** section of the **Business Service Configuration**.

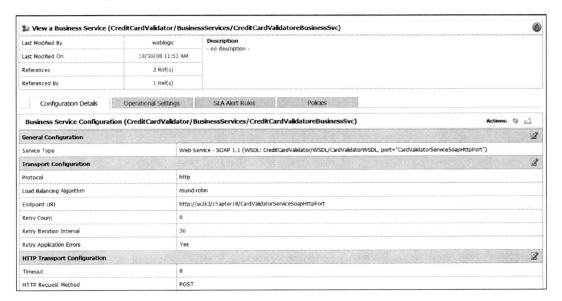

From the **HTTP Transport Configuration** screen we can specify that we want **Basic** authentication. Selecting this requires us to provide a **Service Account** to associate with the authentication.

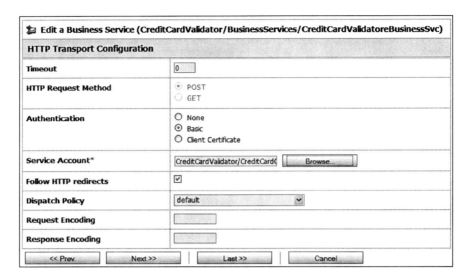

Clicking **Browse** enables to select the service account from a list.

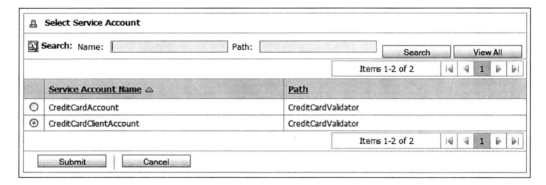

Having selected a service account we can then click **Last>>** to enable us to review the details before clicking **Save**. Remember to activate changes in the Service Bus Change Center. Whenever a request is now made to this business service the given user credentials will be added as HTTP Basic authentication parameters in the HTTP header.

Managing service bus user accounts

By default service bus users are managed by the internal LDAP server within WebLogic. This is fine for small scale configurations but for most deployments it will be necessary to configure an external LDAP server as a security provider. This will allow the selection of users and groups from that external server when applying security policies to proxy services. For test environments then the **Security Configuration** tab of the service bus console provides **Users**, **Groups**, and **Roles** tabs that allow management of users.

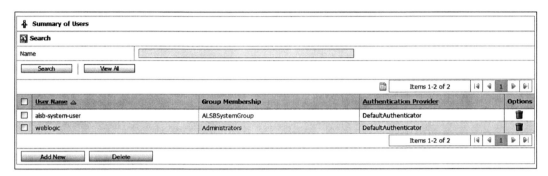

We can add a new user by selecting the **Users** tab and then clicking **Add New**. This then prompts us for the username and password of the new user and invites us to assign the user to groups.

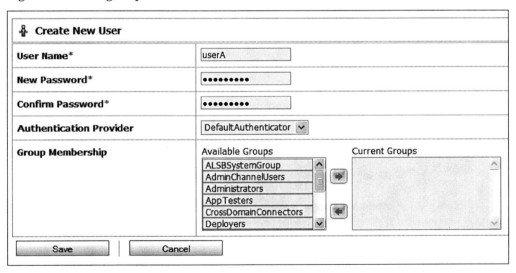

Clicking the **Save** button will create the new user, add the requested group memberships and take us back to the **Summary of Users** screen.

Service bus roles

The service bus has the concept of security roles that enable users and groups to be assigned a role based on a variety of operational conditions such as time of day. Rather than protect proxy services by user rules it is preferable to do it through roles. To create a role we go to the **Security Configuration** tab of the service bus console and select the **Roles** tab. This provides us a list of currently active roles.

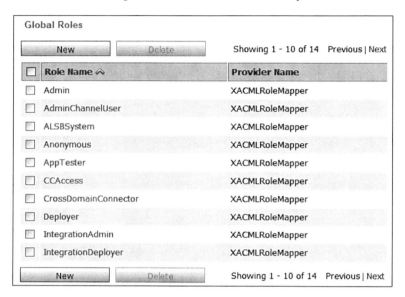

Clicking **New** takes us to the new role dialog where we specify a name for the role and then save it by clicking **OK** which takes us back to the **Global Roles** screen.

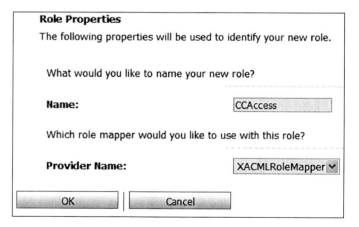

Having created a role we now need to define when the role is activated. This is done by clicking on the role name in the **Global Roles** screen.

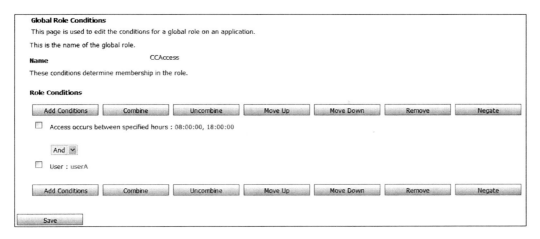

Here we can add the conditions that specify when the role is active. We use the **Add Conditions** button to insert conditions. This takes us to a screen asking what kind of rule or predicate we wish to add. As can be seen there are an extensive array of predicates that cover users, groups, time, and message content as well as others.

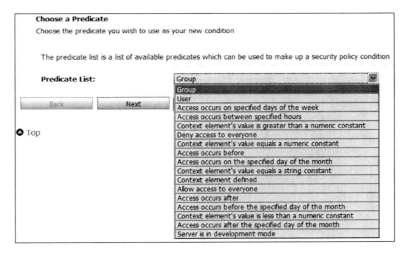

Choosing **User** and selecting **Next** will take us to the **Edit Arguments** screen where we configure the predicate according to the specific requirements we have. In this case we need to add a username. Note that the username must exist in the list of users.

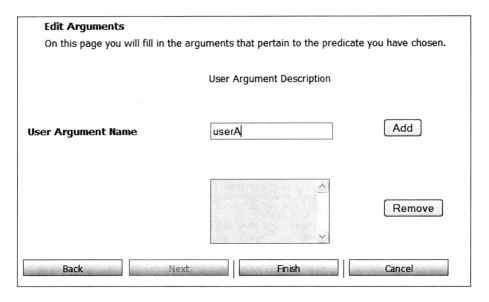

Note that we need to click **Add** to add the user before clicking **Finish** which will save the predicate and take us back to the **Global Role Conditions** screen. It is possible to combine predicates to form complex Boolean expressions. Grouping is managed by the **Combine** button. When we are happy with our changes we can save them by clicking **Save**.

We now have a role that can be used across many different proxy services.

Using a role to protect a proxy service

We can protect the proxy service by requiring requestors to be within a role before being allowed access. We do this by editing the **Proxy Service**. First if our role requires an authenticated user we must ensure that the service is configured to accept user credentials, such as HTTP basic authentication. This is done by selecting the appropriate transport configuration, in this case **HTTP Transport Configuration**, and ensuring that the correct authentication option is selected.

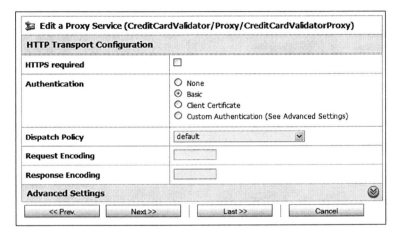

We must then select the **Security** tab of the proxy service screen and drill down into the **Transport Access Control**.

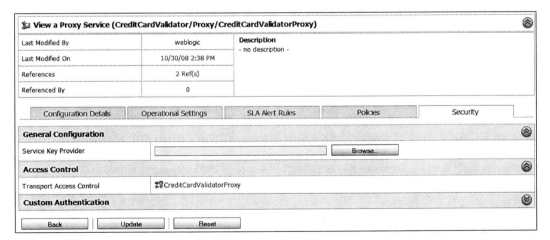

From here we can specify conditions (predicates) in the same way as in the roles screen. However, when using the roles screen we can reuse the predicate combinations or policy across many proxy services; any configuration on this screen is unique to this proxy. It is generally best to just add roles onto this screen. Note that there is a default policy for all proxy services of everyone being allowed access to the proxy. We add a single condition with a predicate of the **Role** that we created earlier. This effectively makes the access policy for this proxy follow the role that we set up.

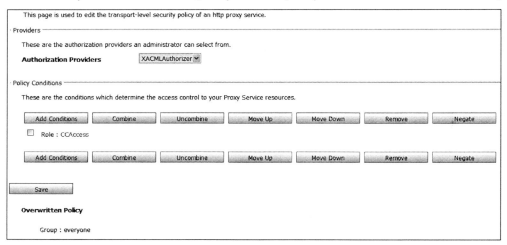

Clicking **Save** completes our application of the role and we can then apply the changes in the change center. We would now only be able to invoke this service in compliance with the role we set up, which may for instance require HTTP basic authentication of a user and restrict access to working hours.

Final thoughts on security

The examples used in this chapter have been based upon HTTP basic authentication because that does not require configuration of certificate stores. To properly secure services it is recommended that a public key infrastructure is used in conjunction with an LDAP server to provide secure message delivery and centralized user management. The steps used above are appropriate for use in development and test environments without access to an LDAP store or a PKI infrastructure.

Monitoring services

In addition to defining policies to be applied to requests, the Web Services Manager can also monitor the performance of services and raise alerts if they exceed a previously set threshold.

Both Web Services Manager and service bus can monitor services. Web Services Manager is unique in being able to monitor the service directly by using an agent that resides in the same container as the target service. The Web Services Manager is also able to provide out of the box reports on the security aspects of service invocation, tracking the number of failed authentication, or authorizations. The service bus provides an extremely capable monitoring and reporting framework for services that can be used alongside the Web Services Manager reporting framework.

Monitoring overall service statistics in OWSM

The **Snapshot** tab under **Operational Management** provides a quick overview of all a components services or an individual service.

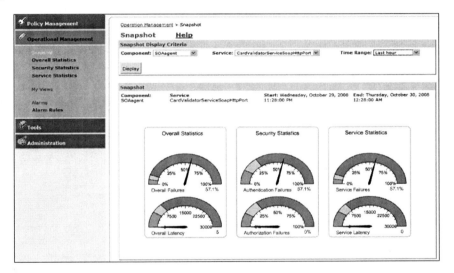

After selecting the **Component**, **Service**, and **Time Range** for which statistics should be displayed then clicking **Display** will update the dashboard. The statistics report the security failures as a percentage of total requests, as well as all service failures including security. They also provide a measure of latency or response time.

Defining a Service Level Agreement in OWSM

Service Level Agreements may be reviewed by selecting the **SLA Compliance** tab underneath **Operational Management** and **Overall Statistics**. Like the snapshot tab it is possible to select the component, service and time period to review. The displayed report provides percentages of service invocations that were too slow (**Success with high latency**), invocations that failed for some reason (**Failure**) and invocations that met service level agreements (**Success with low latency**).

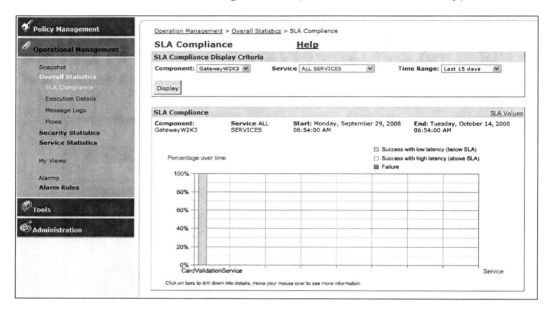

Note that a default SLA is provided for services. When displaying individual service SLA compliance then the report also provides information on service uptime and measures it against the SLA. SLAs can only be set against individual services by clicking on the **SLA Values** link. Although there is a link to set SLA levels for all services on a component it just leads to a selection box that forces the choice of a single service to set SLA levels for.

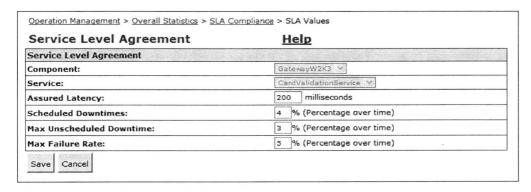

The SLA values that can be set include response time (**Assured Latency**), scheduled and unscheduled downtime and maximum failure rate. Apart from latency all these measures are as a percentage over time. Clicking **Save** will update the SLA with the new values.

Other monitoring and measuring features in OWSM

It is also possible to access the content of messages that have been logged by a component by clicking on the **Message Logs** tab under **Overall Statistics** and then selecting the component and individual message that you are interested in. Other features of OWSM provide access to the number of authorization and authentication failures as well as the total throughput for services and components in terms of number of messages and total bytes processed.

It is also possible to set alarms that can either be monitored through the console, or more usefully can be used to trigger a remote web service, send an email or perform some other notification event.

Monitoring in service bus

Like OWSM, the service bus is also able to monitor services. Like security policies, the service bus is not currently consistent with OWSM in its service monitoring. Service Level Agreements can also be specified in service bus, but they are enabled in a different fashion to OWSM SLAs.

Creating an Alert Destination

Any breaches of service level in the service bus will cause an alert to be raised. An alert must be associated with a destination. So before we begin, we need to define an alert destination. This is done by adding an **Alert Destination** resource to our project in the service bus. Selecting **Alert Destination** from the **Create Resource** list takes us to the **Create Alert Destination** dialog.

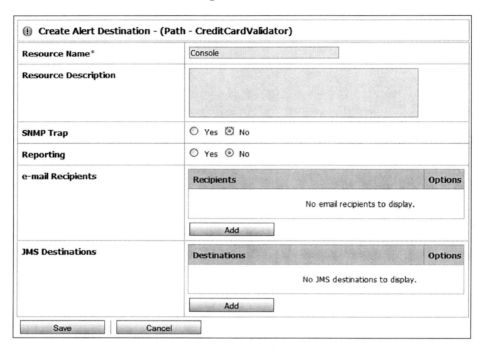

In this dialog we need to provide a name for the alert destination and specify the targets for this destination. The console is always included as a destination, but we may also send alerts to SNMP for integration with system managements systems such as Oracle Enterprise Manager or HP OpenView. Other destinations include Email, JMS queues, and internal reporting. Once we click **Save** then we have an alerting destination that can be used by many alerts.

Enabling service monitoring

To improve performance by default service monitoring is disabled for proxy services. To enable service monitoring we need to go to the proxy service edit screen and select the **Operational Settings** tab.

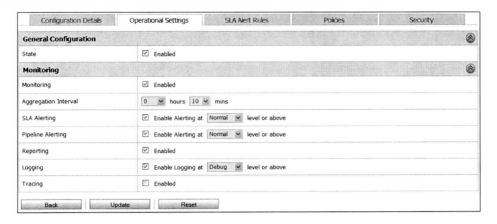

After selecting the **Monitoring** check box to enable monitoring for this service, review the other potential properties. The **Aggregation Interval** is the rolling time period over which SLAs for this proxy will be monitored. **Alerting** and **Logging** specify the monitoring level at which events will be tracked. **Reporting** allows inclusion of this proxy service in reports on the console. Finally **Tracing** can be enabled to help debug the service. Selecting **Update** will save the new configuration.

Creating an alert rule

Having enabled monitoring for our service we can now create an alert rule by selecting the **SLA Alert Rules** tab. Selecting **Add New** takes us to the **New Alert Rule** dialog where we can start to configure our rule.

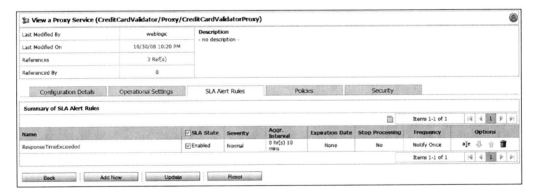

After providing a name for the alert rule we need to specify the destination. It is possible to limit applicability of the rule by restricting the time window in which the rule applies, by setting an expiry date, or by explicitly suspending the rule by setting **Rule Enabled** to `false`. The alert severity indicates the importance of this alert. The **Alert Frequency** is used to control whether the alert works as an edge trigger, firing only when the threshold is first exceeded, or as a level trigger, firing whenever the metric is above the threshold.

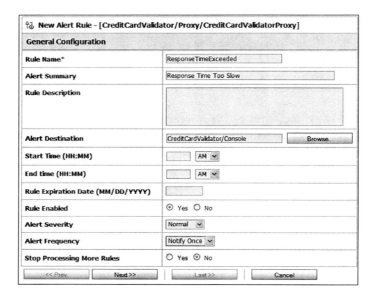

We also need to specify a destination for any alerts resulting from this rule. This is done by clicking the **Browse...** button next to the **Alert Destination** field and selecting an appropriate destination from the list presented in the **Select Alert Destination** dialog.

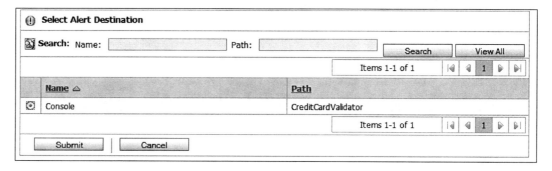

Having selected **Next>>** we can now construct our rule by defining the expression or expressions that we wish to use as an SLA. Expressions are created by first selecting the type of expression and then selecting the actual measurement. The expression type may be a count, a minimum, a maximum, or an average. Actual metrics for count may be error or message counts and success or failure ratios. Metrics for minimum, average, and maximum may be response times. Multiple expressions may be combined with Boolean operators. Expressions are added to the SLA rule by clicking **Add**.

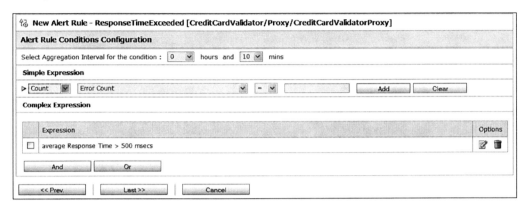

Clicking **Last>>** takes us to the summary screen where we can use the **Save** button to confirm our selections.

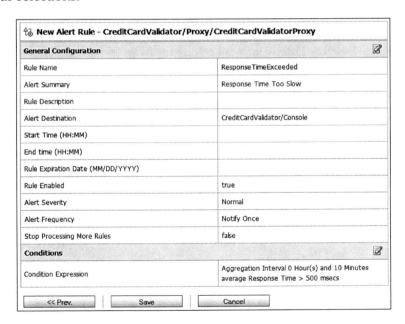

We can then do a final review of our modifications before selecting **Update** on the **SLA Alert Rules** tab. Remember to activate changes from the change center. Our SLA is now established and any violations will be reported.

Monitoring the service

We can monitor the health of our services by using the **Dashboard** tab found under the **Operations Monitoring** tab. This gives an immediate overview of alerts generated within the last thirty minutes.

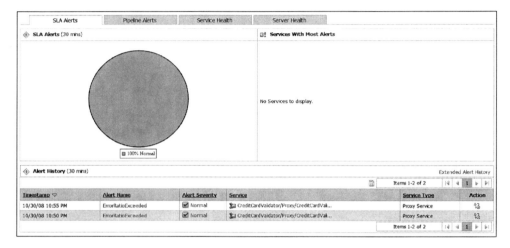

In addition to the dashboard, further information about the services can be obtained by examining the **Service Health** tab, which gives an overview of service behavior, throughput, error rates, and response times.

What makes a good SLA

SLAs should not be restricted just to report violations that are unacceptable. It can be a good practice for a given metric to set two or even three SLAs. The worst SLA should be the one that is unacceptable and is the real SLA. The other SLAs should be used to warn that the metric has gone outside of normal operating bounds or to warn that it is approaching the worst SLA. These latter SLAs can be used to help operators diagnose problems and take corrective action before they become critical.

Summary

The Web Services Manager and the service bus allow security and monitoring to be applied to services without modifying their core functionality. These policies may be applied consistently through the policy manager and enforced through the service bus, gateways, and agents. This model of security, as a service and as a facet, is applied to existing services allows for new security standards to be easily incorporated into the SOA infrastructure. In addition, it is possible to monitor the health and performance of groups of services and of individual services, including monitoring for compliance with service level agreements.

Index

Thank you for buying
Oracle SOA Suite Developer's Guide

About Packt Publishing

Packt, pronounced 'packed', published its first book "*Mastering phpMyAdmin for Effective MySQL Management*" in April 2004 and subsequently continued to specialize in publishing highly focused books on specific technologies and solutions.

Our books and publications share the experiences of your fellow IT professionals in adapting and customizing today's systems, applications, and frameworks. Our solution based books give you the knowledge and power to customize the software and technologies you're using to get the job done. Packt books are more specific and less general than the IT books you have seen in the past. Our unique business model allows us to bring you more focused information, giving you more of what you need to know, and less of what you don't.

Packt is a modern, yet unique publishing company, which focuses on producing quality, cutting-edge books for communities of developers, administrators, and newbies alike. For more information, please visit our website: www.packtpub.com.

Writing for Packt

We welcome all inquiries from people who are interested in authoring. Book proposals should be sent to author@packtpub.com. If your book idea is still at an early stage and you would like to discuss it first before writing a formal book proposal, contact us; one of our commissioning editors will get in touch with you.

We're not just looking for published authors; if you have strong technical skills but no writing experience, our experienced editors can help you develop a writing career, or simply get some additional reward for your expertise.

BPEL Cookbook

ISBN: 1904811337   Paperback: 188 pages

Ten practical real-world case studies combining business process management and web services orchestration

1. Real-world BPEL recipes for SOA integration and Composite Application development

2. Combining business process management and web services orchestration

3. Techniques and best practices with downloadable code samples from ten real-world case studies

Oracle Web Services Manager

ISBN: 978-1-847193-83-4   Paperback: 236 pages

Securing your Web Services

1. Secure your web services using Oracle WSM

2. Authenticate, Authorize, Encrypt, and Decrypt messages

3. Create Custom Policy to address any new Security implementation

4. Deal with the issue of propagating identities across your web applications and web services

Please check **www.PacktPub.com** for information on our titles

Printed in the United Kingdom by
Lightning Source UK Ltd., Milton Keynes
137863UK00001B/178/P